THE BRITISH AND THEIR LAWS IN THE EIGHTEENTH CENTURY

Edited by
David Lemmings

THE BOYDELL PRESS

First published 2005
The Boydell Press, Woodbridge

ISBN 1 84383 158 9

The Boydell Press is an imprint of Boydell & Brewer Ltd
PO Box 9, Woodbridge, Suffolk IP12 3DF, UK
and of Boydell & Brewer Inc.
668 Mt Hope Avenue, Rochester, NY 14620, USA
website: www.boydellandbrewer.com

A CiP catalogue record for this book is available
from the British Library

Library of Congress Cataloging-in-Publication Data
The British and their laws in the eighteenth century / edited by David Lemmings.
p. cm.
Summary: "New analysis and interpretation of law and legal institutions in the long eighteenth century"–Provided by publisher.
Includes index.
ISBN 1-84383-158-9 (hardback : alk. paper)
1. Law–Great Britain–History–18th century. 2. Rule of law–Great Britain–History–18th century. 3. Legislation–Great Britain–History–18th century. 4. Justice, Administration of–Great Britain–History–18th century. 5. Criminal justice, Administration of–Great Britain–History–18th century. I. Lemmings, David. II. Title.
KD614.B75 2005
349.42'09'033–dc22
2005006654

Contents

Contributors

Christopher Brooks is Professor of History at the University of Durham. His publications include *Lawyers, Litigation and English Society since 1450* (London, 1998), and he is currently completing a book on law, society, and politics in early modern England (1485–1640).

Simon Devereaux is Assistant Professor of History at the University of Victoria, Canada. He is the author of several articles on law and the state in Hanoverian England. Most recently he has co-edited *Penal Practice and Culture, 1500–1900: Punishing the English* (Basingstoke, 2004). His monograph *Criminal Justice and English Government, 1750–1810: Convicts and the State* is forthcoming from Palgrave. His current research deals with the administration of the capital code in Hanoverian London.

Douglas Hay teaches legal history in the faculty of law and department of history at York University in Toronto. Recent work appears in *Masters, Servants and Magistrates in Britain and the Empire 1562–1955* (Chapel Hill, NC, 2004), ed. D. Hay and P. Craven. He is currently writing on the history of English criminal law, aspects of Scots and Irish employment law, and the judicial politics of the English court of King's Bench.

Joanna Innes is Fellow and Tutor in Modern History at Somerville College, Oxford. She has published widely on government and legislation and public debate in the UK 1688–1840, especially in relation to social policy. She is currently preparing a collection of her essays on eighteenth-century social policy for publication.

Bruce Kercher is a Professor of Law at Macquarie University in Sydney. He is the author of *An Unruly Child: A History of Law in Australia* (St Leonards, NSW, 1995) and *Debt, Seduction and other Disasters: The Birth of Civil Law in Convict New South Wales* (Sydney, 1996). He is interested in the legal history of the nineteenth-century British empire, and is currently working on the interaction of law and custom on merchant ships.

David Thomas Konig is Professor of History in Arts and Sciences and Professor of Law in the School of Law at Washington University in St Louis. He is the author of *Law and Society in Puritan Massachusetts: Essex County, 1629–1692* (Chapel Hill, NC, 1979), and co-author and editor of *Devising Liberty: Preserving and Creating the Conditions of Freedom in the New American Republic* (Stanford, CA, 1995). He is currently writing a book on the invention of due process in colonial Virginia and a study of Thomas Jefferson's legal thought and practice.

David Lemmings is an Associate Professor of History in the School of Liberal Arts, University of Newcastle, Australia. He is the author of *Gentlemen and Barristers: The Inns of Court and the English Bar, 1680–1730* (Oxford, 1990), and *Professors of the Law: Barristers and English Culture in the Eighteenth Century* (Oxford, 2000). He is currently completing a book on law, governance, and English society in the eighteenth century.

Michael Lobban is Professor of Legal History at Queen Mary, University of London. He is the author of *The Common Law and English Jurisprudence, 1760–1850* (Oxford, 1991). He is currently the holder of a British Academy Research Readership, and is engaged in research on the law of obligations in the nineteenth century. This work will form part of the Victorian volumes of the Oxford History of the Laws of England.

Randall McGowen is a Professor of History at the University of Oregon. He is co-author (with Donna Andrew) of *The Perreaus and Mrs. Rudd: Forgery and Betrayal in Eighteenth-Century London* (Berkeley, CA, 2001). He has written many articles on the cultural history of the death penalty, and is currently at work on a book on forgery and criminal law reform in early nineteenth-century England.

Wilfrid Prest is currently a Professorial Fellow in the Law School at the University of Adelaide. He has written two books and numerous articles on the inns of court and the legal profession in early modern England, as well as an outline history of England 1660–1815 (*Albion Ascendant*, Oxford, 1998). His edition of the correspondence of Sir William Blackstone is forthcoming with the Selden Society.

Acknowledgements

This book started life as a conference at the Humanities Research Centre of the Australian National University, Canberra, held at the end of September, 2001. The meeting brought together a group of British, North American, and Australian legal historians to discuss the changing roles of 'law' in English society and at the edges of the British empire and their relations to the development of a more 'imperial' state. I am grateful to the HRC for financial support and to Leena Messina for her kindness and efficiency in helping to administer the event. Generous financial support was also provided by the Faculty of Arts and Social Science (as it was then) at the University of Newcastle. The conference benefited greatly from the participation of Alastair MacLachlan and Cindy McCreery, who helped to chair some of the sessions. Turning the proceedings into a collection of essays has been a pleasure because the contributors have been so prompt and forbearing in their responses to my editorial requests. I would also like to thank the commissioning editor for Boydell and Brewer, Peter Sowden, for his constant enthusiasm and support. As always, Claire Walker has been a constant source of inspiration and encouragement, and I thank her warmly too.

David Lemmings

Acknowledgements

1

Introduction

DAVID LEMMINGS*

> [I]t is one of the characteristic marks of English liberty, that our common law depends upon custom; which carries this internal evidence of freedom along with it, that it probably was introduced by the voluntary consent of the people.
>
> Sir William Blackstone (*Commentaries on the Laws of England* (Oxford, 1765–9), i. 74)

> [S]ince with us no Punishment is first settled without the whole Legislative Power, and the People in general as represented in Parliament, as well as the Royal Power, are all concern'd in appointing divers kinds of Punishment, whether they are more or less severe, none can say there is any Thing done without the Nations owns Consent and Act.
>
> George Ollyffe (*An Essay Humbly offer'd, for an Act of Parliament to prevent Capital Crimes, and the Loss of so many Lives; and to Promote a desirable Improvement and Blessing in the Nation* (London, 1731), 6–7)

> Oh! If such a despicable reptile shall annoy mankind with Impunity, if such a contemptible miscreant shall have it in his power to do such deeds of inhumanity and oppression, what avails the law?
>
> Tobias Smollett, satirizing a corrupt and oppressive JP (*The Life and Adventures of Sir Launcelot Greaves*, ed. P. Wagner (Harmondsworth, 1988[first publ. 1762]), 136)

Law matters: the eighteenth century, historians, and the laws

In the eighteenth century the English inherited a powerful sense of *The Law*. Englishmen congratulated themselves on enjoying rights and benefits in law that could not be overridden at the whim of kings and ministers: above all, freedom from arbitrary arrest, equal treatment with their betters before courts,

* I would like to thank Claire Walker for reading this chapter in draft and making helpful suggestions.

and trial by a jury of their peers in the case of criminal prosecution. These advantages, supposedly enshrined in iconic constitutional landmarks such as Magna Carta, the Petition of Right and the Habeas Corpus Amendment Act, and derived from the time-honoured procedures of the common law, stood in sharp contrast, they believed, with the oppressed condition of other European peoples. Or at least that is what they were told, time after time, as judges and magistrates trumpeted the good news about liberty under the rule of law in their charges at the regular meetings of assizes and quarter sessions.[1] Indeed, it has been argued that after the Glorious Revolution of 1688 the rule of law displaced religion and divine right monarchy as the principal legitimating ideology of the governing elite.[2] Certainly around this time law was normally associated with proceedings in courts, where all sorts of people met and negotiated justice, normally according to the rules of common law. And as Edward Thompson and other scholars have shown, by 1700 concepts, processes, rules and definitions established by the common law courts had become second nature to many aspects of everyday life and administration in English society, especially local government, productive relations, inheritance, and property ownership generally.[3]

Yet some of these legal customs were challenged and completely overturned by legislation over the next century, and in this period acts of parliament were passed in unprecedented numbers, as permanent parliamentary sessions became an established feature of government from 1689.[4] Certainly by 1800 statute was 'the dominant form of regulation'; most famously over the previous century a whole body of acts attempted to reconstitute ideas of criminal deviance in relation to particular forms of property and attached a variety of different penalties to offences.[5] In these circumstances one might expect significant shifts in understandings of 'law', and perhaps some popular disenchantment with its supposedly libertarian benefits. Indeed, perhaps it is appropriate to speculate that in the eighteenth century – a period when improving legislative governance became the norm, sensational crimes, trials and punishments were a staple of the press and the novel, and ideologies about rights under law confronted parliamentary statute across the Atlantic ocean – the rule of law first

[1] See e.g. *Charges to the Grand Jury 1689–1803*, ed. G. Lamoine (Camden soc., 4th ser., 43, 1992).

[2] D. Hay, 'Property, Authority and the Criminal Law', in D. Hay *et al.* (eds), *Albion's Fatal Tree: Crime and Society in Eighteenth-Century England* (Harmondsworth, 1975), 58–9.

[3] E.P. Thompson, *Whigs and Hunters* (Harmondsworth, 1977), 261.

[4] See e.g. J.M. Neeson, *Commoners: Common Right, Enclosure and Social Change in England, 1700–1820* (Cambridge, 1993), esp. chs 7–8; D. Hay and N. Rogers, *Eighteenth-Century English Society* (Oxford, 1997), esp. ch. 7. For legislation see J. Hoppit, 'Patterns of Parliamentary Legislation, 1660–1800', *The Historical Journal*, 39 (1996), 109.

[5] J. Brewer, 'The Eighteenth-Century British State: Contexts and Issues', in L. Stone (ed.), *An Imperial State at War: Britain from 1689–1815* (London, 1994), 57.

'came to its maturity' as an English historical tradition capable of adaptation to an infinite variety of circumstances.[6]

What then did the rule of law mean to contemporaries, and how did it connect with changing experiences of law in all their bewildering complexity? Given the powerful claims for their importance in the governance of English society, it is appropriate that over the last quarter-century or so many social historians have engaged productively with eighteenth-century law and legal institutions. But despite widespread agreement about *Law*'s significance as a key to unlock so much that was central to life in this period, taken as a whole the work of recent historians offers a fragmented and sometimes quite contradictory picture of the *laws* in their social meanings and actions during the Georgian age. Of course the story of law is bound to be complex, given the range of laws and administrative jurisdictions which applied in England (not to mention the colonies), and their differential connections with various social groups and local environments. In fact there is a variety of stories about eighteenth-century English laws, courts, and communities, accounts that – legitimately enough – emphasize somewhat different perspectives, and suggest both positive and negative experiences.

High political and constitutional narratives of the eighteenth century as a period of 'settlement' and 'stability' under the rule of law and the supremacy of parliament, which were based upon contrasts with the seventeenth-century constitutional crisis on the one hand, and the nineteenth century as 'the age of reform' on the other, have been problematized by detailed scholarly research on law in society and related studies.[7] In the aggregate this body of scholarly work has constituted a new social history of English law and government, a history which has taken multiple perspectives in three principal areas: crime and the administration of criminal justice; civil litigation and the legal professions; and the growth of legislation and its implications for relations between the state and local society.

The most extensive body of published research has been on crime and criminal justice. Pre-eminent among the inspirational sources of this material are the classic studies of the 'Warwick school', dating from the 1970s, which emphasized oppressive features of the administration of justice, especially its manipulation by members of the governing elite to enforce their own economic and political power. They also argued that much of the new capital legislation created in bulk by parliament after 1689 enforced commercial approaches to property at the expense of customary rights, and suggested that

6 Thompson, *Whigs and Hunters*, 267. See also *idem*, *Customs in Common* (Harmondsworth, 1993), 34.

7 D.L. Keir, *The Constitutional History of Modern Britain 1485–1937* (3rd edn, London, 1947), ch. 6; J.H. Plumb, *The Growth of Political Stability in England 1675–1725* (Harmondsworth, 1967).

some forms of criminal activity – clipping and counterfeiting coin, poaching, stealing from wrecks and smuggling – should be interpreted as quasi-political forms of resistance against the dominant social and political order.[8] While not always explicitly disagreeing with these interpretations, another body of work about the history of crime and punishment in the eighteenth century, partly inspired by John Beattie's studies of London and its environs, stresses rather different factors, especially the administrative imperatives felt by magistrates, judges, and ministers.[9] Beattie himself has shown that early Georgian governments were remarkably responsive to panics about rising crime in the metropolis, in so far as parliament passed legislation introducing more practical alternatives to capital punishment, and the grass-roots metropolitan authorities took their own steps to improve policing and prosecution. His emphasis on hitherto largely unstudied changes in penal law between 1689 and 1720 has largely overturned the previous orthodoxy, which confined reform of criminal justice to the later eighteenth century.[10] And Peter King has drawn attention to the importance of discretionary decision-making at all levels of the criminal justice system; in procedures which empowered people from the middle ranks of society, as well as the ruling elite.[11] Moreover in a series of incisive studies of the criminal trial John Langbein has demonstrated that from the 1730s the judicial bench responded to the incipient professionalization of policing and prosecution proceedings in London by 'evening up' the administration of justice with more restrictive rules of evidence, and by allowing lawyers to represent defendants, both in pre-trial proceedings and at the trial itself.[12] So under this broad revisionist optic, while hardly benign or egalitarian in its application to individuals, and certainly subject to manipulation for political purposes, eighteenth-century criminal justice appears as an irregular but broadly rational apparatus which was amenable to a range

[8] See especially *Albion's Fatal Tree*; Thompson, *Whigs and Hunters*; P. Linebaugh, *The London Hanged: Crime and Society in the Eighteenth Century* (Harmondsworth, 1991).

[9] J.M. Beattie, *Crime and the Courts in England 1660–1800* (Oxford, 1986); *idem*, *Policing and Punishment in London 1660–1750* (Oxford, 2001).

[10] See, e.g., J. Beattie, 'London Crime and the Making of the "Bloody Code", 1689–1719', in L. Davison *et al.* (eds), *Stilling the Grumbling Hive: The Response to Social and Economic Problems in England, 1689–1750* (Stroud, 1992), 49–76.

[11] P. King, *Crime, Justice and Discretion in England 1740–1820* (Oxford, 2000), 355–8.

[12] J.H. Langbein, 'The Criminal Trial before the Lawyers', *University of Chicago Law Review*, 45 (1978), 263–316; *idem*, 'Shaping the Eighteenth-Century Criminal Trial: A View from the Ryder Sources', *University of Chicago Law Review*, 50 (1983), 1–136; *idem*, 'The Prosecutorial Origins of Defence Counsel in the Eighteenth Century: The Appearance of Solicitors', *Cambridge Law Journal*, 58 (1999), 314–65; *idem*, 'The Historical Origins of the Privilege against Self-incrimination at Common Law', *Michigan Law Review*, 92 (1993–4), 1047–85; *idem*, *The Origins of Adversary Criminal Trial* (Oxford, 1993). See also J.M. Beattie, 'Scales of Justice: Defense Counsel and the English Criminal Trial in the Eighteenth and Nineteenth Centuries', *Law and History Review*, 9 (1991), 221–67.

of people and opinions, rather than a 'system' calculated to buttress elite hegemony.[13]

Partly because of the very high standard maintained by these studies, where it finds its way into general surveys of Hanoverian England, law is often dominated by accounts of crime and punishment, especially the treatment of alleged felons at the assizes and the Old Bailey, the 'theatres of power' which applied the most serious penal sanctions.[14] But without wishing to doubt the importance of serious criminal proceedings for popular experiences of law and government, it is essential to understand that in early modern England more people encountered law in what we would recognize as regulatory, or civil contexts, even among the relatively disadvantaged sectors of society, and especially among those of middling and substantial property.[15] For example at the county meetings of justices in quarter sessions, while the JPs' judicial business was carried out using the procedure of presentation and indictment, much of its substance was about local government as we would understand it today, meaning the routine maintenance of highways, bridges, and public buildings, the regulation of sports and popular pastimes, and the prevention of nuisances by individuals.[16] Criminal law procedures therefore covered a variety of 'offences', and were utilized for different purposes. Even indictments for riot and assault were quite likely to be undertaken for compensation rather than punishment, and were frequently dropped on the parties' settlement, therefore approximating to civil suits.[17] Certainly in their parlours individual JPs were frequently preoccupied with petty interpersonal disputes, especially abusive or violent quarrels between neighbours, acquaintances, and family members, complaints which were often brought to some resolution, rather than legal judgment and punishment.[18] Moreover, as William Blackstone pointed out at the time, in the eighteenth century criminal law proceedings were becoming dominated by magistrates sitting alone and without juries, who were empowered by an ever-growing body of statutes to try and administer penalties

[13] See also J. Brewer and J. Styles (eds), *An Ungovernable People: The English and their Law in the Seventeenth and Eighteenth Centuries* (London, 1980).

[14] See esp. J. Rule, *Albion's People: English Society 1715–1815* (Harlow, 1992), ch. 9; F. O'Gorman, *The Long Eighteenth Century: British Political and Social History 1688–1832* (London, 1997), 286–94. For broader accounts, see Hay and Rogers, *Eighteenth-Century English Society*, chs 6–7; R. Porter, *English Society in the Eighteenth Century* (2nd edn, 1990), 133–42; P. Langford, *A Polite and Commercial People: England 1727–1783* (Oxford, 1989), 296–304; W. Prest, *Albion Ascendant: English History 1660–1815* (Oxford, 1998), 65–6, 199–205, 257–60; J. Hoppit, *A Land of Liberty: England 1689–1727* (Oxford, 2000), ch. 14.

[15] C. Brooks, *Lawyers, Litigation and English Society since 1450* (London, 1998), 27.

[16] W. Holdsworth, *A History of English Law* (London, 1922–72), x. 146–9.

[17] N. Landau, 'Indictment for Fun and Profit: A Prosecutor's Reward at Eighteenth-Century Quarter Sessions', *Law and History Review*, 17 (1999), 507–36.

[18] See e.g. *The Justicing Notebook of William Hunt 1744–1749*, ed. E. Crittall (Devizes, Wiltshire Record Soc., xxxvii, 1982), 12–16.

for a range of 'disorderly' offences summarily, on the complaint of third parties. While it would be inappropriate to assume all these JPs applied the law like Smollett's Justice Gobble, Blackstone feared that in the absence of substantial restraints upon the exercise of their powers they could well 'be prostituted to mean and scandalous purposes, to the low ends of selfish ambition, avarice, or personal resentment'.[19] At the very least, here again contemporary experience of the laws would have been rather different from the ideal of freedom under *Law* associated with the jury and Magna Carta.

Given the social reach of the civil as well as criminal aspects of the law, it is appropriate that studies of litigation and the legal professions have constituted another area of recent growth in the social history of eighteenth-century law. Across England and Wales interpersonal litigation was the mainstay of many jurisdictions among the patchwork of courts which had been inherited from medieval times. Disputes over commercial matters, landholding and land usage, inheritance, marriage, and defamation preoccupied the local courts of manors and boroughs, hundreds and counties, and archdeaconries and dioceses, as well as the superior courts at Westminster and the principal ecclesiastical courts of Canterbury and York. Civil litigation also sustained those most 'interested' in law, the learned professionals: barristers, attorneys, and solicitors in the secular courts, and advocates and proctors in the courts administered by the Church of England. Many of their lay contemporaries had a critical interest in civil litigation too, because maintaining 'civil suits' seemed to be so difficult in the face of tedious delays, rising fees, and the precarious chances of success. Indeed, against the usual generalizations about 'the Excellency of our Laws', the administration of interpersonal suits attracted considerable criticism and recommendations for reform, especially in the early eighteenth century.[20]

In this context, the most interesting feature of recent scholarship on civil litigation is that by contrast with the later sixteenth and early seventeenth centuries, when participation in litigation proceedings seems to have been at a peak, research on the period between 1680 and 1760 suggests that in most jurisdictions there was a major decline in law suits, a recession which was only partially arrested after 1800.[21] Although there are significant variations from

[19] Blackstone, *Commentaries*, iii. 278–80. See epigraph above.

[20] [Sollom Emlyn,] *A Complete Collection of State Trials* (2nd edn, London, 1730), i. 3. W. Prest, 'Law Reform in Eighteenth-Century England', in P. Birks (ed.), *The Life of the Law* (London, 1993), 117–21; D. Lemmings, *Professors of the Law: Barristers and English Legal Culture in the Eighteenth Century* (Oxford, 2000), 9–15.

[21] Brooks, *Lawyers, Litigation and English Society*, esp. ch. 3; H. Horwitz and P. Polden, 'Continuity or Change in the Court of Chancery in the Seventeenth and Eighteenth Centuries', *Journal of British Studies*, 35 (1996), 24–57; H. Horwitz, 'Chancery's "Younger Sister": The Court of Chancery and its Equity Jurisdiction 1649–1841', *Historical Research*, 72 (1999), 160–82; C. Muldrew, 'Credit and the Courts: Debt Litigation in a Seventeenth-

court to court, overall it appears that courts and lawyers were much less generally utilized by the mid-eighteenth century than they had been a hundred years earlier, not only in London, but also in the provincial cities. Admittedly, the complex causes and meanings of the decline in numbers of cases are not yet well understood. Most studies have drawn attention to parallel changes internal to the administration of the law, especially sharply rising costs and lengthening delays in bringing suits to judgment. Several have also noted the possible influence of broader economic, social, and cultural trends in English society, including changes in the way business people enforced debts, the relative stability of life in the countryside (by contrast with social turmoil in the previous two centuries), and the possibility of growing 'civility' in interpersonal relations. Any sufficient explanation for the eighteenth-century recession of litigation will have to account for what several historians have identified as a broad convergence among the data across several different forms of litigation and jurisdictions (including borough courts, as well as the central courts of common law at Westminster, and the network of ecclesiastical courts), despite major differences in their constituencies and processes.[22] But whatever its causes, it appears that there was diminishing engagement between the people and this aspect of the law.

Assuming that 'the Great Litigation Decline' was a meaningful historical event, it is important to consider some of its possible implications for the experience of law.[23] Historians of sixteenth- and seventeenth-century England have stressed the importance of broad access to the courts for the legitimation of governance and general social integration.[24] Recently Michael Braddick has argued that 'going to law' constituted one of the most important elements in the formation of the early modern English state as a 'collective' authority; and Steve Hindle has agreed that the law was an 'incorporative force . . . , creating and intensifying links not only between individuals, but also between the communities of parish, county and realm'.[25] Indeed these scholars suggest

Century Urban Community', *Economic History Review*, 46 (1993), 23–38; *idem*, *The Economy of Obligation: The Culture of Credit and Social Relations in Early Modern England* (Basingstoke, 1998); W.A. Champion, 'Litigation in the Boroughs: The Shrewsbury *Curia Parva* 1480–1730', *Journal of Legal History*, 15 (1994), 201–22; *idem*, 'Recourse to the Law and the Meaning of the Great Litigation Decline, 1650–1750: Some Clues from the Shrewsbury Local Courts', in C.W. Brooks and Michael Lobban (eds), *Communities and Courts in Britain 1150–1900* (London, 1997), 179–98.

22 Champion, 'Recourse to the Law', 179–80; Muldrew, *Economy of Obligation*, 237–42. See also M.J. Braddick, *State Formation in Early Modern England c.1550–1700* (Cambridge, 2000), 160–1.

23 See Wilfrid Prest's chapter below.

24 J.A. Sharpe, 'The People and the Law', in B. Reay (ed.), *Popular Culture in Seventeenth-Century England* (London, 1985), 244–70.

25 Braddick, *State Formation*, 162–3; S. Hindle, *The State and Social Change in Early Modern England* (Basingstoke, 2000), 89.

that the business of government was both strengthened and legitimized by open legal institutions and cheap processes that allowed a large proportion of the population to access elements of official power in furtherance of their daily concerns, while aiming to contain conflict within formal structures. In this period government was largely executed through legal instruments and courts of law, and widespread use of the courts was arguably the most important expression of the grass-roots participation and local–central exchange typical of the early modern polity.[26] A remarkably wide range of people had first-hand knowledge of legal processes and concepts; and while the Tudor–Stuart state's social projects were hardly uncontested, it has been argued that in the mass this tendency to existential law-mindedness helped to reconcile local needs and initiatives with the government's abiding interest in promoting order. Moreover, as citizens who knew the law through personal experience, the English people had clear expectations of good governance.[27]

If this was so then any major decline in the social reach of the courts and the common law may have had very significant implications. Most obviously, in the apparent absence of alternative machinery for meaningful and relatively broad participation in government, did the eighteenth-century British state become hegemonic, and perhaps even imperial, in the domestic sphere as well as in its dealings with the American colonies? More particularly, in a period when unrepresentative parliaments mass-manufactured statutes, perhaps 'the law' itself assumed the proportions of an instrument of government for promoting values and objectives which were exclusive, rather than normative, in so far as it enforced the interests of particular elites, instead of representing a cross-section of the population?[28]

These rather vague speculations assume a little more flesh in the context of recent writing about the eighteenth-century state and parliamentary legislation, another principal point of growth in law-related studies of this period. John Brewer's work on the growth of the British state has raised important questions about the changing nature of government in the Georgian period; especially its associations with the coercive force of British naval and military power and the administrative strength of its fiscal machine. In this century of semi-continuous warfare the government raised more revenue from taxation than ever before, increasingly in the form of intrusive customs and excise regulations, and maintained unprecedented numbers of soldiers and sailors, including many Englishmen who were recruited against their will, sometimes under statutory powers.[29] Naturally an expanded bureaucracy was needed to

[26] Braddick, *State Formation*, 25–6, 36–9, 161–4; Hindle, *The State and Social Change*, 23–4, 29–32, 89–93, 232–5.

[27] Hindle, *The State and Social Change*, 115, 236–7.

[28] I am not suggesting that the law, or the state, were controlled exclusively by any particular class. See below for the 'concessive' nature of parliamentary law-making.

[29] The crown's power to impress men for naval service rested on immemorial usage, but

organize such an extensive fiscal–military effort, and there were complaints about the unparalleled bureaucratic power associated with the new 'army' of state servants, especially the officers of the burgeoning revenue departments, who represented the bogey of centralized direct administration.[30] The officers of the excise were particularly resented because of their remarkable powers of search and surveillance, and their direct dependence on the central government, which offended against traditions of personal freedom and local self-policing. Indeed, because they combined a ubiquitous national presence with unique statutory powers, and were answerable only to a central board of commissioners, for contemporaries the excisemen symbolized a radical and threatening departure in executive government under administrative law. More generally Brewer has noted the 'increased separation between government and public, between state and society', with the growth of an administrative culture which depended on professionals who acknowledged their first loyalty to the crown.[31]

In the eighteenth century, as previously, government continued to have other important functions, besides the raising of taxes and provision of soldiers and sailors. Its principal domestic responsibilities were the maintenance of public order, the administration of justice, and the regulation of economic life. In some of these areas too there were significant changes that arose from the growth of a more powerful state after the Glorious Revolution, and the continuity in legislative 'policy' made possible by regular parliamentary sessions.[32] Joanna Innes has demonstrated how several hundred acts of national scope helped to shape 'social policy', in areas such as the regulation of the poor, insolvency, and crime.[33] The plethora of laws relating to criminal offences and punishments appears to be an obvious example of positive legislative intervention from the centre, and Innes has also drawn particular attention to Georgian governments' sustained focus on the various problems connected with raising and demobilizing the armed forces.[34] Certainly by the mid-1750s at least leading parliamentarians 'saw the necessity of statute for the daily

the Mutiny Act of 1705 provided for capital convicts to be enlisted in the army on condition of pardon, and from 1704 magistrates were empowered to conscript able-bodied men for the army if they appeared to be unemployed (2 & 3 Anne c. 19; 4 Anne c. 10).

30 J. Brewer, *The Sinews of Power: War, Money and the English State, 1688–1783* (London, 1989), ch. 3. For the 'structural differentiation' of the institutions of central government from local government see also N. Landau, 'Country Matters: The Growth of Political Stability a Quarter-Century On', *Albion*, 25 (1993), 266–7.

31 Brewer, *Sinews of Power*, 83, 85, 101–14, 214–15.

32 Beattie, 'London Crime and the Making of the "Bloody Code"', 51–2.

33 J. Innes, 'Parliament and the Shaping of Eighteenth-Century Social Policy', *Transactions of the Royal Historical Society*, 5th ser., 50 (1990), 63–92.

34 J. Innes, 'The Domestic Face of the Military Fiscal State: Government and Society in Eighteenth-Century Britain', in L. Stone (ed.), *An Imperial State at War: Britain from 1689–1815* (London, 1994), 108–17.

government of the nation'.[35] Eighteenth-century administration was not usually big government in the modern sense, however. Rather than being a product of the executive, much of the general legislation was promoted by interested 'backbenchers' or (less frequently) voluntary bodies, and it was usually implemented by local authorities. Moreover it was notorious that many statutes were either not implemented at all or applied partially, according to the prevailing opinions of intermediate authorities.[36] Indeed, parliaments of this period were suspicious of general measures with a centralizing tendency, especially during the first half of the century, when the 'country persuasion' operated as a powerful check (if not checkmate) on the growth of executive power.[37]

In fact most of the acts passed in the eighteenth century were of a specific, rather than a general nature, and they usually originated at the grass-roots. A recent study has categorized nearly three-quarters of all acts of parliament passed between 1689 and 1800 as either highly local or personal in their application.[38] As Paul Langford has shown, MPs were highly responsive to all sorts of local interests, and invested many with significant administrative powers, as a mass of legislation on urban improvement commissions, poor law corporations, small debt courts, and communications projects reveals.[39] In these cases legislation followed a request from the locality. Typically the promoters of a river navigation project, a turnpike, or some other 'improvement' would organize a petition from the magistrates and leading inhabitants assembled at the assizes or quarter sessions setting out the advantage to be gained from the project and explaining why legislation was necessary to accomplish it. The petition would subsequently be presented in the House of Commons by a local member, who would move to bring in a bill and pilot it through the various stages of discussion and debate.[40] After mid-century, when the number of local acts increased sharply, petitioners became ever more confident that parliament was willing to grant their applications, even dispensing with the formal allegation of some defect in existing law.[41] Indeed it has been argued that from the 1770s some active county magistrates helped to develop what assumed the proportions of a national 'policy' in the legislative

[35] R. Connors, '"The Grand Inquest of the Nation": Parliamentary Committees and Social Policy in Mid-Eighteenth-Century England', *Parliamentary History*, 14 (1995), 312.

[36] Langford, *Polite and Commercial People*, 296–7.

[37] Brewer, *Sinews of Power*, 155–61; and see C. Brooks, 'The Country Persuasion and Political Responsibility in England in the 1690s', *Parliaments, Estates and Representation*, 4 (1984), 135–46.

[38] Hoppit, 'Patterns of Parliamentary Legislation 1660–1800', 116–17.

[39] P. Langford, *Public Life and the Propertied Englishman 1689–1798* (Oxford, 1991), 150–75.

[40] See e.g. the legislation discussed in S. Handley, 'Local Legislative Initiatives for Economic and Social Development in Lancashire, 1689–1731', *Parliamentary History*, 9 (1990), 14–37.

[41] Langford, *Public Life*, 168–9.

reform of penal institutions.[42] In this sense a considerable part of the proliferation of law-making after 1689 represented 'concessive' or 'empowering' governance, rather than the orders of a centralized state.[43]

Nevertheless (and leaving aside the important question about who was empowered), it is important to understand that parliament had a 'centralist perspective' of its role in the eighteenth century. It was a self-consciously national institution which developed a high doctrine of sovereignty and formally rejected any suggestions of accountability to particular constituencies or to the public at large.[44] In these circumstances it is appropriate to question whether even the most localized acts of parliament can be distinguished from centralized government, especially at a time when MPs were spending more time in London and the growth of communications and the press were integrating the governing elites of country and city in the activities and preoccupations of national life. In 1770 Burke noted that since the Revolution of 1688 the House of Commons had abandoned its traditional role of a control on executive government for 'the constant habit of authority', and he bemoaned 'this separation of the representatives from their constituents' which he identified in their recent refusal to accept Wilkes as MP for Middlesex.[45] After 1689 the Commons was clearly a part of the government, as much as the watchdog of the executive, and most MPs recognized the utility of parliamentary sovereignty in its ability to serve and protect the interests of property.[46] Indeed, despite the constitutional importance of the Revolution settlement, the Septennial Act, and the legislation which asserted its power over the colonies, probably the most significant aspect of parliament's growing capacity for law-making was that experienced at a more obscure level, with the aggregated impact of so many specific acts effectively implementing 'policy' of general scope.[47] Individually they conferred 'an astonishing array of legal powers' on

[42] D. Eastwood, *Governing Rural England: Tradition and Transformation in Local Government 1780–1840* (Oxford, 1994), 244–6, 247–51; *idem*, *Government and Community in the English Provinces, 1700–1870* (Basingstoke, 1997), 108–9.

[43] Langford, *Public Life*, 175; J. Innes, 'The Local Acts of a National Parliament: Parliament's Role in Sanctioning Local Action in Eighteenth-Century Britain', in D. Dean and C. Jones (eds), *Parliament and Locality 1660–1939* (Edinburgh, 1998), 26–7, 39.

[44] D. Eastwood, 'Parliament and Locality: Representation and Responsibility in Late-Hanoverian England' in D. Dean and C. Jones (eds), *Parliament and Locality, 1660–1939* (Edinburgh, 1998), 68–77; Langford, *Public Life*, 188–90.

[45] E. Burke, *Thoughts on the Present Discontents* (1770), in *The Writings and Speeches of Edmund Burke*, ed. P. Langford (Oxford, 1981), ii. 293–5.

[46] Brewer, *Sinews of Power*, 159, 247; H.T. Dickinson, 'The Eighteenth-Century Debate on the Sovereignty of Parliament', *Transactions of the Royal Historical Society*, 5th ser., 26 (1976), esp. 199–200. See also E.S. Morgan, *Inventing the People: The Rise of Popular Sovereignty in England and America* (New York, 1988), esp. ch. 2. Cf. P.D.G. Thomas, *The House of Commons in the Eighteenth Century* (Oxford, 1971), ch. 2.

[47] D. Lieberman, *The Province of Legislation Determined: Legal Theory in Eighteenth-Century Britain* (Cambridge, 1989), 23; cf. Beattie, *Policing and Punishment*, 464.

local commissioners and magistrates, some of whom stood to benefit materially from the project in question at the expense of the poorer members of their communities.[48] Certainly, with numerous acts of government mediated through MPs and JPs who were formally at arm's length from the executive, the English 'became habituated, as the century passed, to multiple forms of centrally-directed governmental activity, at which their ancestors might have balked'.[49] The acculturation process of this increase in government deserves more attention. It is especially important to consider what it meant for people's relations with the law, and the integration of state and society.

Discussion of these historiographies about law and government in the eighteenth century therefore raises some important issues for understanding the nature and experience of government and the endurance of the common law tradition. It is striking that they are usually discussed separately, thereby inhibiting a full appreciation of what contemporaries understood as 'law'. Although I am hardly suggesting that the British legal realm was monolithic, there seems to be considerable potential for adding value to this literature by analyses of law in England and British settler colonies that consider broadly the issues of participation, central–local relations, and the maintenance of common law traditions in the context of increasing legislative interventions and grants of statutory administrative powers. The chapters in this volume revisit and re-evaluate different aspects of the British and their laws in this period along these lines.

The nature and locus of legal authority

Legislative governance was hardly invented in the eighteenth century. For example the almost universal adoption of poor rates in England within a century of the acts that authorized them indicates the power and legitimacy of parliamentary statute in the late sixteenth and seventeenth centuries.[50] And of course the Reformation parliament carried through a revolution in the organization and doctrine of the national church within a few generations. But what was different after 1689 was the scale and scope of parliament's legislative enterprise. For while the law-making capacity of parliament had historical legitimacy, and individual acts of parliament had demonstrated social traction, legislative power had never been exercised so extensively before. Given the centrality of common law processes and institutions to what the

[48] Brewer, 'The Eighteenth-Century British State', in L. Stone (ed.), *An Imperial State at War: Britain from 1689–1815* (London, 1994), 64–5; Langford, *Public Life*, 245–51.

[49] J. Innes, 'Politics, Property and the Middle Class', *Parliamentary History*, 11 (1992), 291.

[50] J. Innes, 'The State and the Poor: Eighteenth-Century England in European Perspective', in J. Brewer and E. Hellmuth (eds), *Rethinking Leviathan: The Eighteenth-Century State in Britain and Germany* (Oxford, 1999), 238.

English perceived as being distinctive about their relations with government, one therefore wonders whether contemporaries noticed a shift in the nature of legal authority. Certainly, writing in the aftermath of the Gordon riots in 1781, the painter Allan Ramsay argued that the authorities were impotent because the Riot Act was generally believed to *encompass* the law, with the result that the more flexible common law provisions against public disorder were forgotten:

> It is easy to see that all this is merely statuary; that it is merely an act of legislative power; such as would equally make it felony to eat buttered peas, or to wear leather breeches. It is, *sic volo, sic jubeo* [so wished, so ordered]. In the mean while the Common law of England, and the law of common sense, which ought to be the corner stone of every positive institution, are kept entirely out of sight; by which the minds of those who read this act are suffered to be impressed with the idea that these leading formalities are the essentials of it; and that, as all statutes are *stricti juris*, an exact observance of these formalities was to be followed in all its subsequent clauses.[51]

So for Ramsey, who was a strong supporter of parliamentary sovereignty, statute fetishism had nevertheless sapped the legitimate foundations of legal authority and rendered the common law nugatory.

Michael Lobban's chapter (Chapter 2) investigates the prevailing views about the nature of legal authority among elite lawyers and legal theorists from the seventeenth century to the end of the eighteenth, paying special attention to reconciling parliamentary sovereignty with ideas about fundamental rights and customary legal development associated with the common law. He argues that although notions of natural law and community consent continued to inform legal theory and popular discourse into the eighteenth century, the writings of Selden and Hale insisted that municipal law depended on the command and sanction of a sovereign, and these ideas were reinforced after 1700 by the publication in England of strongly positivist continental writings. Blackstone, indeed, articulated a high doctrine of positive sovereignty as the source of law, and at this time sovereignty was identified with the king in parliament. Even the common law was partly assimilated to this positivist jurisprudence, in so far as many of its principal elements were tracked to the codes and settlements of medieval kings or parliaments.

While they acknowledged the imprimatur of the sovereign was essential to authorize law, Lobban shows clearly that eighteenth-century jurists conceived of legal development as a continuous organic process, rather than the product of arbitrary sovereign command. Like Coke, judges continued to advance the generation of common law rules by making decisions in cases consonant with the principles applied in previous judgments, a system that they characterized

[51] Allan Ramsay, *Observations upon the Riot Act* (London, 1781), p.8.

as developing the law in conformity with its ancient foundations. In some cases, as in Chancery generally, decisions were made and rules were developed on the grounds of natural justice; or, as in the area of commercial law constructed by Lord Mansfield, according to community practice. However, although common law judges sometimes evinced considerable concern about activist law-making by parliament, their jurisprudence provided no grounds for challenging the practical achievement of legislative sovereignty.[52] The limitations of legal theory applied even to the American patriots, who like the English radicals were the inheritors of a more authentically Cokean constitutionalist language based on fundamental rights under common law. Lobban argues that while the seventeenth-century idiom provided useful rhetorical ammunition in the developing crisis of relations with imperial Britain, it did not furnish compelling legal arguments against the sovereignty of king in parliament, and it was largely abandoned for Lockean political theory after 1770. Thus in England and America, henceforth 'controlling abuses of power by parliament was . . . to be done by political, rather than legal means'; although in the American case the tensions between parliamentary absolutism and the common law tradition left indelible traces in the form of fundamental laws and a supreme court which developed powers of legislative review.[53]

It therefore appears that the high culture of the common law world was moving away from enduring popular notions that identified English law with fundamental rights, institutions such as trial by jury and habeas corpus, and 'historical landmarks' like Magna Carta and the Revolution of 1688. This is to adapt a useful distinction made by Douglas Hay in his chapter (Chapter 3), which considers the 'low law' of magistrates' judicial authority in England and the British empire and its connections (or lack of connections) with the 'high law' of the legal establishment centred on Westminster Hall. Hay makes an important point about the nature of law at its sharp end by noting that in eighteenth-century Staffordshire over 80 per cent of criminal cases were tried summarily by JPs sitting alone or in pairs, rather than by juries at quarter sessions or assizes. In criminal matters this 'low law' was therefore far more important than the common law elaborated and administered by the professional lawyers and judges at Westminster. The substance of 'low law' was delegated parliamentary authority over the activities of the labouring population: magistrates acted under statutory powers which gave them very wide discretion to prosecute acts which could be construed as criminal in cases of vagrancy, offences against the poor laws, petty theft, poaching, or breach of contract. Hay notes that this jurisdiction continued a statutory tradition that

52 Blackstone, *Commentaries*, i. 10; Lemmings, *Professors of the Law*, 321–2; D. Lieberman, *The Province of Legislation Determined* (Cambridge, 1989), 14–19, 56–67.

53 See below, p. 41. D. Lemmings, 'Law', in I. McCalman (ed.), *An Oxford Companion to the Romantic Age: British Culture 1776–1832* (Oxford, 1999), 77.

dated from the fourteenth century, but it grew rapidly during the eighteenth century with fresh draughts of legislative power, and Blackstone's criticisms captured the concern of conservative common lawyers about what they saw as illegitimate modes of trial.[54] For them, if the rule of law was to apply continuously, there was a need for the magistrates' summary jurisdiction to be supervised by the court of King's Bench, either by writ of certiorari or via criminal information for misdemeanour. However Hay shows that in the Staffordshire cases he has examined only a tiny fraction of the thousands of convictions were reviewed in this way, and in none of them did the magistrate suffer any punishment. Indeed there had been a shift in judicial attitudes from the early eighteenth century, when judges had generally been suspicious of summary jurisdiction. Lord Mansfield reduced the scope for finding a criminal information against magistrates, and although his successor Kenyon tried to buck the trend, the evidence suggests 'the critical eye of the high court was increasingly shut to the behaviour of inferior justices from the late eighteenth into the early nineteenth centuries'.[55]

This account of the late Georgian judiciary's attitude towards the magistrates' statutory powers is therefore entirely consistent with Lobban's exegesis of high legal theory. In the absence of common law supervision the poor in England were left to the mercies of 'low law'. Hay's analysis of the master and servant cases determined by JPs under summary procedure shows the judges' strict conformity to the words of statutes in these cases too, even when they were in derogation of Coke's fundamental principle that the courts must protect subjects against official oppression or misgovernment.[56] Thus the judges refused to interfere in the Staffordshire magistrates' almost absolute power to commit labourers to prison for alleged breaches of contract, rejecting arguments for an appeal to quarter sessions. An even greater degree of complaisance towards coercive local authority seems to have prevailed with respect to colonial jurisdictions, at least in so far as the quasi-military and unlawful justice meted out in mid-eighteenth-century Quebec was fully supported by the government at home and its law officers. Hay also shows that the law of master and servant which conferred such power on magistrates in England was largely replicated across the second British empire as it grew, and its provisions frequently circumvented the inconveniences of superior court supervision, especially where the control and exploitation of non-white labour was its target. So it appears that in its criminal aspect the eighteenth-century 'project of law' largely represented the further development of a long tradition by which parliamentary legislation empowered the local representatives of the state, with the crucial difference that the common law was now irrelevant. Indeed according to Hay, when they were asked to intervene against oppressive JPs

[54] Blackstone, *Commentaries*, iv. 343–4.

[55] See below, p. 71.

[56] See J.H. Baker, *An Introduction to English Legal History* (3rd edn, London, 1990), 165.

its guardians simply looked the other way, conscious of the overriding need to support the magistracy.

Parliament, legislation, and the localities

How did the magistrates keep up with the law? In Chapter 4 Simon Devereaux considers another aspect of the relations between the magistracy and the central authorities, the promulgation of new parliamentary statutes by the British government. His chapter shows that at the end of the eighteenth century, when parliament was making new statutes at an unprecedented rate, there was concern among reformist lawyers and social commentators about the ability of ordinary people to know the laws that governed them, especially the burgeoning penal code. But mainstream opinion was more worried about the potential for ignorance among the law's 'enforcers', and the need to communicate the statutes to the provincial magistracy was the focus of the government's attention. Thus under the guidance of Charles Abbot, from 1797 the Pitt administration attempted to impose some uniformity in the administration of the law by arranging for the systematic transmission of sets of statutes to selected JPs and other officials all over the country, rather than just the MPs and London-based officials who had previously received them. Indeed this was a development that seems to mark a departure from the broadly laissez-faire attitude towards the localities which is the prevailing tone of government for the previous century.

Devereaux's analysis complements Douglas Hay's chapter by showing that English magistrates were certainly instruments of a statutory legal regime, rather than the common law world of judges and high courts. (Certainly many eighteenth-century representations of the JPs show collections of statutes as well as Burn's *Justice* or some other working manual.[57]) However he points out that the number of copies of the statutes distributed was inadequate to ensure coverage across the whole population of country magistrates, and it appears that the Home Office, which had responsibility for implementing the scheme, did not devote much administrative energy to this drive for central control. It is significant, nevertheless, that over the succeeding years many justices petitioned the government to be added to the list of recipients: perhaps indeed they were complicit in the gradual centralization of authority. Of course there is no way of knowing how far this system of communicating the statutes ensured more uniformity in the administration of law. But at least it is clear that at the end of the eighteenth century a rising number of JPs positively identified themselves with the prestige of the state and the will of parliament,

[57] E.g. *Midas; or the Surry Justice* (1768); T. Rowlandson after E.M. Woodward, *Country Characters No. 2: Justice* (1799); *The Country Justice* (1785).

if only by proudly displaying the volumes of bound acts on the shelves of their justice rooms.

Given the centrality of parliamentary acts to the eighteenth-century legal regime demonstrated by Devereaux and Hay, one of the key questions about statute law is then: who had access to parliament, and how much external participation was there in the increasingly fashionable process of law-making? At first sight general questions about access seem to produce uniformly negative answers. It is well known that in the borough constituencies parliamentary decisions resulted in the narrowing of many franchises, and there were few electoral contests in the counties after 1720. Certainly the Septennial Act reduced formal participation in electoral politics, and while the political influence of the men of large property and patronage increased, ultimately they became more dependent on government.[58] Interpreting the falling temperature of parliamentary elections as an indicator of frustrated participation in governance may be anachronistic, however: there were other, more direct, and possibly more important ways to take part.[59] In particular, as discussed previously, Paul Langford has stressed parliament's responsiveness to a variety of commercial and local interests who promoted or opposed legislation.[60] His optimism about the 'functional effectiveness' of the legislature for all propertied people may seem misguided when one considers extra-parliamentary politics and the movement for parliamentary reform.[61] But in Chapter 5 Joanna Innes identifies three forms of increasing public engagement with the legislative process during the later eighteenth and early nineteenth centuries.

First, Innes shows that from 1760 more and more material relating to parliamentary business was published: after a struggle, extensive reporting of parliamentary debates was allowed, publication of the Commons and Lords *Journals* became more contemporary, and there was separate publication of some bills, committee reports, accounts, and other papers. In the early years of the new century Charles Abbott, the hero of statute promulgation, also arranged for the systematic publication of sessional papers as the 'Blue Books'. Some of the formal material certainly found its way into public libraries, and samples were used to inform public debate on controversial issues, becoming fodder for proponents and opponents of legislative intervention. Secondly, despite legislative restrictions passed in 1661, 1795, and 1819, there was a considerable rise in the number of petitions to parliament relating to public issues and general legislation from the 1760s, with very large increases in the

58 J.H. Plumb, *The Growth of Political Stability in England 1675–1725* (Harmondsworth, 1967), ch. 3.

59 See M. Goldie, 'The Unacknowledged Republic: Officeholding in Early Modern England', in T. Harris (ed.), *The Politics of the Excluded, c. 1500–1850* (Basingstoke, 2001), 158–9.

60 Langford, *Polite and Commercial People*, 709–11, 713.

61 N. Rogers, 'Paul Langford's "Age of Improvement"', *Past and Present*, 130 (1991), 205–6.

1780s, 1810s, and later 1820s. Indeed by the end of this period some petitioning campaigns had burst their constitutionally defined local authority boundaries to become institutionalized and national in scope. To what extent all this represented enhanced agency in legislative processes for relatively humble people is not clear: one supposes that the petitions which initiated or challenged local legislation were dominated by members of the county or borough elites. But the sheer scale of petitioning in the early nineteenth century does indicate that in a broad sense British people were being mobilized and politicized by unprecedented engagement with parliament.

Innes's third and most interesting case of public participation in the making of legislation is the development of parliamentary inquiries. These varied in their nature, ranging from the select committees that considered petitions for specific legislation, through committees which discussed bills after their second reading, to more general inquiries into public issues. They also proceeded in various ways, taking written as well as oral evidence from official and non-official sources, although by 1700 there was already an established custom for committees sitting on local or personal legislation to take evidence from interested parties as witnesses. It is not clear whether early eighteenth-century committees of inquiry into crime and poverty examined witnesses, but the Commons' inquiries into the conditions of metropolitan gaols in 1729–30 seem to have done so, and by the early nineteenth century 'a tradition of witness interrogation' had become established as a principal feature of parliamentary inquiry into domestic government and remedial legislation. Of course the most important question from the perspective of participation in law-making is who was selected to appear, and how. In cases of general legislation the committees themselves and their nominees seem to have controlled selection, and Innes gives examples from the 1820s of committees which were reluctant to hear evidence from plebeian sources. In one of these cases artisans' representatives won a hearing by determined petitioning and the assistance of sympathetic MPs, however, and they subsequently had a major influence over legislation. Clearly the institutionalization of parliamentary inquiry requires more detailed research, as does the grass-roots origins of legislation generally. We still know very little about the nature and extent of popular engagement with law-making, and Innes rightly cautions against equating participation with power. Nevertheless, her chapter does suggest that external access to legislative processes was growing in the later eighteenth century, although it remained limited, and was challenged after 1800 by a contrary trend towards more control on the part of the government.

The administration of justice and participation

As discussed previously, historians of civil litigation have suggested that there was a 'massive' decline in law suits over fifty years or so from the end of the seventeenth century, and that this occurred across both local and central jurisdictions, as cases which were derived from the English provinces ebbed away from central and local courts.[62] Certainly there was a revival of litigation in the nineteenth century. But it has been hypothesized that the early modern legal regime of widespread communal participation in the government of interpersonal relations was never recovered, and this was a significant social loss, not fully replaced by parliamentary democracy.[63] Two chapters in this volume consider the subject, while another looks at changing attitudes towards popular participation in capital punishment.

In Chapter 6, Wilfrid Prest cautions about placing too much interpretive weight on the statistical evidence for an eighteenth-century litigation crash. He questions whether the various counts of law suits in the courts between the mid-seventeenth century and the mid-eighteenth are comparable as units of measurement, whether there are enough observations to justify the identification of any general trends, and indeed, whether civil litigation is a meaningful category of analysis. For Prest, following Craig Muldrew, taking account of all the variations across local and central courts means dating the decline in litigation from the seventeenth century, and characterizing it as a return to normal levels, rather than a recession. There is not space to discuss all these points at length here. However it should be pointed out that Muldrew concluded that it was only after 1700, 'when both absolute and "per household" numbers of suits fell to such low levels, that the drop in litigation must have become socially obvious'.[64] Certainly a mid-Georgian nadir would coincide with demonstrated reductions in the numbers of barristers and enrolments at the inns of court, phenomena which in themselves seem to indicate poor prospects for making a living from litigation.[65] Moreover, an eighteenth-century dearth of law suits does not only help to explain significant changes in the numbers, working lives, education, and professional organization of lawyers. Henry Horwitz has suggested it may also account for what appears to have been declining pressure in parliament for reform of litigation procedure, by contrast with the seventeenth century.[66]

62 For a concise summary see H. Horwitz, 'Changes in the Law and Reform of the Legal Order: England (and Wales) 1689–1760', *Parliamentary History*, 21 (2002), 306–7.

63 Brooks, *Lawyers, Litigation and English Society*, 106–7, 127–8; *idem*, 'The Longitudinal Study of Civil Litigation in England 1200–1996', in W. Prest and S. Roach Anleu (eds), *Litigation Past and Present* (Sydney, 2004), 35–7; Lemmings, 'Law', 73–81; *idem*, *Professors of the Law*, 319–20.

64 Muldrew, *Economy of Obligation*, 241. Considering generally the nature of litigation in the eighteenth century, Muldrew also insisted 'the great decline in litigation was undoubtedly a social change of some importance' (242).

65 D. Lemmings, 'Blackstone and Law Reform by Education: Preparation for the Bar and Lawyerly Culture in Eighteenth-Century England', *Law and History Review*, 16 (1998), 221–2, 249–50.

66 Horwitz, 'Changes in the Law and Reform of the Legal Order', 309–11, 324.

Prest is surely right when he calls for more detailed qualitative research on the grass-roots origins of litigation as a means to penetrate the formal veneer of legal records and elucidate its various subjective meanings. Like participating in the legislative process, going to court was not necessarily an empowering experience. Much of the early modern glut of law suits in the central courts consisted of actions for debt on sealed bonds, and they were unlikely to have generated extensive proceedings (although litigation over debts was not necessarily 'routine', especially in borough courts, where the process was more substantial).[67] In addition, it is difficult to show conclusively that law and lawyers had less currency among the population during the Georgian period than they had in the age of Coke and Selden, and it is true that information about law and legal proceedings became a staple of eighteenth-century newspapers and the print media generally. Nevertheless, there is an important question about how far the rule of law depends upon substantial, rather than vicarious, participation in its proceedings. This issue is taken up by Christopher Brooks in Chapter 7, as well as in the conclusion to this introduction.

Brooks, whose work on the seventeenth- and eighteenth-century courts has inspired much of the current interest in litigation, argues that there are identifiable shifts in the relations between government and society across the early modern period which can be associated with changing patterns of civil litigation. In his wide-ranging essay, he places considerable emphasis on the implications of declining litigation for popular participation and agency. Certainly he agrees that for Elizabethan and early Stuart England, 'going to law' had been a valued source of individual agency in interpersonal relations and a vital component of political consciousness. Indeed, diminishing recourse to the borough and central courts around 1700 may have been part of a more general change by which individual participation in all kinds of grass-roots juridical institutions – manorial courts, courts leet, quarter sessions, and ecclesiastical courts – went into steep decline, and popular ideas about rights lost their concrete connections with law. According to Brooks, the primary institutions governing ordinary people after 1750 – the vestry, the individual JP, and the courts of requests – were oligarchical or patrician centres of authority that were hardly touched by common law or amenable to community influence. In these circumstances, he suggests, popular participation in the governance of late Hanoverian Britain was more symbolic than substantial, despite the dramatic events of the Wilkite agitation, and other radical public demonstrations.

[67] In the borough courts actions for debt were normally litigated in the form of trespass on the case, because they were based on informal agreements, rather than sealed bonds, and suits of this kind were more likely to be defended. See Muldrew, 'Credit and the Courts', 25–6; Champion, 'Litigation in the Boroughs', 213–14; *idem*, 'Recourse to the Law and the Meaning of the Great Litigation Decline', in C.W. Brooks and M. Lobban (eds) *Communities and Courts in Britain 1150–1900* (London, 1997), 180.

Randall McGowen's chapter on the expectations and disappointments which were read into the executions of criminals at Tyburn in the mid-eighteenth century (Chapter 8) demonstrates that the idea of popular participation was integral to the administration of justice in early modern England. He shows that for contemporary commentators the efficacy of public execution depended on shared understandings that the appearance of the criminal on the scaffold represented the existential Christian choice between good and evil. The crowd was invited to witness the penitence of the condemned and thereby freely affirm the justice of the sentence, drawing the appropriate moral lesson, that divine judgement would inevitably follow a wicked course of life. However he argues that from the end of the seventeenth century there was increasing criticism that the ritual was not working according to the script, in so far as the proceedings were not sufficiently solemn, the crowd was often irreverent and riotous, and the condemned was encouraged to be obdurate, thereby sending the wrong dramaturgical signals.[68] In fact it is not clear that there had been any change in the behaviour of the people who attended at Tyburn; rather the problem was that polite opinion no longer had confidence in their ability to recognize moral justice, and was increasingly disgusted by the violence and disorder associated with popular culture. McGowen argues that these sentiments began to prevail among educated people around the middle of the eighteenth century, in the context of fears about rising crime, disorder, and general moral degeneration among the common people. The result was a 'crisis of punishment': the urban elites no longer believed that executing criminals in the face of the people would serve to promote the kind of moral discipline which was the event's primary objective.

McGowen's discussion of solutions to the problem of the Tyburn execution carnival implies that adherence to the traditions of participatory punishment died hard. Certainly the presence of the crowd was still required, if only for the purpose of deterrence: the procession from Newgate to Tyburn survived until 1783, and public hangings went on into the mid-nineteenth century. But the evidence of the pamphlets he cites suggests that by 1750 some polite commentators believed that there was no longer any positive moral role for public executions, mainly because enlightened sensibility destroyed their appreciation of the drama, and especially the common people's allotted role in it. This has considerable implications for our understanding of eighteenth-century criminal justice generally. As McGowen shows, in 1730 Sollom Emlyn had singled out public proceedings as the distinguishing characteristic of English criminal justice, a feature that he believed made it superior to continental justice systems. In this connection he mentioned the importance of exemplary deterrence, but made it clear that the common people were not invited simply to be intimidated and terrorized: rather justice had to be seen

[68] On this point, see also A. McKenzie, 'Martyrs in Low Life? Dying "Game" in Augustan England', *Journal of British Studies*, 42 (2003), 167–205.

to be done and understood, if English subjects were truly free.[69] Executions, in other words, were civic events, like the trials that preceded them. However if elite opinion was progressively disinclined to believe that ordinary people were capable of appreciating the moral difference between guilt and innocence, then how could they play a full role in criminal trials, either as witnesses, or jurors? Here indeed McGowen may have hit upon a problem in the administration of justice generally, and not just a crisis of punishment.

British law in the colonies

Finally, two chapters in this collection consider the experience of British law in the administration of settler colonies. In Chapter 9 David Konig moves our focus to Virginia in British North America and discusses the law as it was variously created, administered, and interpreted by the colonial high courts, the royal governors who presided over them, and the Privy Council in London. According to Konig's interpretation of the complex issues between the parties, attention to the litigation and legal politics generated by the clashing interests of Virginian planters, English merchants, and colonial governors in the early eighteenth century reveals a growing contest over the meanings and purposes of law. For their part governors attempted to subject the colonists and their courts to closer control by authoritarian personal intervention from the bench, the use of prerogative powers, encouragement of appeals to metropolitan authorities and jurisdictions, and the creation of new courts. At the same time, under the influence of British merchants in the tobacco trade the Privy Council overturned the decisions of colonial juries and threatened to abolish customary mercantile and common law procedures, thereby encouraging growing discontent in Virginia about the apparently arbitrary application of law from the centre. From the perspective of some leading Virginians, in the context of metropolitan discretionary intervention, law was becoming quite unpredictable; and parliamentary statute was an imperialist instrument that threatened them with rules of justice inferior to those enjoyed by their fellow Englishmen.

Such a story is important for two reasons. First, as Konig points out, it helps to revise the conventional historiography of the Atlantic seaboard colonies in the eighteenth century, which paints a picture of stability under the ascendancy of local legislatures until they were challenged by the new assertiveness of the Westminster parliament after the Seven Years War. This view, based as it is on the study of colonial assemblies, fails to take account of the much more long-standing 'pattern of legal contest between imperial interests and local usage' which is revealed by Konig's research on the

69 A *Complete Collection of State Trials*, ed. T.B. Howell (London, 1809–26), i. xxv–xxvi (repr. of Emlyn's preface to 1730 edition of the *State Trials*).

arguments over the administration of justice. Secondly, the Virginians' shocked reaction to the Council's determination in *Perry* v. *Randolph* suggests their high expectations of justice conformable to 'the Laws and Customs of England' were associated above all with trial by jury and 'due process', as well as the *local* determination of facts in dispute. Indeed Michael Lobban draws attention to the arguments of some American constitutional historians that the colonists' understandings of law were associated with custom and community consensus, rather than positive enactment. Certainly, besides their emphasis on trial by jury as the settled process of law, the Virginians insisted on the legal force of customary dealings between merchants, whereby interest was not due on running accounts and 'set-offs' of money owed from plaintiff to defendant were allowed to negate debts. In these disputes, therefore, there is evidence to support J.P. Reid's arguments about an American concept of law that appealed to seventeenth-century ideas about consent and usage, a concept that was being eclipsed in English government circles by associating law narrowly with parliamentary enactments.[70]

In Chapter 10 Bruce Kercher takes an Australian perspective on the changing nature of British law in the colonies and considers whether judges educated in 'the common law tradition' were resistant to positivist applications of statute or other kinds of legal authority. He shows that several early New South Wales judicial rulings recognized issues of local custom and usage to justify departures from English statutes on the basis of the implied consent of the community. For the majority of judges in the Supreme Court in 1833, 'law was a matter of custom, not positive rule, gaining its legitimacy by its use or non-use by the people of New South Wales'.[71] It appears there are parallels with the Virginians' take on the law here, and their identification of law that was independent of positive authority. Certainly the chief justice talked subsequently about 'the fundamental laws of the land' in connection with English law, by which he appeared to mean fundamental constitutional principles and rules which could not be overturned by colonial statutes, at least in the absence of clear legislation from the Westminster parliament. Ultimately, as the decision of Chief Justice Forbes in *R* v. *Hayes* (1829) showed, the New South Wales judges recognized the supreme authority of the imperial parliament, but Kercher's exegesis of Forbes's decisions reveals a basic instinct for what he discerns as 'the old common law method'. Although he departed from it in individual cases, his guiding principle was that what was law (whether judicial rules or statutes) should be determined through popular consent and local suitability, as signified by usage. But as Kercher shows, even in the 1830s (and in some of Forbes's decisions) this method was showing signs of giving way to the future of law as authority, indicated by relying strictly on the words of statutes and the precedents of previous rulings.

70 See e.g. J.P. Reid, *In Defiance of the Law* (Univ. Park, PA, 1977), esp. chs 5, 20.
71 See below, p. 239.

Just as it is hard to find uncompromising adherence to the common law tradition among judges in early New South Wales, so it is difficult to identify an authentically commanding 'imperial state at law' in their colonial and metropolitan superiors. It is true that some of the first New South Wales governors and legislative councils appear to have been firmly positivist in their approach to law-making. But for their part the imperial law officers and officers of the Colonial Office are represented by Kercher as fairly liberal, at least in so far as they agreed with Forbes's flexible interpretations of English law, and even upheld his point of view on several occasions when he was in conflict with the governor. On the other hand, as in America the imperial structure of authority rendered the New South Wales legal establishment firmly subservient to metropolitan control. Colonial judges' powers of judicial review were subject to scrutiny by the law officers; and their tenure depended on the good opinion of the government in London. So whatever their cultural predispositions were, they were more directly creatures of the state than their counterparts in Westminster Hall. But it is tempting to regard the drift to positivism on the New South Wales bench as part of a more general loss of confidence by judges in their ability to declare the law; a cultural shift which should be linked with the growing institutional power of parliament, rather than the orders of officials.[72]

Conclusion: from consent to command?

The chapters in this book take several different perspectives on the issue of whether British law became more positivist and less participatory or consensual in the eighteenth century, with the apparent decline in the currency of common law traditions and the rise of parliamentary government. However they are hardly comprehensive in scope: for example there is nothing here on policing, and little detail on criminal trial process, even for England. In these areas there is further evidence for a trend away from popular participation in the administration of justice.

Recent work on policing the metropolis of London has demonstrated important eighteenth-century continuities with Peel's new police.[73] In Westminster, metropolitan Middlesex and the City of London after 1700 the night watch was progressively remodelled as local authorities obtained acts of parliament which enabled them to raise rates and organize dedicated bodies of paid men. At the same time London constables were increasingly likely to be paid substitutes who served for several years, rather than citizens who took their

[72] See P.S. Atiyah, *The Rise and Fall of Freedom of Contract* (Oxford, 1979), 383–4.

[73] R. Paley, '"An Imperfect, Inadequate and Wretched System"? Policing London before Peel', *Criminal Justice History*, 10 (1989), 95–130.

turn for twelve months.[74] Following the example set by the Fieldings at Bow Street, in 1785 and 1792 there were also movements towards the centralization of metropolitan policing under a paid magistracy.[75] Although these trends were not fully realized until the foundation of the metropolitan police in 1829, it is clear that 'community self-policing' had largely been eliminated from London by 1750. Indeed the transition to quasi-professional policing increased the scope for active government. During the second half of the century there was a growing consciousness on the part of metropolitan authorities that the arrangements for hiring watchmen and constables had created a new instrument of legal authority for managing the people and the streets.[76] London was exceptional in its precocity, however; even after 1800 changes in policing were complex and uneven across England and Wales.

Professionalization is also clearly evident in the English jury trial, the central legitimizing element of the administration of criminal justice, and it came at the expense of lay participation. Like many contemporary comments on the justice system, sessions charges celebrated the constitutional role of juries, even describing them as 'the Representatives of the People of England', in that they formed a microcosm of the country, whose consent was required for the king to unsheath the sword of justice.[77] But although its formal decision-making power was not diminished, and its autonomy increased somewhat, the jury was largely silenced by the intervention of lawyers in the criminal trial, beginning in the mid-eighteenth century.[78] By the beginning of the nineteenth century, although only a minority of trials at the Old Bailey featured counsel, and only a tiny proportion had counsel on both sides, the overall impact of the lawyers' work was becoming apparent.[79] The defendant was often substantially excluded from the proceedings; witnesses were clearly being selected and carefully prepared for what they would prove according to the solicitor's brief; and members of the jury were reduced to interested but passive spectators of the trial: they voted, but had no active voice. In other words, the criminal trial was well on the way to assuming its modern forms.[80]

74 E.A. Reynolds, *Before the Bobbies: The Night Watch and Police Reform in Metropolitan London, 1720–1830* (Stanford, CA, 1998), chs 2–3; Beattie, *Policing and Punishment*, chs 3–4.

75 L. Radzinowicz, *A History of English Criminal Law and its Administration from 1750* (London, 1948–56), iii. 29–62, 108–37.

76 Beattie, *Policing and Punishment*, 155–7.

77 E.g. *Charges to the Grand Jury*, ed. Lamoine, 375–6, 379: charges of 1752 and 1767.

78 Langbein, *Adversary Criminal Trial*, 319–31.

79 A. May, *The Bar and the Old Bailey, 1750–1850* (Chapel Hill, NC, 2003), 34–5.

80 Langbein, *Adversary Criminal Trial*, ch. 5. See also C. Cottu, *On the Administration of Criminal Justice in England; and the Spirit of the English Government* (1822 [1st edn, 1820]), 33–7, 86–9, 93–4, 105–6; Langbein, 'Criminal Trial before the Lawyers', 273, 307; *idem*, 'Prosecutorial Origins', 328–32.

Viewed from these angles, around 1800, popular relations with law had been transformed from the sixteenth and early seventeenth centuries, when it had been integrated with many aspects of everyday life and culture. Certainly there was widespread (and growing) participation in the administration of justice and in parliamentary politics through the consumption of newspapers and magazines, as well as popular associations. However as Christopher Brooks suggests below, it is important to understand that this was *virtual* experience. Increasingly people connected with law and government as readers of the stories about trials, executions, and parliamentary debates that were staple copy for authors and editors, rather than as face-to-face participants. Indeed, thinking about the nexus between crime, scandal, the press, and parliament takes us into the realm of moral panics about 'social problems' and the reflex 'law and order' legislative responses that are a staple of modern politics. If this was consent for law, it was inclined to over-reaction and susceptible to political manipulation. It remains for further research to demonstrate how far the Westminster legislative process allowed space for direct popular influence, but there can be no doubt that by the end of the eighteenth century parliament, rather than the courts, was the centre of the English legal universe, in practice as well as theory. Admittedly the agencies of central government remained relatively weak, outside the fiscal–military establishment, and as Douglas Hay has pointed out, the 'low law' of positive magisterial authority at the grass-roots was of medieval origin, rather than a new development. But eighteenth-century legislation expanded the province of this kind of administrative authority out of all proportion, while the reach of the common law and its communal traditions of governance seems to have diminished, at least outside British North America. Here, perhaps, were the outlines of a legal regime appropriate for an imperial state, rather than 'an ungovernable people'.[81]

[81] See Brewer and Styles (eds), *An Ungovernable People*, for a collection of essays that emphasizes the ability of the common people to negotiate with legal authority by using customs, ideas, and processes associated with common law tradition.

2

Custom, nature, and authority

The roots of English legal positivism

MICHAEL LOBBAN*

Introduction

Scholars have long acknowledged the political significance of parliamentary sovereignty after 1688, and the increasing importance of legislation in the eighteenth century.[1] The era which saw a significant growth in parliamentary activity has also been associated with a transformation in English legal thought, initiated by Jeremy Bentham's critique of Sir William Blackstone's attempts in his *Commentaries on the Laws of England* to explain the common law as a customary system based on natural law.[2] Bentham's jurisprudence seemed to herald an age in which law would be seen neither as an expression of community consensus manifested through its customs, nor as the articulation of timeless principles of reason or natural law, but rather as the express or tacit commands of a sovereign ruler with absolute power. While in this historiography, Blackstone represents the *ancien régime*, for historians of the American Revolution, his defence of parliamentary sovereignty reflected a new metropolitan rejection of the notion of the fundamental rights of Englishmen which

* An earlier version of this chapter was delivered to the Yale Law School in December 2001, as well as in Canberra. I am grateful to participants in both places for their comments. I am also grateful to the British Academy for the award of an Overseas Conference Grant to cover travel expenses to Australia, and to the Humanities Research Centre for assistance in Australia. The arguments presented here will be developed at greater length in my contribution to volume 9 of *A Treatise on Legal Philosophy and General Jurisprudence* (12 vols, general ed. Enrico Pattaro, forthcoming).

[1] See Julian Hoppit, 'Patterns of Parliamentary Legislation 1660–1800', *Historical Journal*, 29 (1996), 109–32; Hoppit, *Failed Legislation, 1660–1800* (London & Rio Grande, 1997); and J. Innes, 'The Local Acts of a National Parliament: Parliament's Role in Sanctioning Local Action in Eighteenth Century Britain', *Parliamentary History*, 17 (1998), 23–47.

[2] David Lieberman, *The Province of Legislation Determined: Legal Theory in Eighteenth Century Britain* (Cambridge, 1989).

Americans were keen to preserve, and a move towards a positivist mentality.[3] The 1760s, it has been argued, thus saw a parting of the ways between an English view of law, stressing the power of a supreme parliament and an American view, which looked to older fundamental common law rights derived from custom, nature, and community consensus, which would subsequently be translated into the fundamental law of the American constitution.[4]

The very ambiguity of many of Blackstone's arguments, which meant that the *Commentaries* could be drawn on by American Whigs seeking to justify resisting Westminster as well as by metropolitan Tories defending the position of the Declaratory Act,[5] might itself seem to be evidence that this was a key moment of transformation in legal thought, which required a Bentham to give it clearer articulation. However, in what follows, it will be suggested that Blackstone's ambiguous language to some degree masks how far the views of many mainstream English jurists had already departed from the Cokean view so beloved of American Whigs. It will be suggested that the dominant view among English lawyers did not see law as a reflection of popular custom or as a system of natural reason, nor was there a belief in a body of fundamental law which could override or limit the power of parliament. Instead, from the early seventeenth century onwards, law had been defined in terms of the commands or impositions of superior sovereigns. In England, it was argued, sovereignty was located in the crown in parliament as a result of an historical original contract, which generated the criteria for determining the validity of legal rules. This sovereign was the formal source of the common law. While most jurists shared Blackstone's mistrust of the quality of parliamentary legislation, wanting as little legislative interference with the common law as possible, they saw the common law as a body developed within the official forum of the courts, which derived their authority from the sovereign. While judges might develop that law in accordance with the needs of the public, nothing was law which had not been so recognized within the judicial forum.

[3] See Thomas C. Grey, 'Origins of the Unwritten Constitution: Fundamental Law in American Revolutionary Thought', *Stanford Law Review*, 30 (1978), 843–93, and Edward S. Corwin, *The Higher Law Background of American Constitutional law* (Ithaca, NY, 1955).

[4] See John Philip Reid, 'The Irrelevance of the Declaration', in Hendrick Hartog (ed.), *Law in the American Revolution and the Revolution in Law: A Collection of Review Essays on American Legal History* (New York and London, 1981), 46–89; John Philip Reid, *Constitutional History of the American Revolution* (Madison, Wisconsin & London, 1986–93); Jack P. Greene, 'From the Perspective of Law: Context and Legitimacy in the Origins of the American Revolution', *South Atlantic Quarterly*, 85 (1986), 56–77; Jack. P. Greene, *Peripheries and Center: Constitutional Development in the Extended Polities of the British Empire and the United States, 1607–1788* (New York, 1986), 144–50.

[5] Gerald Stourzh, *Alexander Hamilton and the Idea of Republican Government* (Stanford, CA, 1970), ch. 1.

Defining the nature of law

If Sir Edward Coke was the champion of the notion that the common law was 'the perfection of reason',[6] his contemporaries took a view which looks more positivist. Both John Selden and his follower Matthew Hale saw law in terms of the commands of a superior.[7] In an unpublished work, Hale defined a law as:

> a rule of moral actions, given to a being endued with understanding and will, by him that hath power or authority to give the same and exact obedience thereunto *per modum imperii*, commanding or forbidding such actions under some penalty expressed or implicitly contained in such law.[8]

For a law to exist, he argued, 'there must be an author thereof as a legislator' who 'must be distinct from the person to whom it is given or that is to be obliged by it'.[9] Like Selden, Hale said that a law required the existence of a sanction.[10]

The natural law which stood at the centre of Selden and Hale's jurisprudence was one derived from God's commands. In Selden's view, natural law was revealed to men, particularly in the seven *praecepta Noachidarum* given after the Flood, which forbade homicide and theft, and obliged people to maintain the religious and civil order. The most important precept was 'You must abide by your contracts and forms of government agreed on by the citizens, and you must keep your word.'[11] As Hale pointed out, one of the *praecepta* commanded men to institute government: there was 'a kind of natural propension in the human nature to have some imperative and coercive power lodged in the society'.[12] Alongside this positive source of the divine commands sat a second source by which natural law was known. This was the faculty possessed by every rational being, the *intellectus agens*, which enabled them to see natural law, just as light enabled them to perceive objects. Through

[6] Edward Coke, *The First Part of the Institutes of the Laws of England, or, a Commentary upon Littleton*, ed. Francis Hargrave and Charles Butler (15th edn, London, 1794), 97b.

[7] See *Table Talk of John Selden*, ed. Sir Frederick Pollock (London, 1927), 116, cf. 69–70.

[8] *Treatise of the Nature of Lawes in Generall and touching the law of nature*, British Library MS Hargrave 485, f. 3. See the discussion in Alan Cromartie, *Sir Matthew Hale (1609–1676)* (Cambridge, 1995), 90–4.

[9] Hale, *Nature*, f. 7.

[10] *Nature*, f. 12, see also f. 48. For Selden, see Richard Tuck, *Philosophy and Government, 1571–1651* (Cambridge, 1993), 215.

[11] J. Selden, *Opera Omnia* (London, 1725), i. 150, quoted in Tuck, *Philosophy and Government*, 216–17.

[12] Hale, *Nature*, f. 42v.

it, God's commands could be known to individuals, for instance in the consciences of those who were not under the power of their sensual lusts.[13]

The two sources were not contradictory: a subject could not disobey the command of a ruler by claiming to follow what was revealed to him by the *intellectus agens*. Selden and Hale did not conceive of natural law as a complete set of immutable, timeless principles which operated independent of government. Rather, law was a social institution, located in a context. As Selden put it in his edition of Fortescue's *De Laudibus Legum Angliae*, all systems of law derived from the same foundation in nature, and were equally ancient: however, they had taken different paths in their development.[14] Nor could natural law be applied in the abstract. Hale wrote,

> though it may be true, that the consequences and deductions, that may be made by reason, may be ramifications of the law of nature; yet possibly it may be hard to conclude, that all those deductions and inferences are that law of nature, which was intended for the common rule or law of mankind; because, though they might be truths; yet every man is not capable of that perspicacity to follow the consequences so far.[15]

For Hale, positive laws were needed 'to settle that variety and inconstancy of particular applications and conclusions, which, without some established rule, would be found in most men, though of excellent parts and reason, and agreeing in common notions'.[16] Moreover, the

> great variety of circumstances which accompany moral actions [. . .] strangely diversify the application of the general lawes which we may suppose natural, whereby those, that perchance subscribe to the same universal lawes of nature, yet are contradictory in their conclusions touching particular moral actions.

For that reason, matters of detail, were best 'left to the guidance, lawes and customes of people'.[17] Hale's notion of the law of nature, like Selden's, saw its expression through the development of positive laws in context. The legitimacy of law was ultimately underpinned by the command of God's natural law:

[13] J.P. Sommerville, 'John Selden, the Law of Nature, and the Origins of Government', *Historical Journal*, 27 (1984), 437–47.
[14] Selden, *Opera Omnia*, iii. 1891.
[15] Hale, *Nature*, ff. 17–17v.
[16] 'Sir Matthew Hale's Preface to Rolle's Abridgement, published 1668', in [F. Hargrave (ed.)] *Collectanea Juridica, consisting of tracts relative to the law and constitution of England: volume the first* (London, 1791), 274–5.
[17] Hale, *Nature*, ff. 18v, 83v. Cf. *Considerations touching the amendment or alteration of laws*, in Francis Hargrave (ed.), *A Collection of tracts relative to the law of England, from manuscripts* (Dublin, 1787), i. 259–60.

but it was articulated through the commands of an earthly superior and earthly judges.

Definitions of law which sought to root it in the rules laid down by God and government continued to predominate in the eighteenth century, particularly in the wake of the publication of a number of continental treatises which were more accessible than Selden's and Hale's theories.[18] Samuel Pufendorf's *Of the Law of Nature and Nations*, which was translated in 1703, was particularly influential.[19] As Ian Hunter has written, Pufendorf rendered 'natural law immanent to the exercise of sovereignty, thereby opening the doctrine of natural law to the theories of "absolute" (secular) sovereignty elaborated by Bodin', and others.[20] J. J. Burlamaqui's *Principles of Natural and Politic Law*, itself influenced by Pufendorf, was also translated into English in 1748. For Burlamaqui, the sovereign was: 'he who has a right to command in the last resort. To command, is directing the actions of those who are subject to us, according to our own will, and with the authority or the power of constraint.'[21] This is not to suggest that views which saw law in terms of superior commands always predominated. In his *Institute of the Laws of England* of 1720, for instance, Thomas Wood wrote:

> As *Law* in General is an Art directing to the knowledge of Justice, and to the well ordering of Civil Society; so the Law of *England* in particular, is an Art to know what is Justice in *England*, and to preserve Order in that Kingdom.[22]

Other jurists invoked the language of Justinian's *Institutes*, that 'Jurisprudence is the knowledge of things divine and human, the science of the just and the

[18] Selden's huge *De Jure Naturali et gentium juxta disciplinam Ebraeorum* was republished in his *Opera Omnia* in 1725, but was never translated into English. However, it was used by some, including John Taylor, *Elements of the Civil Law* (Cambridge, 1755), at 99. Hale's works remained largely in manuscript, though they do appear to have circulated among some prominent lawyers. See, e.g., Alexander Fraser Tytler, *Memoirs of the Life and Writings of the Honourable Henry Home of Kames* (Edinburgh, 1807), ii. 238; *The Parliamentary History of England*, xvi. 169–70.

[19] The third edition of 1717 included Jean Barbeyrac's notes. Thomas Wood pointed out that young lawyers were expected to read both Grotius and Pufendorf: *Some Thoughts concerning the Study of the Laws of England, particularly in the two universities* (2nd edn, London, 1727), 8.

[20] Ian Hunter, *Rival Enlightenments: Civil and Metaphysical Philosophy in Early Modern Germany* (Cambridge, 2001), 193.

[21] J. J. Burlamaqui, *Principles of Natural and Politic Law*, trans. T. Nugent (2nd edn, London, 1763), i. 80; cf. 78.

[22] *An Institute of the Laws of England* (London, 1720), 6. Cf. John Ayliffe, *A New Pandect of the Roman Civil Law* (London, 1734), 1–2, 9. It should be noted however that Wood prefaced a translation of Jean Domat's *Treatise of Laws to his A New Institute of the Imperial or Civil Laws* (London, 1730).

unjust.'[23] Nor were anti-positivist interpretations of law dependent on Roman maxims. The common law and ancient statutes, wrote the Whig barrister Capel Lofft in 1779, 'spring not from the will of any earthly *superior*, for THE PEOPLE OF ENGLAND acknowledges *no superior* but God'. He went on to argue that the common law 'depends in its *chief*, *essential*, and *noblest* part upon *natural law*; that it sprang from the *bosom* of *liberty*, hath been educated in the *shrine* of *justice*, [and] approved by COMMON CONSENT'.[24]

If positivist language was far from universal, it was nonetheless commonly used by jurists. John Taylor's *Elements of Civil Law*, published in 1755, argued that the reasonableness of an action did not of itself impose an obligation. Rather, 'legal Necessity must come from a superior and directing hand.' If natural law was the command of God, civil law

> Is either MERVM *et simpliciter Civile*, mere arbitrary, positive Institutions of a Lawgiver, and such only, as bind from the Sanction given them by his Authority [. . .] Or, what may be called *Jus Civile* MIXTVM, where positive Institutions make some Alteration in the Law of Nature, either by adding to it, or taking from it, or else by determining and limiting what by the former Law was indeterminate.

For Taylor, the laws of nature were immutable only 'in the Abstract or in Principle' but not 'in Application'.[25]

Taylor's work was admired by Blackstone,[26] who himself put forward a strongly positivist conception of law. Municipal law, he wrote, was 'a rule of civil conduct prescribed by the supreme power in a state, commanding what is right and prohibiting what is wrong'. In all governments, there must be 'a supreme, irresistible, absolute, uncontrolled authority, in which the *jura summi imperii*, or the rights of sovereignty, reside'. Law 'always supposes some superior who is to make it' – so that God was the legislator of natural law. Human legislation was essential for society, for if the 'absolute rights' of Englishmen were 'founded on nature and reason' their 'establishment (excellent as it is)' was 'still human'.[27] Analysing the parts of a law, Blackstone argued that the 'declaratory' part depended 'not so much upon the law of revelation or of nature, as upon the wisdom and will of the legislator'. He acknowledged there were some rights established by God and nature which did not need positive

[23] See Thomas Bever, *A Discourse on the Study of Jurisprudence and the Civil Law* (Oxford, 1766), 3. Such language was also to be found on the bench: See *Millar* v. *Taylor* (1769) 4 Burrow 2343–4.

[24] Capel Lofft, *Elements of Universal Law; and Particularly of the Law of England* (London, 1779), xlviii–xlix, lx. In the following year, Lofft was one of the founders of the Society for Constitutional Information.

[25] Taylor, *Elements*, 132–3, 143.

[26] Blackstone called him 'a very judicious writer': *Commentaries on the Laws of England* (Oxford, 1765–9), i. 36 (henceforth as 1 *Comm.* 36).

[27] 1 *Comm.* 44, 49, 43, 123.

declaration: however this was because they were so obviously harmful that every man was presumed to know that their violation would be punished. Offences against such rights (such as murder or perjury) contracted 'no additional turpitude from being declared unlawful by the inferior legislature'. Other rights which arose from the law of nature, however, did require the laws of the land to set out 'the particular circumstances' under which acts against them were determined to be right or wrong. Besides these 'mixed' matters, finally, there were wholly indifferent matters left to the determination of the legislator. Discussing the 'vindicatory' part, Blackstone noted that 'the main strength and force of a law consists in the penalty annexed to it. Herein is to be found the principal obligation of human laws.' It was human punishment which established the distinction between crime and sin. This meant that while some crimes were offences against the law of nature and others not, 'yet in a treatise of municipal law we must consider them all as deriving their particular guilt, here punishable, from the law of man.'[28]

Blackstone's positivism was to some degree masked by the use he made of the language of natural law. Though his theoretical discussion of the law of nature was largely perfunctory, the distinction running through his text between absolute and relative rights appeared to set up an external standard by which to judge positive law. Blackstone wrote that absolute rights were those which people would have 'merely in a state of nature, and which every man is intitled to enjoy whether out of society or in it'. Echoing Locke, he said the aim of society was 'to protect individuals in the enjoyment of those absolute rights, which were vested in them by the immutable laws of nature', and 'which in themselves are few and simple'. By contrast, rights which were 'social and *relative* result from, and are posterior to, the formation of states and societies'; and were much more numerous and complicated.[29] This appeared to make a clear distinction between natural rights, which came from God, and indifferent matter, which came from human legislation. However, we should not be misled by the use of this language at the start of the work. It has often been recognized that Blackstone's 'absolute' rights were not really such: the rules of property came from positive imposition and even the right to life could be forfeited.[30] Moreover, Blackstone himself argued that 'human laws can have no concern with any but social and relative duties; being intended only to regulate the conduct of man, considered under various relations, as a member of civil society.'[31] Equally, within the text, Blackstone

[28] 1 *Comm.* 54–7, 4 *Comm.* 42. At 4 *Comm.* 8, he argued that the power to punish came from human laws, for all individuals gave up to society the power they had by natural law to punish.
[29] 1 *Comm.* 119–21.
[30] See Robert P. Burns, 'Blackstone's Theory of the "Absolute" Rights of Property', *University of Cincinnati Law Review*, 54 (1985), 67–86.
[31] 4 *Comm.* 41.

appeared to devote far more space to the 'absolute' than the 'relative' rights, although he had said at the outset that the latter were more numerous. The conundrum is resolved when we acknowledge that in the body of the text, Blackstone did not use the terminology of absolute and relative rights to distinguish between those which were pre-social and those which derived from society. Instead, the division was an organizational one, and followed Hale's adaptation of the institutional scheme in his *Analysis of the Law*.[32] The distinction was one between those rights which could be considered without reference to a person's status – such as the rights of life or liberty – and those which had to be explained in the context of social relationships.[33]

Blackstone was not alone in describing law in terms of positive imposition. The laws 'with which we have any concern', Sir Robert Chambers told his students, 'are those only that flow either expressly or by inference *from the will of a superior*.' Chambers made an important distinction in noting that 'the subjects of each state are governed by these its positive institutions, as the *rule* of their *civil conduct*, and owe an obedience to the laws of God and of nature, as the *rule of their moral behaviour*.'[34] His successor, Richard Wooddeson, began with a discussion of the law of nature in which he criticized Hobbes's view than men must obey whatever the sovereign commanded, arguing that when civil laws 'grossly and manifestly contradict' the supreme law of God, 'such immoral or irreligious ordinances ought in conscience to be disobeyed.' However, when subsequently discussing whether positive laws made against natural law were void, he qualified this view:

> The principle is infallibly true; the application of it, and the conclusion, dangerous. We must distinguish between right and power, between moral fitness and political authority. We cannot expect that all acts of legislators will, or can be, entirely good, ethically perfect; but, if their proceedings are to be decided upon by their subjects, government and subordination cease.[35]

He went on to describe legislation as the most exalted degree of sovereignty, perhaps the only supreme power in the state.

[32] M. Hale, *The Analysis of the Law* (3rd edn, London, 1739). Hale's method also influenced Thomas Wood's *Institute*. Blackstone's method can be seen succinctly stated in his own 'Analysis of the Laws of England' in his *Tracts, chiefly relating to the Antiquities and Laws of England* (3rd edn, Oxford, 1771), 14–15, 18–19.

[33] Blackstone followed Hale's same model, although he insisted more than his predecessor that the right to property was one of the absolute rights of persons, a categorization which did cause him some discomfort. 1 *Comm.* 134–6, 3 *Comm.* 138.

[34] Sir Robert Chambers, *A Course of Lectures on the English Law delivered at the University of Oxford 1767–1773*, ed. Thomas M. Curley (Oxford, 1986), i. 84, 88, 91. Emphasis in original unless otherwise stated.

[35] Richard Wooddeson, *Lectures on the Law of England*, 2nd edn, ed. W. R. Williams (London, 1834), i. 30, 48 (original pagination).

The location of sovereignty

If the power of municipal law derived from a sovereign power, what constituted that power? Common lawyers from Selden to Blackstone located the origins of political society in an original contract. However, it was not a Lockean vision that was put forward. For radical Whigs such as Locke, sovereignty always lay with the people, who retained rights derived from a pre-social natural law. '[L]aw, in its true notion', Locke said, 'is not so much the limitation as the direction of a free and intelligent agent to his proper interest, and prescribes no farther than is for the general good of those under that law.' Natural law existed in the state of nature, where men could acquire property in things through adding their labour. They entered society to protect their property, which included life, liberty, and estate. Since men could only give to the legislature the power they possessed in the state of nature, and since in that state each man had 'no arbitrary power over the life, liberty, or possession of another, but only so much as the law of Nature gave him for the preservation of himself and the rest of mankind, this is all he doth, or can give up to the commonwealth.' All government was thus inherently limited: 'the supreme power cannot take from any man any part of his property without his own consent.' Since the legislature was 'only a fiduciary power to act for certain ends, there remains still in the people a supreme power to remove or alter the legislative, when they find the legislative act contrary to the trust reposed in them.'[36]

By contrast, the common lawyers we have been examining did not see the government created in an original contract as a fiduciary acting on behalf of a sovereign people. Nor did jurists such as Hale envisage a law of nature in the pre-social state, which was to be secured by society. There was only a limited legal regime in the state of nature, based on the *praecepta Noachidarum*, which was not sufficient for all the needs of humanity. In the state of nature, Hale admitted, things did exist in which individuals had property, regardless of contract or agreement. For example, everyone had property in his own life, and could sell himself into servitude.[37] While he also admitted the possibility that property could be acquired in that state by occupation or labour, he hesitated from drawing this conclusion, instead noting that 'most of the methods of acquisition of property seem to be by institution.' In any event, 'the full complement of settling of properties' required government.[38]

[36] John Locke, *Second Treatise*, in Locke, *Two Treatises of Government*, ed. Peter Laslett (Cambridge, 1988), §§ 57, 123, 135, 138, 149.

[37] Similarly, Hale argued that adultery was against the law of nature, even in the absence of any pact between the adulterer and the husband. This was because the husband had property in the body of his wife, as a result of the marriage contract, which could not be violated by the adulterer. Hale, *Nature*, f. 36v.

[38] Hale, *Nature*, ff. 36v, 42.

For Hale, just as the forms of property created in different societies could vary according to different contracts, so could the forms of government created by the original contract.[39] This constitution could be changed over time, even where the prince had been given absolute powers. While the people could not resume the powers they had given away, since that would violate their agreement with the prince and constitute a breach of faith, 'yet by that consent of all persons interested [the constitution] may receive an alteration in part or in all.' Such consent could be manifested in a number of ways:

> sometimes by the treaty and conclusion itself of the prince and people, as by acts of parliament, sometimes by the charters of the prince recommunicating some regality back to the people, sometimes by long custom and usage, which binds both prince and people, as well upon the presumption of such an agreement as by introducing a law, by long uninterrupted tacit submission and consent of both.[40]

To be sure, the sovereign was created by consent: but once the parties creating the sovereign had promised, they were bound by their obligation to God to maintain that sovereign according to the terms of the original contract. Under the English constitution, Hale added, the king had 'his rights absolutely, perpetually & hereditarily & cannot be deprived of them either in whole, or part, without his consent', according to the original contract.[41] Equally, the people had their liberties preserved. While there was no authentic evidence of either set of rights in any original document, Hale argued that its existence had to be presumed from the evidence of long usage and frequent confirmation.[42] Under the English constitution, therefore, law was made not by the consent of all the people but '[b]y the immediate consent of that person or those persons in whom by the constitution of the commonwealth that power is placed'. Just as the English monarchy was not subject to any foreign power, 'neither is it subject to the power of the people either distributively, collectively or representatively' since 'the people have either by express or tacit consent transferred the sovereignty unto the king according to the just extents thereof.'[43]

What if the holder of sovereign power acted against the public good? For Locke and the radical Whigs of the 1680s, the people had the power to remove the ruler who had broken his trust. Four decades earlier, John Selden faced a similar dilemma in the spring of 1642. In his view,

[39] Hale, *Nature*, f. 10. Cf. Hale, *The Prerogatives of the King*, ed. D.E.C. Yale (Selden Society, London, 1976), 3.

[40] Hale, *The Rights of the Crown*, quoted in *Prerogatives*, 5n.

[41] British Library, Add. MS 14291, f. 222v.

[42] M. Hale, 'Reflections by the Lord Cheife Justice Hale on Mr. Hobbs his Dialogue of the Law', British Library Add. MS 18235, f. 22v (reprinted in W.S. Holdsworth, *A History of English Law* (London, 1924) v. 500–13).

[43] Hale, *Prerogatives*, 169, 13.

> To know what obedience is due to the prince, you must look into the Contract betwixt him and his people, as if you would know what Rent is due to the Landlord from the Tenant, you must look into the Lease. When the Contract is broken, and there is no third Person to judge, then the [decision] is by arms.[44]

This was to suggest that if the original contract was breached, there would be no superior to judge, and the constitution would dissolve – as appeared to occur in the 1640s. Hale, in calmer times, took the view that the constitution itself generated certain criteria of validity for the king's acts. Most importantly, the king could neither tax nor legislate without parliamentary assent. His subjection to law was confirmed by the presence of 'other additional Laws which either Custome or the Kings assent in Parliament have provided to be perpetual or temporary bounds of the K[in]g's power'.[45] This meant that 'exceeding the royal power is beyond the bounds of law & custome'. It was subject to a *potestas irritans* in many areas: where the king's *ultra vires* actions would simply be ignored.[46] If the king was limited and subject to a kind of control, by contrast, parliament had 'sovereign and sacred Authority in making, confirming, repealing and expounding Laws'. It had, he added, borrowing a phrase from Coke, 'transcendent and absolute' powers.[47] Legislation was, in his words, 'a *Tripartite Indenture*, between the King, the Lords and the Commons'.[48]

Later writers agreed that law did not depend on the immediate consent of the people, but depended rather ultimately on parliament. For John Taylor, societies operated like partnerships. He wrote:

> upon my Entrance into this Partnership I covenant to be concluded in my Negociations, either by the Direction of *One* Man, in whom I may be considered to have reposed a great Confidence; or by the Sentiments and Counsel of the most Substantial and *most considerable*; or lastly by a Majority of the *Whole*.

Thus, law could at the same time be seen to be 'the Direction of a *Superior*, and the mutual Combination of *Equals*': for it was consent that gave to the superior the power to make rules. This applied whether superiority was vested in one man, or remained 'the Superiority of the general Voice'. 'Now this

44 Selden, *Table Talk*, 137. Pollock writes 'division' for 'decision'. On Selden's position, see Richard Tuck, '"The Ancient Law of Freedom": John Selden and the Civil War', in John Morrill (ed.), *Reactions to the English Civil War 1642–1649* (London, 1982), 137–61.

45 BL Add. MS 14291, f. 243r–v. Cf. Hale, *Reflections*, f. 17v.

46 BL Add. MS 14291, f. 245.

47 M. Hale, *The Original Institution, Power and Jurisdiction of Parliaments* (London, 1707), 49, 46, quoting Coke, *Institutes*, iv. 32.

48 M. Hale, *The History of the Common Law of England*, ed. Charles M. Gray (Chicago, 1971), 3. Quoted also in Edward Wynne, *Eunomus: or, Dialogues concerning the Law and Constitution of England* (2nd edn, London, 1785), iii. 124.

Superiority', Taylor said, 'gives this united *Consent* the formal *Ratio* or *Precept*, calls forth the Obligation, and supports and invigorates the Execution.'[49]

The views of late eighteenth-century holders of the Vinerian chair at Oxford echoed Hale's. Though sceptical about the historical idea of an original contract, Blackstone nonetheless referred to the legislature as 'originally set up by the general consent and fundamental act of the society'. For him the very formation of government required some superior, whose commands the members of the community were to obey. Like Hale, he quoted Coke's view that parliament had absolute and transcendent powers, before adding his own gloss that it could do 'every thing that is not naturally impossible'.[50] Blackstone's successors shared his scepticism about the history of the original contract, and shared his notion that the constitution could only be changed through constitutionally valid means. Chambers spoke of the evolution of civil government out of patriarchal authority. The first care of any new society, he said, was 'to select and establish governors, and its first law must constitute the power by which future laws are to be made.' Unlike his predecessor or successor, Chambers therefore defined public law as a distinct head,

> that law of government by which the supreme power in a state regulates its own conduct and that of its subordinate officers, which constitutes the existence, and modifies the operations of the supreme legislative magistrates, [and] which directs and limits (where it is limited) the agency of the supreme executive.[51]

Perhaps the most controversial endorsement of an anti-Lockean position came from Wooddeson. Another sceptic on the original contract, who felt that the constitution developed through gradual change, he nonetheless asserted (in a manner reminiscent of Hobbes) that popular consent to the constitutional arrangement was not subsequently revocable, 'at the will even of all the subjects of the state, for that would be making a part of the community equal in power to the whole originally, and superior to the rulers thereof after their establishment'.[52]

What security did eighteenth-century jurists feel the subject had against misrule? In the wake of the Glorious Revolution, there were two aspects to this question. First, there was the problem of executive misbehaviour. Blackstone acknowledged the autonomous position of the crown. By law, he said, 'the person of the king is sacred, even though the measures pursued in his reign be completely tyrannical and arbitrary: for no jurisdiction upon earth has power to try him in a criminal way.' For Blackstone, 'cases of ordinary public

[49] Taylor, *Elements*, 152.
[50] 1 *Comm.* 48, 52, 156.
[51] Chambers, *Lectures*, i. 89, 90.
[52] Wooddeson, *Lectures*, 22.

oppression' could be controlled, for the king could not misuse his powers without assistance from wicked ministers who would be subject to punishment. However, this would be ineffective for 'such public oppressions as tend to dissolve the constitution'. Any oppression which sprang from 'any branch of the sovereign power' could not be covered by any express rule, but would have to be dealt with by the 'prudence of the times'. Clearly uncomfortable when explaining the events of 1688, he avoided arguing along Selden's lines, that such a clash would lead to a breakdown of society, and preferred endorsing the Convention's interpretation of the events as an endeavour by James II to break the original constitution, but which resulted in his abdication. However, Blackstone also accepted Locke's view that in these circumstances a ruler could be deposed, since 'whenever a question arises between the society at large and any magistrate vested with powers originally delegated by that society, it must be decided by the voice of the society itself.'[53] Locke's views were thus of some use in justifying the deposition of a tyrant king.[54]

In the mid-eighteenth century, attempts to use the prerogative powers of the crown in a way which appeared to bypass parliament and dispense with laws were met with loud constitutional protests, cast in legalistic language reminiscent of the 1670s and 1680s.[55] However, it was found much harder to use a legalistic argument against parliament itself. Blackstone famously wrote that '[s]o long . . . as the English constitution lasts, the power of parliament is absolute and without control.' Did this mean that parliament was bound to observe the constitution, or could constitutional fundamentals be altered? If Blackstone accepted Lockean views to control the *executive*, he rejected Locke's argument that the people had a supreme power to alter the *legislature*, arguing that any dissolution of the whole form of government would, 'by annihilating the sovereign power [repeal] all positive laws whatsoever before enacted', and return all to a natural state of equality. No laws, he said, could contemplate a case which would destroy all law: which was to say that there was no fundamental law which controlled or stood behind parliament. Moreover, he admitted that key component parts of the constitution had been altered in the past, including the succession to the crown, the established religion, 'and even the constitution of the kingdom and of parliaments themselves'.[56]

Nevertheless, late eighteenth-century jurists felt uncomfortable with the idea that there were no bounds to what parliament could do. Richard Wooddeson spoke of the constitution as a set of fundamental rules which were a kind of cement holding the government together. They developed in time

[53] 1 *Comm.* 235–8, 205.

[54] Cf. Wynne, *Eunomus*, i. 72–3.

[55] See, e.g., the debates in 1766 over a bill of indemnity introduced by Chatham's administration for those who acted under an Order-in-Council which imposed an embargo on the export of wheat: *Parliamentary History*, xvi. 245ff.

[56] 1 *Comm.* 157, 156.

in Burkean fashion: 'the finished fabric of a well-ordered constitution', he said, 'is to be the work of succeeding generations, and gradually to be improved by progressive experience.' However, he argued that while there were no bounds to the power of legislative authority in general, the case was 'materially varied' if the legislature attempted to nullify its own essential constitution, as had been done by the statute 31 Hen. VIII c. 8, giving the king's proclamations the force of law.[57] His predecessor at Oxford, Chambers, referred to this statute as unconstitutional but legal, while noting that it was a constitutional fundamental that no parliament could bind its successor. Explaining why this should be so, he noted that 'no power can effect contradictions. That power should limit itself is impossible, and if power destroys itself it ceases to be power.'[58] Common lawyers, in short, were ambiguous on the ultimate power of parliament to change the constitution: while there were no legal limits on its power, it was acknowledged that actions which amounted to an abolition of the institutions themselves would be beyond its powers.[59]

This was a high threshold. It meant that it was within parliament's powers to alter or even abolish what were popularly regarded as ancient common law rights. Thus, the right to trial by jury, which seemed so foundational, was in practice only a 'default position': if a statute was silent as to the mode of trial when a new offence was established, the trial was to be by jury.[60] However, jury trial was not used in the ecclesiastical courts, nor in equity, nor in the myriad of new courts of request set up under statute in many eighteenth-century towns. The right to a jury was further undermined by the extension of summary jurisdiction given by statute to justices of the peace and commissioners of excise. Legal commentators found it difficult to trace the origins of justices' summary powers; but they acknowledged the practical need for them.[61] However, while it was clearly legal for parliament to restrict rights such as jury trial, how far it was constitutionally acceptable was found to be a matter which needed careful consideration.[62] In many areas, what was constitutionally

[57] Wooddeson, *Lectures*, 42–3, 51.

[58] Chambers, *Lectures*, i. 141. It should be noted that Blackstone condemned the Henrician statute, but did not comment on its constitutionality, merely observing that it was subsequently repealed: 1 *Comm.* 261; 4 *Comm.* 424.

[59] The most obvious example is the rule, stated equally by Coke, that no parliament could bind its successors. However, the common lawyers' unease with legislation which might render a man judge in his own case may be seen as a parallel example. For a discussion of an eighteenth-century debate on this, see Philip A. Hamburger, 'Revolution and Judicial Review: Chief Justice Holt's Opinion in *City of London* v. *Wood*', *Columbia Law Review*, 94 (1994), 2091–53.

[60] *Reg.* v. *Sturmey* (1702) 7 Mod. 99.

[61] See, e.g., William Paley, *The Law and Practice of Summary Convictions on Penal Statutes by Justices of the Peace*, 2nd edn by James Dowling (London, 1827), xxxi, xxii.

[62] See, e.g., William Paley, *Principles of Moral and Political Philosophy* (London, 1785), 504–5; 4 *Comm.* 278.

acceptable was a much more complex – and political – question than what was legally permissible.[63]

For mid-eighteenth-century jurists, controlling abuses of power by parliament was thus to be done by political, rather than legal means. This explains how Blackstone, the apparent champion of an unlimited parliament, could at the same time express country Tory suspicions of parliament. It was vital, he said, that members of parliament were of the highest mental and moral standards, since 'England could never be ruined but by a parliament.'[64] He commented further that while the nominal power of the crown had diminished in the period since the Revolution, its real power had not: that real power was based on the influence and patronage which came with the development of the military–fiscal state. Like many country party ideologists, Blackstone was alive to the need to maintain the balance of the constitution. Each element of the constitution must be kept in balance, while the people had to be 'loyal, yet free; obedient, and yet independent'.[65]

Custom and the origins of the common law

If common lawyers had a command-based abstract notion of law, and saw law as derived from a sovereign, how did they explain the origin of the common law, which had long been explained by English jurists in customary terms? Custom was clearly an important source of law. 'All the law you can name', John Selden told the Commons in 1628, 'is reduced to these 2: it is either ascertained by custom or confirmed by act of parliament.'[66] While early seventeenth-century writers like Sir John Davies rooted custom in community

[63] The ambiguity of these constitutional arguments can be seen, for instance, in the protests generated by the excise on cider in 1763, which allowed excise officers to search private dwelling houses, as it laid a duty not merely on the trader, but on anyone who produced cider. In his pamphlet *The Right of Appeal to Juries in causes of excise asserted* (London, [1770]), David Hartley argued that a general excise was unconstitutional, while a 'limited excise [on traders] may be called a constitutional excise . . . [b]ecause it may be consistent with the liberty of the subject' (4). However, he only argued for a right to appeal to a jury against the acts of the excise officers, arguing that if it were given, 'tho' you tax, we will still be free' (27). For other attacks on commissioners, see [Philalethes], *English Liberty in some cases worse than French Slavery: exemplified by animadversions upon the tyrannical and anti-constitutional power of the Justices of the Peace, Commissioners of Excise, Customs and Land Tax etc* (London, 1748), 6, 8.

[64] 1 *Comm.* 156–7. See in general Robert Willman, 'The Politics of Blackstone's *Commentaries*: Whig or Tory?' in G.J. Schochet, P.E. Tatspaugh and C. Brobeck (eds), *Politics, Politeness and Patriotism* (Washington, DC, 1993), 279–308.

[65] 1 *Comm.* 326. Cf. 1 Comm 149.

[66] Robert C. Johnson, Mary Frear Keeler, Maija Jansson Cole, and William B. Bidwell (eds), *Commons Debates 1628* (New Haven & London, 1977), iii. 33. Cf. J. Selden, *Jani Anglorum Facies Altera*, in *Tracts Written by John Selden*, trans. Redman Westcot.

practice,[67] later lawyers took care to distance themselves from any view which would suggest that the common law had existed in the same form since time immemorial, or that it intrinsically embodied the customary practices of the people. For Selden and Hale – whose historical works were highly influential on eighteenth-century jurists – the common law was to be found by searching legal records.

While Hale stressed that much of what was considered as customary probably derived from legislation, he did not however argue that *all* the common law had a statutory origin.[68] For Hale, the 'formal and obliging Force and Power' of the common law 'grows by long Custom and Use'.[69] However, this very fact carried a presumption that it originated 'from the just legislative authority of him or them that first had it'. It implied the consent of the community bound by it, and 'of the legislative authority that tacitly consents to it'. This meant that while customary law 'hath not the formality of other instituted lawes, yet it hath the substance and equivalence of an institution by the legislative authority'.[70] Rather than seeing law originating in a vague distant common consciousness, these historians therefore sought as far as possible to trace the precise origins of legal rules.[71] In this process, Selden in particular delighted in disproving the assumptions of his profession.[72]

An historical approach which saw law as deriving from moments of positive imposition,[73] and which sought to trace ancient common law rules to their precise origins, can be found in many eighteenth-century legal judgments,[74]

[67] Sir John Davies, *Les Reports des Cases & Matters en ley, resolves & adjudges en les courts del roy en Ireland* (London, 1674), preface.

[68] On his 'legislative' view of the common law see Hale, *History of the Common Law*, 44, and Richard Tuck, *Natural Rights Theories: Their Origin and Development* (Cambridge, 1979), 136ff. But compare Hale's view of the manner in which some Norman customs became settled 'insensibly' after the conquest in *History*, 67. Note also his comment elsewhere that many of the key rules of inheritance, conveyance, and contract, 'have not their Authoritie or Institution by Acts of Parliam^{t}'. BL Add. MS 18235, f. 33v.

[69] Hale, *History of the Common Law*, 17.

[70] *Nature*, f.10v. Compare *Prerogatives*, 169. Cf. also Taylor, *Elements*, 245: 'The power of all Law is from the *express*, and that of Customs from the *supposed*, will of the Legislator.'

[71] For Selden, law was controlled by experts even in the era of the ancient Britons, when '*Druids* were wont to meet, to explain the Laws in being, and to make new ones as occasion required': *Jani Anglorum*, 93; cf. *England's Epinomis* (London, 1683), 4. From the Saxon era, he contended, new laws were made in assemblies.

[72] Thus, he pointed out that estates in tail could be found before *De Donis* in the laws of Alfred: Selden, *Opera Omnia*, ii. 926. On the other hand, rules regarding shipwreck, which lawyers reckoned 'among the most ancient Customs of the Kingdom', derived from a statute of Henry I: Selden, *Jani Anglorum*, 66.

[73] Sir Thomas Clarke MR observed, 'I admit most of our law as to its foundation is positive': *Burgess* v. *Wheate* (1759) 1 W. Bl. 123 at 149.

[74] See, e.g., *R.* v. *Dwyer* (1724) Gilb. Rep 267 (on murder); *Reg.* v. *Mawgridge* (1707) Kelyng 119 (on murder); *R.* v. *Wiseman* (1718) Fortescue 92 (on sodomy); *Loyd* v. *Williams* (1771)

as well as in the texts of jurists. Blackstone's debt to Hale in this area was considerable: indeed, several historical passages in the *Commentaries* were little more than transpositions of Hale's *History of the Common Law*, albeit lacking Hale's subtlety.[75] While stating that the common law received its binding force from immemorial usage, Blackstone showed that its origins could be dated, and traced back to positive institution. Accepting Selden's qualification of Fortescue, that the common law included the different customs of Saxons, Danes, and Normans, Blackstone argued that they were moulded into a single code by several kings. Building on foundations laid by Alfred, Edward the Confessor 'extracted one uniform law or digest or laws, to be observed throughout the whole kingdom'. In this process of creation, 'each district mutually sacrific[ed] some of it's own special usages, in order that the whole kingdom might enjoy the benefit of one uniform and universal system of laws.' The codes of law drawn up by these Saxon kings 'gave rise and original to that collection of maxims and customs, which is known by the name of common law'.[76] Yet Blackstone noted that not all of what was regarded as common law was Anglo-Saxon: most importantly, 'the fundamental maxim and necessary principle' that all lands in England were held of the crown[77] derived from the feudal system which, following Sir Martin Wright's *Introduction to the Law of Tenures*,[78] Blackstone dated to the reign of the conqueror.[79] Blackstone repeated Wright's view that the fiction that the king was universal lord of all his territories was one 'nationally and freely adopted' with the consent of the *Commune Concilium*, and that the oppressive consequences associated with feudalism only ensued when crafty Norman lawyers began to manipulate the rules they had penned.[80]

This approach made it hard to treat any aspect of the law as immemorial and timeless in the way Coke's *Prefaces* had suggested. Many of the rules

3 Wils. KB 250 at 259–60 (on usury); *Swann* v. *Broome* (1764) 3 Burr. 1595 (on court days). It should be observed that it was not only the works of Selden and Hale that were used, but also William Lambarde, Henry Spelman, and other seventeenth- and eighteenth-century antiquarians.

[75] Compare, e.g., 1 *Comm.* 68 with *History of the Common Law*, 17–18, and 1 *Comm.* 63 with *History of the Common Law*, 16–17.

[76] 1 *Comm.* 64–6, 74, 67. See also 4 *Comm.* 405, which discusses the role of Edgar.

[77] 2 *Comm.* 51, 4 *Comm.* 411. See also 2 *Comm.* 105.

[78] This was published in 1730, and built on the work of Craig. See John W. Cairns and Grant McLeod, 'Thomas Craig, Sir Martin Wright, and Sir William Blackstone: The English Discovery of Feudalism', *Journal of Legal History*, 21 (2000), 54–66.

[79] Sir Robert Chambers also drew on the work of Selden, Hale, and Wright, and concluded that 'much of our *private law* therefore as depends on general and immemorial usage, must be acknowledged to be in great measure Norman' though 'the great outlines however of our *public law*, like the bulk of our people, are manifestly of Saxon origin'. Chambers, *Lectures*, i. 103.

[80] Wright, *Tenures*, 58–9, 71–2, 78–81. For Blackstone's version, see 2 *Comm.* 48–50, 4 *Comm.* 407–8.

Blackstone discussed as 'general customs' could only be explained in the context of positive institutions. For example, he pointed out that it had been determined 'time out of mind' that a brother of the half-blood should not succeed to his half-brother's estate, but that it should escheat to the king or superior lord. 'Now this', he said, 'is a positive law, fixed and established by custom, which custom is evidenced by judicial decisions.'[81] But this was no simple custom hardened into law, for the feudal rule of escheat, referred to here, was traced by Blackstone to the post-conquest statutory agreement. When common lawyers spoke of 'immemoriality', therefore, they generally meant that there was no authoritative way to trace the rules prior to 1189, the limit of legal memory.[82] Whether or not a rule predating 1189 should be regarded as customary or statutory in origin was ultimately a purely academic question; and often an unanswerable one. What was clear from Hale's *History*, however, was that these ancient foundations were the sources of the *capitala legum*, the fundamentals of English law, such as the course of descent in property, which formed 'the great *Substratum* that is to be maintain'd'.[83]

The jurists' view that law derived from moments of positive enactment can even be found in their attitude to the binding force of local customs. According to Matthew Bacon's *Abridgement*,

> The frequent repetition of an act, which at first was assented to by the people of a certain place for their mutual conveniency and advantage, is called a custom, and every such custom, being certain and reasonable in itself, and commencing time immemorial, and always continuing without interruption, has obtained the force of a law, and in such places shall prevail, though contrary to the general laws of the kingdom.[84]

In deciding whether a custom was reasonable, it was often asked whether it could have had a reasonable *origin*, for however reasonable, new customs could not arise in derogation of the common law.[85] Their status was therefore to be explained by the notion that they were the product of a positive institution in an era prior to the establishment of the common law. As Blackstone put it, they were 'the remains of that multitude of local customs before mentioned, out of which the common law, as it now stands, was collected first by king Alfred'.[86] Customary rights thus were to be anchored to

81 1 *Comm*. 70.

82 2 *Comm*. 31. Hale, whose structure and general arguments he follows, did discuss the relevance of the loss of records before 1189 more thoroughly.

83 Hale, *History of the Common Law*, 46.

84 M. Bacon, *A New Abridgment of the Law* (London, 1832), tit. Customs (A).

85 See Bacon's *Abridgement*, tit. Customs (C): 'Every custom ought to appear to have had a reasonable commencement, and that at first it was voluntarily agreed to.'

86 1 *Comm*.74. At 1 *Comm*. 76, Blackstone argued that if the origin of a custom could be traced, then it would not be valid: this was to assume (understandably) that it would not

moments of legal origin, and not left to mere usage, practice, or even popular belief.[87]

Judicial reasoning and the growth of common law and equity

While lawyers took a restrictive view of customs, they had an expansive view of the common law. As Hale put it, the further the laws were from their original institution, the more numerous they grew, as judges developed the law on the foundations of the *capitala legum*.[88] Hale gave some guidance as to how cases should be decided which had not been determined *in terminis* before. First, the judge was to enquire 'with all Imaginable Industrie' to see what had formerly been done in such cases; and not depart from such resolutions 'without very Evident and cleare & unanswerable Reason'. If there were no precedent resolutions, the judge should 'keep his Reason as Neare as may be within the Cancelli of the Reason of the Law' and make analogies with similar cases, in order to maintain certainty. A mischievous certain law, Hale observed, was better than an arbitrary one, for the former could be amended by act of parliament, whereas 'there is no cure for the Inconveniences of an Arbitrary Law.' Only when there were no similar cases could 'Reason att large' be used.[89] In this way, the laws became the product of the experience of many ages; for it required 'much time and much experience, as well as much wisdom and prudence successively to discover defects and inconveniences, and to apply apt supplements and remedies for them'.[90] Hale was especially concerned with the generation of rules. 'Itt is one of the things of greatest Moment in the profession of the Common Law', Hale wrote,

> to keepe as neare as may be the certainty of the Law, and the Consonancie of it to it selfe, that one Age and one Tribunall may Speake the same things and carry on the same thred of the Law in one uniforme Rule as neare as is possible; for otherwise that which all Ages and Places have contended for in Lawes, Namely Certainty and to avoide Arbitrariness and that Extravagance that would fall

be possible to trace the origin of specific local customs in Anglo-Saxon times. In *Weekly v. Wildman* (1699) 1 Ld Raym 405, counsel sought to argue that all reasonable customs should be presumed to have begun by statute: but Treby CJ rejected this, saying that such a presumption would make all unreasonable customs binding as well.

[87] See also the discussion of legal attitudes to rights of common in E.P. Thompson, 'Custom, Law and Common Right', in his *Customs in Common* (London, 1991), 97–184 and Andrea C. Loux, 'The Persistence of the Ancient Regime: Custom, Utility and the Common Law in the Nineteenth Century', *Cornell Law Review*, 79 (1993), 183–218.

[88] Hale, *History of the Common Law*, 40–1.

[89] BL Add. MS 18235, ff. 32–33v.

[90] Hale, 'Preface to Rolle's Abridgement', 266–7.

out, if the Reasons of Judges and Advocates were not kept in their Traces would in halfe an Age be lost.[91]

Common lawyers remained keen to develop this system into a larger body of 'positive laws' by analogy and extension.[92] The way in which law was developed by the judicial process was explained by Justice Wilmot in giving an opinion to the Lords in 1758 on the operation of the writ of habeas corpus outside the Caroline statute. Wilmot argued that writs of *habeas corpus* in cases of private custody had originated in the era of the Restoration, by 'a warrantable extension of a legal remedy in one case, to another case of the same nature'. The legality of this first extension, he said, was confirmed by its continued application by the judges for eighty years. He went on,

> The principle upon which the usage was founded, lay in the law; and the usage is nothing but a drawing that principle out into action, and a legal application of it to attain the ends of justice. It is upon this foundation only, that an infinite variety of forms, rules, regulations, and modes of practice in all Courts of Justice must stand, and can only be supported.[93]

The courts, he said, moulded and modified their practice from experience and observation to administer justice better to the people. However, this was a strictly controlled *legal* process:

> all acts done by Judges at their chambers, and by officers of the Court, either in term or out of term, are under a delegated authority from the Court. They are controulable by the Court, and obedience to them must be enforced by the Court. And the acts done in Court and out of Court, taken together, form that system of practice by which the benefit of the law is dealt out to the people.

[91] Hale, *Reflections*, ff. 12v–13.

[92] Eighteenth-century lawyers often referred to settled legal practices which had developed in court as 'positive laws'. While this phrase often referred to a statute, it could also mean any settled rule or practice of the common law. Thus, in *Williamson* v. *Hancock* (1675) 1 Mod. 192, Maynard Sjt observed in argument that 'the present case is upon a collateral warranty, which is a positive law, and a thing so remote from solid reason and equity, that it is not to be stretched beyond the maxim.' Equally, in *Lisle* v. *Grey* (1679) T. Raymond 315, 320 the court declared 'the rule in *Shellie's case* to be a positive law, of which there can no reason be given, but is a land-mark by which other cases are bounded'. See also the use of the phrase by counsel in *R.* v. *Bishop of London and Lancaster* (1693) 1 Shower KB 441 at 444 and by Lord Mansfield in *Lindon* v. *Hooper* (1776) 1 Cowper 414 at 417.

[93] *Opinion on the Writ of Habeas Corpus* (1758) Wilmot 77 at 96. Thomas Hedley told the Commons in 1610 that 'the common law is extended by equity, that whatsoever falleth under the same reason will be found the same law': Elizabeth Reed Foster (ed.), *Proceedings in Parl 1610. Vol 2 House of Commons* (New Haven, 1966), 175–6.

Hale's advice had made pure reason the last place for the judge to look. However, in a number of areas of increasing importance – notably the law of obligations – there were few 'positive' rules to be extended by analogy, and resort had perforce to be made to 'reason and convenience, adapted to the circumstances of the times'.[94] In these areas, the common law acted more like a system of remedies than as one of rules, enforcing obligations whose content was derived from outside the law.[95] At the same time, the court of Chancery's jurisdiction – of growing importance to the propertied and commercial society of the eighteenth century – was seen to be rooted in notions of equity and good conscience, as opposed to positive rules. An examination of legal reasoning in many eighteenth-century cases on the law of obligations might suggest that judges were simply enforcing a system of natural rules, or rules generated by community practice, making any positivist conception of the law untenable. Nevertheless, eighteenth-century jurists maintained that the judges derived their authority from the sovereign, rather than autonomously from a natural law itself or from the people. If the content of the rules came from outside the law, their formal binding authority and their validity came from within the system.

For Blackstone, the remedies offered by the common law for breaches of obligations through the action on the case were to be traced to a positive origin in the second statute of Westminster,[96] which empowered the issuing of writs which were adapted to the individual circumstances of the alleged wrong. Common law judges were thus authorized by statute to enforce all manner of 'natural' obligations: but these obligations only became positive by the decision of the court, after which point they became precedents to be referred to in the future elaboration of rules.[97] How free were judges to resort to nature and reason, within this system of remedies, disregarding earlier decisions? At first glance, it might appear that they had a great deal of discretion: for jurists frequently asserted that legal decisions were only evidence of the law, rather than the law itself, and that the common law was a system of principles, not precedents.[98] Blackstone's own statement that it was the judges in court, 'the living oracles, who must decide in all cases of doubt', seemed to give them great power to decide according to their own views of natural law: for where precedents were 'most evidently contrary to reason', the judge could depart from the old rule, not to make a new law, but to vindicate 'the old one

94 2 *Comm.* 385.

95 See M. Lobban, *The Common Law and English Jurisprudence, 1760–1850* (Oxford, 1991), ch. 4.

96 3 *Comm.* 51.

97 See 2 *Comm.* 397, cf. 2 *Comm.* 438.

98 See Lord Mansfield's comment in *Jones* v. *Randall* (1774) 1 Cowp. 37 at 39. See also Jim Evans, 'Changes in the Doctrine of Precedent during the Nineteenth Century', in Laurence Goldstein (ed.), *Precedent in Law* (Oxford, 1987), 35–72.

from misrepresentation'.[99] Despite such statements, however, the system of precedent was more strongly acknowledged by jurists in the eighteenth century than has sometimes been admitted.[100] Moreover, if Blackstone's comments proved controversial, his point was rather less ambitious than it seemed. For the example he gave of a judge's decision which would not be law was the extreme one of a judge, familiar with the rule against the half-blood inheriting, deciding that an elder brother could therefore seize lands purchased by his half-brother. Such a decision would be a merely arbitrary judgment without any legal foundation. To say that a judge could mistake the law was to describe what later judges referred to as a decision *per incuriam*, made in ignorance of authority. Such an opinion was hardly novel: as Sir John Vaughan observed in 1674, one court was not obliged to follow the decision of a prior court 'unless it think that judgment first given was according to law. For any court may err, else errors in judgment would not be admitted, nor a reversal of them.'[101]

If the flexible adjudication of the common law could be related back to an empowering statute, jurists faced another problem in explaining the jurisdiction of the Chancery. The very existence of a jurisdiction grounded in conscience seemed to acknowledge that the common law was a system of inflexible rules which could be unconscionable. It also implied that natural equity could trump the common law. How were jurists to explain the Chancery's jurisdiction without accepting that all law might ultimately be subject to the sensibilities of one judge's conscience, which could vary from one chancellor to another just as the length of their feet differed?[102] By the eighteenth century, equity lawyers were certainly keen to assert that their jurisprudence was based on settled principles rather than on the subjective will of the incumbent lord chancellor.[103] However, they often

[99] 1 *Comm.* 69–70.

[100] On the development of precedent from cases of first impression, see Wynne, *Eunomus*, iii. 177–8. Wynne recognized a clear hierarchy (at iii. 191–5). The lowest value were precedents *sub silentio*; followed by the single opinion of a judge at *nisi prius*; then the determination of one court in Westminster Hall; then the confirmation of this by another court on a writ of error; and finally the determination of a writ of error in the Lords, which had the same authority as a statute. See also the comments of Lord Loughborough in *Graham* v. *Johnstone* (1796) 3 Ves Jr 198: 'all questions of succession are in their nature questions of positive law; and if the argument had raised a doubt in my mind, and I were not inclined to follow the rule, that has prevailed in other cases, I am bound by repeated decisions in the House of Lords to make the decree, I intend to make.'

[101] *Bole* v. *Horton* (1674) Vaughan 360 at 383. See also *Bishop of Exeter* v. *Hele* (1693) Shower PC 88 at 100.

[102] Selden, *Table Talk*, 43.

[103] See D.E.C. Yale (ed.), *Lord Nottingham's 'Manual of Chancery Practice' and 'Prolegomena of Chancery and Equity'* (Cambridge, 1965), 194; *Cook* v. *Fountain* (1733) 3 Swanst 585 at 600, and the preface to *Reports of Cases Taken and Adjudged in the Court of Chancery in the Reign of Charles I Charles II and James II* (London, 1693).

described those principles in terms of natural law or 'the original and eternal Rules of Justice'.[104]

To see how lawyers explained the function of the Chancery, we need to examine their understanding of equity. The role of 'equity' was classically to deal with situations where the application of a strict rule of law would produce injustice in individual cases. However, its operation could be viewed in a number of ways. One interpretation was to see it as a power inherent in the judges to interpret laws equitably, by extending or restricting the reach of the law to cases which fell or did not fall within its meaning. This power had long been seen to inhere in the common law judges; and did not call for a separate jurisdiction.[105] A second approach was to see the power as inherent in the ruler, who could by his or her absolute power go beyond the ordinary rules of law to see justice done.[106] Many seventeenth- and eighteenth-century writers agreed that this was the origin of the equitable function. It was argued that in the early stages of political society, before the settlement of positive laws or the writing down of customs, cases had been decided on the basis of equity, usually by a wise man chosen to act as ruler. The courts themselves, it was argued, had originated as wise rulers – notably Alfred, following the example of Moses – delegated their power to others: but in this process, the right of subjects to seek the equitable judgment of the king himself, when they could not get justice at home, was preserved.[107]

However, the notion of an equitable power inherent in the sovereign to set aside unjust laws was an awkward explanation of present practice: by the eighteenth century, not only was this power delegated to a court, but the court had no power to relieve against an express act of parliament.[108] Instead, the

[104] [Richard Francis], *Maxims of Equity, collected from and proved by cases out of the Books of the best authority, in the high court of Chancery* (London, 1727), 2. For a theory of equity built on natural law foundations, see [Henry Ballow], *A Treatise of Equity*, 5th edn, with notes by John Fonblanque (London, 1820).

[105] See, e.g., Georg Behrens, 'Equity in the *Commentaries* of Edmund Plowden', *Journal of Legal History*, 20 (1999), 25–50; 'A Dialogue betwixt two students of the Common Law concerning equity' [written in the 1640s] BL MS Egerton 3357; *R* v. *Philips* (1757) 1 Kenyon 531.

[106] See, e.g., Sir John Fortescue, *De Natura Legis Naturae* in Thomas Fortescue, Lord Clermont, *The Works of Sir John Fortescue, Knight* (London, 1869), i. 214–15; 'A Learned Treatise concerning the High and Honourable Court of Chancery written by the Famous Sir Robert Cotton', BL MS Hargrave 227, f. 41; Yale (ed.) *Nottingham's 'Manual of Chancery Practice'*, 189.

[107] See Coke's statement in *Calvin's case*, 7 Co 13a; William Lambarde, *Archeion: or a Discourse upon the High Courts of Justice in England*, ed. Charles H. McIlwain and Paul L. Ward (Cambridge, MA, 1957), 10–17; William Dugdale, *Origines Juridiciales* (2nd edn, London, 1671), 1, 19; Yale (ed.) *Nottingham's 'Manual of Chancery Practice'*, 188; Henry Spelman, *The English Works of Sir Henry Spelman* (London, 1723), 219.

[108] [Ballow], *Treatise*, 16–18.

equitable function was now seen in terms of giving new forms of remedy which were unprovided for at common law. But since the common law was meant itself to provide a remedy for every wrong, the separate existence of the Chancery still needed some explanation. Rival explanations of its origins were provided by partisans and opponents of the court, some seeing it as equal in age with the courts of common law, others as a later statutory creation, subject to the fundamental common law.[109] By the early eighteenth century, however, most related its origins as a court to developments after the passing of the second statute of Westminster. For instance, Jeffrey Gilbert argued that this statute had been passed because Chancery officials had proved reluctant to grant writs in cases for which there were no precedents, preferring to see parties petition parliament for a remedy. If this paved the way for a more flexible system of remedies at common law, the Chancery's rise as a separate jurisdiction was the result of later clerical manipulation. Gilbert claimed that the statute was used conservatively until the reign of Richard II, when the clerical chancellor, John Waltham, used his power to devise the new writ of subpoena, in order to develop a jurisdiction over uses, which had been devised to evade the Statute of Mortmain.[110] This view of the origins of the Chancery could explain why the legal system offered both the flexible common law action on the case, and the jurisdiction of the lord chancellor, both of which seemed to have the 'equitable' function of providing just remedies adapted to the party's situation.[111]

Whatever its origins, by the eighteenth century all commentators were bound to admit that the Chancery provided remedies which were not available at common law, by its power to probe and direct the conscience of the parties, and obtain answers from the defendant. It was admitted that the common law did not have the machinery to examine matters of fraud, accident, and trust:[112] and that the capacity of individuals to commit acts of injustice

[109] Compare *Arguments, proving from antiquity the dignity, power and jurisdiction of the Court of Chancery* (written between 1644 and 1654 and printed in the end of *Reports of Cases Taken and Adjudged in the Court of Chancery* (London, 1693; 2nd edn, 1715) and in F. Hargrave, *Collectanea Juridica*, 20–78) and Roger Acherley, *The jurisdiction of the Chancery as a court of equity researched* (3rd edn, London, 1736; 1st edn, 1733). The argument was sometimes made that the court derived its equitable function from the statute 36 Edw. III c. 9: see, e.g., *King* v. *Standish* (1668) 1 Levinz 241 at 242, and the *Certaine Observations concerning the office of the Lord Chancellor* (London, 1651), 27–8, the authorship of which was misattributed to Ellesmere.

[110] J. Gilbert, 'Forum Romanum', in *The History and Practice of the High Court of Chancery* (Dublin, 1758), 28–30. This argument was repeated by Blackstone, 3 *Comm.* 51–2. Cf. Lambarde, *Archeion*, 39.

[111] For an early expression of such a view, see Edward Hake, *Epieikeia: A Dialogue on Equity in Three Parts*, ed. D.E.C. Yale (New Haven, 1953), 103–6.

[112] Acherley, Jurisdiction, 35–6. Cf. John Mitford, A *Treatise on the Pleadings in Suits in the Court of Chancery by English Bill* (2nd edn, London, 1787), 3. Blackstone said that

by fraudulent means was potentially unbounded. It was thus less a question that the rules of the common law were hard than that its procedures were too strict. This point was made by John Reeves's *History of English Law*, which agreed in locating the origin of the equitable jurisdiction in the reign of Edward I, and accepted that the rise of uses increased its importance; but which argued that the jurisdiction derived from a delegation of the king's council to the lord chancellor to act according to conscience. Reeves pointed to the problems caused by the rigid procedures of the common law, which facilitated proceedings in most cases, but denied justice in others. He cited the argument of the sixteenth-century *Replication* that all the courts knew what reason and conscience dictated: but some courts simply had their own procedural customs which prevented them from hearing certain pleas.[113]

The courts of both common law and equity were thus seen as deriving their authority from the sovereign power; and both were seen to be able to use reason or natural law as a source of rules. Indeed, it was necessary to use sources from outside the ancient common law: if the law of property could be seen as originally derived from a set of rules agreed by the king and his council, it was much harder so to see the law of obligations or trusts in those terms.[114] Nonetheless, lawyers drew a clear distinction between the obliging force of positive law as recognized and developed in a court, and the moral obligation of natural law. For despite the occasional rhetoric which suggested that the law of nature was enforced by English courts,[115] even the most equitably minded of judges acknowledged that the enforceability of natural obligations was limited by positive law.[116] As one early seventeenth-century judge pointed out, even if *jura naturae sunt immutabilia*, they could be bound by 'law of policy . . . in point of form and circumstance, it being better to admit a mischief in particular,

the action on the case 'might have effectually answered all the purposes of a court of equity; *except that of obtaining a discovery by the oath of the defendant*', 3 *Comm.* 51 (emphasis added).

113 John Reeves, *History of the English Law* (London, 1787), 3. 188–9, 373. See also J. A. Guy (ed.) *Christopher St. German on Chancery and Statute* (Selden Society, Supplementary series, 6, London, 1985), 111; and Philip Yorke's argument in *R* v. *Hare and Mann* (1719) 1 Stra. 146 at 150–1.

114 It was agreed, for instance, that the original duty of a trustee (or feoffee to uses) was merely the confidence reposed in him by the beneficiary and settlor, which was subsequently enforced by a court. See (e.g.) Lord Mansfield's comments in *Burgess* v. *Wheate* (1759) 1 W Black. 123 at 156.

115 Thus, Talbot LC spoke of 'it being the business of this court [of Chancery] to relieve against all offences against the law of nature and reason': *Bosanquet* v. *Dashwood* (1734) Cases temp Talbot 38.

116 For instance, Lord Mansfield noted in 1768 that while '[t]he justice of allowing cross demands is supported by natural equity, . . . the common and established forms of law have, in general, directed separate remedies to be mutually had by different actions . . . And Courts of Equity have followed this rule, because it was the law': *Green* v. *Farmer*, 1 W Black. 651 at 652.

even against the law of nature, than an inconvenience in general'.[117] Indeed, courts recognized that some obligations regarded as natural would simply not be enforced.[118]

The common law, natural law, and the American Revolution

The vision of the common law held by the mainstream jurists and lawyers we have discussed was far from universally held in the wider political world. The common law continued to occupy an important place in popular conceptions of the constitution, and from the 1760s, 'law was integral to the culture of opposition.'[119] Radicals and Whigs looked to it as a guarantee against arbitrary and tyrannical rule in terms quite different from those we have encountered hitherto. As Junius put it, '[t]he power of the legislature is limited not only by the general rules of natural justice, and the welfare of the community, but by the forms and principles of our particular constitution.'[120] For writers like this, the common law represented a series of fundamental rights which the government was bound to protect, which could not be altered without the people's consent. For them, the common law was not the preserve of the lawyers. In the era of Mansfield's attempts to restrict the power of the jury in cases of seditious libel, many opponents of government questioned the judiciary's willingness to preserve popular rights, and Junius pointed out how the people were roused by unconstitutional measures, whether they were 'supported only by the power of government, or masked under the forms of a court of justice'.[121] While opponents of the government were often able to achieve spectacular courtroom successes which rested on a mastery of legal argument,[122] their view of the nature of the common law rested less on its technical details than on institutions such as trial by jury and habeas corpus, and by historical landmarks, such as Magna Carta and the Glorious Revolution. John Thelwall, for example,

[117] *Anne Needler* v. *Bishop of Winchester* (1615) Hobart 220 at 224.

[118] E.g. *Fursaker* v. *Robinson* (1717) 1 Eq. Ca. Ab. 123, Prec. Ch. 475.

[119] Richard Price, *British Society, 1660–1880: Dynamism, Containment and Change* (Cambridge, 1999), 254.

[120] Quoted in Reid, *Constitutional History*, iii. 83.

[121] *The Letters of Junius*, ed. John Cannon (Oxford, 1978), 33 (letter 1, 21 Jan., 1769).

[122] On the use of law by and against the radicals, see John Brewer, 'The Wilkites and the Law, 1763–74: A Study of Radical Notions of Governance', in J. Brewer and J. Styles (eds), *An Ungovernable People: The English and their Law in the Seventeenth and Eighteenth Centuries* (London, 1980), 128–71; T. A. Green, *Verdict According to Conscience: Perspectives on the English Criminal Trial Jury, 1200–1800* (Chicago, 1985), 318–55; M. Lobban, 'From Seditious Libel to Unlawful Assembly: Peterloo and the Changing Face of Political Crime, c.1770–1820', *Oxford Journal of Legal Studies*, 10 (1990), 307–52; and John Barrell, *Imagining the King's Death: Figurative Treason, Fantasies of Regicide 1793–1796* (Oxford, 2000).

hailed the common law as 'that still surviving fragment of the free and glorious Constitution of our Saxon ancestors!'[123]

Over time, however, the rhetoric of opposition began to be cast decreasingly in terms of the ancient constitution and increasingly in Lockean, natural law terms.[124] One reason for this was that it was found increasingly difficult to counter the notion of parliament's absolute supremacy by using legalistic language. This trend is particularly apparent in the American crisis of the 1760s and 1770s, which saw a development away from a common law constitutionalist language to one based on natural law principles which did not depend on an immemorial law.[125] American political argument in the 1760s was full of constitutionalist rhetoric about the fundamental rights of Englishmen and the common law.[126] Echoing the language of Sir Edward Coke, lawyers such as James Otis argued that acts of parliament against the constitution or against natural equity were void.[127] Otis denied 'that the supreme power should have the right to alter the constitution' or that 'those who are entrusted with sovereignty by the people have a right to do as they please'.[128] Given the often ambiguous and uncertain status of common law rules in America,[129] it came to be seen more as a general set of fundamental rights than as a set of firm rules or technical procedures.

In an era when parliamentary intervention in the colonies was rare, the association of the ancient common law with a *mentalité* of rights could flourish: but problems were inevitably raised by parliament's increasing intervention from the mid-1760s. While much political debate might be generated by the notion of 'virtual representation', from the legal point of view it was difficult either to assert that statutes should not bind those who had not assented to

[123] John Thelwall, *The Natural and Constitutional Rights of Britons*, in Gregory Claeys (ed.), *The Politics of English Jacobinism: Writings of John Thelwall* (University Park, PA, 1995), 21.

[124] Wilfrid Prest, *Albion Ascendant: English History, 1660–1815* (Oxford, 1998), 280.

[125] See also J.C.D. Clark, *The Language of Liberty, 1660–1832: Political Discourse and Social Dynamics in the Anglo-American World* (Cambridge, 1994), 93–110.

[126] See, e.g., Robert J. Taylor, Mary-Jo Kline, and Gregg G. Lint (eds), *Papers of John Adams* (Cambridge, MA, 1977), i. 86.

[127] See Charles Francis Adams (ed.), *The Works of John Adams* (Boston, MA, 1850), ii. 521. See also Otis, *The Rights of the British Colonies asserted and proved*, in Bernard Bailyn (ed.), *Pamphlets of the American Revolution, 1750–1776, vol. 1 1750–1765* (Cambridge, MA, 1965), 454. Cf. Taylor, Kline, and Lint, *Papers of John Adams*, i. 152.

[128] James Otis, *The Rights of the British Colonies asserted and proved* (Boston, MA, 1764), in Bailyn (ed.), *Pamphlets*, 477.

[129] For the relationship between English and colonial law, see Jack P. Greene, *Peripheries and Center*, 26 and Joseph Henry Smith, *Appeals to the Privy Council from the American Plantations* (New York, 1950), 562–72, 487–95. On the local adaptation of common law rules, see, e.g., Julius G. Goebel, 'King's Law and Local Custom in Seventeenth Century New England', *Columbia Law Review*, 31 (1931), 416–48; George Lee Haskins, *Law and Authority in Early Massachusetts: A Study in Tradition and Design* (New York, 1960), ch. 8; D. T. Konig, *Law and Society in Puritan Massachusetts: Essex County 1629–92* (Chapel Hill, NC, 1979), 37. See also Prof. Konig's chapter in this collection.

them either directly or by their chosen representatives, or to challenge the right of parliament to legislate for the colonies.[130] A number of writers after 1774 therefore put forward a new argument that the sole connection between the Americans and the English came through the person of the king. 'Those who launched into the unknown deep, in quest of new countries and habitations', James Wilson wrote in 1774,

> still considered themselves as subjects of the English monarchs, and behaved suitably to that character; but it nowhere appears, that they still considered themselves as represented in an English parliament, or that they thought the authority of the English parliament extended over them.[131]

If such arguments were a convenient way to evade the sovereignty of parliament, they ran the risk of seeing all American rights as deriving from the gift of the king, particularly since it was the king who had granted colonial charters. While some pamphleteers flirted with arguments linking the allegiance to the king with feudal ties,[132] others soon saw the danger of such arguments. John Adams argued that American settlers received lands in charters which presumed regal authority only because they were misled by canon law and feudal ideas. This argument could be used to prove American independence from parliament, while doubting the royal power.[133] According to Thomas Jefferson,

> America was not conquered by William the Norman, nor its lands surrendered to him, or any of his successors. Possessions there are undoubtedly of the allodial nature. Our ancestors, however, who emigrated hither, were farmers, not lawyers. The fictitious principle that all lands belong originally to the king, they were early persuaded to believe real; and accordingly took grants of their own lands from the crown.[134]

As the debate progressed between 1774 and 1776, so many began to abandon legalistic arguments, and to look more to the political notions to be found in

[130] As Thomas Wood put it (*Institute*, 8, citing 1 Co. Rep 47, 4 C. Rep 76, 1 Inst. 95b, 333a) 'To an Act of Parliament every Man in Judgment of Law is Party.'

[131] James Wilson, *Considerations on the Nature and Extent of the Legislative Authority of the British Parliament* (Philadelphia, 1774), in James DeWitt Andrews (ed.), *The Works of James Wilson* (Chicago, 1896), ii. 537. See also Alexander Hamilton, *The Farmer Refuted*, in Harold C. Syrett and Jacob E. Cooke (eds), *The Papers of Alexander Hamilton: vol. 1 (1768–1778)* (New York & London, 1961), ii. 90.

[132] For an argument suggesting a feudal link, see Hamilton, *Farmer Refuted*, 108.

[133] John Adams, *Novanglus*, in Taylor, Kline, and Lint, *Papers of John Adams*, ii. 331.

[134] Thomas Jefferson, *A Summary View of the Rights of British America*, in Joyce Appleby and Terence Ball (eds), *Jefferson: Political Writings* (Cambridge, 1999), 78.

Locke. For Adams and Jefferson, the American situation was to be explained in terms of an original contract with English kings. According to Jefferson, the settlers had a natural right to emigrate in search of new habitations, 'and of there establishing new societies, under such laws and regulations as to them shall seem most likely to promote public happiness'.[135] This argument led to the position that the relationship with the king was one which came from an original contract with the Americans.[136] The binding force of charters, 'both upon the crown and us, is wholly from compact and the law of nature'.[137] In this context, the common law heritage was related not to an immemorial constitution, but to a positive choice. Adams, for instance, stressed that the common law had no authority outside the four seas. 'How then do we New Englandmen derive our laws?' he asked:

> I say, not from parliament, not from the common law, but from the law of nature and the compact made with the king in our charters. Our ancestors were intitled to the common law of England when they emigrated, that is, to just so much of it as they pleased to adopt, and no more. They were not bound or obliged to submit to it, unless they chose it.[138]

The common law was now seen to have had its foundation in the pure law of nature. Alexander Hamilton wrote that

> The sacred rights of mankind are not to be rummaged for, among old parchments, or musty records. They are written, as with a sun beam, in the whole *volume* of human nature, by the hand of the divinity itself; and can never be erased or obscured by mortal power.[139]

Following Locke, he argued that as no man in a state of nature had the right to deprive another of his life, liberty, or property, all governments must arise from compacts between the ruler and ruled, and 'be liable to such limitations, as are necessary for the security of the *absolute rights* of the latter; for what original title can any man or set of men have, to govern others, except their own consent?'[140]

By 1775, American thinkers had effected the intellectual separation of the colonies from parliament. They acknowledged two remaining links,

135 *Summary View*, 65. See also Adams, *Novanglus*, 317.

136 Adams, *Novanglus*, 321.

137 *Novanglus*, 354. This meant that if a charter were revoked, the king would lose all his authority, rather than becoming absolute again: ibid., 333. See also Hamilton, *Farmer Refuted*, 90.

138 Adams, *Novanglus*, 328. Cf. Jefferson, *Summary View*, 66.

139 *Farmer Refuted*, 122.

140 *Farmer Refuted*, 88.

which secured co-operation between the parts of the empire. First, the king could exercise a veto over legislation in all parts of the empire, in order to ensure that there was co-ordination.[141] Secondly, in matters relating strictly to external commerce, the Americans 'cheerfully consented' to British legislation. However, as Adams put it, this was 'not by any principle of common law, but merely by the consent of the colonies, founded on the obvious necessity of a case, which was never in contemplation of that law'.[142] For all other purposes, they were autonomous societies with their own legislatures. In the following year, the Declaration of Independence signalled their separation from the crown. The Declaration's preamble was written in the language of natural law, proclaiming the 'self-evident' truths that all men were created equal and endowed with unalienable rights to life, liberty, and the pursuit of happiness. The main body of the text was an indictment of the king, relating 'a history of repeated injuries and usurpations, all having in direct object the establishment of an absolute tyranny over these states'.[143] The first series of charges against the king complained of his tyrannical acts, which upset the institutional aspects of the constitution. The second set related to his combining with the British parliament to subject Americans 'to a jurisdiction foreign to our constitution', notably by imposing taxation without consent, and by 'taking away our charters, abolishing our most valuable laws, and altering fundamentally the forms of our governments'. This was a catalogue of rights violated. Finally, there was a general set of accusations, including the charge that he had 'abdicated government here, by declaring us out of his protection and waging war against us'. This was America's 1688.[144] It was what Adams in 1775 called the revolution principles 'of Aristotle and Plato, of Livy and Cicero, of Sidney, Harrington and Lock'.[145]

The era of the American Revolution and its aftermath saw a growth of radical and reformist activity in England. As in America, so in England, the language of opposition was increasingly cast in Lockean and natural law terms, finding its most prominent expression in Thomas Paine's *Rights of Man*. By the 1790s, common law rhetoric was as likely to be invoked by conservative defenders of the status quo as by reformers: Edmund Burke's defence of the constitution was thus framed in terms of precedent that owed much to the common lawyers. At the same time, the government newspaper *The True Briton* took as its motto *nolumus leges Angliae mutari*; and pamphleteers invoking the

[141] Bailyn, *Pamphlets*, 133.

[142] The phrase comes from the Declaration of Rights and Grievances of the First Continental Congress; *Novanglus*, 246.

[143] Appleby and Ball, *Jefferson: Political Writings*, 102–3.

[144] Jefferson saw the parallel: *Papers* 1: 311, quoted in David N. Mayer, *The Constitutional Thought of Thomas Jefferson* (Charlottesville & London, 1994), 37.

[145] *Novanglus*, 230. He added that 'a manifest design on the part of the Prince, to annul the contract on his part, will annul it on the part of the people' (230–1).

same phrase spoke of the 'outlines and general principles' of the common law being 'written on the hearts of the people'.[146]

Conclusion

The elite lawyers we have been discussing did not have a monopoly of common law discourse: the common law stood for more than the lawyers' vision we have seen. Nor was the view taken of the law by the late eighteenth-century holders of the Vinerian chair and those of their antecedents the only one possible for lawyers to hold: in America, in place of the positivist jurisprudence which took root in England, the constitution drawn up in Philadelphia in 1787 sought to reconcile notions of popular sovereignty and natural rights which owed much to different American interpretations of the common law tradition.[147] However, it was the dominant view in mid-eighteenth-century England.

The common lawyers we have discussed did not want an activist parliament generating a large body of legislation: jurists like Blackstone retained the typical lawyer's distrust of parliamentarians' skills.[148] But in practice, much of the law that was of interest to the barristers of Westminster Hall – land law, contract, tort, or trust – was largely ignored by the legislature in the eighteenth century. Equally, the growth of the regulatory legislation of the fiscal–military state did not elicit much of a legal response. Men like Blackstone were certainly keen, in country party vein, to control the executive through the removal of placemen, and to maintain a balanced constitution. It is notable, however, that legal writers in the eighteenth century took relatively little notice of the development of 'public law' remedies which might have provided a focus for controlling government; while the courts themselves made few efforts to subject the central executive to legal control. The seventeenth and eighteenth centuries did see the development of new remedies such as mandamus to control the acts of public officials.[149] *Mandamus* extended rapidly in the

[146] [John St. John], *A Letter from a Magistrate to* Mr. *William Rose*, in Gregory Claeys (ed.), *Political Writings of the 1790s* (London, 1995), 5, 190.

[147] See Thomas C. Grey, 'Origins of the Unwritten Constitution: Fundamental Law in American Revolutionary Thought', *Stanford Law Review*, 30 (1978), 843–93; Gordon S. Wood, *The Creation of the American Republic 1776–1787* (New York & London, 1969); James R. Stoner, Jr, *Common Law and Liberal Theory: Coke, Hobbes, and the Origins of American Constitutionalism* (Lawrence, Kansas, 1992); Sylvia Snowiss, *Judicial Review and the Law of the Constitution* (New Haven & London, 1990); Charles F. Hobson, *The Great Chief Justice: John Marshall and the Rule of Law* (Lawrence, Kansas, 1996).

[148] See David Lieberman, 'Codification, Consolidation, and Parliamentary Statute', in John Brewer and Eckhart Hellmuth (eds), *Rethinking Leviathan: The Eighteenth Century State in Britain and Germany* (Oxford, 1999), 359–90.

[149] See Edith G. Henderson, *Foundations of English Administrative Law: Certiorari and Mandamus in the Seventeenth Century* (Cambridge, MA, 1963).

eighteenth century. For Lord Mansfield, 'it ought to be used upon all occasions where the law has established no specific remedy, and where in justice and good government there ought to be one.'[150] It was a remedy 'issuing regularly only in cases relating to the public and the government', rather than to private matters,[151] and was aimed to 'provide as effectually as it can that all official duties are fulfilled, wherever the subject-matter is properly within its control'.[152] Yet it is striking that eighteenth-century writers of legal treatises very largely ignored these new remedies. Blackstone's discussion of mandamus was limited, coming in the book on private wrongs;[153] and no treatise was published in the eighteenth century on this topic.[154]

If common lawyers were not positivist in the sense of desiring an active interventionist legislature, they were positivist in that they conceived of law in the abstract as consisting of commands backed by sanctions. Law for them was not equated either with popular custom or an autonomous natural law: the common law may have reflected the desires of the people, and grown with its needs, but it was law because it was developed by judges in court. The authority of these judges, and the validity of their judgments, came from the fact that they acted within a system based on a historical original contract;[155] not because their decisions promoted the public good, or accorded with natural law, or reflected the will of the people. For the Vinerian professors teaching in Tory Oxford, this was not a Lockean contract in which sovereignty rested with the people. If these lawyers were no champions of an activist parliament, then, they did not have a vision of law which would challenge a sovereign active parliament. When Bentham and Austin shed the language of natural law and history, for a more rigorous positivist theory, they therefore found a receptive audience among English lawyers.[156] If they had not sought it, an activist nineteenth-century parliament proved to be no challenge to their vision of law.

[150] *R* v. *Barker et al.* (1762) 3 Burr 1265 1267. See also *R* v. *Blooer* (1760) 2 Burr 1043.

[151] Bacon, *Abridgement*, tit. Mandamus, A. See also *Daniel Appleford's Case* (1671/2) 1 Mod. 82, *R* v. *Bank of England* (1819) 2 B & A 620, where Bayley, J ruled (at 622) 'The Court will never grant this writ except for public purposes, and to compel the performance of public duties.'

[152] Thomas Tapping, *The Law and Practice of the High Prerogative Writ of Mandamus, as it obtains in England and in Ireland* (London, 1848), 9.

[153] 3 *Comm.* 110, 264.

[154] It was discussed in the second volume of Robert Gardiner's *Instructor clericalis* (London, 1724), and was treated in abridgements of the law. However, the first treatise was published only in 1826: Walter J. Impey, *A Treatise on the Law and Practice of the Writ of Mandamus.*

[155] For a modern discussion of positivism and the concept of validity, see H.L.A. Hart, *The Concept of Law* (Oxford, 1961).

[156] See Lobban, *The Common Law and English Jurisprudence*, chs 5–8.

3

Legislation, magistrates, and judges

High law and low law in England and the empire

DOUGLAS HAY*

> You a Justice you be damned You are no more fit for a Justice than my arse God damm you I can make as good a Justice out of My Arse as you are; You a Justice You're a Devil.
>
> William Hill, Staffordshire woolcomber, to the Reverend George Malbon, Justice of the Peace, 1762 (Staffs. Record Office (SRO), Q/SR 1762 Easter)

Introduction

The contrast between superior and appellate courts on the one hand, and lower level tribunals on the other, is familiar to every criminal lawyer. In common law jurisdictions inferior courts have usually been distinguished by large numbers of defendants, relatively few apparent legal issues, many very apparent human problems, and not much legal assistance for those accused. Direct or indirect descendants of the jurisdiction of the English county and borough magistrates, inferior courts spread throughout the empire, sometimes as direct transplants, sometimes as adaptations of already established European traditions. In newly conquered Quebec the British made use of the *capitaines de milice* before establishing justices in 1764, giving them also a summary jurisdiction in debt not shared by their counterparts in England; in South Africa, the *landdrost* acted in the Cape until 1827; in both early New South Wales and Newfoundland, antecedent military and naval jurisdictions, and in Australia conflict between free settler and ex-convict populations, gave a strong local flavour to the institution or popular attitudes toward it.[1] Their

* An earlier version of this chapter was presented at the conference 'Law and the Enlightenment: the British Imperial State at Law, 1689–1832', Humanities Research Centre, Australian National University, September 2001. I am grateful to the participants and to the organizer, David Lemmings, for suggestions and criticisms.

[1] On Quebec, see Adam Shortt and Arthur G. Doughty (eds), *Documents Relating to the*

later development in different countries has been equally distinctive. On one of the most significant issues, the place of lay magistrates, there are great differences in current practice. In Ontario, Canada a largely professional magistracy came into being in the mid-nineteenth century, and the few surviving lay magistrates quietly expired about 1990.[2] In England, in contrast, lay magistrates still do something like 95 per cent of criminal adjudication, albeit sometimes guided with a strong hand by their clerks. The incursions of stipendiaries in the mid-nineteenth century were reversed in England, although the Blair government is apparently moving in the direction of professionalization. Even in Scotland, usually thought to have had a minimal lay jurisdiction until the present, there was considerable activity by the justices and other lay judges both before and after 1707, and an actual expansion of jurisdiction as late as the mid-1970s, hotly debated by the profession and the parties.

The contrast between the high law of the judges and other professional lawyers, and the low law of magistrates' courts, has important implications for understanding the nature of law in the empire.[3] For a vast amount of the law imposed and suffered, used and resisted, was low law, in the hands of laymen, acting without juries. It was often hardly touched by high law, although the courts of high law could not have operated in its absence. The ubiquity of low and/or lay justice in Britain and its former empire, in scores of jurisdictions, may appear almost incredible to European lawyers, for good historical

Constitutional History of Canada 1759–1791 (Ottawa, 1918), 207–8. The inferior bench, originally restricted to Protestants, was later reconstituted and opened to Catholics; for its subsequent evolution see Donald Fyson, 'Criminal Justice, Civil Society and the Local State: The Justices of the Peace in the District of Montreal, 1764–1830' (Ph.D. diss., Université de Montréal (1995)). On the *landdrost*, see Richard Elphick and Hermann Giliomee (eds), *The Shaping of South African Society, 1652–1840* (Middleton, Conn., 1988), 290–1, 497. David Neal, *The Rule of Law in a Penal Colony: Law and Power in Early New South Wales* (Melbourne, 1991), ch. 5; Jerry Bannister, *Rule of the Admirals: Law, Custom, and Naval Government in Newfoundland, 1699–1832* (Toronto, 2003).

[2] Confusingly, Ontario still has justices of the peace, limited largely to bail hearings, and summary hearings of 'provincial offences' not falling within the federal Criminal Code. See Anthony N. Doob, Patricia M. Baranek, and Susan M. Addario, *Understanding Justices: A Study of Canadian Justices of the Peace* (Toronto, 1991). The magistrates, all lawyers, are now called judges of the Ontario Court of Justice (distinguished from high court judges in the Superior Court of Justice).

[3] For this use of the terms 'high law' and 'low law' see also Douglas Hay, 'Time, Inequality and Law's Violence', in Austin Sarat and Thomas R. Kearns (eds), *Law's Violence* (Ann Arbor, Mich., 1992), 166ff., and 'Introduction' to Douglas Hay and Paul Craven (eds), *Masters, Servants and Magistrates in Britain and the Empire* (Chapel Hill, NC, 2004), note 186. Recently Peter Karsten, *Between Law and Custom: High and Low Cultures in the Lands of the British Diaspora – The United States, Canada, Australia, and New Zealand, 1600–1900* (Cambridge, 2002) uses the term 'low law' much more broadly, to include customary practices, local beliefs, popular understandings of high law, and also magistrates' powers, in a way that blurs distinctions that I consider important in state law itself.

reasons.[4] Two comparisons are illuminating. First, the vast numbers of magistrates in England in the eighteenth century (not to speak of commissioners of courts of request, and other inferior tribunals of more ancient origin) stand in sharp contrast to the small numbers of the high court judges, a mere dozen in the common law courts, a few more in Chancery. Second, the contrast of English and European high courts is striking. There were 240 professional judges in the Parlement of Paris alone in the eighteenth century, and some 1,200 in all thirteen French appellate courts.[5] French judges had powers and obligations greater than those of the common law, and a large bench was thus necessary. Their investigations generated the creation of the prosecution dossier, they decided on guilt without the assistance of juries, and higher courts were obliged to hear appeals of most serious cases, whereas appeals were virtually unknown in England. But judges in France also lacked the assistance of anyone resembling that highly characteristic figure of English law, the justice of the peace. In England, justices of the peace and borough magistrates carried out a great many of the duties entrusted to professional judges on the continent in the administration of the criminal law. English magistrates were empowered to do so by a large amount of legislation, and encouraged to do so by a deliberate policy of minimal supervision by the high courts.

Hence the dichotomy of my subtitle. What follows is a consideration of some of the implications of having both high law and low in the eighteenth century, the law of the judges and the law of the justices. I discuss three issues: the importance of statute; the relationship between the highest and lowest criminal jurisdictions in England in case law and practice; and the domestic and imperial manifestations of low justice as enacted in one, very important, corpus of legislation, the law of master and servant.

England: legislation and practice in the work of the justices

The principal jurisdictional levels outside London are well known: high court judges on circuit at county assizes hearing capital and some non-capital jury trials; lay justices at county quarter sessions, also with juries, dealing with most lesser felonies and misdemeanours; justices and borough magistrates hearing and determining without juries certain summary offences under statutory authority, sitting either singly or in pairs ('the double justice'), depending on the terms of legislation that gave them jurisdiction for specific offences.[6]

[4] Made clear to me in conversation with a German lower court judge, in Alice Springs in October 2001: I think he thought my account of English lay justice, which he clearly found extraordinary, was the result of too much sun.

[5] R.C. Van Caenegem, *Judges, Legislators and Professors: Chapters in European Legal History* (Cambridge, 1987), 133–4.

[6] This greatly simplified account ignores cities and boroughs with county status, visited on circuit by the judges; and some with exclusive jurisdictions under charters giving the

Although in this chapter I emphasize the importance of this statutory jurisdiction for summary conviction, and the freedom of action enjoyed by the justices, two other aspects of their work in criminal law were of course very important. Recent work has greatly clarified the role of magistrates in bail and committal proceedings, including investigation, in felonies, which almost always came before them first, before being tried at quarter sessions or assizes.[7] Secondly, we should note that by the early nineteenth century the justices in quarter sessions were superseding the work of the judges to an increasing extent on jury trials also. As calendars lengthened with greater population and more vigorous prosecution, and trials began to lengthen with more voluble lawyers elaborating defences (and the case law), the magistrates took up the load. In the county of Staffordshire, for example, quarter sessions benches between 1740 and 1800 heard about 31 per cent of all jury trials, and the assize judges about 69 per cent. From 1800 to 1820 the average was 52 per cent at quarter sessions, 48 per cent at assizes. Viewed another way, in the second decade of the nineteenth century the judges were sitting on about four times as many Staffordshire jury trials as they had heard in the 1740s; but quarter sessions was hearing over ten times as many.[8]

Yet the judicial role of justices in quarter sessions was dwarfed by their activity in summary conviction. It is impossible to establish accurate comparable figures for the growth of summary convictions, but there is little doubt that there was a great increase in the course of the century, due both to legislation and prosecutorial initiative, in most if not all counties. Some evidence is considered below. What is clear is that the numbers of convictions before the judges was a tiny fraction of the numbers of convictions before magistrates sitting without juries. In Staffordshire by the early nineteenth century single and double magistrates were sentencing to prison four times as many offenders as the high court judges were sentencing in all ways at assizes; the number of all convictions at assizes was perhaps only 2 per cent of the number before single and double justices.[9] At the other extreme, a very few criminal cases

magistrates authority to hear even capital cases (Lichfield City and Borough, for example), although the practice was rare. London's jurisdictional complexity, a subject in itself, is illuminated in J.M. Beattie, *Policing and Punishment in London, 1660–1750* (Oxford, 2001).

[7] J. M. Beattie, *Crime and the Courts in England 1660–1800* (Princeton, 1986), ch. 6; John H. Langbein, *The Origins of Adversary Criminal Trial* (Oxford, 2003), 40–8; Peter King, *Crime, Justice and Discretion in England 1740–1820* (Oxford, 2000), 87–98. For Canada, see Susan Lewthwaite, 'Pre-trial Examination in Upper Canada', in Greg T. Smith, Allyson N. May, and Simon Devereaux (eds), *Criminal Justice in the Old World and the New: Essays in Honour of J.M. Beattie* (Toronto, 1998), 85–103.

[8] Based on a stratified sample of 2,928 cases at quarter sessions and assizes between 1741 and 1817, of which 1,552 went to trial. The sources are Staffordshire Record Office (SRO), series Q/B, Q/Be, Q/SR, Q/SO, Q/SM, Q/SPr2, and others, and National Archives [Public Record Office], series ASSI 2, ASSI 4, ASSI 5, ASSI 9, and others.

[9] Sentences to the Stafford house of correction only, by single and double justices, 1802,

were reviewed by the judges of King's Bench on writs of *certiorari*, or considered in applications for criminal informations, and informations *ex officio*; informations, if they went to trial, were tried at assizes, but in the *nisi prius* (civil) court.[10] In the eighteenth century, my current estimates suggest that King's Bench dealt with less than 1 per cent of Staffordshire cases, the judges at assize jury trials about 11 per cent, justices at quarter sessions jury trials about 5 per cent, and justices out of sessions about 83 per cent.[11] Of course, poaching hares,[12] or pilfering turnips, potatoes, cabbages, parsnips, peas, or carrots,[13] is not the same as murder, rape, or burglary. But the sheer volume of summary proceedings compared to prosecutions on indictment, and the relative immunity from supervision that I describe below, invites consideration of the significance, as well as extent, of this realm of 'low law'.

First, it was entirely statutory, and the legislation that conferred jurisdiction was large in volume, and both recent and ancient in origin. To enumerate all the statutes in force, and enforced, is impossible here: as Bacon's *Abridgement* observed in 1768, 'The jurisdiction herein given to justices of peace by particular statutes is so various, and extends to such a multiplicity of cases, that it were endless to endeavor to enumerate them.'[14] In one area alone of their summary jurisdiction, adjudicating disputes between masters and workmen (usually with criminal penalties for the latter when in breach), about eighty statutes had been enacted by 1800; some twenty-six were still relevant in the eighteenth century, including important clauses of the Statute of Artificers,

1807, 1817; guilty verdicts at Staffordshire assizes for the same year; sources those in preceding note, and Staffs. RO, D(W) 1723/1,2. The estimate of justices' total convictions (a minimum of 10,000) is based on rough estimates of the proportion of prison sentences to all convictions in eleven justices' notebooks and petty sessions registers from a number of counties, 1687–1824: see D. Hay, 'England, 1562–1875: The Law and its Uses', in Hay and Craven (eds), *Masters, Servants and Magistrates*, 59–116, Table 2.1.

10 D. Hay, *Criminal Cases on the Crown Side of King's Bench: Staffordshire, 1740–1800* (forthcoming, Staffordshire Record Society), cited below as *Crown Side Cases*, which calendars 13 informations against justices, 35 informations qui tam, 15 informations ex officio, 10 writs of habeas corpus, 23 certioraris on indictment, and 13 certioraris on summary convictions. Only the informations might result in trials; very few did.

11 Such estimates have a wide and unknown margin of error, because of the fact that numbers of summary convictions can only be estimated from a variety of sources, and with a variety of assumptions. The relative orders of magnitude are nonetheless clear.

12 Punishable summarily by 14 & 15 Hen. VIII c. 10 (1523), 1 Ja. I c. 27 (1603), 22 & 23 Cha. II c. 25 (1670), 9 Anne c. 27 (1710), 13 Geo. III c. 80 (1773): all cited in Richard Burn, *The Justice of the Peace and Parish Officer* (14th edn, London, 1780). Here and throughout I have changed dates of enactment and chapter numbers of statutes where necessary to correspond to the conventions of *Chronological Table of the Statutes* (London: HMSO, 1966 and other dates).

13 Fine of ten shillings or one month in prison on summary conviction before one justice: 13 Geo. III c. 32 (1772).

14 Matthew Bacon, *Abridgement of Law and Equity* (3rd edn, 1768), iii. 292.

5 Eliz. I c. 4 (1562).[15] Game was another large criminal jurisdiction;[16] and powers under such broad categories as the poor law could also confer what amounted to criminal jurisdiction, particularly in the punishment of vagrants.[17] The expansive definitions of rogues and vagabonds (among others, 'common players of interludes, and all persons who shall for hire, gain, or reward, act, represent, or perform, or cause to be acted, represented, or performed, any interlude, tragedy, comedy, opera, play, farce, or other entertainment of the stage, or any part therein, not being authorized by law') allowed justices to whip and commit to the house of correction a wide variety of transient and suspect poor; if committed until sessions, further punishment could follow by the full bench.[18] The theft of wood and vegetables and dogs, and a wide range of embezzlement in different trades, were also within the jurisdiction of justices out of sessions.[19] So too was much enforcement of the excise laws, and criminal penalties against smuggling, sabbath-breaking, gambling, liquor offences, and lotteries. There were many other summary offences, useful for occasional social discipline, such as swearing.[20] Most of this legislation was enacted to make criminal, and to punish summarily, acts which were not crimes at common law. The most common prosecutions were for vagrancy and other poor law offences, breach of contract (master and servant), poaching offences under the game laws, wood theft, vegetable theft, and embezzlement of materials in industry, with different counties and parts of counties showing very different patterns, changing also over time. Often the case loads of individual magistrates were also distinctive, reflecting local industries and personal prejudices.

By the later eighteenth century, some justices in Staffordshire were hearing hundreds of summary cases a year; a few hyperactive magistrates accounted for the great majority. The distribution of summary convictions probably mirrors that of committals for trial: in Staffordshire two or three justices in any given decade after 1740 each committed over 8 per cent of those going to trial,

[15] Usually cited as 1563. See Hay, 'England, 1562–1875', in Hay and Craven (eds), *Masters, Servants and Magistrates*.

[16] Peter B. Munsche, *Gentlemen and Poachers: The English Game Laws 1671–1831* (Cambridge, 1981); Roger B. Manning, *Hunters and Poachers: A Cultural and Social History of Unlawful Hunting in England 1485–1640* (Oxford, 1993).

[17] Before the enactment of 17 Geo. II c. 5 (1743), servants were often imprisoned under the vagrancy provisions of 7 Ja. I c. 4 (1609).

[18] 17 Geo. II c. 5 (1743) s. 2.

[19] Wood: 43 Eliz. I c. 7 (1601), 15 Cha. II c. 2 (1663), 1 Geo. I st. 2 c. 48 (1715), 6 Geo. I c. 16 (1719); dogs: 10 Geo. III c. 18 (1770); vegetables: see above n. 13. On the embezzlement statutes, see John Styles, 'From an Offence between Men to an Offence against Property? Industrial Pilfering and the Law in the Eighteenth Century', in M. Berg, M. Sonenscher, and P. Hudson (eds), *Manufacture in Town and Country Before the Factory* (Cambridge, 1983), 173–205.

[20] 19 Geo. II c. 21 (1745).

with two very active magistrates committing over a third of all cases for trial in each of two decades.[21] Similarly, most summary convictions resulting in committals to the house of correction were the work of relatively few men: again, four men each committed 7 per cent to 12 per cent of those sent to the house of correction in Stafford between 1792 and 1814; a few others accounted for 2 per cent or 3 per cent, but almost all the other magistrates, about 100 men, each accounted for fewer, often far fewer, than 1 per cent of all cases. Similar evidence has been compiled for other counties.[22]

Most accounts of the summary convictions of the justices mention Blackstone's reservations about their large and growing jurisdiction in the eighteenth century, as incursions on jury trial: 'new and arbitrary methods of trial, by justices of the peace . . . fundamentally opposite to the spirit of our constitution'.[23] It is an observation that captures the constantly expanding summary jurisdiction of the justices, but conveys the false impression that they were unimportant in earlier centuries. More recently, historians of medieval law have remarked that the justices and their statutory authority were born together, an express delegation of jurisdiction at a very early date, probably as the result of the systemic and legal disruptions occasioned by the Black Death.[24] That fact reminds us that low law in the sense in which I am using it has a pedigree almost as old as that of the common law itself, the high law found and applied in Westminster Hall by the royal judges.

What was the nature of the articulation between high law and low, the law of Westminster Hall and the forum of the single or double justice? We can consider this in terms of case law and the actual activity of the court of King's Bench in the eighteenth century, in its supervisory role over inferior justice.

King's Bench: the supervisory role of high law

The older literature suggests a close supervision, effected by the prerogative writs, mainly certiorari, and by prosecutions of magistrates, which in the case of King's Bench took the form of criminal informations for misdemeanour in their office.[25] With the writ of *certiorari* a defendant could move all proceedings

[21] Joseph Turton of Wolverhampton (committals 1763–72); Alexander Bunn Haden, vicar of Wednesbury (committals 1793–1802); calculated from assize and quarter sessions gaol calendars, SRO.

[22] King, *Crime, Justice, and Discretion*, Table 4.4, 113; Norma Landau, *The Justices of the Peace 1679–1760* (Berkeley, 1984), Table 3, 178.

[23] William Blackstone, *Commentaries on the Laws of England* (12th edn, 1795), iv. 350. Blackstone was also writing about the summary powers of commissioners of excise, a branch of penal law providing very high fines and long sentences.

[24] See below.

[25] William Holdsworth, *A History of English Criminal Law* (London, 1922–72) x. 249–50;

into King's Bench, where the judges could quash a summary conviction for insufficiency; a prosecution on a criminal information was a charge brought against the magistrate himself.[26] However, the archival evidence of all the criminal informations and *certioraris* involving Staffordshire magistrates 1740–1800 shows that there were very few. Only thirteen applications for criminal informations against fifteen different magistrates for misdemeanour in office, and eleven writs of certiorari to eight magistrates, questioning the summary convictions of sixteen defendants, were filed in King's Bench. In total, then, there were in all twenty-four separate proceedings against twenty-four magistrates.[27] Yet there were perhaps 10,000 summary convictions and committal proceedings by several hundred lay magistrates in the county commission of the peace and in boroughs during this period.[28] As with all legal proceedings, wholly opposite conclusions may be drawn from the statistics alone: that there were few magisterial transgressions needing reproof, or that it was unwise, for a variety of reasons, to bring such cases. The detail of the evidence in these twenty-four cases, and the terms of the case law developed by the royal judges on the subject of magisterial misbehaviour, both suggest very strongly that the common law judges deliberately made it difficult to proceed against magistrates by criminal informations or *certiorari*, both in procedural and substantive terms.

This is particularly the case with respect to the criminal information. There were important procedural barriers to its use, whether used against ordinary citizens or magistrates, but with a few additional requirements of notice and limitation in the case of magistrates.[29] Costs were very high, and since all

Sidney [Baron Passfield] and Beatrice Webb, *English Local Government, Volume I: The Parish and the County* (London, 1906; repr. 1963), 306, 333, 336, 349, 389–90, 419–20. Other writs, including *habeas corpus*, *mandamus*, and prohibition, were in practice of lesser importance.

[26] For a fuller discussion, and the evidence on which the following paragraphs are based, see Douglas Hay, 'Dread of the Crown Office: The English Magistracy and King's Bench 1740–1800', in Norma Landau (ed.), *Law, Crime and English Society 1660–1840* (Cambridge, 2003), 19–45.

[27] All the cases from 1740 to 1800 are reproduced in Hay, *Crown Side Cases*, parts B and E, where full references are given, and the process of the court described. The manuscript series exhaustively used in the study for the whole period 1740–1800 were National Archives [PRO], ASSI 4, KB 1, KB 11, KB 15, KB 16, KB 20, KB 21, KB 29, KB 39 (indices to KB 1), and the Great Docket Books (indexes to KB 28). Soundings were also made in KB 28, KB 33, and KB 36. Cases from 1800 to 1820 will be described in other publications. The separate issue of civil suits for damages did not require KB to comment on magisterial practice directly; there were very few such cases in the county (see Hay, 'Dread of the Crown Office' for one instance). There were no proceedings on indictment against magistrates in sixty years. The few instances of mandamus related to administrative matters.

[28] See note 9.

[29] In outline summary: a criminal information was begun by the filing of affidavits by the prosecution, including affidavits of notice to the defendant, who either filed affidavits in

persons who made affidavits in a case were held to be prosecutors, witnesses were hard to find and failure of a prosecution could have disastrous consequences for many people. But judicial policy in the high court was the most important disincentive to such proceedings.

Early in the eighteenth century the case law suggests that the judges were more willing to allow prosecutions of magistrates, perhaps because some of the reported cases arose out of the sharp party conflict of the period. But after Mansfield's appointment as chief justice in 1756 much narrower grounds for an information against a JP were elaborated. Mansfield required proof of corruption in a pecuniary sense, although some of the earlier cases had also used tests of malice and revenge. Later in the century, post-Mansfield, there was a suggestion in 1788 that the court would re-admit tests other than purely pecuniary corruption, but the moment was brief.[30] It is absolutely clear from the case law that the need to support the justices of the peace, and not to discourage a magistracy that acted (at least notionally) without recompense, and the identification of free service with gentlemanly integrity, all made the granting of criminal informations an extremely rare occurrence, particularly outside London. The most severe judicial response was to grant a rule absolute for an information, raising the possibility of a jury trial. In only two of the Staffordshire cases (involving three justices) was a rule absolute made; in all the other cases the prosecution was unsuccessful. Nor did those three justices actually face trial: the defendants were discharged (possibly, but not likely, with a financial settlement), or the prosecutions dropped before a jury could hear them. In only one case (against two borough justices) did King's Bench obliquely express disapproval, requiring the otherwise unpunished magistrates to pay their own costs (which otherwise fell on the prosecution); in one other case, the JP had also to pay the costs of the prosecutor.

In *certiorari*, although much contemporary comment, lay and professional, suggested that the judges were extremely exacting of convictions removed into the court, the numbers of such cases were very few, largely due to the danger of crushing costs.[31] Of the Staffordshire cases, one conviction was affirmed,

answer or reserved his defence until after motions on the prosecution affidavits for a rule *nisi* were made in term time. Argument on the merits by counsel either resulted in dismissal or a rule absolute, which allowed an information to be exhibited. If not dropped or compromised, the case was then tried in the *nisi prius* court at assizes in the county where the cause originated; a verdict delivered into Westminster by a postea was followed by judgment there, unless there were motions in arrest of judgment or for a new trial. Additional affidavits could be filed before sentence in mitigation or aggravation, and in connection with costs. For details see Hay, *Crown Side Cases*.

30 Hay, 'Dread of the Crown Office', 28–30.

31 A truck statute, 29 Geo. II c. 33 (1756), revising an earlier enactment, 12 Geo. I c. 34, noted that 'several prosecutions have been carried on against offenders for offences committed in breach of the said act, in manner therein prescribed, but the trials thereupon have been removed by Certiorari into some or one of his Majesty's courts of record at

four were quashed, two were dismissed for failure of the prosecutor to respond, and for three outcomes are unknown but were probably abandoned or compromised.

The evidence in the Staffordshire cases, and in other contemporary sources, leads to the conclusion that poorer persons, those most likely to be abused by magisterial misbehaviour, had virtually no prospect of successful legal recourse in the eighteenth century. The very few magistrates whose behaviour was brought before King's Bench were likely to find themselves there because for some reason, often extrinsic to the case, the usual amity of the bench had broken down, and men of their own class were prepared to countenance proceedings against them. A justice of the peace had to behave in an extremely ungentlemanly way before other gentlemen and justices were prepared to retaliate. The few King's Bench informations against Staffordshire JPs appear to have arisen in such circumstances.[32] In none of these cases were the misbehaving magistrates punished: after all, they were not actuated by 'corrupt motives' or 'interest' in the narrow terms defined by the high court judges. And country magistrates clearly knew they were in little danger from King's Bench. One wealthy JP, John Gough of Perry Hall, had survived five attempts to get criminal informations against him when a newly aggrieved farmer arrived at his door with an attorney in 1802. 'I'll prosecute you and have you in the Kings Bench . . . I'll have no lawyers here . . . I'll have you in the King's Bench for this I'll play the Devil with you', shouted Gough from an upper window of Perry Hall.[33] Yet the affidavits in the few cases brought before the court, in this and other counties, show much egregious and oppressive behaviour. Such evidence is impossible to recover from justices' notebooks, the eighteenth-century press, and most private correspondence, all sources heavily self-censored or largely indifferent to the plight of ordinary defendants before inferior magistrates.[34]

Westminster, and such prosecutions have been dropped upon account of the expense of carrying them on.'

[32] Hay, 'Dread of the Crown Office'; for earlier examples, see A.J. Fletcher, 'Honour, Reputation and Local Officeholding in Elizabethan and Stuart England', in Anthony Fletcher and John Stevenson, *Order and Disorder in Early Modern England* (Cambridge, 1985), 100–1. However, Tudor and Stuart magistrates also were much more closely directed by the Privy Council than were their Hanoverian counterparts, notably with respect to marketing and public order offences.

[33] For full details see Hay, 'Dread of the Crown Office'. Gough's opponent in this case successfully brought a civil suit and received £500 damages and double costs, in what appears to be the uniquely successful case in the county. It is reported in part: *Osborne* v. *Gough* (1803), 3 Bos & Puller 550–6, a report of Gough's subsequent, unsuccessful attempt to have the verdict set aside on grounds of excessive damages and a defect in process.

[34] My impression is that published imagery also was largely uncritical of magistrates before the early nineteenth century. Hogarth satirizes the Lord Chief Justice and his brethren in his painting and engraving of *The Bench*, portraying Willes and the puisnes as sleepy

It is true that the case law is replete with statements of judicial suspicion of summary convictions, comments fairly general in the late seventeenth and early eighteenth centuries, sporadic at other periods, depending on the judges, the nature of the conviction, and the decade. Blackstone's comment about 'new and arbitrary methods of trial' simply echoes these judicial reservations. Chief Justice Holt, speaking for the court in *R* v. *Chandler*, a case argued over several terms in 1699 to 1702, took the view that a deer-stealing conviction on 3 Wm. and Mary c. 10 was good, without following all the forms of indictments:

> He said, that in these convictions by justices of peace in a summary way, where the ancient course of proceeding by indictment and trial by jury is dispensed with, the Court may more easily dispense with forms; and it is sufficient for the justices, in the description of the offence, to pursue the words of the statute; and they are not confined to the legal forms requisite in indictments for offences by the common law. For though all Acts, which subject men to new and other trials, than those by which they ought to be tried by the common law, being contrary to the rights and liberties of Englishmen, as they were settled by Magna Charta, ought to be taken strictly; yet when such a statute is made, one ought to pursue the intent of the makers, and expound it in so reasonable a manner, as that it may be executed.

'But [he added] it is also incumbent upon Judges, to take care, that in the execution of this law they [the justices] do not go beyond the Act of Parliament.'[35] In *R* v. *Whistler*, another *certiorari* for a conviction on the same statute a few years later, Holt's language was stronger:

> Everybody knows, that this being a penal law, ought by equity and reason to be construed according to the letter of it, and no farther . . . That this act is penal is most plain . . . the defendant is put to a summary trial different from Magna Charta, for it is a fundamental privilege of Englishmen to be tried by jury, which privilege has been secured to us by our ancestors many hundred years ago. Then when there is a penalty inflicted, and a different manner of trial from Magna Charta instituted, and instead of being openly tried by his neighbours in a Court of Justice, he shall be convicted by a single justice of peace in a private chamber, upon the testimony of one witness, I fain would know if upon the consideration of such a law, we ought not to adhere to the letter of the law, without carrying words farther than the natural sense of them?[36]

nonentities or pompous voluptuaries. But his most famous image of a magistrate is the tenth plate of *Industry and Idleness*, in which the good apprentice Goodchild, now alderman of London, recoils in agony as he recognizes the bad apprentice brought before him, impeached by an accomplice. But he will do his duty: the next plate is the hanging at Tyburn.

[35] 1 Ld Raymond 581–2; also 5 Mod 446, 1 Ld Raymond 545, 1 Salk. 378, Holt KB 214.

[36] 7 Mod 134–5. The issue was whether a confederate, not actually present, was within the statute. The rest of the court held that he was. See also 2 Salk. 542–3, Holt KB 215–16, 2 Ld Raymond 846, 11 Mod 28.

The rest of the court were not persuaded, but Blackstone's much quoted remark is a summary of this tradition of judicial suspicion of the procedural informality of justice of the peace law; in the same decade, the King's Bench made an often quoted observation (in a case, *R* v. *Corden*, in which a gentleman had been summarily convicted of angling in a private fishery) that 'a tight hand ought to be holden over these summary convictions.'[37]

In fact, probably few of the judges had extensive personal experience of provincial magisterial activity, at quarter sessions or boroughs or in the county commission of the peace. One who did was Lord Kenyon (chief justice of King's Bench 1788–1802), who first as an attorney's clerk, and then as a young barrister, had had a great deal of petty and quarter sessions experience. He remarked from time to time on the variability of JP law. In *R* v. *Stone* (in which a gentleman appealed a poaching conviction), Kenyon deplored any loosening of requirements for a valid conviction on the game laws:

> It is necessary for Courts of Justice to hold a strict hand over summary proceedings before magistrates, and I never will agree to relax any of the rules by which they have been bound. Their jurisdiction is of a limited nature, and they must shew that the party was brought within it. Shall it be sufficient for the witness to say, that he saw such a person (perhaps a nobleman of the highest rank and largest fortune in the kingdom) out a shooting on such a day; and shall that be sufficient to convict him, because the information, which is not upon oath, contains in point of form an allegation that the defendant was not qualified. If this were sufficient to warrant a conviction, unless the defendant proved his own qualification, it may be necessary for him to bring his title deeds and witnesses from the furthest part of the kingdom, in order to shew his qualification. The proposition is monstrous; and the inconvenience and vexation would be insufferable. I know not how far it may not extend. The Legislature only intended to subject persons not having certain qualifications to this summary jurisdiction. The defendant must therefore be shewn to be such a person. And if Lord Mansfield, Mr. Justice Dennison, and Mr. Justice Foster thought that all this was necessary above forty years ago, surely the length of time which has since elapsed, without their decision having been called in question, has not weakened but rather confirmed the authority of it.[38]

Kenyon's hypothetical was of a peer being wrongly accused of poaching, by an inferior magistrate; the facts of the case resembled those in *Corden*. From these and other examples, it is clear that summary convictions on the game laws caused the judges particular concern. Game was a subject about which feelings ran high, the cases put gentlemen at odds and sometimes at risk of the law, and

[37] *R* v. *Corden* (1769), 4 Burr 2281.

[38] 1 East 650–1, 102 English Reports 252–3. The issue was whether the conviction need expressly show that the lack of qualification to hunt had been proved in evidence.

penalties were often heavy.[39] In this case the court was divided, to the chief justice's disgust. A review of a wide range of other case law suggests that the critical eye of the high court was increasingly shut to the behaviour of inferior justices from the late eighteenth into the early nineteenth centuries. Widespread riot and fears of democratic sedition apparently convinced many high court judges that magistrates should be protected against criminal prosecutions whenever possible.[40]

One important aspect of the archival evidence suggests a qualification: a high proportion of the few Staffordshire cases in fact involved misdeeds of borough magistrates, who were easier to sue or intimidate. Usually of inferior social standing to the gentlemen in the county commission of the peace, and owing their office to municipal rather than national politics, the mayors and aldermen, usually tradesmen, who acted as magistrates in boroughs were less likely to have the protection of magnates and gentlemen. The concerns of the judges, that magistrates in the commission of the peace not be discouraged, did not apply to these borough justices. They were magistrates ex officio: they were obliged to act, unlike those in the commission of the peace, who could simply neglect to take out the formal qualification, the dedimus, or having done so, simply turn complainants away from their doors.

Another perspective: the contract of employment

In assessing the meaning of lay and low justice in both England and the empire we can turn to one group of cases that occupied much of the time of some of the most active magistrates in England: those arising out of the law of master and servant. This body of law was also of critical importance in many parts of

[39] There were higher penalties for deer-stealing, most likely to be the acts of yeomen and labourers. The penalties on summary conviction on 3 Wm. and Mary c.10, the statute at issue in *Chandler* and *Corder*, included penalties of £30 or, on failure to pay, prison for a year and exposure in the pillory, on summary conviction by one justice of the peace. Kenyon in other cases did evince more concern for the poor defendant than did many other judges of the period: *The Oxford Dictionary of National Biography* (Oxford, 2004), 'Lloyd Kenyon'.

[40] This is a large argument that I pursue elsewhere. For one instance of a case before Lord Ellenborough that coincided with early Luddism, *R* v. *Hoseason* (1811) 14 East 605, see D. Hay, 'Patronage, Paternalism and Welfare: Masters, Workers and Magistrates in Eighteenth-century England', *International Labor and Working-Class History*, 27 (1998), 40–5, and D. Hay, 'Master and Servant in England: Using the Law in the Eighteenth and Nineteenth Centuries', in Willibald Steinmetz (ed.), *Private Law and Social Inequality in the Industrial Age: Comparing Legal Cultures in Britain, France, Germany and the United States* (Oxford, 2000), 245–6. Hoseason, a Norfolk justice, sentenced Generel Batterbee, a labourer working on Hoseason's own farm, to a prison sentence and a whipping for insolence to the magistrate's bailiff, under 20 Geo. II c.19 (1747).

the empire, inviting us to rethink regimes of 'common law' as in fact two parallel systems of law, high and low, with often minimal connections between them.[41]

The regulation of employment relations was one of the oldest duties of magistrates. Indeed, it has been argued that it was *the* foundation duty of that office when it was first created: that the creation of magistrates as the local representatives of the central state is intimately connected with the enforcement of the unprecedented central policies embodied in the Ordinance of Labourers (1349), the Statute of Labourers (1351), and further statutes of 1361 and 1388.[42] Palmer in fact sees in this dual event the means by which the class of gentry itself emerged.[43] The law was elaborated over succeeding centuries of legislation. By the end of the eighteenth century the law conferring summary jurisdiction rested on the Statute of Artificers, 5 Eliz. I c. 4 (1562), and on another twenty-six enactments, many still contingent on the 1562 Statute. From the last the judges also invented remedies, such as summary wage recovery for servants, before legislation explicitly conferred jurisdiction in 1747.[44] The statutory penal sanctions of master and servant, providing for one to three months' imprisonment for breach of contract, were notorious by the nineteenth century. Yet, as will be seen, these summary decisions were for practical purposes unreviewable in Westminster Hall.

It has been difficult to assess how much of the average magistrate's case load in the eighteenth century was comprised of master and servant cases.[45] We know that in the later nineteenth century it was about 2.5 per cent nationally, although as high as 10 per cent or 12 per cent in some counties in some years. That percentage obviously also depends upon the denominator, the range of other business brought before the local magistrates. Soundings in a variety of published and unpublished JPs' notebooks shows a higher proportion in the eighteenth century (consistent with the fact that there were fewer other kinds of cases in their jurisdiction than would be the case a century later). Averages range from 3 per cent to 25 per cent, the latter being that of Sir Thomas Ward in the 1760s, in an area of Northamptonshire with rural industry as well as agricultural labour. The importance of master and servant in penal terms is also suggested by imprisonment figures. Thus in Staffordshire between 1792 and 1814, almost 40 per cent of all men and women in the largest house

[41] Regimes of civil or partly indigenous law in the empire were bifurcated in a similar way: see below.

[42] 23 Edw. III; 25 Edw. III st. 2; 34 Edw. III cc. 9–11; 12 Ric. II cc. 3–9.

[43] Robert C. Palmer, *English Law in the Age of the Black Death 1348–81: A Transformation of Governance and Law* (Chapel Hill, NC, 1993), ch. 3.

[44] Hay, 'England, 1562–1875', in Hay and Craven (eds), *Masters, Servants and Magistrates*.

[45] The following paragraph is based on Hay, 'Master and Servant in England', in Steinmetz (ed.), *Private Law*, 233ff., 257ff., and Hay, 'England, 1562–1875', in Hay and Craven (eds), *Masters, Servants and Magistrates*.

of correction were there for labour offences (forty a year); in one of three bridewells in Gloucestershire at about the same period they comprised 32 per cent of prisoners, about forty-nine a year. In the Staffordshire case, it is clear that some magistrates had very heavy case loads, particularly if they were the justice of resort by local manufacturers. In fifteen years the Reverend Edward Powys committed 179 potters to the Stafford house of correction for master and servant offences (66 per cent of those he sent there); he heard perhaps 2,000 employment cases in all during those years, about 130 annually. Looking at all the committals of master and servant cases in the county, again extrapolating, there were possibly about 8,000 cases decided by all magistrates in the period 1792–1814.

These figures for summary convictions dwarf the activities of both magistrates at quarter sessions and high court judges at assizes in the same period by about a factor of four. It is suggestive that only one of these 8,000 employment cases was ever considered by King's Bench. It was also reported, and was probably a test case to try to expose, and change, a statutory interpretation clearly disadvantageous to workers. Joseph Thompson, a 36-year-old collier from Tipton, served two months in the house of correction in 1810 for absenting himself from work.[46] His lawyers (probably engaged by his union) sought a writ of mandamus to force quarter sessions to hear an appeal. But the relevant statute allowed appeals to quarter sessions *except [on] an order of commitment*, and Thompson's conviction was included in such an order. King's Bench ruled that the statutory basis for an appeal was absent.

The exception clause in the statute, and the ruling of King's Bench that upheld it, helps to explain why in the 929 committals of workers to the Staffordshire house of correction between 1792 and 1814, the 20 per cent of servants released before serving half their sentences were freed by the permission of their masters, not by the courts. *R* v. *Justices of Staffordshire*, the report of Thompson's case in King's Bench, also takes us back to the connections, or rather disjunctions, between high law and low. In this case, as in others, high law provided a venue for the determination of the exact meaning of the statute, and a chance to seek a remedy. King's Bench granted a rule *nisi* for a writ of mandamus, some of its many clerks filed the affidavit and entered the rules in the crown book and in the rolls, its judges listened to arguments by counsel (and incidentally shared in the fees, as chief justices did until the 1830s).[47]

46 *R* v. *Justices of Staffordshire* (1810), 12 East 572; 104 English Reports 223 (application for mandamus for sessions to hear appeal; refused because a warrant of commitment is excepted from appeal to quarter sessions by 6 Geo. III c. 25, and in the present case the record of conviction is contained in the warrant of commitment, and cannot be severed from it).

47 National Archives [PRO], KB 1/36 Trin. 50 Geo. III, no.1, bundle 17; KB 21/49, 462 (rule *nisi* for mandamus), 481 (rule discharged).

The lawyers cited a range of other cases, but also urged that Thompson be allowed to appeal on grounds of policy and probability. Surely, they argued, it was not the intention of parliament to allow employers to appeal against wage orders of 'a few shillings', but to prohibit workers from contesting unjustified imprisonment? But that is in fact what the judges decided the exception clause meant. Workers committed to prison by justices of the peace, in a county in which active magistrates were increasingly likely to be deeply involved in mining and manufacturing, had no legal grounds for appeal even to the county bench.[48] Thus the attempt to find justice in the high courts, at great expense, had the sole effect of entrenching an interpretation of the statute that was deeply prejudicial to servants.

Imperial variants

The structure of English law was replicated, to a greater or lesser extent, in most colonies. It was not always replicated quickly, as a few examples may illustrate. In eighteenth-century Quebec, for example, after the military conquest of 1760, the occupying army constituted all law, high and low, and tried civilians by the procedure of courts martial until 1763, to the vast indignation of Scots, American, and English merchants prosecuted, tried, and convicted by army officers. The governor and his officers were finally informed by the Judge Advocate General in London that all such proceedings (including death sentences that had been carried out) had no basis in law. But no one sued; the gaffe was not made public.[49] The subsequent establishment of a full structure of civil courts in Quebec in 1764 created justices of the peace on the English model (after 1774 they included French Catholics, some of whom had occupied the roughly analogous position of *capitaine de milice* in New France). High law was somewhat compromised by the fact that in the 1770s and 1780s the judges in commission for the Quebec court of King's Bench had not a lawyer among them. When confronted with *habeas corpus* proceedings by American sympathizers gaoled without charge or trial for the duration of the American rebellion the bench evinced an insuperable inability to understand what habeas corpus was all about, which suited the governor, Haldimand, very well. A few years earlier Chief Justice Livius had been dismissed from office for insisting that *habeas corpus* was, or should be, law in Quebec. In the context

[48] 20 Geo. II c. 19 (1747); 6 Geo. III c. 25 (1766); the next significant enactment, 4 Geo. IV c. 34 (1823), made all determinations, including wage orders, final and without appeal.
[49] The following paragraph is based on D. Hay, 'Civilians Tried in Military Courts: Quebec, 1759–64', and D. Hay and J.-M. Fecteau, '"Government by Will and Pleasure instead of Law": Military Justice and the Legal System in Quebec, 1775–1783', in F. Murray Greenwood and Barry Wright (eds), *Canadian State Trials: Law, Politics, and Security Measures, 1608–1837* (Toronto, 1996), 114–28, 129–71.

of rebellion and sedition, it suited the home government and the law officers to leave wonderfully vague whether *habeas corpus* could be said to be part of the law of Quebec. After the war one of the detainees, a Scots cooper named Charles Hay, successfully sued the governor in the English court of King's Bench (high law) for unlawfully detaining him. Haldimand had to enter bail for £3,000. In spite of the argument of Erskine, his counsel, that it was 'not to be imagined, that every officer was sufficiently a lawyer to know what may be the point of law in every part of his conduct', Hay got damages of £200 and costs. High law vindicated Charles Hay at last, 3,000 miles away and four years later. A year later the government granted Haldimand £2,500 for 'law expenses'.

High law in Quebec was often highly politicized, in a tradition common in other colonial jurisdictions, in Canada and elsewhere in the empire. Much of it arose from the lack of qualified judges. Some of it was the result of the central role of the colonial judiciary in politics, as speakers in executive and legislative councils, in the drafting of legislation, as well as on the bench. They also held office only at pleasure. There were some equivalents to these conditions in England, especially in the mid-eighteenth century, when Lord Chief Justice Mansfield sat in cabinet for many years, and the argument is persuasive that judicial independence in England was in some measure myth, given the fact that chief justiceships were rewards for prior loyal service as crown lawyers in parliament. But the calibre of judicial appointments in England was high, and the judges of Westminster Hall did not face the problems of their weaker colonial brethren, who struggled against military governors and fractious colonial assemblies that did not afford them much respect.[50]

Low law was copied in colonial settings with even greater enthusiasm, albeit much variation. In Quebec, for example, where eventually the British conceded the retention of French civil law, while insisting on the introduction of English criminal law, master and servant penal sanctions were enacted soon after the conquest for *voyageurs* in the fur trade, and for seamen. Conflict between the conquering and conquered representatives in the assembly by 1802 led to the delegation of legislative power to municipal governments, but the main emphases of English penal sanctions for breach of contract were retained: fines, and imprisonment up to two months.[51] Contracts of

[50] Peter Oliver, 'Power, Politics and the Law: The Place of the Judiciary in the Historiography of Upper Canada', in *Essays in the History of Canadian Law*, vol. 8, *In Honour of R.C.B. Risk*, ed. G. Blaine Baker and Jim Phillips (Toronto: University of Toronto Press for the Osgoode Society, 1999), 443–68; David Lemmings, 'The Independence of the Judiciary in Eighteenth-century England', in Peter Birks (ed.), *The Life of the Law: Proceedings of the Tenth British Legal History Conference Oxford 1991* (London, 1993), 125–49; John McLaren, '"The judicial office . . . bowing to no power but the supremacy of the law": Judges and the Rule of Law in Colonial Australia and Canada, 1788–1840', *Australian Journal of Legal History*, 7 (2003), 177–92.

[51] Paul Craven, 'Canada 1670–1935: Symbolic and Instrumental Enforcement in Loyalist North America', in Hay and Craven (eds), *Masters, Servants and Magistrates*, 175–218.

employment were understood by the terms of French civil law, but they were enforced by the methods of English criminal law. Those who enforced them were the lay magistrates.

A similar adoption and evolution can be seen in Madras, where the English domestic law of master and servant, at least its more punitive sides, was first established by municipal statute to meet the problem posed by labour that was 'idle', 'unruly', given to 'shameful impositions', and 'addiction to riot'. Local weavers were denounced as 'lazy', 'profligate', 'drunken', 'deceitful', 'tumultuous', and 'dissolute'. The response was a series of demands and experiments from 1764, through the 1770s and 1780s, culminating in copies of the most relevant parts of English master and servant law, to be administered by magistrates, in 1811. Corporal punishment was somewhat more prominent, however, and sentences longer:

> All servants, and all workmen, Lascars or others hired to work in any employ who shall refuse to work or shall desert their employ or wilfully disobey or behave disrespectfully or insolently to their Masters or Mistresses, employers or lawful superiors or who shall neglect their duty, shall be subject, at the discretion of the magistrates, to whipping not exceeding 2 dozen of stripes and hard labour for a period of four months, or either of those punishments on conviction before two magistrates.

Employers illegally punishing servants, or refusing to pay them, were to be fined the large sum of 20 pagodas (about £8). (Masters had been warned in 1796 that battering a servant to death was not within their authority.) Other clauses of the 1811 regulations were inspired directly by the Statute of Artificers (1562), and the principal English statutes of 1747 and 1766[52] dealing with master and servant, under which the Norfolk labourer Batterbee and the Staffordshire collier Thompson were convicted respectively at the same time, on the other side of the world.[53] The Indian variants of the English acts provided corporal punishment and imprisonment and large fines for a variety of labour offences, and also re-created that great innovation of fourteenth- and sixteenth-century English labour legislation, statutorily fixed wages, for which a few country gentleman traditionalists in England still felt great affection, although now from a paternalist perspective that was quite at odds with prevailing sentiment in parliament.[54] Over thirty master and servant statutes were enacted in British India. The most important was (India) n. 13 of 1859, for Madras, Bombay and Calcutta, rapidly extended by notification to almost

[52] See note 48.

[53] Above, notes 40, 46.

[54] Ravi Ahuja, 'The Origins of Colonial Labour Policy in Late Eighteenth-century Madras', *International Review of Social History*, 44 (1999), 159–96, at 185.

all of India, and repealed only in 1926 (India, n. 12 of 1925).[55] Again, enforcement was in the hands of inferior magistrates.

Everywhere in the empire were found equivalents of the English magistracy, of master and servant and vagrancy and a host of other laws, tied together in the intimate bundle of authority and coercion that first arose in fourteenth-century England. The colonial variants in master and servant law alone are immensely interesting. The single point I wish to emphasize here is that they were almost without exception, some 1,400 of them, enacted in the model of English employment law: inferior justice, low law.[56] This vast legislative exercise considerably exceeded in verbiage the law of God, both old and new testaments.[57] The enormous prolixity of employment legislation is partly a product of the number of jurisdictions: each small Caribbean island had its own succeeding statutes, for example. But it also was generated by the constant concern of colonial employers and governments to find and coerce as much labour as possible into bounded markets of low wages (lower wages than workers otherwise would accept) in order to make a profit in an increasingly competitive world. In the eighteenth century it was complemented, of course, by a parallel corpus of slavery statutes; in the nineteenth, fully half the legislative corpus regulated in the most detailed way the vast inflow of indentured labour after the 1840s. It was a flow of labour that was subject to the kind of coercion we have seen embodied in the early Madras legislation, as England was leaving that most direct use of state power behind.

In practice and very often in enacting language, notably in limits on appeals and judicial review, most of this vast magisterial authority was protected from the scrutiny of high courts, particularly in the non-white empire. In the eighteenth century, and again in the later nineteenth, the racist bias is clear.[58]

[55] Michael Anderson, 'India 1858–1930: The Illusion of Free Labor', and P. Mohapatra, 'Assam and the West Indies, 1860–1920: Immobilizing Plantation Labor', in Hay and Craven (eds), *Masters, Servants and Magistrates*, 422–54, 464–7.

[56] Paul Craven and Douglas Hay, 'The Criminalization of "Free" Labour: Master and Servant in Comparative Perspective', *Slavery & Abolition*, 15 (1994), 71–101.

[57] Based on the total number of words in a database of master and servant law held at York University. It comprises what we call 'core' master and servant statutes, some 700 of the most important of the total of 1,400, and only the clauses of them that specifically deal with the creation, supervision, and ending of the employment contract, and the powers of the justices to supervise it. It is therefore a proportion only of the full range of master and servant law, not to speak of labour law, excluding most material on labour standards, collective bargaining, etc. (There are other databases containing all the core statutes in coded rather than full text form, so that content can be compared regardless of language.)

[58] Indeed, the mandarins in the Colonial Office of the late Victorian empire frankly and openly held the view (at least in the precincts of Whitehall) that master and servant law was peculiarly fitted for 'inferior races': M. K. Banton, 'The Colonial Office 1820–1955: "Constantly the subject of small struggles"', in Hay and Craven (eds), *Masters, Servants and Magistrates*, 251–303.

As the more distant empire grew, from its seventeenth-century beginnings to its twentieth-century apotheosis, imperial law replicated, in many hundreds of statutes applied to many millions of people, most of them not of European ancestry, the summary punishments and procedures originally deemed suitable for working people in medieval and early modern England. It was enacted, like its English equivalent, by wholly undemocratic governments.[59]

Conclusion

The law of master and servant, while unusually important, formed only a portion of the jurisdiction of inferior justices in both England and the empire. What does this vast mass of legislation say about the tradition of the common law? One conclusion is that the notion of a 'common law regime' is in some ways deeply misleading, for England itself and for the wider empire. In spite of the existence of a number of intermediary kinds of courts (and the fully professionalized magistrates' courts found in London by 1792, in some urban areas in England and some of the dominions by the 1840s, fit that description to a limited degree), in England and in the empire such 'mid-level' law was rare. High law was rarer still. For the greatest part of five hundred years, a mass of statutes deliberately confining remedies and punishments of offences primarily of working people to an inferior tribunal, were enacted and re-enacted in enormous variety. In the case of master and servant law, analysis of the legislation shows a range of penalties wholly excluded from contractual relationships in the high courts, ranging from double-time service for absence from work, to the use of corporal punishment for very minor infractions of work discipline. The emphasis on subordination of a threatening 'other', whether in Norfolk or Bengal, whether in the sixteenth century or the nineteenth, produced a legal order quite unlike that of the high courts. For many other offences, such as excise and liquor offences, high fines and prison sentences of up to a year gave low law real bite. For a vast array of petty and not-so-petty offences, lay justices exercised what was in practice almost always the final determination.

The fact that a great deal of legislative and judicial ingenuity was expended on ensuring separation between high law and low law, and not only in labour cases, as I argue in the first part of this chapter, reinforces the conclusion that to speak simply of a common law tradition is actively misleading. The judges for the most part ignored low law in the eighteenth century, except where it concerned the interests of the propertied. To argue that the eighteenth-century project of law (or indeed the nineteenth) owed a great deal to the enlighten-

[59] The fact that universal suffrage in England came so late is a large part of the explanation for the persistence, and application, of penal master and servant law there long after it had become unthinkable in the United States, and largely unapplied in Canada.

ment, and was embodied in the procedural guarantees found in civil litigation and increasingly in criminal trials before juries, is to ignore the experience of most of those who came before the justices. In that jurisdiction, the imperial state at law inherited, and greatly developed, cheap, informal, and final measures of coercion and control.

4

The promulgation of the statutes in late Hanoverian Britain

SIMON DEVEREAUX*

> The plain fact is this; that the magistrates, who are entrusted with the execution of the laws, have not any correct and speedy means of knowing the laws which they are required to enforce; and his majesty's subjects in general are exposed to the hazard of dissolving [i.e., breaking] laws of which they have no direct communication whatever.
>
> Charles Abbot, MP, 2 November 1796 (*The Parliamentary History of England* (1806–20), xxxii. 1240)

> Whether the number of copies allotted to particular places, or the places themselves, are in all respects selected according to the best possible arrangement, I will not venture; but the reasons are assigned in the Report, and open to consideration. . . . On the other hand, the County Magistrates, even those who do not always serve the public by acting, have been in some parts very clamourous for a larger distribution to decorate their Libraries. All these things therefore must be judged together.
>
> Charles Abbot, speaker of the House of Commons, 29 March 1809 (National Archives, PRO 30/9/14 part 2)

This chapter examines the first efforts by the national government of Great Britain (and, from 1801, of the United Kingdom of Great Britain and Ireland) to ensure that the men principally responsible for administering the laws prescribed by parliament, specifically the magistrates who bore the greatest – and rapidly expanding – burden of regulatory duties during the Hanoverian era, uniformly carried those laws into their proper effect in every jurisdiction throughout the realm. There had of course always been some means available to government to make known to these oft-maligned local administrative

* I owe thanks to the University of Queensland for grant support during the final stages of researching and writing this article; and I am grateful to Donna Andrew, John Beattie, David Lemmings, Andrea McKenzie, and Bruce P. Smith for their comments on an earlier version of it.

workhorses the will of the metropolitan centre as prescribed by law. It may come as something of a surprise to learn, however, that it was not until the end of the eighteenth century that systematic provision was at last made to ensure that some justices of the peace in all parts of the realm actually received complete copies of the statutes of the realm in regular and systematic fashion.

For all its seemingly self-evident relevance to any study of the expansion of central state power vis-à-vis the domestic locality, little has been written on the subject of 'the promulgation of the statutes' after 1796. The chapter which Sheila Lambert devotes to the topic in her indispensable study of eighteenth-century *Bills and Acts* (1971) is in fact principally concerned with the related issue of the new mode of classifying the statutes, while a recent article by John Prest is primarily concerned with the situation in 1835.[1] This study uses the parliamentary papers, Home Office records, and the personal papers of statesmen to examine the scope of the problem that confronted legislators by the late eighteenth century – with particular reference to the increasingly controversial issue of England's 'bloody code' of capital statutes – as well as how the ambitions of the first comprehensive scheme to promulgate the statutes were limited and refined owing to the limits of central governance at the time. On the one hand, it foregrounds a clear and explicit effort by authorities at the national centre to impose a significant degree of uniformity in the local administration of the law: an effort which might look somewhat surprising after more than a decade's scholarship on the 'local origins' of the modern administrative state in eighteenth-century Britain. At the same time, however, the actual scale on which this effort was made – the number of local officials who received copies of the laws with the regularity prescribed by parliament – was far smaller than so splendid-sounding a title as 'the promulgation of the statutes' might lead one to assume. Even so, it will be suggested that the effort itself and subsequent magisterial responsiveness to it suggests a growing role in the British provinces for the authority of central government.

The growing burden of the Hanoverian magistrate

Historians once took it largely for granted that there was no administrative state to speak of in Britain before the early nineteenth century. This conviction was rooted in a prevailing tendency to see 'the state' solely as an arrangement of clearly structured and explicitly defined authority relations, with instructions flowing outwards (and downwards) from a central authority and activity being undertaken on the ground by officials whose response to the dictates of the centre, as this new structure of authority expanded and developed during the

[1] S. Lambert, *Bills and Acts: Legislative Procedure in Eighteenth-Century England* (Cambridge, 1971), ch. 9; J. Prest, 'The Promulgation of Statutes', *Parliamentary History*, 17 (1998), 106–12.

Victorian era, became increasingly immediate, direct, and uncomplicated. The hallmarks of this modern administrative arrangement included an ever more formidable and detailed capacity to gather information from the localities and the growing capacity of the centre to ensure that its dictates were carried out with uniform dedication through a structured, routine system of inspection. The driving force of this seemingly straightforwardly necessary and desirable line of development was the massive social and economic dislocation of the Industrial Revolution, which not only generated a far greater sense of urgency for an interventionist, regulatory state but also highlighted the utter failure of traditional local authorities and personal philanthropy to meet the scale of need.[2] This perspective was shaped by the rise to maturity of the first generation of historians of the state during the heyday of Britain's post-war welfare state and its total administrative ambitions, a development which was taken implicitly to mark the zenith of the line of development they described.[3]

More recently, the pre-Victorian state has been seen in more positive and dynamic terms. Historians such as Michael J. Braddick and Steve Hindle argue for an early modern English state in which the requirements and wills of local officials and central government were regularly and effectively conveyed to one another along a variety of communicative channels – parliament, proclamations, Privy Council directives – all of which might seem either invisible or ineffective to a mentality which views governance solely in centralized, hierarchical terms.[4] Joanna Innes, indeed, believes that, before its supersession by a variety of administrative offices at Westminster from the late seventeenth century onwards, the early modern Privy Council actually provided a more aggressively centralizing force in English administration than was seen during most of the eighteenth century.[5] At the same time, the general picture of neglect amongst the provincial magistrates of eighteenth-century England has

[2] O. MacDonagh, *Early Victorian Government, 1830–1870* (London, 1977); U.R.Q. Henriques, *Before the Welfare State: Social Administration in Early Industrial Britain* (London, 1979); S. Checkland, *British Public Policy, 1776–1939: An Economic, Social and Political Perspective* (Cambridge, 1983); D. Fraser, *The Evolution of the British Welfare State: A History of Social Policy in the Industrial Revolution* (2nd edn, Basingstoke, 1984).

[3] For the particular role of Sidney and Beatrice Webb's eleven-volume history of *English Local Government* in shaping this perspective, see J. Innes, 'Parliament and the Shaping of Eighteenth-Century Social Policy', *Transactions of the Royal Historical Society*, 5th Series, 40 (1990), 64–6. For a provocative discussion of the underlying politics of changing views of English state history, see M. J. Wiener, 'The Unloved State: Twentieth-Century Politics in the Writing of Nineteenth-Century History', *Journal of British Studies*, 33 (1994), 283–308.

[4] M.J. Braddick, *State Formation in Early Modern England, c.1550–1700* (Cambridge, 2000); S. Hindle, *The State and Social Change in Early Modern England, c.1550–1640* (Basingstoke, 2000).

[5] J. Innes, 'The Domestic Face of the Military–Fiscal State: Government and Society in Eighteenth-Century Britain', in L. Stone (ed.), *An Imperial State at War: Britain from 1689 to 1815* (London, 1994), 96–127 (esp. 97–101).

been powerfully qualified in the work of historians such as Paul Langford, who have detected a significant core of active and dedicated JPs, most strikingly amongst the 'squarsons' (churchmen who did double-duty as magistrates) who once seemed the epitome of administrative turpitude.[6] And the work of David Eastwood seems to turn the old model on its head, arguing that most dimensions of modern administrative practice, most notably the systematic gathering and application of statistics and other forms of information, actually originated in the responses of local authorities to the social and economic crises of the late Hanoverian era.[7]

However active or effective individual justices of the peace might have been before 1800, the sheer scale of tasks which they were assigned to perform by statute law was vast and growing rapidly. By the late eighteenth century, indeed, it seemed to be growing more swiftly than ever. Whereas parliament passed less than three thousand statutes between 1485 and 1688, it passed approximately 13,600 from 1689 to 1801, a five-fold increase during the eighteenth century by comparison with the two centuries which had preceded it. Moreover, the bulk of this growth appears to have been concentrated on the last four decades of the eighteenth century.[8] Peter Thomas estimates that the reign of George III saw an average of more than three times as many acts passed in each parliamentary session as in those of his predecessor, and more than four times as many as in those of George I.[9] The difference is more imposing still when recalculated to reflect the length of each session: 0.36 acts per day before 1688, compared with 1.95 after 1760.[10] 'During this sessions his majesty has given the royal assent to 95 public bills, and 101 private,' marvelled *The Gentleman's Magazine* in 1766. 'What an addition this, to the statutes at large, which, in time, at this rate of accumulation, must be carried with the judges in a baggage-wagon, if no method is contrived to digest the statute law into one body.'[11] It can be little wonder then, as David Lieberman has shown, that the questions of codification and rationalization came to preoccupy Daines Barrington, William Blackstone, Jeremy Bentham, and other late eighteenth-century commentators on the state of English law.[12]

[6] P. Langford, *Public Life and the Propertied Englishman, 1689–1798* (Oxford, 1991), ch. 6.

[7] D. Eastwood, *Governing Rural England: Tradition and Transformation in Local Government, 1780–1840* (Oxford, 1994); D. Eastwood, *Government and Community in the English Provinces, 1700–1870* (Basingstoke, 1997).

[8] J. Hoppit, 'Patterns of Parliamentary Legislation, 1660–1800', *Historical Journal*, 39 (1996), 109.

[9] P.D.G. Thomas, *The House of Commons in the Eighteenth Century* (Oxford, 1971), 61. Thomas estimates that the reigns of William III and George I both averaged 58 acts per session, those of Queen Anne and George II 78 and 81 respectively, and George III no less than 254.

[10] Hoppit, 'Patterns of Parliamentary Legislation', 110.

[11] *The Gentleman's Magazine*, 36 (1766), 292.

[12] D. Lieberman, *The Province of Legislation Determined: Legal Theory in Eighteenth-Century*

Both the immense number of laws being passed and the increasing speed with which the bulk of the statute book was accumulating posed in dramatic fashion the most pressing consideration of all for those expected to carry the laws into effect. How was the active magistrate to know just what his duties were? Worse still, it has been estimated that fully one-quarter of the legislation of the late eighteenth century consisted of revisions to previously existent statutes (compared to a figure of less than 8 per cent for the Restoration era), a situation sure to generate particularly acute headaches for any magistrate determined to enforce the laws of the land as he was expected to do.[13] Printed editions of the statutes at large, produced by the King's Printer, started to appear in the late fifteenth century, but there is little evidence of English magistrates securing copies for their own use. By the 1760s, rival publishers such as Owen Ruffhead and Danby Pickering were producing comprehensive multi-volume editions for private purchase, though their versions were usually selective as to which measures they reproduced in full.[14] In any event, the typical magistrate, usually a man largely or entirely devoid of formal legal training and unversed in the complexities of legal expression, was far more likely to derive a practical knowledge of the state of the laws and the precise character and extent of his duties from a more practical and readily available source.

Justices' manuals, providing concise summaries of relevant statute law and straightforwardly spelling out the manner in which a magistrate was expected to carry out its requirements, were far more likely to be consulted by the local JP than were the statute books. The prototype of this genre was William Lambarde's *Eirenarcha*, which first appeared in 1581 and went through numerous editions through the early seventeenth century, when it appears to have given way to Michael Dalton's *Countrey Justice* (1618). One of the last editions of Dalton was printed in 1746, only a decade before the first appearance of the volume most often to be found on the shelves of conscientious magistrates in late eighteenth-century England, Richard Burn's *The Justice of the Peace and Parish Officer* (1755).[15] Burn's two-volume work ultimately went through thirty editions – the last, in 1869, was six volumes long – and remained the standard authority in its area until well into the nineteenth century, largely because (in Norma Landau's words) it

Britain (Cambridge, 1989); Lieberman, 'Codification, Consolidation, and Parliamentary Statutes', in J. Brewer and E. Hellmuth (eds), *Rethinking Leviathan: The Eighteenth-Century State in Britain and Germany* (Oxford, 1999), 359–90.

[13] Hoppit, 'Patterns of Parliamentary Legislation,' 111.

[14] W. Holdsworth, *A History of English Law* (London, 1903–66), ii. 307–13; vi. 312–13; xi. 301–8.

[15] Holdsworth, *History of English Law*, iv. 117–19; vi. 332–5; L.M. Boyer, 'The Justice of the Peace in England and America from 1506 to 1776: A Bibliographic History', *Quarterly Journal of the Library of Congress*, 34 (1977), 315–22; N. Landau, *The Justices of the Peace, 1679–1760* (Berkeley, 1984), 334–42; T. Skyrme, *History of the Justices of the Peace* (Chichester, 1991), i. 164–7.

> provided lucid, comprehensive, and accurate instruction. . . . Burn defined every legal term that the justice would encounter. He described every task the justice might perform and carefully outlined, in chronological order, every step in every judicial procedure. . . . The justice could just open his Burn and follow instructions. . . . In Burn, the justice had at last had a complete and virtually indisputable guide to the rules controlling the procedures of his office.

Burn's work became so deeply entrenched a feature of magisterial practice that in 1787 the court of King's Bench chose to accept as valid a summary conviction in fact inadequately supported by evidence but which nonetheless had followed the procedure spelled out in its pages.[16] The authority widely attributed to Burn's *Justice of the Peace*, the fact of its regularly appearing in revised and extended editions, and the frequent appearance of would-be competitors like Samuel Glasse's *The Magistrate's Assistant* (1784), Edward Barry's *Present Practice of a Justice of the Peace* (1791), and Thomas Walter Williams's *Whole Law Relative to the Duty and Office of a Justice of the Peace* (1793) all indicate that there must have been both a healthy demand and strong sense of the need for such works amongst justices, many of whom in turn must presumably have been more active and engaged in the exercise of their duties than earlier portraits of the Hanoverian county bench would have us believe.[17]

The need to promulgate the 'Bloody Code'

Many late eighteenth-century observers believed that the obligation to disseminate knowledge of the laws did not stop simply with keeping officials abreast of the tasks they were expected to carry out. 'There is a preliminary duty with respect to the administration of justice, which is especially incumbent upon the government,' wrote Henry Brougham in 1844. 'It is bound to make the laws known to the people upon whom they are to be enforced; to make the rules which are to govern the administration of justice known by the subjects of that administration.'[18] In no realm of late Hanoverian English law was the need for the broadest public knowledge of its content more urgently felt than in the nation's extraordinarily extensive capital code. It is easy to

16 Landau, *Justices of the Peace*, 341–2.

17 Glasse acknowledged the superior comprehensiveness of Burn's four volumes and that 'no Magistrate ought to be without them', but also claimed that 'as Books of Reference, [they] comprize much more, than it is necessary for a Justice of the Peace to investigate, in the *ordinary* Duties of his Office' and that much of the information they contained was 'not immediately connected with the Duties of a Magistrate' (*The Magistrate's Assistant; or, A Summary of Those Laws which Immediately Respect the Conduct of a Justice of the Peace* (Gloucester, 1784), viii; emphasis in original).

18 H. Brougham, *The British Constitution: Its History, Structure, and Working* (1844); in *Works of Henry Lord Brougham* (Edinburgh, 1873), xi. 301.

overstate the practical significance of the expansion in the array of capital offences from about fifty in 1688 to about 240 by 1820. The majority of trials ending in capital convictions during the eighteenth century in fact proceeded under the major categories of crime – robbery, burglary, housebreaking, pocket-picking, arson, rape, murder – that had been rendered capital offences during the Tudor era.[19] Nevertheless new capital offences continued to be created in the last decades of the eighteenth century and the first of the nineteenth, so it is unsurprising that men who actually knew something of the processes of legislation and enforcement of the law might start to entertain fears that many people might be capitally convicted of offences which they had not even known to exist before being prosecuted for them. Some of the more frequently enforced capital offences created after 1688 included theft from shops (1699), theft from houses (1713), theft of sheep (1741) and cattle (1742), smuggling (1746), and theft from the mails (1765).[20] The most striking and extensive of the newly emergent categories of capital crime, however, was undoubtedly forgery. Forgery of the seal or notes of the Bank of England was made a capital crime in 1697, as was the forging of various duty stamps in 1711, but the decisive shift came with the passage of a short but sweeping statute in 1729. Newly defined categories of forgery continued to be capitalized as late as the 1820s, and even after an act of 1830 effectively eliminated the application of capital punishment to it, forty-two forms remained capital crimes for another two years.[21] By the end of the second decade of the nineteenth century, the disproportionately severe application of death to those convicted of forgery gave it a powerful role in the swiftly expanding debate over capital punishment as a whole.[22] Its threat must have seemed all the greater in so far as it was also

19 L. Radzinowicz, A *History of English Criminal Law and Its Administration from 1750* (London, 1948–86), i. 3–5, 611–59; J.M. Beattie, *Crime and the Courts in England, 1660–1800* (Princeton, NJ, 1986), chs 3–4 (esp. 141–8).

20 For more detailed accounts of the circumstances surrounding the creation of some of these newer offences, see C. Winslow, 'Sussex Smugglers', in D. Hay *et al.*, *Albion's Fatal Tree: Crime and Society in Eighteenth-Century England* (London, 1975), 119–66; J.G. Rule, 'The Manifold Causes of Rural Crime: Sheep-Stealing in England, c.1740–1840', in J. Rule (ed.), *Outside the Law: Studies in Crime and Order, 1650–1850* (Exeter, 1982), 102–29; and J. Beattie, 'London Crime and the Making of the "Bloody Code", 1689–1718', in Lee Davison *et al.* (eds), *Stilling the Grumbling Hive: The Response to Social and Economic Problems in England, 1689–1750* (Stroud, 1992), 49–76.

21 Radzinowicz, *History*, i. 590–5, 604–5, 627–8, 646–50 (esp. 650 n. 76); R. McGowen, 'From Pillory to Gallows: The Punishment of Forgery in the Age of the Financial Revolution', *Past & Present*, 165 (1999), 107–40; McGowen, 'Making the "Bloody Code"? Forgery Legislation in Eighteenth-Century England', in N. Landau (ed.), *Law, Crime and English Society, 1660–1830* (Cambridge, 2002), 117–38.

22 Radzinowicz, *History*, i. 550–1, 555–61, 590–5; V.A.C. Gatrell, *The Hanging Tree: Execution and the English People, 1770–1830* (Oxford, 1994), 408–13. Randall McGowen will soon be publishing a full-scale study of the law of forgery and its application in the eighteenth and early nineteenth centuries.

perhaps the most technically abstruse – the most difficult for the average person fully to know – of all categories of capital crime, hence the need to continue extending its definition as a capital offence until almost the very end of the 'Bloody Code'. It can be little wonder then that compilations of the penal statutes in particular became a prominent sub-genre of compilations for magistrates from the 1770s onwards.[23]

The question of being able to know the burgeoning letter of the capital code was a central concern, and nowhere perhaps more so than amongst those who advocated its reduction and reform.[24] William Eden's *Principles of Penal Law* (1771), one of the most widely read and influential English reformist tracts of its time, devoted an entire chapter to the issues of composition and promulgation of the laws. 'It is . . . essential to political freedom', Eden wrote, 'that the laws be clearly obvious to common understandings, and fully notified to the people.'[25] Fifteen years later Samuel Romilly, who would later lead the first sustained and effective attack on the 'Bloody Code' from within parliament, went even further.[26] He argued that whether or not a person knew the nature of the law for which they were hanged was less important than the broader question of whether or not the offence in question merited so severe a punishment. 'If laws operate in violation of the feelings and understandings of men', he wrote, 'they are unjust and unwise, by however legitimate an authority they were enacted.' Nevertheless he agreed that knowing the full range of capital offences was an essential consideration, and he also believed that few people possessed sufficient time and skill to be able to learn the whole of their vast substance; certainly not the largely uneducated and desperate thieves who invariably formed the largest number of victims of the gallows during the eighteenth century. Indeed, even the best-informed, most well-educated observers were unlikely to be able to keep pace with the legislature, so swiftly were new laws being created and so vast the number of people being put to death during the 1780s. Most people did not even know a new hanging offence existed until someone had paid the ultimate price for it, and 'this can hardly be considered as a promulgation of the law; for who has curiosity or leisure to enquire what has been the crime of every individual among the multitude that are executed?'[27] On one basic point, then, Eden and Romilly

[23] W. Addington, *An Abridgment of Penal Statutes* (London, 1775; 3rd edn, 1786; 4th edn, 1795); G. Clark, *The Penal Statutes Abridged and Alphabetically Arranged* (London, 1777); W. Boscawen, *A Treatise on Conviction on Penal Statutes* (London, 1792).

[24] The most recent survey of late eighteenth-century advocates of criminal law reform is Lieberman, *Province of Legislation Determined*, ch. 10.

[25] W. Eden, *Principles of Penal Law* (London, 1771), 287.

[26] Radzinowicz, *History*, i. ch. 16; R.R. Follett, *Evangelicalism, Penal Theory and the Politics of Criminal Law Reform in England, 1808–30* (Basingstoke, 2001), chs 2–3, 7.

[27] [S. Romilly,] *Observations on a Late Publication, intituled, Thoughts on Executive Justice* (London, 1786), 35–51 (quotes at 38, 43–4). For the unprecedentedly high execution levels of the 1780s, see Beattie, *Crime and the Courts*, 582–92; D. Hay, 'The Laws of God and the

were agreed: the full penalty of the law could not be imposed with justice where there was no confidence that its object had understood that he or she was committing a criminal offence.

The principal responsibility for ensuring that people knew the laws of the realm rested with those whom the people most often saw enforcing it, and at least one major criminal court attempted to supply itself with copies of the statutes during this era. In November 1771 the town clerk of the City of London was ordered to 'provide a set of Pickering's Statutes at large in Octavo for the Sessions house in the Old Bailey', the busiest felony jurisdiction in the country. In purchasing the volumes, City officials expended the not inconsiderable sum of £37 18s.[28] Three years later, London's twenty-five aldermen, all of whom were expected to act as magistrates for the City, were ordered 'to complete' their individual 'Set of the Statutes at Large', though only 'in such manner as [each] shall think proper'. But the order for a full and complete set for use at the Old Bailey was also reiterated on this occasion, as well as the authority of the town clerk to reclaim any further expenses he incurred thereby, and this, as well as a further restatement of the same order only ten years later in October 1784, suggests the lack of success that City officials must have had in ensuring the regular purchase, let alone 'promulgation', of the statutes.[29] Even the senior officials of the nation's busiest criminal jurisdiction could not be assured of quick and authoritative reference to the letter of the law.

'It is a well-known maxim of the law', wrote an anonymous correspondent (possibly William Wilberforce) to *The Gentleman's Magazine* in 1792, 'that a want of knowledge of the law excuses no man from the penalty of it. This clearly demonstrates the very great necessity there is for a better promulgation of the laws than we at present possess.' He invoked the example of Thomas Bayley, an active and reform-minded magistrate of Lancashire, who had recently suggested that 'extracts of all the penal statutes [should be] inserted in the public newspapers'. However, this correspondent believed that even this tactic would not work, as 'The number of individuals who have an opportunity of reading the newspapers is truly small, in comparison with those who neither read nor see them for months or years. . . . [T]he majority of the poorer sort of

Laws of Man: Lord George Gordon and the Death Penalty', in J. Rule and R. Malcolmson (eds), *Protest and Survival: The Historical Experience: Essays for E.P. Thompson* (London, 1993), 61–5; and P. King, *Crime, Justice and Discretion in England, 1740–1820* (Oxford, 2000), 273–8.

28 Corporation of London Records Office (CLRO), Repertories of the Court of Alderman, vol. 175, pp.14, 88. The scale of the expenditure may be measured against estimates that £50–75 per annum constituted a minimal to average middle-class income at the time; see P. Langford, *A Polite and Commercial People: England, 1727–1783* (Oxford, 1989), 62–3; and J. Rule, *Albion's People: English Society, 1714–1815* (London, 1992), ch. 3.

29 CLRO, Repertories of the Court of Alderman, vol. 178, p.151; vol. 188, pp. 332–3. For the role of aldermen as magistrates, see J.M. Beattie, *Policing and Punishment in London, 1660–1750: Urban Crime and the Limits of Terror* (Oxford, 2001), ch. 2.

the people . . . will still remain involved in the same gloomy veil of ignorance.' He proposed a different solution:

> The sheriffs of every county should be commanded, at the close of each session of parliament, to transmit to the constables of the respective townships a plain and simple abstract of the contents of the penal statutes that have been passed, directing them to get the same read on the Sunday following at the end of the morning and evening service at the door of the next parish church or chapel. By this means, the young and old, the rich and poor, would gain without any expense or trouble an accurate and early communication of the laws; and no longer could it be said, to the disgrace of Englishmen, 'you have wise and salutary laws to restrain the passions of men; but how little do they avail, when the greater part of that class of people, who are the most liable to infringe the rules of justice, know not that such laws exist, unless by fatal experience!'[30]

Such scrupulous concern for the knowledge of the criminal law by its offenders appears to have been a minority sentiment, however, as Wilberforce himself clearly understood. Far more widespread was concern that its principal enforcers should be fully informed of all changes in the statute book as soon as possible. 'The late immoderate additions to the statute law of this country, abounding with penal clauses of the most oppressive kind', wrote the Rev. Edward Barry in 1791, rendered an accurate statement of all the duties incumbent on local magistrates 'absolutely necessary, to those who wish to act with propriety in their respective offices and situations'.[31] Six years later, efforts were at last made to regularly supply them with full-text copies of the acts at parliamentary expense.

Charles Abbot and the committee of 1796

Charles Abbot, first Baron Colchester (1757–1829) is little known outside parliamentary history circles, but he is the sort of figure who, had he

[30] *The Gentleman's Magazine*, 62 (1792), 807–8. The letter is signed 'W.W.', and when the first motion for a committee to consider the promulgation of the statutes was moved in November 1796, William Wilberforce enthusiastically seconded it (*The Parliamentary History of England, from the Earliest Period to the Year 1803* (London, 1806–20), xxxii.1241). He had indeed been specifically chosen to do so, presumably from a prior knowledge of his interest in such a measure; see Lord Colchester (ed.), *The Diary and Correspondence of Charles Abbot, Lord Colchester, Speaker of the House of Commons, 1802–1817* (London, 1861), i. 73. For Thomas Bayley's activity as a reforming Lancashire magistrate, see M. DeLacy, *Prison Reform in Lancashire, 1700–1850: A Study in Local Administration* (Stanford, CA, 1986), 70–82, 95–8.

[31] *The Present Practice of a Justice of the Peace; and a Complete Library of Parish Law* (London, 1791); quoted in *The Critical Review*, 2nd series, 2 (1791:2), 30.

never existed, a less scrupulous historian might be tempted to invent.[32] He entered parliament in June 1795 and rose rapidly to prominence, largely on the patronage of Henry Addington, speaker of the House of Commons and an intimate friend of prime minister William Pitt. When Addington assumed the premiership in February 1801, he briefly made his protégé chief secretary for Ireland before supporting his succession to the speaker's chair in February 1802, a position in which Abbot served conscientiously until 1817.[33] But it is with Abbot's prior legislative activities that we are most concerned. During this earliest phase of his parliamentary career, Abbot was the principal moving force behind several major innovations in legislative and administrative practice which might well be reckoned amongst the benchmarks of modern state activity. Within a year of his first entering parliament, he secured the first of what subsequently became annual committees to determine 'Expiring Laws' (that is, temporary laws whose provisions had lapsed after a specified interval), a vital element of any set of efforts to master the country's vast array of statutory law.[34] It was also thanks to Abbot's efforts that a new, tripartite division of legislation into 'Public General', 'Public and Local', and 'Local and Personal' Acts was initiated in 1797.[35] His was also the guiding hand behind the thirty-six Reports of the Select Committee on Finance 1797–8, a sweeping attempt by parliament to review and reform virtually the whole range of government activity and expenditure.[36] Finally, in the last weeks of 1800, Abbot shepherded through parliament the first legislation providing for a national census (41 Geo. III c.15), a measure which he promised Pitt 'may be essentially useful towards the formation of any permanent Plan for preventing the recurrence of the pressure which we now experience' in the provision of food to the population at large, a vital consideration in light of the famine conditions which existed in some parts of the country during the late 1790s and subsequent

[32] The most detailed account of Abbot's life and career remains the three volumes of the *Colchester Diary*, which publishes a large selection of his extensively preserved papers (National Archives [NA], PRO 30/9). The sole modern account is that provided in R.G. Thorne (ed.), *The History of Parliament: The House of Commons, 1790–1820* (London, 1986), iii. 1–8.

[33] P. Ziegler, *Addington: A Life of Henry Addington, First Viscount Sidmouth* (London, 1965), 134–5; Thorne (ed.), *House of Commons*, iii. 1–4.

[34] *Colchester Diary*, i. 50. The inability even of government to know the substance of the law could be a source of profound embarrassment and political discomfort. In 1794 it had been discovered that several Scotsmen convicted of sedition and sent to New South Wales had, in fact, been transported without legislative authority, the act allowing for the transportation of Scottish felons not having been renewed when required. See *Parliamentary History*, xxx. 1298–1310, 1346–53, 1449–61, 1486–76; xxxi. 54–83, 263–8.

[35] Lambert, *Bills and Acts*, 180–6.

[36] The critical impact of the twenty-eighth of these reports, that concerning 'Police, including the Convict Establishments' (26 June 1798), is treated at length in my *Criminal Justice and English Government, 1750–1810: Convicts and the State* (Basingstoke, forthcoming).

outbursts of food rioting. A national census, argued Abbot, would 'lay the basis for a periodical numeration of the People which may shew the increasing or decreasing demand to which the supply of provisions is to be accommodated; And at all events the Result of it will be very serviceable for many of the great purposes of Legislation or Government, Civil and Military.'[37]

Abbot's activity, and the legislative and administrative reforms which followed on from much of it, reflected the growing influence of a new generation – or, perhaps more accurately, a new mind-set – of parliamentarians that was coming to the fore during the last decade of the eighteenth century. These men, whose leading figures included Addington, Abbot, and many of their closest associates, took a more serious and high-minded view of the character and conduct of national politics and public administration than had the passing generation. In the coming years, this quality would be physically manifest in a transition from a generally varied and often colourful mode of personal dress amongst members of parliament to a more sober and professional, uniformly dark one, as well as a cooler and more reserved personal demeanour in public.[38] Many of these new men were particularly determined to create a mode of governance for the British nation that was more efficient, somewhat more (though as yet far from completely) centralized, and not least of all, more fiscally responsible.[39] It would be tempting to read further significance into the fact that Abbot was the step-brother of that omnivorous advocate of legal codification and reform Jeremy Bentham, but from the evidence of Bentham's voluminously preserved correspondence, the two appear to have had relatively little professional or even personal involvement with one another during their long careers.[40] The scope of Abbot's activity, independent of his more vocal but ultimately far less influential step-brother, more than justifies his

[37] NA, PRO 30/58/3/86, Charles Abbot to William Pitt, 5 November 1800. (I am grateful to Mr G.A.F.E. Adams for permission to quote from the papers of his ancestor.) For the food shortages, famine, and disturbances of the 1790s, and especially 1799–1801, see R. Wells, 'English Society and Revolutionary Politics in the 1790s: The Case for Insurrection', in M. Philp (ed.), *The French Revolution and British Popular Politics* (Cambridge, 1991), 191–5, 215–26. See also A. Charlesworth (ed.), *An Atlas of Rural Protest in Britain, 1548–1900* (London, 1983), 97–103.

[38] For this transition, see P.J. Jupp, 'The Landed Elite and Political Authority in Britain, *ca.* 1760–1850', *Journal of British Studies*, 29 (1990), 53–79; and P. Langford, 'Politics and Manners from Sir Robert Walpole to Sir Robert Peel', *Proceedings of the British Academy*, 94 (1997), 103–25.

[39] For this latter theme especially, see P. Harling and P. Mandler, 'From "Fiscal–Military" State to Laissez-faire State, 1760–1850', *Journal of British Studies*, 32 (1993), 44–70; and P. Harling, *The Waning of 'Old Corruption': The Politics of Economical Reform in Britain, 1779–1846* (Oxford, 1996).

[40] Abbot's widowed mother Sarah married Bentham's widowed father Jeremiah on 14 October 1766 (Abbot's ninth birthday!), when Bentham was 18 years old; see J.H. Burns *et al.* (eds), *The Correspondence of Jeremy Bentham* (London and Oxford, 1968–), i. 99n.

characterization by one historian as 'one of the most distinguished ornaments of the Administrative Revolution'.[41]

With Addington's encouragement, Abbot had begun investigating the various subjects relating to statute law by February 1796, only seven months after he had first entered parliament. By the middle of June 1796, and after consultation with the King's Printer Andrew Strachan, he had settled the scheme of promulgation which he proposed to present to parliament.[42] By mid-October he had 'chiefly turned my thoughts' to that subject, assuring Addington that he had 'endeavored to devise such a mode [of printing and distribution] as might render the Promulgation most effectual without prejudicing any private right or enhancing the public expense'.[43] By the end of that month, the two had met twice to agree on the final form of the report and to plan the membership of the committee which would present it to parliament. 'We agreed', wrote Abbot in his diary, 'that the less said to expose the deformed and shapeless condition of the present mode of giving publicity to our laws, the more discreet it would be.'[44] And so Abbot's motion in the Commons on 2 November 1796 to form a committee on the subject was careful to deflect blame from local magistrates and parliament alike. 'The plain fact is this', he told the House,

> that the magistrates, who are entrusted with the execution of the laws, have not any correct and speedy means of knowing the laws which they are required to enforce; and his majesty's subjects in general are exposed to the hazard of dissolving [i.e., breaking] laws of which they have no direct communication whatever.

However, the present difficulties were not the result of any failing on the part of either an overworked parliament or of indolent magistrates. 'The truth is', he continued,

> that the evil has come upon us by the change of customs which naturally belongs to a change of times; and when the older usage of proclaiming statutes by the sheriff was suspended by the introduction of printing, we can only wonder, that our

[41] R.B. Pugh, 'Charles Abbot and the Public Records: The First Phase', *Bulletin of the Institute of Historical Research*, 39 (1966), 69–85 (quote at 69).

[42] *Colchester Diary*, i. 32–4, 42–3, 52–4, 56–7, 60–1.

[43] Devon Record Office, Sidmouth Papers, 152M/C1796/OZ/13, Abbot to Addington, 15 October 1796.

[44] *Colchester Diary*, i. 71–3 (quote at 72). They also discussed the possibility of 'making a thorough revision' of the contents of all existing statutes to date, but Abbot was loathe to assume a task that he deemed to be an 'undertaking which far exceed[s] the industry and talents of any individual, however zealous for the public Service' (quoted in note 43 above). Addington 'urged' him 'to prosecute it strenuously' and 'insisted that the whole must depend upon [Abbot], and that if it was not now done it could never be looked for' (*Colchester Diary*, i. 73). But the superhuman task of English statute consolidation would have to wait another generation yet.

ancestors did not at that era substitute some better method of promulgation by the very means of which they had acquired the facility [i.e., distribution of printed copies]. But no such steps were taken; and the grievance has since grown gradually, with the annual multiplication of our statutes to such a magnitude as demands an immediate and effectual remedy.[45]

A more extended account of Abbot's speech on this occasion is explicit regarding the particular role of criminal law concerns to secure a more effective publicizing of the statute law. Under the old system of shrieval proclamation, Abbot insisted,

The laws were in fact no sooner capable of promulgation than they were generally and publicly known. Whether or no such a practice actually prevented the commission of crimes, it was not for him positively to say; but one thing he knew, that there was less danger of crimes being committed then than now. At present, indeed, the fact was, that men were tried, convicted, and sometimes lost their lives, according to the tenor of laws, the existence of which was unknown to them. . . . The evil was, therefore, in this point of view, truly serious – truly worthy of consideration.[46]

Finally, ever mindful of parliament's anxiety about mounting expenses, especially in time of war, Abbot hastened to assure his fellow MPs

that means will probably be found arising out of the business, and out of the very improvement of the present system, which may furnish an effectual distribution upon a scale of very considerable extent, even without enhancing the public expenditure in any degree whatever.[47]

The Commons unanimously endorsed Abbot's motion to form his committee.

It remained for the committee's report, ordered for printing a month later, to spell out in detail how Abbot proposed to resolve the tensions between a full and expeditious promulgation of the statutes on the one hand and the potentially exorbitant expense of printing and distribution of them on the other.[48] The problems of scale and cost were crucial, for Abbot's committee

[45] *Parliamentary History*, xxxii.1240.
[46] *The Senator; or, Clarendon's Parliamentary Chronicle* (London, 1790–1802), xvi. 175.
[47] *Parliamentary History*, xxxii.1240.
[48] Unless otherwise indicated, all quotations in this and the following three paragraphs are from the Report from the Committee for Promulgation of the Statutes (5 December 1796). This has been most recently and authoritatively reprinted in Sheila Lambert (ed.), *House of Commons Sessional Papers of the Eighteenth Century* (Wilmington, Del., 1975), civ. 1–72. I used the version that appears in the micro-opaque edition of the *British Sessional Papers 1731–1800: House of Commons Reports* (New York: Readex Microprints, 1960), xix. no.137 (1796/7).

proposed to triple the number of copies presently circulated at public expense. From the total 1,126 copies of statutes currently distributed to 'a very limited Circle of Persons' (p. 7) by the King's Printer, Abbot proposed an increase to 3,550.[49] His solution to the problem of cost was to deploy his new classification scheme in order to minimize the number of statutes that had actually to be printed in full-text format. Of the three types of acts now recognized, only the Public General acts were to be promulgated according to the new system. On the basis of the last ten years of legislative activity at Westminster, Abbot estimated that these, 'the first and most important Class' of statutes, comprised only 'a very small Proportion of the whole Mass' (two-sevenths) of printed pages generated in the statute book during a given year (p. 16). Larger by far was the proportion of paper devoted to reproducing 'Local' acts (four-sevenths), while a further seventh was comprised solely of the abstracts of both (p. 18n.). For 'the purposes of Economy and mere Multiplication', then, only the Public General acts would be printed and distributed nationwide at public expense (p. 17).[50] These volumes would be 'carrying forth to the Nation, as Public Laws, those only which profess to be founded on principles of general Policy and unusual Obligation' (p. 19). Thus, even though Abbot rejected any notion of further economies of production by reducing the paper and font sizes used in printing the acts for fear of 'the Loss of other Conveniences' of consultation (pp. 17–18), the proposed increase in circulation by a multiple of three would in theory be more than offset by a reduction of more than two-thirds in the total volume of the annual statute book.[51]

As a mode of extending the reach of central authority into the provinces, however, Abbot's scheme of promulgation seemed to look in two directions at once. On the one hand, it undoubtedly gave the systematic promulgation of the statutes in Great Britain a far wider geographical basis than it had ever before possessed. Indeed, in so far as the 1,126 copies distributed at public expense before 1797 went solely to officials based in London, the vast majority

[49] The King's Printer could always have printed and sold any copies of the Acts which individuals might request, but the Report noted that no one had requested a full set of the statutes 'for Many Years past' (p. 7).

[50] The local and private acts were also to be printed at public expense, but there were only to be two hundred copies of them, almost half of them for the use of London-based officials and institutions and the bare minimum of one each for distribution to the clerks of the peace (pp. 23–6, 70–1).

[51] Thus, as Abbot observed more than a decade later, 'the Plan then proposed and finally adopted (whatever the qualities it might have) at least had not that of extending the scale of expence beyond its antecedent amount' (NA, PRO 30/9/14 part 2, Charles Abbot to Henry Thornton (copy), 29 March 1809). By 1809 however this assumption was breaking down under the pressure of prolonged warfare, during which time 'the Public General Acts exceed the proportion of 1/3, and therefore since 1797, the total expense has exceeded the previous enumeration. The number of . . . Public Acts being so large' (NA, PRO 30/9/14 part 2, undated note, *c.* 1808–9).

of whom would have had little or no practical use for them (members of the House of Lords and the House of Commons alone comprised more than 900 of the recipients), the addition of more than 2,000 copies for distribution outside the capital looks an impressive, inevitably centralizing innovation (pp. 37–8).[52] As the report noted, 'every complete End for the Promulgation of Laws must be commensurate with the System of Jurisdictions by which the Laws are or may be administered' (p. 15). To this end, it continued, 'The principal Objects, and for which the greatest Effort should be made, are the numerous Jurisdictions into which the whole Kingdom is sub-divided' (p. 21). And the report even seemed to end with something very much like an explicit, ringing endorsement of the power of parliament to legislate for every corner of the realm and ensure that local officials carried its will into force in a consistent and uniform manner. The conclusion declared that 'the correct, speedy and general Promulgation of the Laws is essentially concerned with the Dignity of the Legislature, the Efficacy of all Government, and the universal Principles of Justice' (p. 32).

Yet, upon closer examination, the actual scheme of distribution seems to propose a system which could scarcely have carried through on such splendidly confident wording, for the actual number of jurisdictions in Great Britain, comprising England, Wales, and Scotland, was immensely large. Appendices III, IV and VI of the report identified no fewer than 106 commissions of the peace, 368 cities, boroughs, or corporate towns, 10,353 parishes, and 14,599 rateable districts (pp. 41–52, 57–61). Appendix V additionally noted the presence in counties and towns of 4,119 'resident acting justices', that is, magistrates known to be conducting their official duties in a largely regular and reliable fashion (pp. 53–6). For so immense a range of jurisdictions and magistrates, the 2,372 copies of the statutes not allocated to high officials in London could not be expected to go very far at all in terms of making new laws known even to every one of their enforcers, let alone those subject to it. Abbot's proposed strategy for circumventing this difficulty was that many copies assigned to individual jurisdictions would be entrusted to local officials as a source of permanent reference to other officials of the jurisdiction rather than the personal possession of one. Thus one copy each would be transmitted to the sheriff of each of the 85 counties, to 'be lodged and preserved, for public Inspection' in the office of the under sheriff, while another would be distributed

52 Even then mishaps could occur, one of which suggests how often copies must have gone astray. An accounts book from the Treasury Office records that in March 1813 a nearly complete run of the statutes at large for the reign of George III was purchased for £1 11s 6d, with a view to securing immediately copies of the volumes for 1809 and 1812, even though that office was formally allocated no less than thirteen copies free of charge. See British Library, Add. MS 29472, f. 93; and Report from the Committee for Promulgation of the Statutes of the United Kingdom, throughout all parts of Great Britain and Ireland (28 April 1801), p.5, in *Sessional Papers of the House of Commons 1801–1900*, 1801 (49) iii. 87–126.

to each of the 106 clerks of the peace, to be similarly 'deposited in their respective Offices, and assigned to their Successors, and to be employed for the Public Use at the Times of holding the several Sessions, Great Sessions, and Assizes' (p. 21). Another 379 copies were to be sent to the senior officials of various towns (pp. 62–4). All of this, it was hoped, would 'produce a very general Notification of [the statute book's] Contents, although it might not be in exact Proportion to the Surface [i.e., the geographical area] or Population of the Districts to which they were communicated' (p. 22).

Ultimately, though, the core of the scheme lay in its numerically largest group of recipients, the resident acting magistrates. Many of these men would be obliged to carry on their immense burden of administrative duties far from the towns where the sheriffs and clerks of the peace would be retaining copies for consultation and on many occasions in between the assizes and sessional meeting times when those copies would be close to hand. It is amongst this crucially important group above all that the pattern of distribution starts to look peculiar by comparison with what common sense might seem to dictate. No less than 1,788 copies, just over half of the total number printed and distributed at government expense, were to be allocated to these crucial 4,119 officials. In order to maintain a sense of impartiality, however, a numerical scheme of distribution was imposed which inherently favoured the least populous regions. In districts that had fewer than ten resident acting justices, every one of them would get his own copy of the statutes. But districts with ten to twenty such justices received only ten copies, those with twenty to fifty received only twenty, and those with fifty or more received only twenty-five, 'to divide them amongst themselves by their own Authority, according to any Mode which they should conceive to be best adapted to the Advancement of Justice and the more effective Execution of the Laws' (pp. 22–3, 64–9). This produced some extraordinary disproportions, with places like Bedford and the Isle of Ely receiving their complete complements of two and nine respectively, while larger jurisdictions might be immensely hard-pressed, the maximum of twenty-five being assigned equally to Cornwall's sixty-two active magistrates, Gloucester's seventy-two, Surrey's ninety-seven and Essex's one hundred and ten. The sole exception to this seemingly bizarre rule was Middlesex, the county in which lived the vast majority of the population of metropolitan London, the nation's largest city with 12–14 per cent of the population of England and Wales between 1800 and 1830, and even Middlesex's 158 active magistrates were allocated only an extra five copies above the county's prescribed twenty-five (pp. 64–9).[53]

Not surprisingly then, this component of the numerical scheme was substantially increased only four years later when the Act of Union with Ireland

[53] B.R. Mitchell, *British Historical Facts* (Cambridge, 1988), 11, 25. On the other hand, Middlesex's small size was perhaps expected to ensure that copies would be close to hand for those magistrates who might need to consult one.

necessitated the addition of Irish officials into a larger scheme of promulgation for the United Kingdom as a whole. No other measure, the centrally minded Abbot confidently assured the Commons in February 1801, 'would tend more to that identity of habits and manners, so necessary to the identity of interests, throughout every part of the United Kingdom'.[54] In the scheme of 1801, the number of statutes provided to the acting magistrates of England and Scotland was increased by more than a thousand, with Middlesex, to take perhaps the most striking example, now receiving eighty-five copies rather than thirty.[55] But these latter numbers remained largely unchanged when Victoria ascended the throne thirty-six years later, by which time they must have seemed even more vastly out of step with social, economic, and demographic developments than they had done under the first proposed scheme of 1796.[56]

It is possible (though I know of no instances) that some, perhaps even many members of parliament quietly passed along their assigned copies of the statutes to some magistrate with whom they had connection or whom they knew to be active in the locality they represented or in which they resided. Additionally, although the local schemes of distribution amongst resident acting justices are hidden from view of the sources deployed in this article, it may well be that careful account was taken to ensure that those magistrates who were most remote from the offices where copies of the acts were kept for general consultation were the prioritized recipients of individual copies. In general though, one gets the distinct impression that many of the people who might be expected to have had the greatest need for immediate reference to the statute book were by no means assured of receiving their own copy of it. In this measure more than any other perhaps, Abbot's scheme for the promulgation of the statutes, while perhaps the best which could be devised within the limits of overriding concerns for economy, must have been at best only a partial and limited measure of centralization in late Hanoverian Britain. In this respect at least, it should come as little surprise that the request of local magistrates to become recipients of their own copies of the acts became an increasingly common feature of the final decades of that era.

The responsibility for overseeing the promulgation of the statutes was vested in the Home Office, a department of government which in 1797 had only

[54] *Parliamentary History*, xxxv. 1003.

[55] 1801 Report on Promulgation of Statutes, pp. 4–37 (esp. 27–8) in *Sessional Papers of the House of Commons 1801–1900*, 1801 (49) iii. 87–126. Gloucester, Surrey, and Cornwall now received thirty, but Cornwall still received only twenty-five.

[56] Promulgation of the Statutes: Statement of the Number of the Statutes sent to each Office, County and Borough for the Year 1837 . . . (16 August 1838; 8 pp.); in *Sessional Papers of the House of Commons 1801–1900*, 1837–8 (733) xxxvi. 439–46. Only eighty more copies were assigned to acting magistrates between 1801 and 1837; the other figures were scarcely altered at all. Cornwall's quota had been raised from twenty-five to thirty-six during the intervening years, but Essex had only been increased to thirty-five, and Gloucester and Surrey still received only thirty each (ibid., 445).

existed for fifteen years, during the first ten of which Home Secretaries had generally sought to avoid taking on board any wider a scope of administrative duties than the equivalent offices had possessed under the old division of the Secretariat of State.[57] Accordingly the Home Office managed to keep a considerable share of the burden of distributing the acts off its shoulders, in this case by leaving the practical arrangements to be worked out by Abbot and the King's Printer, Andrew Strachan. By the end of June 1797, the two had devised a system whereby the first sets of statutes were to be distributed by post.[58] It was left to the justices of quarter sessions in each county to determine the further distribution of copies for the use of petty sessions and acting magistrates alike, but within a year difficulties had arisen in this part of the system.[59] By late August 1798, Strachan informed Abbot that

> Various complaints have been made that the Justices at the Petty Sessions held in different Districts of the same County are not so quickly furnished with the Acts as might be, owing to the Delay occasioned by the Clerks of the Peace having to send them to the Clerks of the Petty Sessions instead of the latter receiving them immediately from our Office by the Post.[60]

Abbot forwarded his letter to the Home Office, noting that this was already the second time that such complaints had been received from various parts of the country and endorsing Strachan's recommendation that the Home Office should secure a list of places for which petty sessions were held and authorize the direct dispatch to them of their assigned copies of the statutes.[61] One month later, after the Home Office had sent a circular to all clerks of the peace requesting the addresses all clerks of petty sessions, Abbot suggested that the system be further elaborated by requiring the clerks of petty sessions to inform the post office of the addresses of all resident acting justices in their jurisdictions, so that the latter too could have the acts directly dispatched to them, rather than being obliged to await a formal meeting of sessions before final distribution of the statutes could take place at the local level.[62] Accordingly, a second circular went out to the clerks of the peace, requiring 'in future' that

[57] M.A. Thomson, *The Secretaries of State, 1681–1782* (Oxford, 1932), ch. 4; R.R. Nelson, *The Home Office 1782–1801* (Durham, 1969), chs 6–9; S. Devereaux, 'The Criminal Branch of the Home Office, 1782–1830', in G.T. Smith, A.N. May, and S. Devereaux (eds), *Criminal Justice in the Old World and the New: Essays in Honour of J.M. Beattie* (Toronto, 1998), 270–308.

[58] *Colchester Diary*, i. 111, 112–13, 114; NA, Home Office Papers (HO) 42/41, ff. 89, 90, 92–3, 94.

[59] *Colchester Diary*, i. 113; NA, HO 42/41, f. 323.

[60] NA, HO 42/44, f. 153.

[61] NA, HO 42/44, ff. 152, 155.

[62] NA, Secretary of State Papers (SP) 44/416, Wickham to the Clerks of the Peace for England and Wales (circular), 31 August 1798; NA, HO 42/44, f. 187.

any changes in the names and addresses of the acting magistrates of the county to receive copies of the statutes (to be determined by the justices in quarter sessions) should be sent to the Home Office, which would in turn issue 'new instructions immediately . . . to the King's Printer to make the alteration suggested without delay, provided that the numbers required do in no case exceed' those originally allotted to the county.[63] It was presumably some time in the course of refining the system of distribution that upward adjustments were made in the number of copies distributed to each county, yielding the figures noted in the parliamentary report of 1801 compared with the original proposal of 1796.

The interesting thing in all of this is not only the relative passivity of the Home Office, but also the striking number of demands for timely receipt of the statutes amongst justices and clerks of the peace from various parts of the country. Such demands did not suggest that local officials were merely passive recipients of initiatives from the central government; rather, many of them were, if anything, more actively desirous of the connection than officials at the centre appear to have anticipated. Nowhere is this more strikingly apparent during the earliest days of the scheme than in the reaction of the clerk of the peace for the Isle of Ely, who noted in March 1799 that the nine copies assigned for the acting magistrates of his jurisdiction far exceeded the actual number required (a mere four) and who proposed an altered scheme of distribution that would take cognizance of magistrates in five other market towns nearby. He also complained to the Home Office that the acts

> Are sent so extremely irregular, sometimes only part of the Number at once, and the Remainder a Month or More afterwards, and very Seldom the total Number ever Arrives, [so] that I am continuously applied to for the Acts before they Arrive; . . . I hope you Will have the Goodness to give the Necessary Directions for sending the Acts with due Regularity.[64]

Clearly then much, perhaps even the most important part of the distribution of the statutes at the county level was not directed from the centre at all but left to the discretion of local officialdom. From the outset, indeed, the Home Office merely insisted that, while the magistrates of quarter sessions might alter the local allocation of the acts in whatever manner they saw fit, they must under no circumstances demand a greater number overall than that already assigned to them. This insistence was first iterated in January 1799 and almost

[63] NA, SP 44/416, Wickham to the Clerks of the Peace for England and Wales (saving those in note 65 below, as well as Huntingdonshire, Leicestershire, and Warwickshire): circular, 1 January 1799. The only surviving reply to this circular that I have found is at NA, HO 42/46, f. 303.
[64] NA, HO 42/46, f. 349.

invariably persisted throughout the next four decades.[65] Though Abbot clearly intended the promulgation of the statutes to achieve a more unified and consistent application of the law throughout the country, considerations of economy would almost always militate against that centralizing aim.

Conclusion

Here, on this note of qualified success, the story of parliamentary engagement for the promulgation of the statutes ended for several decades. It is not clear how effective this new measure was in making the substance of law known to every British magistrate who ought to be informed of it. The records of the Home Office between 1800 and 1830, which record a growing number of requests from justices of all localities to be made recipients of the scheme, certainly suggest that the desire to express the legislative will of parliament was felt among some magistrates as keenly as was that of MPs to see it promulgated.[66] Abbot himself entertained serious doubts on that score, confiding to a friend in 1809 that 'the County Magistrates, even those who do not always serve the public by acting, have been in some parts very clamorous for a larger distribution to decorate their Libraries.'[67] Indeed, for a local justice of the peace, to be in receipt of a personal copy of the statutes was not simply a means of reinforcing personal dedication to an increasingly burdensome array of administrative tasks. Both to themselves and to anyone else who might behold the undoubtedly impressive sight of the bound copies of the acts stacked end-to-end, it must also have served as a powerful token of the individual magistrate's special standing with the government in London. And this in turn implies the growing authority of the central government in the localities, if only amongst elites rather than the increasingly numerous and sometimes turbulent people over whom they ruled. The operative reality of centralizing ambitions may not have been felt by most residents of local English society much more often or more forcefully than it had been before, but its ongoing potential was now much more immediately conveyed by the physical presence of the statutes themselves, whether or not they were actually consulted in the course of proceedings. The judges of the central courts still returned to London when the county assizes ended, and the magistrates of quarter sessions dispersed to their home towns and villages after their quadrennial sittings were done. The pomp and ceremony associated with those meetings, so crucial to asserting and legitimating the authority of central and local officialdom alike, soon

[65] NA, SP 44/416, Wickham to the Clerks of the Peace for Norfolk and the East and West Ridings of Yorkshire (circular), 1 January 1799.
[66] I hope before long to examine the possible significance of the numbers and geographical distribution of such requests.
[67] NA, PRO 30/9/14 part 2, Abbot to Thornton (copy), 29 March 1809.

dissipated, and the rhythms of daily life in a nation still largely rural and agricultural, though strikingly more urban and unsettled in more and more places, reasserted themselves.[68] But the statutes themselves, embodying the will of the central state, and more assiduously promulgated by it from the outset of the nineteenth century, were there to stay.

[68] For the social and symbolic importance of assizes and quarter sessions ceremonial, see D. Hay, 'Property, Authority and the Criminal Law', in Hay *et al.*, *Albion's Fatal Tree: Crime and Society in Eighteenth-Century England* (London, 1975), 26–31; Landau, *Justices of the Peace*, ch. 9; Beattie, *Crime and the Courts*, 316–18; Skyrme, *History of the Justices of the Peace*, ii. 41–7; B.J. Davey, *Rural Crime in the Eighteenth Century: North Lincolnshire, 1740–80* (Hull, 1994), ch. 7; and Eastwood, *Government and Community*, 100–2.

5

Legislation and public participation 1760–1830

JOANNA INNES

It has long been appreciated that the Reform Act of 1832 represented a node of change in only one strand of the multi-stranded relationship between the Westminster parliament and its public. In the late eighteenth and early nineteenth centuries, many strands in this relationship assumed new forms – mostly through much less clearly defined and formal processes of change. These broader patterns were marked by two, converse trends. On the one hand, these years saw a trend towards increased public activism and access – evident, for example, in the increased number of electoral contests fought around public issues; in the growing readiness of politicians to speechify in public; in the emergence of political 'movements' as political phenomena; and in the appearance of a subset of MPs who developed working relationships with extra-parliamentary associations and movements.[1] On the other hand, these years also saw a trend towards closure – evident in, for example, the increasing tendency of government to take the initiative across a wide range of policy issues; the increased share of parliamentary time devoted to government measures and the rise of party organization.[2]

This chapter explores certain strands within this broader story. It focuses not on the much studied electoral relationship, but rather on more direct forms

[1] Frank O'Gorman, *Voters, Patrons and Parties: The Unreformed Electoral System of Hanoverian England, 1734–1832* (Oxford, 1989); John Belchem, 'Henry Hunt and the Evolution of the Mass Platform', *English Historical Review*, 93 (1978), 739–73. For MPs as mediators, see Peter Jupp, *British Politics on the Eve of Reform: The Duke of Wellington's Administration 1828–30* (Basingstoke, 1998), 365.

[2] Peter Fraser, 'The Growth of Ministerial Control in the Nineteenth Century House of Commons', *English Historical Review*, 75 (1960), 444–63; Valerie Cromwell, 'The Losing of the Initiative by the House of Commons, 1780–1914', *Transactions of the Royal Historical Society*, 5th ser., 18 (1968), 1–23; Miles Taylor, *The Decline of British Radicalism 1847–60* (Oxford, 1995); and G.W. Cox, *The Efficient Secret: The Cabinet and the Development of Political Parties in Victorian England* (Cambridge, 1987). See also James Vernon, *Politics and the People: A Study in English Political Culture c.1815–67* (Cambridge, 1993).

of public engagement with parliament as a law-making body: with legislative process. In this connection, it charts three forms of increasing public 'activism and access': the increasing availability of material about parliament's proceedings; the growth of petitioning, with a view to obtaining, or shaping the character of legislation; and, finally, the growth of parliamentary inquiry, especially inquiry involving the interrogation of witnesses. In all these contexts, it is clear that practice was transformed in the half-century and more preceding the Reform Act: access vastly increased, and the scale of public engagement changed dramatically.

All these topics have received some attention from historians. The first has been well mapped; the second, quite well mapped; only the third – the growth of parliamentary inquiry – remains ill charted. In relation to the first two themes, I add little to what is known; in relation to the third, I raise as many questions as I answer. Because what has been written about these themes receives, in general, much less notice than what has been written about the franchise and elections, I hope, none the less, that this account may prove instructive. I hope also to have identified some topics deserving further research.

Experience suggests that I cannot emphasize too much the limited implications of what is described here. In modern usage, 'access' and 'participation' have overwhelmingly positive connotations. They are heralded as good things in themselves; sometimes it seems to be assumed that they automatically bestow power. In fact, however, power in the political as in other domains is a very complicated matter. 'Access' may open the road to power; it does not guarantee its achievement. The late eighteenth- and early nineteenth-century 'public' was, moreover, not a coherent entity with a single mind; when members of the public gained access to political processes, they commonly gained no more than the opportunity to join in an argument. Not all had equal access and not all were equally sympathetically heard. This period of growing 'public access' was also a period when many experienced themselves as being ignored by key decision-makers; that perception helped to fuel campaigns for parliamentary reform. This does not undermine the claim that 'access' and 'participation' increased. It merely underlines the limited significance of those developments, taken by themselves. As I have stated in the opening paragraph above, moreover, trends favouring access and participation were by no means the only trends evident in public life in these years. I suggest in the conclusion to this chapter that increased 'access' helped to prompt the development of new forms of management: moves towards 'closure'. That dialectic is one that has played itself out many times in the history of political cultures.

Publicizing parliament's proceedings

In the aftermath of the 1688 Revolution, parliament won for itself a secure place at the heart of English government. Since 1689, parliament has met every year, for several months in the year. Certain of the measures it passes every year, notably fiscal measures, are crucial to the operation of government. During the eighteenth and early nineteenth centuries, ministers' demands upon parliament by no means exhausted MPs' time and energies. They used the time remaining to promote – sometimes successfully, sometimes unsuccessfully – a wide range of other national and local measures.[3]

The main business of both houses was carried out in public session. Respectable members of the public might be admitted to the galleries. Others hung around the lobby and accosted members. Some had the chance to state their views before parliamentary committees (a subject to which I shall return). At times of political excitement, crowds might gather outside parliament: making their views known, demonstrating more or less favour for particular MPs.[4] For most of the first century after the Revolution, none the less, despite the importance of the business parliament transacted from many points of view, those who neither attended themselves nor had close contact with members had few opportunities to gain information about parliament's doings. The picture did not change significantly until the 1760s. Thereafter, an increasing quantity of reasonably authoritative information found its way into print.

In the decades immediately following the Revolution, routine, official publications fell into two series: the texts of public acts, and the *Votes* of the House of Commons. The *Votes* were first printed in the 1640s, routinely only from the 1680s; they offered a daily, formal record, not of debates in the Commons, but simply of the business transacted there: of petitions received, bills introduced, stages in the consideration of bills, numbers dividing each way on bills (when divisions occurred), and so forth. Parliament occasionally authorized the publication of the texts of bills under discussion, reports of

[3] For legislation: Julian Hoppit, 'Patterns of Parliamentary Legislation 1660–1800', *Historical Journal*, 39 (1996), 109–31; Julian Hoppit and Joanna Innes, 'Introduction', in *Failed Legislation, 1660–1800: Extracted from the Commons and Lords Journals*, ed. J. Hoppit (London, 1997); Innes, 'Parliament and the Shaping of Eighteenth-Century English Social Policy', *Transactions of the Royal Historical Society*, 5th ser., 40 (1990), 63–92; Paul Langford, *Public Life and the Propertied Englishman, 1689–1798* (Oxford, 1991), esp. ch. 3. For parliamentary procedures: P.D.G Thomas, *The House of Commons in the Eighteenth Century* (Oxford, 1971), and the volumes produced by the History of Parliament Trust, esp. the magisterial D. Hayton (ed.), *The House of Commons, 1690–1715, Vol. 1. Introductory Survey* (Cambridge, 2002) (henceforth Hayton, Survey).

[4] Surprisingly little has been written on the physical presence of the public around parliament, but see for an earlier period, Chris R. Kyle and Jason Peacey, '"Under Cover of so much Coming and Going": Public Access to Parliament and the Political Process in Early Modern England', in Kyle and Peacey (eds), *Parliament at Work: Parliamentary Committees, Political Power, and Public Access in Early Modern England* (Woodbridge, 2002), 1–231; also Perry Gauci, *The Politics of Trade: The Overseas Merchant in State and Society, 1660–1720* (Oxford, 2001), 223–4.

parliamentary committees, or accounts and papers presented – but only a few such items appeared each session.[5]

This meagre output was supplemented by various unofficial forms of publication. Promoters of local and private bills were expected to publish drafts of bills. Newspapers and magazines might carry brief notes on parliament's doings. Some published accounts of debates on major public issues – but such reporting was not officially countenanced; it was always highly selective and of dubious quality, and varied in scale from time to time, depending on the enthusiasm and commitment of publishers. Because parliament remained reluctant to countenance printed reports of debates, handwritten 'newsletters' long remained an important vehicle for parliamentary reporting – continuing to serve this purpose even into the 1780s. In this context, personal contacts were at a premium for anyone anxious to know what parliament was about. Some MPs kept parliamentary 'diaries' – their own notes of proceedings and debates. Many wrote brief reports for their own 'men of business' or key constituents.[6]

This remained broadly the picture until the 1760s. The scene was set for significant change when, in 1742 (following the fall of Walpole), parliament agreed to publish its 'Journals' – a handwritten, formal record of daily transactions, interspersed with various other matter. But initial volumes were historic: not until the mid-1760s did they become more nearly current.[7]

It is not easy to gauge just how far information diffused in these circumstances. It could be obtained by the persevering. In the 1690s, Moses Pitt, a bookseller imprisoned for debt, and an active promoter of imprisoned debtors' efforts to persuade parliament to pass an 'act of grace' for their relief, was apparently able to obtain copies of the *Votes* (his background in the trade may have helped).[8] Many commercial and manufacturing groups clearly were

[5] For the *Votes*, see *The Parliamentary History of England* (1806–20), iv. 1306–8, and for the broader picture, the following compilations by Sheila Lambert, *Printing for Parliament 1641–1700* (List and Index Society, Special Series xx, London, 1984), *List of House of Commons Sessional Papers 1701–50* (List and Index Society, London, 1968) (henceforth Lambert, *List*), and *House of Commons Sessional Papers of the Eighteenth-Century: Introduction and List* (Wilmington, Del. 1975) (henceforth Lambert, *Introduction and List*). Also F.W. Torrington (ed.), *House of Lords Sessional Papers of the Eighteenth Century* (New York, 1972–8).

[6] Hayton, *Survey*, 24–8; R. Sedgwick (ed.), *The History of Parliament: The House of Commons 1715–54* (London, 1979), i. 16, 125. For the survival of parliamentary newsletters into the 1780s, see Christine Ferdinand, *Benjamin Collins and the Provincial Newspaper Trade* (Oxford, 1997), 8 and n.

[7] *Commons Journals*, xxiv. 262–6. See however n. 13 below.

[8] Pitt, *The Cry of the Oppressed* (London, 1691), unpaginated preface [xix]. See Hayton, *Survey*, 371 for distribution of the *Votes* both through MPs and commercially. Institutions, such as coffee houses, which subscribed to newspapers might also take the *Votes*; Ferdinand, *Benjamin Collins*, 157 cites an advertisement to this effect from a Winchester coffee house, 1757.

assiduous at lobbying, and did get the ear of, and information from, MPs.[9] In the case of local and private legislation, the expectation was that parliament should provide a forum within which interested parties might hammer out their differences and gain sanction for what they agreed: it was not expected that any one group should, by operating secretly, be able to steal a march on others (though no doubt this sometimes happened).[10] Clearly local proposals were often debated locally, as well as before parliamentary committees, and relevant material was printed to inform debate. There survives in the Essex Record Office a printed record of the proceedings of the parliamentary committee considering the county's application to rebuild its gaol in 1770.[11] Many more such records may have been printed and discarded, leaving no trace in libraries. None the less, not much information was readily, publicly available; much depended on having the right contacts. John Smith, when revising his *Memoirs of Wool* in the 1750s, was able to obtain information from papers presented to parliament – but only thanks to the aid of a friendly MP, who consulted Commons archives on his behalf.[12]

Following the accession of George III, in 1760, the picture began to shift significantly. Records of business transacted were published in much more voluminous form, and made more widely available. At the same time, parliament abandoned attempts to constrain the publication of debates.

During the 1760s, the previously agreed publishing programme unfolded to the point where published Commons and Lords *Journals* became more nearly current.[13] They had been tending to become bulkier by the year, as the volume of parliamentary business increased. Some trend towards including more in the way of committee reports and accounts and papers in the text of the *Journals* can be discerned over time; practice does not appear to have changed sharply as their content became more topical. However, it was decided to issue a parallel series of volumes containing relatively lengthy committee reports – some dating from past decades, most more current. Work also began on an index to

[9] John Brewer, *The Sinews of Power: War, Money and the English State 1688–1783* (London, 1989), ch. 5; Gauci, *Politics of Trade*, ch. 5.

[10] Kazuhiko Kondo, 'The Workhouse Issue at Manchester: Selected Documents, 1729–35. Part One', *Nagoya University Faculty of Letters Research Bulletin*, 3 (1987), 1–96 (copy deposited in Oxford University Modern History Faculty Library) cites (24) Manchester anti-workhouse petitioners saying they only got to know about the scheme to establish a workhouse when the initial petition was reported in the *Votes* (though, in a counter case (26), the proponents denied this, saying the petitioners' agents were in fact in the house when the bill was brought in).

[11] Essex Record Office D/DBe 01 (Benyon papers).

[12] John Smith, *Chronicon Rusticum Commerciale, or Memoirs of Wool* (2nd edn, London, 1757), ii. 279.

[13] Though, according to Parliamentary Papers (House of Commons), 1828 vol. IV, 503, until a reform of printing practice in 1817, volumes usually appeared only two to three years after the end of a session. In that context, the *Votes* remained the chief source for *recent* transactions.

the *Journals*.[14] Meanwhile, separately printed bills, reports, accounts, and papers continued to appear, also on a gradually increasing scale.[15] By the end of the century, minutes of the proceedings of some committees were printed daily for the use of members, though with the injunction that they not be shown to non-members.[16]

Within a couple of years of the establishment of the 'imperial parliament' in 1801, the rationalizing speaker, Charles Abbot, moved to systematize the publishing of 'sessional papers'. These were grouped into four numbered series: Bills, Reports, Financial, and Other Accounts, and collections were made for the use of the House and government departments. From 1815, all the Commons committee rooms were equipped with a set. Commonly termed the 'Blue Books' (from the colour in which they were bound as separates), they became a favourite reference source for activists and social analysts (Marx's extensive use of this source is well known).[17]

The significance of the *Journals* seems to have decreased as that of the Blue Books grew: even libraries which now possess copies of the eighteenth-century *Journals* much more rarely possess their nineteenth- and twentieth-century counterparts. From 1801, reports, accounts, and papers were relegated to an appendix to the *Journals*, and within a few decades there was talk of discontinuing that. In 1832, the clerk of the journals and papers stated that 'we endeavour now to keep the *Journals* as small as possible'.[18]

The *Votes* meanwhile continued to appear – arguably serving a different, shorter-term need. Indeed, they grew bulkier as the habit of petitioning parliament grew, for it was customary to record the substance of petitions in the *Votes*. Speaker Abbot also instituted a 'shorter mode of printing the votes'. By 1810, this was reported to be saving £1,000 p.a. In 1817, petitions were relegated to a separate appendix – an appendix bulkier than the main substance of the *Votes*.[19]

The early years of George III's reign marked a turning point in another respect too. In the early 1770s – following a confrontation with City radicals – parliament ceased to attempt to inhibit the printing of parliamentary debates. In fact, newspaper reporting of debate on issues of major public interest had become standard by that point. The main consequence of this change was that the scale and range of parliamentary reporting increased. Newspapers began

14 Lambert, *Introduction and List*, 49–53; also drawing on my own inspection of the *Journals*.
15 Lambert, *List*. For increases in numbers of copies of individual reports, Parliamentary Papers (House of Commons), 1837 vol. XIII, App. V.
16 Lambert, *Introduction and List*, 45.
17 R.G. Thorne (ed.), *The History of Parliament: House of Commons 1790–1820* (London, 1986), i. 337 (henceforth Thorne, *Commons*). See also T.P. O'Neill, *British Parliamentary Papers: A Monograph on Blue Books* (Shannon, 1968).
18 Parliamentary Papers (House of Commons), 1828 vol. IV, 530; 1831–2 vol.V, 343 (also reprinted as 1833 vol. XII).
19 Parliamentary Papers (House of Commons), 1831–2 vol. V, 342–3.

to cover debates about regulatory legislation: about crime and punishment, the treatment of the poor, and the like. Reporting remained selective, both in so far as speeches were not repeated verbatim, and in as much as not all debates were covered. Although there were calls for an official record of debate in the 1830s, private enterprise reporting was to hold the day until the early twentieth century.[20]

Some of these newly voluminous reports were subsequently gathered into printed collections, some initially issuing in weekly, fortnightly, or monthly parts. Coverage in these collections was more selective than newspaper coverage, and not identical: members might be invited to correct the texts of their speeches (some in fact sent in their own versions to newspapers).[21] The first ventures in this field again date from Walpole's fall; production became continuous from the 1760s.[22] In the early nineteenth century, William Cobbett launched both an unprecedentedly comprehensive series of *Parliamentary Debates*, and a retrospective collection, the *Parliamentary History*. Though the *History* includes only what Cobbett considered the most important debates, its relatively wide availability helps ensure that today, this is the source most frequently consulted by students of the eighteenth century. Finding his finances overtaxed, Cobbett within a few years handed over control of the *Debates* to their printer, T.C. Hansard (whose father had published the *Commons Journals* from 1774). It is as 'Hansard' that the *Debates* series is best known.[23]

During the eighteenth century, a handful of speeches were published as one-off pamphlets. The practice seems to have grown alongside the growth of more systematic reporting – as publishers gained confidence that they might publish, and find an audience for such material, and MPs became accustomed to seeing their words in print. Reports of single speeches multiplied slowly through the 1770s and 1780s, more rapidly from the 1790s. Burke was an early contributor to the genre. The first collection of his speeches appeared as early as 1777; other collections of this kind were few until the early nineteenth

[20] P.D.G. Thomas, 'John Wilkes and the Freedom of the Press, 1771', *Bulletin of the Institute of Historical Research*, 33 (1960), 86–98; A. Aspinall, 'The Reporting and Publishing of the House of Commons Debates 1771–1834', in R. Pares and A.J.P. Taylor (eds), *Essays Presented to Sir Lewis Namier* (London, 1976), 227–57; and William C. Lowe, 'Peers and Printers: The Beginnings of Sustained Press Coverage of the House of Lords in the 1770s', *Parliamentary History*, 7 (1988), 241–56.

[21] Sir Lewis Namier and John Brooke (eds), *The History of Parliament: The House of Commons 1754–90* (London, repr. with corrections 1985), i. 522; Thorne, *Commons*, i. 368–70; Aspinall, 'The Reporting', 245–8.

[22] [H. Hale Bellot *et al.*], 'General Collections of Reports of Parliamentary Debates for the Period since 1660', *Bulletin of the Institute of Historical Research*, 10 (1933), 171–7.

[23] M.L. Pearl, *William Cobbett: A Bibliographical Account of his Life and Times* (2nd edn, Westport, Conn., 1971), 76–7; I owe this reference to John Stevenson. For fuller discussion of the various rival collections of reports on debates, see Aspinall, 'The Reporting', 251–7; Jupp, *British Politics*, 203–5.

century. A collection of Pitt's speeches appeared after his death in 1806. Wyndham, Fox, Sheridan, and others were later similarly memorialized.[24]

How widely available was this material at the time? Copies of the *Votes* and Blue Book material were supplied free to all MPs, both for their own use and for further distribution by them, and production for this group accounted for the bulk of production, though copies of the *Votes* were also produced for public sale. Copies of such material were sometimes given to those it was desired to influence – thus the report of Joseph Hume's select committee on the combination laws of 1824. The British Library was supplied with as complete a set of Blue Books as could be mustered (thus becoming available to Karl Marx); further copies went to other 'public libraries': Oxford and Cambridge university libraries, and, after 1825, the library of the Society of Advocates, Edinburgh, and Trinity College Dublin. 'All the clubs' were said to have collections of parliamentary papers. In 1832, it was reported that, in the previous year, some 400 copies of the *Votes* had been sold to the public – though in only 100 or so cases had the purchaser also acquired the appendix of petitions. MPs, it is said, often sold their copies of such material on, through 'buttermen' to 'stall-book-sellers'. Booksellers could acquire copies more cheaply by such means than through official channels: the clued-up (and metropolitan-based) private purchaser could probably find at least recent publications on this market. However, demand was usually short-lived, and the bulk of the issue would be sold on again for use in wrapping produce.[25] Newspaper reports of debate one would have supposed to be relatively widely available – and the more so as new printing technology increased print runs. Provincial papers cut and pasted such metropolitan reports as they thought would interest their readers.[26]

My sampling of a small selection of early nineteenth-century library catalogues suggests that the more serious libraries routinely held *some* parliamentary material, though only the most ambitious were likely to hold sets of *Journals*, *Reports*, or *Debates*, and then perhaps only as the result of a donation. Subscription and circulating libraries were more likely to hold a selection of single speeches and reports. Library catalogues commonly refer to but do not

[24] This paragraph draws on an electronic search of titles in the Bodleian collection. A number of speeches had been published in the early eighteenth century (see Hayton, *Survey*, 373 for discussion), but during the Whig ascendancy the practice dwindled, reviving only from the 1770s.

[25] O'Neill, *British Parliamentary Papers*, 22–3; Lambert, *Introduction and List*, 15–17. For clubs, see Parliamentary Papers (House of Commons), 1828, vol. IV, 499. For sales of the *Votes*, see 1831–2, vol. V, 339. For reprinting of reports for propaganda purposes, see S.E. Finer, 'The Transmission of Benthamite Ideas 1820–50', in G. Sutherland (ed.), *Studies in the Growth of Nineteenth-Century Government* (London, 1972), 26–7.

[26] Hannah Barker, *Newspapers, Politics and English Society 1695–1855* (London, 2000), esp. chs 2, 3, and 5. Parliamentary Papers (House of Commons), 1817, vol. III, 347 reports the claim that all (presumably London) newspaper editors subscribed to the *Votes*.

always list periodicals routinely received; these sometimes included newspapers and may have included the *Votes*; it is not always clear whether backfiles were kept (see Table 5.1).[27] When, in 1835, it was agreed to organize the sale of a variety of parliamentary papers on a more systematic basis than before, it was anticipated that there would be significant demand from libraries.[28]

Table 5.1

Library	Collected debates	Misc. speeches	Journals	Collected reports	Misc. reports
Royal Institution	y	—	Lds: –1773; Cms: –1793	–1773	y
Norwich and Norfolk Lit. Inst.	—	y	Lds: –1816; Cms: –1823	–1773	y
Willan's Library, Liverpool	—	y	—	—	y
Hookham's Circ. Lib., Old Bond St	–1800	y	—	—	y
Horne's Library, Cheapside	—	—	—	—	—
Rowley's Circ. lib., Edmonton	—	—	—	—	—

Notes: Journals: Lds = Journals of the House of Lords
Cms = Journals of the House of Commons
y = some relevant holdings
– date = series held up to the named date

Probably the number of people who ever read Blue Book material, or the *Votes*, or even who consistently and assiduously read newspaper reports of debate was small. But the increased availability of such material facilitated its use by publicists and intermediaries, who in turn brought some of it to the attention of a wider public. Sometimes such material was reprinted in something close to its original form: thus, anti-slavery campaigners produced and circulated multiple copies of abstracts of evidence against the slave trade after their defeat in parliament in 1791. Opponents of the first Sir Robert Peel's 1802 Health and Morals of Apprentices Act subsequently printed and circulated reports of debate on this bill (according to Peel, inaccurate reports).[29]

[27] I have scanned catalogues of the following libraries: Royal Institution (1809); Norfolk and Norwich Literary Institution (1825); Horne's Public Library, Queen St, Cheapside (1824); Willan's British and Foreign Public Library, Liverpool (1820); Hookham's Circulating Library, Old Bond St (1829); and Rowley's Circulating Library Edmonton (1829). Table 5.1 provides an overview of their holdings of debates, speeches, *Commons* or *Lords Journals* and collected or miscellaneous reports.

[28] Parliamentary Papers (House of Commons), 1837 vol. XIII, 196–7.

[29] Roger Anstey, *The Atlantic Slave Trade and British Abolition, 1760–1810* (London, 1975); *Manchester Mercury*, 22 February 1803.

Probably more commonly, material was selectively quoted or deployed in other publications. Fiscal data laid before parliament provided the basis for a series of publications about Britain's trade and resources, beginning with James Postlethwayt's *History of the Public Revenue* (1759).[30] Such books could often be found in serious library collections. Parliamentary inquiries into administration and finance provided much of the data for John Wade's radical exposé of 1820, *The Black Book, or Corruption Unmasked*; the release of new material made it possible for him both to expand and in some ways to reorient the book in its revised 1832 edition.

Magazines and newspapers sometimes drew upon reports, accounts, and papers: for example county totals of rate expenditure on the poor, derived from returns to parliament, were carried in the press in the mid-1780s. *The Times* carried items relating to parliamentary committees on corn and bread, and on the secret committee on seditious activity in the 1790s and first years of the nineteenth century; on the 'finance committee' appointed to control public expenditure in 1807; on the bullion committee, and committees on the poor laws and the police of the metropolis in the 1810s; on committees on many of the same topics, and on emigration in the 1820s. In 1827, when a new select committee was set up to consider asylums for pauper lunatics, *The Times* reprinted evidence previously presented to an 1815 select committee on madhouses.[31] The review journals reviewed certain select committee reports: the *Edinburgh Review*'s first venture of this kind also related to madhouses, focusing on the report of an 1817 committee.[32] In 1828, the recently founded 'Society for the Diffusion of Useful Knowledge' sought to diffuse, among other things, useful knowledge gathered by parliamentary committees through its *British Almanac*.[33]

Increased publicity attending parliament's proceedings increased the significance of a role parliament had always had, as an engine of publicity in its own right. Activists worked to mobilize witnesses for committees of inquiry not only because they wanted to shape the views of MPs, but also because they knew that reports of this evidence had the potential to reach a wider public, and to pack all the more symbolic punch because of its status as 'evidence presented to parliament'.[34]

30 J. Hoppit, 'Political Arithmetic in Eighteenth-Century England', *Economic History Review*, 2nd ser., 49 (1996), 530.

31 These reports can be traced in Samuel Palmer, *Index to The Times* (London, 1868–1943), now most conveniently consulted in the CD-ROM version published by Chadwyck-Healey. The reports noted in *The Times* are also those which figure most commonly in library catalogues as separates.

32 *Edinburgh Review*, 28 (August, 1817), 431–71.

33 Jupp, *British Politics*, 216.

34 Cf. Finer, 'The Transmission', 20.

Petitioning

Medieval parliaments had received a promiscuous variety of petitions: the character of parliamentary business was not then stereotyped, nor was parliament clearly distinguished from other courts; subjects might seek redress of individual or collective grievances from any available authority.[35] In colonial American assemblies, this remained the pattern: numbers of petitions were large, and their subject matter various; the underdevelopment of the governmental infrastructure encouraged people to seek remedies to a wide variety of problems by petition to the legislature.[36] Immediately after the 1688 Revolution, something of this sort might have been said of English practice too: the Revolution had brought parliament new power, but it was as yet unclear quite what role it would carve out for itself; executive government had only limited ability to monitor and control its own operations. By that time, however, the capacities of English courts and local government were already relatively well developed; even at that point, therefore, the kinds of business brought to parliament fell into a relatively well-defined range of categories. As the new regime settled down, as the capacities of the executive developed, and as parliament's role within the new order acquired sharper definition, so too understandings about the topics appropriately brought to parliament acquired increasingly clear definition.[37]

This is not to suggest that all scope for argument was eliminated. In 1701, in a notorious incident, members of a Kent grand jury who had censured the government's foreign policy in their 'Kentish petition' were imprisoned for scandal and sedition.[38] The rise of parliamentary reform movements from the 1780s led to renewed testing of the limits of acceptable conduct.[39] The greater part of the eighteenth century, however, was unmarked by controversy of quite this kind, and in general, throughout the period – such occasional controversies apart – all parties appear to have operated with a clear understanding of prevailing conventions.

[35] G.O. Sayles, *The King's Parliament of England* (London, 1975), 117–20. See also Parliamentary Papers (House of Commons), 1831–2 vol. V, 337: recommending that petitions be referred first to a committee in a self-conscious reworking of older practice.

[36] Stephen A. Higginson, 'A Short History of the Right to Petition Government for the Redress of Grievances', *Yale Law Journal*, 96 (1986–7), 142–66.

[37] Hayton, *Survey* does not directly discuss petitioning trends, but see 395–406; light is also shed on the kinds of petitions received and ways they were dealt with in *The Minute Book of James Courthope*, ed. O.C. Williams (Camden Miscellany xx, 3rd series cxxxiii, London, 1953).

[38] There exists no full modern account of this episode, though see Tim Harris, *Politics under the Later Stuarts: Party Conflict in a Divided Society 1660–1715* (Harlow, Essex, 1993), 168. Lord Somers's informative tracts are reprinted in *Parliamentary History*, v. Apps. xvii–xviii.

[39] John Cannon, *Parliamentary Reform 1642–1832* (Cambridge, 1972), 76–9.

Several statutes sought to regulate and constrain the political uses of petitioning. Formal constraints on acceptable modes of petitioning were imposed by the Tumultuous Petitioning Act of 1661, and subsequently by seditious meetings acts in 1795 and 1819. The 1661 act provided that

> no Person or Persons whatsoever shall . . . solicite, labour or procure the getting of Hands, or other Consent, of any Persons above the Number of twenty or more, to any Petition, Complaint, Remonstrance, Declaration, or other Address to the King, or both or either Houses of Parliament, for Alteration of Matters established by Law in Church or State, unless the Matter thereof have been first consented unto and ordered by three or more Justices of that County, or by the major Part of the Grand Jury of the County or Division of the County where the same Matter shall arise, at their publick Assizes, or General Quarter-Sessions, or if arising in London, by the Lord Mayor, Aldermen and Commons in Common-Council assembled.

It also stated that no more than ten people might present a petition. No doubt the statute was informed by memories of the 1620s and 1640s.[40] It was clearly implied that only counties and the City of London had the standing to address parliament on sensitive constitutional matters – and they were to be constrained by local authority.[41]

In 1795, against the background of the French Revolution and an upsurge of domestic radical activity, a new 'seditious meetings' act was passed (itself the focus of much public controversy, of many public meetings and petitions).[42] This act again focused upon meetings called to consider 'any grievance in Church or State' or to petition for the redress of such grievances. Tacitly the act conceded that a much wider range of such meetings might legitimately be held than had been accepted in 1661. It imposed no new constraints on meetings summoned by lord lieutenants, sheriffs, justices, grand juries, mayors, or aldermen (and by implication allowed the governing bodies of all corporate towns to convene such meetings). It accepted even that large meetings of this type might be held without having been convened by these authorities – but subjected meetings of this latter kind to constraints. No such meeting attracting more than fifty people might be held unless it had been advertised in advance in the press, and notified to local magistrates.[43]

Against the background of post-war depression and the rise of the 'mass platform', more severe constraints were introduced in 1819. The 1819 act forbade all meetings called to consider petitioning in relation to 'any Public

[40] See Derek Hirst, *The Representative of the People?* (Cambridge, 1975), 181–4; David L. Smith, *The Stuart Parliaments, 1603–89* (London, 1999), 126–7, 134, 143; Mark Knights, *Politics and Opinion in Crisis, 1678–81* (Cambridge, 1994), chs 8–9.

[41] 13 Cha. II s.1 c. 5.

[42] Chronicled in *The History of the Two Acts* (London, 1796).

[43] 36 Geo. III c. 8.

Grievance, or upon any Matter or Thing relating to any Trade, Manufacture, Business or Profession, or upon any Matter in Church or State', unless summoned by the authorities specified in the previous act, or confined to inhabitants of a single parish or township, who must however notify local magistrates. This act thus broadened the range of subjects dubbed problematic; the inclusion of matters relating to 'any trade or manufacture' reflected the rise of organized protest about changing conditions of labour. At the same time, the act attempted to confine the holding of meetings on all such topics not summoned by constituted authorities to a narrowly local setting. Implicitly testifying to the challenge parliament perceived to be presented by the sheer scale of popular political engagement at this time, the act both reflected and reinforced the rise of the parish as a political forum.[44] Indeed, while clearly in every case constraining in intent, considered in sequence these acts none the less stand revealed as having implicitly accepted and endorsed some aspects of the changing political culture they strove to contain.

Though limited in range and character, petitions to parliament were yet heterogeneous: at least as heterogeneous as parliament's business. Different conventions applied to petitions relating to different aspects of parliament's work. At the end of the spectrum that caused least difficulty, it was expected that local and private legislation would be initiated by petition from interested parties, setting out the problem they wished to see addressed. Such petitions sometimes evoked counter-petitions. Sometimes – in a variation on this theme – individuals or groups petitioned parliament stating grievances bearing particularly on them, but not obviously of a kind appropriately tackled by local or private legislation: these might attract inquiry and some kind of remedial or penal action not taking the form of legislation; sometimes legislation of an essentially public character was subsequently drafted to tackle the grievances alleged. Petitions from imprisoned debtors, imploring parliament to pass an act of grace permitting their release, provide an example of this kind.[45]

Some petitions pertained to general legislative proposals already before parliament, or indeed to legislation previously enacted, inviting its modification or repeal. Legislation thus petitioned upon ranged widely in terms of its subject matter, including religious legislation, fiscal legislation, legislation regulating commerce or manufactures, and criminal law. Most petitions of this kind emanated from those who were and presented themselves as materially

[44] 60 Geo. III & 1 Geo. IV c. 6. For the politicization of labour protest, see e.g. John Rule, *The Experience of Labour in Eighteenth-Century Industry* (London, 1981), 113–19; E.P. Thompson, *The Making of the English Working Class* (revised edn, Harmondsworth, Middlesex, 1968), ch. 14; John Dinwiddy, 'Luddism and Politics in the Northern Counties', *Social History*, 4 (1979), 33–63. For the rise of the parish, see S. and B. Webb, *The Parish and the County* (London, 1903), 94–103, 107.

[45] Joanna Innes, 'The King's Bench Prison in the Later 18th Century', in J. Brewer and J. Styles (eds), *An Ungovernable People: The English and their Law in the Seventeenth and Eighteenth Centuries* (London, 1980), 261.

interested parties – though they also usually strove to show that their interests were aligned with the public interest. Some petitions urged a purely public interest or principled case. This became more common from the late eighteenth century, with the growth of philanthropic lobbying.[46]

At the most problematic end of the spectrum, petitions alleged public grievances against central government bodies or practices, and called for redress, whether by inquiry alone or by inquiry leading to legislation. Petitions along these lines were rarely promoted in the first two-thirds of the eighteenth century; other instruments were preferred, notably, 'instructions' to MPs.[47] In the 1760s, however, the Wilkites revived the practice of petitioning the king – showing clear awareness of the Kentish petition as a precedent, and probably being mindful of seventeenth-century precedents too.[48] In the 1780s, parliament became the preferred target of 'political' petitioning. Nationwide campaigns evoked petitions calling for the reduction of public expenditure, and reform in the system of representation.[49] Petitioning campaigns of such ambition raised in acute form questions of the petitioners' standing. Characteristically they urged their case as if on behalf of the people at large. But, it might be asked, what title had they to do this? In what sense did they represent the people? If their petitions were rejected, what then became of their claim to represent the popular will, as against parliament's claim to do just the same thing?[50]

[46] Brewer, *Sinews*, 246–7; Gauci, *Politics of Trade*, 211–20 and 223–6. Petitions of 1751 calling for action against the scourge of gin-drinking provide an early instance in the moral/philanthropic genre: see Lee Davison, 'Experiments in the Social Regulation of Industry: Gin Legislation, 1729–51', in Davison *et al.* (eds), *Stilling the Grumbling Hive: The Response to Social and Economic Problems in Britain, 1689–1750* (Stroud, 1992).

[47] Thus the Excise Crisis, the fall of Walpole, the 'Jew Bill' and the loss of Minorca all prompted instructions to MPs rather than petitions; the Wilkite agitation likewise began with a campaign of instructions. Peter Fraser, 'Public Petitioning and Parliament before 1832', *History*, 46 (1961), 195–211 notes the chronology.

[48] For this revival (not explored in those terms), see George Rudé, *Wilkes and Liberty: A Social Study of 1763 to 1774* (Oxford, 1962), 149. The fact that the failure of petitioning prompted a shift to 'remonstrating' may reflect imitation of 1640s precedent, as reported e.g. in Catherine Macaulay, *The History of England from the Accession of James I to that of the Brunswick Line* (London, 1763–83), iii (1767). 105–14.

[49] James Bradley, *Popular Politics and the American Revolution in England: Petitions, the Crown and Public Opinion* (Macon, Georgia, 1986), 12–13, 24–5. Cannon, *Parliamentary Reform*, ch. 4 offers the most recent among many accounts of the 1780s 'reform' movement.

[50] For links between petitioning and resistance in seventeenth-century theory, see Mark Knights, 'Petitioning and the Political Theorists: John Locke, Algernon Sidney and London's "Monster" Petition of 1689', *Past and Present*, 138 (1993), 94–111. Later eighteenth-century theories of petitioning have not been much studied, but see John Jebb, *An Address to the Freeholders of Middlesex* (3rd edn, London [n.d. c. 1779]), and T.M. Parsinnen, 'Association, Convention and Anti-Parliament in British Radical Politics 1771–1848', *English Historical Review*, 88 (1973), 504–33.

Petitions expressing public grievances had potentially more challenging implications than any others. Precisely because this was so, however, law and convention especially constrained petitioning of this kind. All sorts of affected parties might and did petition on matters of commerce, in whatever groups they chose to organize themselves. Small masters and journeymen might and did – not commonly, but recurrently – petition parliament seeking redress of grievances they felt as working people: seeking, for example, authority for magistrates to regulate wages, or the suppression of new machinery thought to be causing unemployment. Local authorities sometimes even encouraged protesting workers to petition parliament, in the hope of containing conflict within formal institutional structures.[51]

By contrast, when the practice of petitioning for the redress of public grievances revived from the 1760s, much more restrictive conventions were observed. Practice indeed roughly conformed to the provisions of the 1661 act – though boroughs other than the City of London joined in sending petitions. Moreover, attempts were made to ensure that only people of standing within communities signed: petitions thus were commonly represented as emanating from the nobility, gentry, and freeholders of a county, or from the mayor, aldermen, common councilmen, and freemen of a borough. John Phillips has established that Wilkite county petitions were commonly signed only by freeholders; of ten Wilkite petitions deriving from boroughs, five were signed by qualified electors only, though another five also by other inhabitants.[52] The 1780 'economical reform' campaign evoked petitions from public meetings in no fewer than twenty-six out of forty English counties; eleven towns also petitioned. The fact that the issue was canvassed only in counties and major towns meant that the total could not conceivably have been of a very different order. It is therefore inappropriate baldly to contrast these totals with totals achieved in later reform campaigns conducted according to different conventions (or, indeed, with totals obtained in contemporaneous commercial petitioning campaigns, which were sometimes greater in scale).[53]

During the eighteenth century, protests on constitutional and political matters were commonly vastly outnumbered by loyal 'addresses'. But loyal

[51] Rule, *Experience of Labour*, 113–19.

[52] J. Phillips, 'Popular Politics in Unreformed England', *Journal of Modern History*, 52 (1980), 599–625. All these boroughs had substantial electorates, and might have produced respectably supported petitions from electors alone.

[53] See Jacob Price, 'The Excise Affair Revisited', in S.B. Baxter (ed.), *England's Rise to Greatness* (Berkeley, 1983), 293 for a questionably appropriate comparison between numbers on the one hand of petitions against hawkers and pedlars (including many from small towns) and on the other instructions to MPs to oppose Walpole's Excise Bill, which only larger towns were usually bold enough to issue. To underline the importance of assessing petition numbers in context, we might note that in eighteenth-century America, where petitioning was generally more promiscuous, thousands of petitions were occasionally produced on a single issue – even within single colonies: Higginson, 'A Short History', nn. 56, 93.

addresses commonly emanated from the governing councils of boroughs, who at one of their regular meetings could readily rattle off an address.[54] Such floods of addresses enabled monarchs and ministers to meet protest with a brave face. They also provided reassurance that the sizeable pro-government phalanx of MPs routinely returned by 'corporation boroughs' would stand firm. These different forms of manifestation of 'public opinion' are not otherwise comparable.

During the 1780s, petitioning practice began to change in a number of ways. The sources of change were various; the effects, pervasive. They were to some extent the result of political and constitutional struggles, and helped to shape the forms such struggles took. But changes in the political culture both derived from more, and affected more, than just the cause of 'radical reform'.

The most obvious sign of change is a marked upwards shift in petition totals. Table 5.2 brings together information from two sources – Julian Hoppit's work on legislation 1660–1800, and a report from the clerk of the journals and papers in 1832 – to chart changing numbers of petitions relating to general legislation (petitions relating to private and local bills are omitted).[55]

It is clear that the series exhibits marked fluctuations from year to year. No total for 1792 is available, but if it were it would have marked an early peak – for in that year a previously unprecedented 519 petitions were delivered to the Commons putting the case against the slave trade.[56] The omission of petitions to the Lords from nineteenth-century totals conceals a marked increase in petitions sent to the upper house in 1811, when several hundred petitions sent by Dissenting congregations stifled at birth a proposed bill to regulate itinerant preaching.[57] Nonetheless, inspection of the *Journals* suggests that the table represents general trends reasonably fairly (though addition of Lords' totals for later years would of course increase the scale of the rise). Thus, first, there was a general upwards trend. Secondly, as the table suggests, that trend did not develop smoothly, but rather through a series of steps, lurching upwards in the 1780s, in the 1810s, and later 1820s. (In this context, it becomes easier to understand why in 1817 it should have been decided henceforth to relegate petitions to an appendix to the *Votes*, and why procedures for handling them should again have come under scrutiny in 1828.)

54 For addresses see e.g. Rudé, *Wilkes and Liberty*, 62; Bradley, *Popular Politics*, 69–74.

55 Hoppit, *Failed Legislation*, 19 also gives figures for the *proportion* of bills associated with petitions. Figures for numbers of signatures are not available until 1834; thereafter, see Colin Leys, 'Petitioning in the Nineteenth and Twentieth Centuries', *Political Studies*, 3 (1955), 57. Although signatures per petition probably decreased as petition numbers grew, it seems probable that total signatories none the less increased.

56 Seymour Drescher, *Capitalism and Antislavery: British Mobilisation in Comparative Perspective* (Houndmills, Basingstoke, 1986), 80.

57 *Lords Journals*, xlviii. 298–320; Michael Rutz, 'The Politicising of Evangelical Dissent, 1811–1813', *Parliamentary History*, 20 (2001), 187–207.

Table 5.2 Totals of petitions relating to general legislation received in select parliamentary sessions

Session beginning	Average petitions per session		Totals per session
	Both houses	Commons	
1660	30		
1674	3		
1694	43		
1708	88		
1724	19		
1740	57		
1753	79		
1772	48		
1784–8		176	298, 156, 98, 201, 127
1795	241		
1801–5		205	192, 158, 367, 168, 141
1811–4		900	132, 340, 1,699, 1,479, 848
1828–30		3,568	3,635, 4,074, 4,041, 2,522

Sources: *Failed Legislation 1660–1800: Extracted from the Commons and Lords Journals*, ed. Julian Hoppit (London, 1997), 19; Parliamentary Papers (House of Commons), 1831–2 vol. V, 342.

Fluctuations from year to year often reflect the impact of single campaigns. By contrast, both the upward 'steps' and the general upward trend reflect more broadly based change. Not all legislative proposals attracted any petitions, and many attracted only a few. High petition totals were however characteristic of not just one or two, but instead a cluster of high profile, controversial issues. By the 1820s, even moderately controversial issues were attracting petition totals that were high by the standards of the previous century.

The indexes to the *Commons Journals* for the 1820s, which list petitions by issue, illustrate the diversity of issues in question.[58] In that decade, the campaigns eliciting the highest numbers of petitions were those against the bill of pains and penalties on Queen Caroline (1820); against the house and window tax (1823); for the abolition of slavery (1824, 1826, and 1828); for the repeal of the Test and Corporation Acts (1827, 1828); and for and against Catholic Relief (1825, 1827, 1828, 1829). A purely Irish campaign – for the repeal of 7 Geo. IV c. 29, against subletting – also attracted significant support, while in 1826, Sir Walter Scott managed to arouse most of the parishes in Scotland by an appeal to national feeling in the face of a move to extend to Scotland a bill forbidding the issue of small denomination banknotes.[59] In general, eco-

[58] See also Jupp, *British Politics*, 220–1, 366–76.

[59] [Sir Walter Scott,] 'Malachi Malagrowther', *Thoughts on the Proposed Change of Currency*,

nomic issues – the category of issues which in the eighteenth century had tended to elicit highest petition totals – continued to make a good showing, although they no longer figured at the top end of the list. Fairly impressive numbers of petitions were elicited not only by well-known struggles over the corn laws (1814, 1815, 1818, 1825) and the combination laws (1824, 1825), but also by various issues relating to the leather trade (1801, 1816, 1818), duties on coals (1818, 1819, 1824), and on ale houses (1824).

What were the more immediate causes and effects of these changes in gear? In both the 1780s and the 1810s, it seems probable that certain 'model' campaigns helped to draw attention to petitioning as a tactic, and to encourage those who adopted this tactic to aim higher than they might otherwise have done. But other changes in attitudes, culture, and the resources available to campaigners also contributed.

In the 1780s, the model campaign was that which revived the practice of petitioning parliament to express public grievances: Christopher Wyvill's Association campaign, initially aiming at 'economical', subsequently parliamentary reform. The achievements of this campaign, though limited, were not altogether nugatory. The prime minister, Lord North, found life more difficult thereafter; when he resigned two years later, his successors felt constrained to introduce certain economical and political reforms.

In any case the campaign does seem to have helped to encourage some of those who supported it subsequently to employ similar means for other ends. In the later 1780s, both Dissenters seeking the repeal of the Test and Corporation Acts, and anti-slavery campaigners resorted to petitioning campaigns to promote their ends. When Dissenters had pursued the same goal previously, in the 1730s, they had adopted a much lower profile. The anti-slavery movement was the more innovative in form, blending philanthropic money-raising and propaganda techniques with the practical expertise and networking resources of mercantile and manufacturing supporters. As already noted, this campaign achieved record petition totals for its day: an impressive total of 102 petitions elicited in 1788 was in turn dwarfed by the 519 raised in 1792. Pioneering anti-slavery activists are also said to have been the first to exploit the possibilities opened up by the presentation of a long sequence of petitions, over successive weeks, to keep urging their subject upon legislators' attention.[60]

and other Late Alterations, as they Affect, or are Intended to Affect, the Kingdom of Scotland (Edinburgh, 1826); Michael Fry, *The Dundas Despotism* (Edinburgh, 1992), 364–6.

[60] For Dissenters see N.C. Hunt, *Two Early Political Associations: The Quakers and the Dissenting Deputies in the Age of Sir Robert Walpole* (Oxford, 1961), chs 8–9; G.M. Ditchfield, 'The Parliamentary Struggle over the Repeal of the Test and Corporation Acts, 1787–1790', *English Historical Review*, 89 (1974), 551–77. J.R. Oldham, *Popular Politics and British Anti-Slavery: The Mobilisation of British Public Opinion against the Slave Trade* (Manchester, 1995), ch. 4.

Wyvill's campaign was both trend-setting and conventional: conventional in as much as it mobilized protest within constitutionally defined communities. Yet the power of such conventions rapidly waned. Important in eroding them no doubt was the development during the 1780s of a broad 'reform' programme, encompassing several issues previously approached in different ways: political, religious, and philanthropic campaign styles cross-fertilized. Perhaps important too was the fact that political divisions in this decade cut through the middle of what had recently been a loosely unified, oppositional, reforming camp. When George III made Pitt his prime minister in 1783, Pitt carried with him on to the government side many who had supported Wyvill's campaign. This may help to explain why the flood of addresses which commended the King's dismissal of the Fox–North administration and appointment of the younger Pitt, unusually, bore large numbers of signatures: John Phillips finds that most urban addresses were represented as coming from 'inhabitants'.[61]

Writing his memoirs in later life, Henry Brougham would look back to the campaign against the Orders in Council of 1812 as a model petitioning campaign. In numbers of petitions elicited, it was in truth no mould-breaker. Nonetheless it may – as I have suggested of Wyvill's campaign – have stimulated more innovation than it embodied. It may indeed have helped to spark the rather better-supported campaign against the renewal of the East India Company's charter in 1812–13 – perhaps in part conceived as diversionary, but backed also by liberals who strove in this way to create a broad reforming front.[62]

The single most significant boost to petition numbers in the 1810s was provided by the campaign to promote the Christian religion in India, which attracted some 800 petitions in 1813. These petitions came from Wales, Scotland, and Ireland as well as England, but were predominantly English – emanating from a substantial proportion of all English urban settlements. The proliferation of provincial missionary societies, networked into national organizations under the leadership of metropolitan parent bodies, may have helped to make this possible; growing interest in raising funds for missions was however also an effect of that campaign.[63] In the following year, a campaign supporting further measures against the slave trade elicited petitions of comparable number and range. It may be that the networks supporting moral and religious petitioning were especially well developed. The diversity of issues which, over the next few years, elicited high petition totals, suggests

[61] Phillips, 'Popular Politics', 610–14. For shifts in petitioning styles, see also Drescher, *Capitalism and Antislavery*, ch. 4.

[62] Henry Brougham, *The Life and Times of Henry Lord Brougham, by Himself* (Edinburgh, 1871), ii. 303–6, 313–14. For the campaign see J. Cookson, *The Friends of Peace: Anti-war Liberalism in England 1793–1815* (Cambridge, 1982), ch. 9.

[63] Ford K. Brown, *Fathers of the Victorians: The Age of Wilberforce* (Cambridge, 1967), ch. 7 'Missionaries to England'.

none the less that issue-specific explanations will have limited explanatory power.

In this context we might do more to unpack the idea that some cutting-edge campaigns may have provided 'models'. Two different effects might be separated out, one having to do with ends, one with means. Record-breaking campaigns must have changed ideas about what it was possible to achieve; perhaps also about what it was desirable, even necessary to achieve. Secondly, though not all campaigns employed the same means, means conjured into being to support one campaign might none the less subsequently facilitate others. Corps of local activists with campaigning experience were called into being. Organizing and running local societies, within more or less formally organized national networks, became, for some, a way of life. Sophisticated operators learnt how to employ campaigns to advance their position in local power struggles: by choosing issues that might cut into or across their rivals' support base. Rank-and-file petitioners became accustomed to being asked to turn out for public meetings, to putting their name to public documents – and to having to choose which meetings to attend and which documents to sign, as part of a process of defining their own political identity.[64] It should not be assumed that such organizing activity was always voluntaristic. By the end of the period there were 'offices' in London which organized campaigns.[65]

In 1828, it was argued that the sheer scale of petitioning was overwhelming established parliamentary procedures: too much time was being consumed in the presentation of petitions, while MPs charged with presenting petitions struggled to find opportunities to do so. A balloting system was introduced – but by 1832, procedure was again under review. Thereafter, petitions ceased to be read to the Commons, so ceased to provide an opportunity to launch debate on a topic. This by no means ended the rage for petitioning, however. Numbers of petitions presented on a range of reform issues in the 1830s topped new heights; petitioning of course remained central to Chartist strategy.[66]

Parliamentary inquiries

The history of parliamentary inquiry in this period has yet to be written – and what has been written is often distorted by over-reliance on assertions made

64 I have learnt much from the interesting work of Joshua Civin on this theme. See his forthcoming Oxford D.Phil. thesis, 'Civic Experiments: Community-building in Liverpool and Baltimore, 1785–1835'.

65 Parliamentary Papers (House of Commons), 1828 vol. IV, 492.

66 Leys, 'Petitioning', 48–54; Paul Pickering, '"And Your Petitioners &c": Chartist Petitioning in Popular Politics 1838–48', *English Historical Review*, 116 (2001), 368–88. Both also offer interesting discussions of the function of petitioning, beyond my scope here, as do Hayton, *Survey*, 397; Fraser, 'Public petitioning', 207–10; and Jupp, *British Politics*, 221–5.

to mid- and later nineteenth-century reviews of parliamentary procedure, or assumptions deriving from later nineteenth-century practice. It is, thus, often taken for granted that inquiries, if pursued at all, were pursued by 'select committees of inquiry', meeting to consider an issue and perhaps to generate legislation. Indeed, the term 'select committee' is often treated as synonymous with 'committee of inquiry' (a usage endorsed in Erskine May's 1844 manual of parliamentary procedure).[67]

During the eighteenth and early nineteenth centuries both terminology and practice were more fluid and complex. In the eighteenth century (as attested, for example, by the mid-eighteenth-century guide to procedure known as the 'Liverpool Tractate') two main forms of committee were distinguished: the committee of the whole house and the select committee. The defining feature of the latter was that it included only a subset of MPs, meeting outside the main debating chamber. Both committees of the whole house and select committees performed a wide variety of functions. Either might undertake inquiries.[68] Inquiries into the impact of the orders in council 1812–13, thus, were held before a committee of the whole house; in 1813, Brougham brought more than 100 witnesses to be examined at the bar of the Commons.[69]

Committees of the whole house were credited with an inherent right to send for books and papers or examine witnesses (though not under oath). Select committees could be assigned such powers (though there is some evidence that this was regarded as a trivial formality, and it is not safe to assume that such powers were always sought, or their giving recorded, still less indexed). Usually (but not invariably) they were expected to report, though that report might be oral.[70]

[67] Thus Thomas, *House of Commons*, ch. 14 (in other respects informative). Sir T. Erskine May, *Treatise on the Law, Privileges, Proceedings and Usages of Parliament* (London, 1844), 230.

[68] *The Liverpool Tractate: An Eighteenth-Century Manual on the Procedure of the House of Commons*, ed. C. Strateman (New York, 1937), 36–58. Though note that Williams in *Minutes of James Courthope*, v, says the term 'select committee' was not current in the 1690s – and Thomas, *House of Commons*, 264, that usage was still inconsistent in the later eighteenth century. Hayton, *Survey*, 395–405, offers a characteristically well-informed and open-minded sketch of early eighteenth-century practice, noting *inter alia* that the term 'committee of inquiry' was not then in use. Even Hayton does not however discuss the extent to which committees not convened explicitly to inquire may in fact have carried on inquiries. The idea that committees of inquiry form a distinct and countable class is encouraged and shaped by Journal Indexes. Under 'Committees' these list committees appointed to consider certain things, and to do certain things, but exclude bill-processing committees, however they may have proceeded. Problems of categorization are acknowledged by Lambert, *Introduction and List*, 43–4. Her own list does not include all committee reports printed at length in the *Journals* – excluding, for example, reports on local legislation.

[69] Chester New, *The Life of Henry Brougham to 1830* (Oxford, 1961), 62–5.

[70] Thomas, *House of Commons*, 268. For the early prevalence of punitively minded committees, see Hayton, *Survey*, 399–401 and Thomas, *House of Commons*, 265.

In the eighteenth century, committee inquiries played different roles in different kinds of parliamentary business. In the case of private or local legislation, routine procedure was for business to be initiated by petition, after which a select committee was convened to examine the premises of the petition. If a case for action were thought to have been established, a bill would be brought in. Petitions or charges of a more public nature sometimes prompted the convening of a more open-ended committee of inquiry. In these cases, inquiry might be undertaken in a quasi-judicial spirit, and punitive action might ensue, perhaps in tandem with a motion to bring in a bill to redress some of the wrongs discovered. Alternatively, attention might focus on assessing the scale and nature of a problem, and suggesting legislative routes forwards. Some such committees produced conclusions in the form of resolutions; some, draft bills. Public bills not arising from a preliminary inquiry would none the less, unless rejected at a first reading, proceed to a committee stage. Those not concerned with affairs of state were often referred to select committees for consideration in detail after their second reading; however, some such, as well as all major government bills, went to committees of the whole house.

It may seem that inquiry would naturally have preceded the introduction of legislation, but this was not always the case. Second reading committees might decide to hear representations or make inquiries about a bill. Private bill procedure probably affected modes of operation: indeed, the boundaries between 'private' and 'public' legislation were by no means clearly drawn. In the case of legislation affecting commerce or industry, it was common for those whose interests were affected to be given a hearing at whatever point they indicated their desire to be heard, or the committee judged it appropriate.[71]

Our knowledge of what transpired in committees of all kinds is limited by the fact that by no means all committee reports were printed. Reports of committees of the whole house were never printed as such; by convention, all members were supposed to be present at such sessions, and therefore not to need a report.[72] Before the late eighteenth century, even committees which embarked on substantial inquiries might not print their reports – and the destruction of the Commons records by fire in 1834 has ensured that relatively little manuscript material survives. We are better served in the case of the House of Lords, whose manuscript committee books are still extant.[73]

[71] O.C. Williams, *The Historical Development of Private Bill Procedure* (London, 1949), i. 33. See e.g. *Commons Journals*, xxxvi, index under 'Hatters'.

[72] Separate minutes once existed, but were destroyed in the fire of 1834: Lambert, *Introduction and List*, 4. Reports of debates however sometimes include accounts of proceedings in committees of the whole house, e.g. *Parliamentary History*, xix. cols 708–13.

[73] For the Commons, *Minute Book of James Courthope*, ed. Williams. The House of Lords Record Office holds Lords committee minute books from 1661 to 1836. Historical

Prior to the order for publication of the *Journals*, in 1742, only an occasional committee report was printed by order of either house. When the *Journals* were published, some further reports were belatedly put into print. The first reports published by order at the time were often concerned with inquiries into wrongdoing, political, administrative, or financial. The first Commons committee report contemporaneously printed in the eighteenth century (in 1708), thus, reported on 'the humble petitions of several creditors and proprietors of principal mony, annuities and shares in the Mine-Adventure of England', then in financial difficulty. Yet the retrospectively published *Journals* relating to this decade include a handful of committee reports relating to each session in this decade (most of them very brief).[74]

From the 1770s, lengthy reports were often printed, not in the *Journals*, but in the 'First Series' of *Reports from Committees of the House of Commons*. Some were also printed separately: thus, very bulky returns on parochial poor relief expenditure 1777; reports on the proposal to abolish the slave trade 1790; on seditious practices 1794; and on the high price of corn 1795–6.[75] From the early nineteenth century, numerous reports were printed in the numbered 'Sessional Papers' series. In the first few decades, these ran at around fifteen to thirty a year. Initially, only a fraction of those reports came with printed minutes of evidence. That proportion increased over time: in the 1820s, most printed reports included minutes of evidence. It is not clear to what extent this reflected increased resort to witness evidence, to what extent increasingly comprehensive recording practice, or, finally, increased readiness to publish evidence.[76]

Manuscript volumes surveying House of Lords mss. 1689–1718 calendar much of this material. See Historical Manuscript Commission, *The Manuscripts of the House of Lords* (printed as appendices to reports 12–14, and as vols 1–12 new series – henceforth *Manuscripts of H. Lords* n.s.) (London, 1889–1977). From 1771, separate books of 'evidence' were kept; these apparently relate only to select public issues and private bills. A few sets of Lords 'committee papers' and ms. returns also survive. See M.F. Bond, *Guide to the Records of Parliament* (London, 1971), 43–54, 136, 153. The Lords mounted a number of inquiries into the conduct of the wars of 1689 to 1713, but they seem only rarely to have launched inquiries into public affairs from thence until the end of the century, when they mounted an independent inquiry into the slave trade, for which see Michael W. McCahill, *Order and Equipoise: The Peerage and the House of Lords 1783–1806* (London, 1978), 58–9. In the early nineteenth century, they similarly enquired into (e.g.) child labour (1818) and the poor laws (1819).

[74] Cf. Lambert, *List*, and Lambert, *Introduction and List* for the slant towards the quasi-judicial. See similarly early reports listed in Torrington, *House of Lords Sessional Papers*.

[75] Lambert, *Introduction and List*. Unlike her *List* this does not give bibliographical data on separate printings, but does provide cross-references to separate copies held in the Abbott Collection at the British Library.

[76] My own calculations, achieved with assistance from Chadwyck-Healey's CD-ROM Index to British Parliamentary Proceedings since 1800. Lords sessional papers exhibit a similar pattern: the first 'minutes of evidence' described as such in the Index date from 1785 (commerce with Ireland).

Because 'select committees of inquiry' were not the only parliamentary bodies undertaking inquiries, and because information collected in inquiries was increasingly likely to find its way into print, it is no easy matter to assess trends. David Hayton has recently suggested that ministers' increasing grasp of parliamentary management may have been associated with a *decline* in the incidence of parliamentary inquiry in the early years of the eighteenth century. From mid-century, none the less, the tide seems to have reversed: older practices were not merely revived, but extended and developed in new ways.[77] Merchants and manufacturers were well accustomed to presenting their views to committees. But other groups became more experienced at doing so: including workers, philanthropists, and would-be administrative and governmental reformers. Empirical social and political inquiry was an enlightenment fashion: parliament was working in an environment in which the appetite for empirical information was growing and broadening, and new techniques for collecting and presenting it were being developed.[78] These efforts must have helped to shape expectations as to how parliament should proceed.

Parliamentary inquiries in practice proceeded in a variety of ways. Some requested accounts and papers from government departments. These could be used to shed light on economy and society: in the 1730s, a committee inquiring into allegations from ironmasters that the trade was in depression showed some ingenuity by asking the revenue departments for evidence on revenues from alcohol sales in the region, as a form of check.[79] Sometimes local officials were asked to complete information on standard forms: information about imprisonment for debt, about poor relief expenditure and practice, and about charitable funds was all sought in this way in the latter half of the eighteenth century. Such inquiries might have a wider than intended impact: requests for information on poor relief expenditure in the 1780s prompted Berkshire

[77] H. McD. Clokie and J.W. Robinson, *Royal Commissions of Enquiry: The Significance of Investigation in British Politics* (Stanford, CA, 1938), 62, estimate trends from the volume of printed output. Recent estimates have been more rigorous – though all are more or less self-consciously bedevilled by problems of classification. For Hayton's estimates, see *Survey*, 395–406. He suggests that on average during 1689–1714, some twenty Commons 'committees of inquiry' were convened each session, many being quasi-judicial or regulatory in character. Impressionistically: from the 1740s, the mix shifted towards more policy-oriented forms of inquiry; committees conceived in these terms then multiplied. Jupp, *British Politics*, 210–11 draws on *Journal* Indexes to sketch a rise from seven committees of inquiry p.a. in the 1780s to twenty-one in the 1820s. By the 1820s, the 'select committee of inquiry' had begun to establish itself as a distinct sub-type, with its own baggage of conventions and expectations.

[78] Generally, Daniel R. Headrick, *When Information Came of Age: Technologies of Knowledge in the Age of Reason and Revolution, 1700–1850* (Oxford, 2000). More specifically, Hoppit, 'Political Arithmetic'; David Eastwood, '"Amplifying the Province of the Legislature": The Flow of Information and the English State in the Early Nineteenth Century', *Historical Research*, 62 (1989), 276–94.

[79] Lambert, *Introduction and List*, 63.

clergyman David Davies to wonder how the poor managed, and to begin to seek information on working-class budgets; the corporation of Shaftesbury was jolted into wondering whether its administration of charitable funds was defensible.[80]

A further form of recourse – and the one I shall chiefly be concerned with in what follows – was witness evidence. Interested parties sometimes put their case through learned counsel (sometimes they were directed to do this, rather than to appear in person). But if information was sought, first-hand evidence was potentially more useful. It is possible that such evidence was sought from a wider range of people as the period progressed, though problems of evidence make it difficult to establish the case with certainty.

In some contexts, we can be confident that parliament routinely elicited witness evidence from the beginning of the eighteenth century, and indeed sometimes from a much earlier date. By the end of the seventeenth century, this was clearly standard form for personal and local legislation. In the language of the Lords committee books of this period, people appeared before committees to 'prosecute' their bills. There was also a long-standing practice of hearing witness evidence in relation to commerce and industry. David Dean, in his study of late sixteenth-century legislation, cites several instances in which brewers were summoned to attend committees, those with interests in the Essex/Suffolk cloth industry invited to attend, or merchants urged to attend. In the early eighteenth century, men involved in trade and commerce were frequently examined before both Commons and Lords.[81]

Late eighteenth- and early nineteenth-century inquiries sometimes essentially replicated these traditional patterns, sometimes built upon them. There was nothing inherently innovative about parliament hearing witness evidence on the role of regulation in the Yorkshire cloth industry in 1806–7; or the Combination Acts in 1824. More innovative – though arguably a natural enough extension of existing practice – were those inquiries which pitted philanthropists against economic interest groups: the inquiry into the slave trade in 1790, and into child labour in cotton factories and elsewhere in 1816–18.

Parliament recurrently inquired into conditions in metropolitan debtors' prisons. Evidence taken from imprisoned debtors in the 1690s was subsequently printed at length in the *Journals*; inquiries into the Fleet, Marshalsea and King's Bench in 1729–30 were separately printed at the time. William Hogarth commemorated in both a pencil sketch and in a painting the interrogation

[80] David Davies, *The Case of the Labourers in Husbandry Stated and Considered* (London, 1975), 5–7; F.C. Hopton, *Corruption and Reform: Municipal Government in the Borough of Shaftesbury 1750–1835* (Shaftesbury and District Historical Society, 1975), 16–17.

[81] David M. Dean, *Law-making and Society in Late Elizabethan England: The Parliament of England, 1584–1601* (Cambridge, 1996), 137, 148, 151. Their appearances before Lords committees are abundantly documented in *Manuscripts of H. Lords*.

of a ragged debtor before the 'Gaol Committee'.[82] These inquiries are perhaps best set in the context of the tradition of inquiries into abuse: it may be that parliament felt a special responsibility for protecting the helpless. In 1763, perhaps on the same grounds, parliament probed conditions in private madhouses; in the 1790s, there was a general inquiry into the practice of imprisonment for debt. Around the turn of the century, complaints by imprisoned radicals about the conditions in which they were held produced first a select committee and then a royal commission report on the new Middlesex prison at Cold Bath Fields, and royal commission inquiries into two provincial prisons. The conditions of lunatic care were again probed in the 1810s and 1820s.[83]

Did committees considering legislating on crime or poverty in the eighteenth century have recourse to witness evidence? It is to be expected, and can be shown, that this happened when proposed legislation was local in scope: thus, when particular towns proposed to establish statutory 'corporations of the poor'.[84] Similarly, a Commons committee established in 1706 to scrutinize a bill regulating the night watch in the metropolis apparently 'examined witnesses' relating to one Joseph Billers's account of his thwarted efforts to combat crime.[85] Only in 1750 do we first find a committee charged specifically to *inquire* into crime. In practice it probably focused especially upon the crime-ridden metropolis. The *Journals* are notably uninformative as to how it proceeded. In 1770, the proceedings of such a committee first enter the printed record: Sir John Fielding's evidence to a committee on burglaries was printed in the *Journals*.[86] In the case of poverty, from the 1690s on, parliament repeatedly discussed the possibility of amending the poor laws in a general way, and sometimes set up committees of inquiry. Yet evidence that witnesses were questioned by such committees does not surface in the official record until 1817.[87]

82 *Commons Journals*, xi. 641–80 and xii. 684–7; also Pitt, *Cry of the Oppressed*, unpaginated, preface [xxii–iii], and *Manuscripts of H. Lords* n.s. ii. 396–409, iv. 279–93; Lambert, *List*, 88, 91. Ronald Paulson, *The Art of Hogarth* (London, 1975), plates 5–6.

83 For prisons: see *Commons Journals*, xlvii. 640–73; lii. 441–67; Parliamentary Papers (House of Commons), 1809 vol. IV; 1812–13 vol. V; 1814–15 vol. IV. For lunatic care: *Commons Journals*, xxix. 486–9; Parliamentary Papers (House of Commons), 1816 vol. VI; 1826–7 vol. VI. For royal commissions: 1809 vol. IV; 1812–13 vol. V.

84 E.g. *Commons Journals*, xxi. 643–4, 720. Kondo, 'Workhouse Issue', reprints material from *Commons Journals* and also at 58–9 an account of what transpired at the hearing before a committee of the whole house, as usual not in *Commons Journals*. Lords committee books record numerous local inquiries. It seems to have been usual form to seek evidence for the allegations on which local bills (which normally originated in the Commons) were founded when they reached second reading stage.

85 John Beattie, *Policing and Punishment in London 1660–1750* (Oxford, 2001), 247–8; *A Short State of the Case of Joseph Billers* (London, n.d. c. 1709), 3.

86 *Commons Journals*, xxxii. 878–82.

87 Several such committees were convened in the 1690s, and at intervals thereafter.

In the years immediately following the end of the Napoleonic wars, in 1815, a striking number of committees of inquiry were instituted to inquire into aspects of domestic government and social conditions. Some such inquiries focused on metropolitan conditions and practices: on neighbourhoods at parliament's door. Others were more broadly conceived. A series of committees gathered evidence about mendicity in the metropolis; its prisons and its policing. A committee set up to inquire into the education of the lower orders in the metropolis sought redefinition of its brief, and extended its inquiries to all parts of the British Isles. Other geographically wide-ranging inquiries explored the treatment of lunatics, the poor, and factory children. My own current guess is that metropolitan inquiries, being essentially local in character, will have drawn upon a tradition of witness interrogation, and therefore will have been innovative only in scale; geographically wider-ranging inquiries, by contrast, will have been innovative in kind. It remains to be seen whether this can be substantiated or disproved.[88]

How was committee membership determined, and how did committees proceed? Members of all forms of select committees were nominated on the floor of the house (except in especially fraught and politically sensitive cases, when a ballot might be employed). It has been suggested that in the early eighteenth century, common practice was for names to be promiscuously proposed from the floor of the house. In the early nineteenth century, the onus seems to have shifted to the MP who moved the appointment of a committee. Peter Jupp suggests that he proposed the full list of members; S.E. Finer, that he was entitled to name the majority only.[89] In any case it is clear both that membership was supposed to reflect diverse opinion, and that an MP taking the lead was likely to seek to obtain a majority of his own disposition. Clearly, under both eighteenth- and early nineteenth-century regimes, efforts were sometimes made to bias committee membership – yet in other cases, care was taken to include men of differing views. Whoever was named to a committee, in practice, much might hinge on who attended.[90] It was the chairman's responsibility to draft a report.

See Innes, 'Parliament and the Shaping', 88–9, and 'The "Mixed Economy of Welfare" in Early Modern England: Assessments of the Options from Hale to Malthus (*c.*1683–1803)', in Martin Daunton (ed.), *Charity, Self-Interest and Welfare in the English Past* (London, 1996), 151–2, 154–5, 159–60, 162–3.

[88] I comment on the flourishing of inquiry into the metropolis in 'Managing the Metropolis: Social Problems and their Control 1660–1830', in Peter Clark and Raymond Gillespie (eds), *Two Capitals: London and Dublin, 1500–1840* (Oxford, *Proceedings of the British Academy*, Vol. 107, 2001), 78–9.

[89] Hayton, *Survey*, 355–7; Sedgwick, *House of Commons*, i. 6–9; see also Thomas, *House of Commons*, 266–7; Jupp, *British Politics*, 212; Finer, 'The Transmission', 19. P. Jupp, 'The Landed Elite and Political Authority in Britain ca. 1760–1850', *Journal of British Studies*, 29 (1990), 70 and n. 67 offers a preliminary assessment of changing practice from the later eighteenth century.

[90] For a detailed early account of success in packing a (local bill) committee: Hayton, *Survey*,

Procedures for determining who appeared to testify before committees were not closely regulated. Either the chairman or other committee members might suggest names; some witnesses volunteered themselves.[91] When inquiries were ambitious both in scope and in geographical range, the task of putting together an appropriate list of witnesses must have been challenging. MPs might have their own contacts, but probably also relied on supporters acting in effect as opinion brokers to travel, collect evidence, and make local contacts. In early anti-slave trade agitations, Thomas Clarkson played the 'broker' role.[92] In the early nineteenth century, some witnesses had their expenses reimbursed by special order from the Treasury, or – in the case of poor witnesses – by a whip-round among committee members. After 1818, reimbursement became routine, committee expenses soared, and in consequence there arose pressure to regulate the procedure for choosing witnesses.[93]

There were serial witnesses. Francis Place was one such. He gave evidence before a committee on the tailoring trade in 1810; on mendicity in 1815; and on education in 1816. (Interestingly, his evidence before the mendicity committee was not printed, apparently because judged irrelevant. Minutes of evidence cannot therefore be taken to be a complete record; there may have been an intermediate process of sifting.)[94]

Because committees determined who appeared before them, interested parties could not count on being heard. The committee set up in 1825 to consider reinstating acts against workers' combinations (repealed the previous session) was not minded to hear workers' evidence; the radical MP Joseph Hume advised them to gather in the area outside the committee room and agitate in the hope of embarrassing the committee into admitting them.[95] Committees convened to consider petitions designed to initiate local or private legislation were expected to question petitioning parties. In other cases too,

372; also Kondo, 'Workhouse Issue', 77, 80. Jeremy Bentham claimed that his Panopticon proposal was dismissed by an 'appropriately packed' committee in 1811: *History of the War between Jeremy Bentham and George III*, reprinted in *A Bentham Reader*, ed. M.P. Mack (New York, 1969), 206. Ironically, historians have described Bentham's followers as champion committee-packers: see Finer, 'The Transmission', 19–24. Cf. Lambert, *Introduction and List*, 45 and Jupp, *British Politics*, 212–13.

91 For payment of witnesses' expenses, see Parliamentary Papers (House of Commons), 1840 vol. XV, 268.

92 Oldham, *Popular Politics*, ch. 3, esp. 74–5. Dudley Miles, *Francis Place 1771–1854* (Brighton, 1988). A rare survival among Lords mss. – House of Lords Record Office, House of Lords Committee Papers, Papers of Committee on Dearness of Provisions, 1765, f. 48 – reveals the behind-the-scenes role evidently being played by 'eminent cutting butcher' John Cheese in organizing witnesses to give a notably one-sided view of the issues involved.

93 Parliamentary Papers (House of Commons), 1840 vol. XV, 267–8, 280–1, 289.

94 Miles, *Place*, 90, 100–1, 161. For *post factum* editing of the record, see also Lambert, *Introduction and List*, 46. For other committee-related work by Place, see Miles, *Place*, 99, 135, 163–5, 172–3.

95 Miles, *Place*, 163.

petitions may have represented a bid to be heard – though when they were very numerous, clearly at best only a selection of petitioners might be called.

The case of late 1820s friendly society legislation illustrates both that efforts to gain a hearing were not necessarily rewarded, and that perseverance might win out in the end. Representatives of artisan friendly societies failed to gain a hearing before an 1827 select committee on friendly societies. In the following session, however, when a bill was introduced, they won out by dint of flooding the house with petitions, presented to parliament by sympathetic MPs who took the opportunity to assert the petitioners' right to be heard. Once admitted, the objectors made such an impression on the committee that the original bill was dropped; a bill drafted by the objectors was introduced, and passed in the following session. Iorwerth Prothero comments that it is 'a striking illustration of the "openness" of the British political system in the period of private members' legislation and absence of party discipline, that such an artisan agitation could not only prevent one bill, but secure the passage of one of their own'.[96] In whose favour this 'openness' operated however varied from case to case. The important part played by sympathetic MPs – in this case radical Whigs Brougham and Hobhouse – in getting the protestors a hearing deserves emphasis. Gaining access to parliament depended in important part on having insiders supporting the process.

Conclusions

In these ways, and to this extent, eighteenth- and early nineteenth-century parliaments were open fora. Ministers had, in the early eighteenth century, established effective control over the fiscal programme, and could usually count on getting their way on major constitutional and political issues, thanks in no small part to the support they generally received from dependent MPs. Even in these cases, however, there were times when storms of public protest persuaded them that discretion was the better part of valour: that they had best abandon a course on which they had been set. Rarely did they make any attempt to determine either the content or the fate of other general legislation, or of local and private bills. Such matters were commonly left for ordinary MPs to carry forwards. MPs for their part often felt ill equipped to do this without wider consultation.

I have no wish to exaggerate parliament's openness to external pressure. Parliamentary agendas were highly conventionalized, and shifted slowly; members were often not very receptive to new ideas. They were generally disposed to defend the political order in church and state, to uphold all forms of authority in the face of challenge, and to be wary in the concessions they

[96] I. Prothero, *Artisans and Politics in Nineteenth-Century London: John Gast and his Times* (London, 1979), 232–8.

made to those who represented themselves as oppressed – lest they undercut the foundations of the political and social order, or the springs of national prosperity. Yet parliament was never closed to external pressure, and in the right circumstances even relatively lowly people – protesting artisans, imprisoned debtors – might gain a hearing. Even women were sometimes questioned by committees.[97]

There are plenty of grounds for suggesting that, during the late eighteenth and early nineteenth centuries, parliament's accessibility increased, and a wider range of people saw and took the opportunity to press their views upon it. The increased publicity given to parliamentary proceedings was in part the product of rising public interest and changing expectations; it must also have contributed to enhancing that interest and those expectations. The early nineteenth century saw petitions to parliament put to new uses, and generated on an unprecedented scale. Society was increasingly easily mobilized to express views on public issues, and these mobilizing muscles were increasingly often flexed. Many thousands of activists, from a range of social backgrounds, developed practical political skills (in a broad understanding of that term) and helped to politicize the environment in which their neighbours lived. 'Pressure from without' upon parliament helped to spur the development within parliament of groups of MPs particularly well connected to, and sensitive to the concerns of, extra-parliamentary networks: evangelicals, philanthropists, and radicals. As the fashion for empirical inquiry encouraged parliament to undertake wide-ranging surveys of social conditions across the nation, MPs meanwhile found new needs and uses for extra-parliamentary activists and networks. To participate in the political world, to engage with the legislative process, was not necessarily to gain power: power either to set agendas, or to determine outcomes. But these changes in political culture affected people's experience of politics (if sometimes, chiefly by enhancing their frustrations). When circumstances were just right, access might bring power.

Yet the very openness of the political world, and the zeal with which openness was exploited, also served to put openness under strain. I have noted moves made to reduce the demands the receipt of petitions made upon parliamentary time. From the 1810s, ministers – noting the growing ambition of backbench legislators, and also the difficulty they sometimes experienced in formulating acceptable legislation on complex, controversial issues – increasingly involved themselves, beginning more frequently to initiate legislation on the sorts of issues they had previously been content to leave to backbenchers. Concerned to protect their own access to parliament, ministers moreover moved to institute government order days, on which only government business would be heard (the first such regulation was made in 1811).[98] These contrary forces continued to strain against each other into the late Victorian era, yet by 1830

[97] E.g. *Commons Journals*, xi. 641–2.
[98] See n. 2 above. For Abbot, see Thorne, *Commons*, i. 335–6.

it was already apparent that the trend towards access that had recently been so marked could not be continued indefinitely without beginning to change the nature of the medium within which it worked.

6

The experience of litigation in eighteenth-century England

WILFRID PREST

As for Law in the Courts of Westminster, it is grown a perfect Stranger. Not one Determination of any Moment during the whole Term; & the Courts (except the Chancery) not sitting above one hour in the morning. I believe our Clients mistook the Title of an Act that passed last Sessions, & instead of *Abbreviation* read it 'An Act for the *Annihilation* of Mich[aelm]as Term'.

William Blackstone to Seymour Richmond, London, 7 December 1751 ('Original Letters of Mr Justice Blackstone, No II', *Legal Observer or Journal of Jurisprudence*, 6 (1833), 421)

A generation has passed since historians first learnt to view the discretionary administration of criminal justice as a mainstay of the established order in Hanoverian England.[1] But only during the past decade has the non-criminal business of the law courts begun to attract much attention. Until quite recently civil litigation was assumed to have involved no more than a tiny propertied fraction of the total population, and hence dismissed as of little interest, unless to specialist legal historians. However scholars are now coming to recognize that early modern English men and women were far more likely to appear in court in connection with civil proceedings than a criminal indictment, and to speculate that civil litigation was no less important than the criminal law in upholding the political and socio-economic order.[2] Indeed as Hanoverian criminal justice appears much less an instrument of class rule than once was

[1] *Albion's Fatal Tree: Crime and Society in Eighteenth-Century England*, ed. Douglas Hay, Peter Linebaugh, John G. Rule, E.P. Thompson, and Cal Winslow (Harmondsworth, 1975); E.P. Thompson, *Whigs and Hunters* (Harmondsworth, 1975).

[2] The pioneering work of Christopher W. Brooks is conveniently collected in his *Lawyers, Litigation, and English Society since 1450* (London, 1998). See also *Communities and Courts in Britain 1150–1900*, ed. C.W. Brooks and M. Lobban (London, 1997), esp. chs 10–11; C. Muldrew, *The Economy of Obligation: The Culture of Credit and Social Relations in Early Modern England* (Basingstoke, 1998).

thought,[3] so interest correspondingly shifts to civil litigation, conceived of as a mode of popular representation and social participation. If this enfranchising role presumably peaked with the extraordinary surge of business which swept through both local and central courts during the later sixteenth and early seventeenth centuries, it seems not unreasonable to suppose that any subsequent ebb must have had a contrary effect.

Hence it becomes possible to envisage an eighteenth-century 'crisis of litigation':[4] a massive and sustained slump in the volume of civil business handled by, especially if not exclusively, the central common law courts, part and parcel of a general trend towards a more powerful, centralized, *imperial* state apparatus, which marginalized where it did not totally exclude ordinary people, especially the poor and/or propertyless. Previously the common law had provided an avenue of empowerment, giving the middling and lower sorts opportunities to challenge the pretensions of their socio-economic superiors, enlisting state authority to defend their individual rights. Now inflated costs and procedural deficiencies tended to squeeze all but a few wealthy or imprudent plaintiffs out of Westminster Hall. Influenced by enlightenment rationalism, even they no longer shared the confidence which their Tudor and early Stuart forebears had placed in the laws of the land, but agreed with Edward Gibbon in deriding the gothic absurdity of 'old customs (begun in barbarous ages, and since continued from a blind reverence to antiquity)'.[5]

This chapter seeks to explore the origins, nature, and impact of that alleged crisis. Can a 'considerable decline in the volume and social reach of civil litigation after 1700'[6] be established? If so, did it mark the welcome advent of a society less abrasively combative and dysfunctional, because more 'polite and commercial'?[7] Or ought we rather to deplore a sharp reduction in access to legal process because it signified for most people a diminished political and social agency? Is it indeed possible to form any but the most tentative

[3] Cf. J. Langbein, '*Albion's* Fatal Flaws', *Past and Present*, 98 (1983), 96–120; P. King, 'Decision-makers and Decision-making in the English Criminal Law, 1750–1800', *Historical Journal*, 27 (1984), 25–58; J. M. Beattie, *Crime and the Courts in England, 1660–1815* (Princeton, 1986); V. Gatrell, *The Hanging Tree: Execution and the English People 1770–1868* (Oxford, 1994).

[4] The phrase was used in publicity material for the September 2001 Humanities Research Centre conference 'An Imperial State at Law' at which a first draft of this chapter was presented.

[5] E. Gibbon, 'Remarks on Blackstone's Commentaries', *The Miscellaneous Works of Edward Gibbon*, ed. J. Holroyd (London, 1814), v. 546.

[6] D. Lemmings, 'Ritual, Majesty and Mystery: Collective Life and Culture among English Barristers, Serjeants and Judges, *c.* 1500–*c.* 1830', in *Lawyers and Vampires: Cultural Histories of Legal Professions*, ed. W.W. Pue and D. Sugarman (Oxford, 2003), 27.

[7] Cf. L. Stone, 'Interpersonal Violence in English Society, 1300–1980', *Past and Present*, 101 (1983), 22–33; *idem*, 'A Rejoinder', *Past and Present*, 108 (1985), 216–24. W. Blackstone, *Commentaries on the Laws of England* (Oxford, 1765–9), iii. 326.

hypotheses about the overall direction, let alone the causes and consequences, of long-term trends in the recorded civil case loads of early modern English law courts?

Counting problems

Thanks to the pioneering labours of Christopher Brooks, together with Henry Horwitz, Craig Muldrew, and W.A. Champion, to name only the most notable and innovative workers in this field, we have now at least an outline knowledge of movements in the volume of non-criminal business handled by English courts of law, central and local, ecclesiastical and secular, between the early sixteenth and late eighteenth centuries. We also possess varying amounts of information about how that work was distributed among the various jurisdictions, the relative and changing popularity of different forms of action and process which they entertained, and the social characteristics of those involved as parties to litigation. It seems clear that throughout these centuries the greater part of the business processed by the secular courts, both central and local, arose from disputes over monies owed, or claimed to be owed, typically by borrowers to lenders: in Brooks's words, 'the vast majority of actions concerned some form of the debtor–creditor relationship'.[8] It is also apparent that litigation was not merely a means of maintaining existing economic and social inequalities. On the contrary, as Muldrew has emphasized with reference to his own work on the Guildhall Court of King's Lynn, Norfolk, in the 1650s and 1680s, and following Brooks's earlier insights:

> Local courts were extremely accessible institutions in which the poor as well as the wealthy could obtain justice. . . . There was certainly social bias in the way they functioned, in that the wealthy sue more often than they themselves were sued, but at the same time, the wealthy did not use local courts to prey upon the poor, forcing them to pay a lot of debts, and the poor certainly sued their 'betters' when they failed in their obligations.[9]

Finally, the massive upsurge in recorded business of the courts during the later sixteenth century was not sustained, although (as we shall see shortly) the timing and rate of subsequent decline varied quite widely from one jurisdiction to the next.

But what are we to make of these findings? That their historical significance remains far from certain is hardly surprising, given the very disparate activities

[8] Brooks, *Lawyers, Litigation*, 87. On the importance of debt in all legal systems, see D.J. Guth, 'Centrality of Debt in Western Medieval Sacred and Secular Legal Systems', *Contemporary Law 1994 Droit Contemporain* (Cowansville, 1995), 56–67.
[9] Muldrew, *Economy of Obligation*, 271.

lumped together under the label 'civil litigation', and the variety of social actors engaged, whether directly or indirectly. Evidential gaps and complexities make it very difficult, if not impossible, to produce any meaningful systematic index of national litigation levels, or per capita litigiousness, between c. 1500 and 1800. But even if such figures were available, their interpretation would necessarily involve some tricky moral and political value judgements. Thus while it may be granted that the law was not merely 'a tool of the ruling elite, a weapon useful only for the protection of property and the oppression by the gentry of the rest of the population', we might still question how much and what sorts of agency legal institutions offered, to whom, and with what results.[10] To put it another way, was Gerrard Winstanley entirely isolated and utterly deluded when he claimed in the middle of the seventeenth century that 'most laws are but to enslave the poor to the rich'?[11] After all, in the early twenty-first century we find no unanimity of opinion on current litigation levels among big business, consumer advocates, insurance companies, lawyers, medical practitioners, and politicians.[12] So it is hardly surprising that historians differ in their assessments of how the law was used, by whom, and to what ends, in early modern England.

Any attempt to determine trends in civil litigation during the century or so after the summoning of the Long Parliament encounters complex definitional and evidential problems. To begin with, there was no straightforward distinction between criminal and civil proceedings in early modern England. Thus when 'eighteenth-century prosecutors brought indictments of assault, riot, or other non-felonious offenses against the person, their goal was not punishment of the defendant . . . but instead the extraction of payment, or less frequently an apology'.[13] Whether such actions should now be categorized as criminal or civil is a nice question for us, just as the civil proceedings which led to imprisonment for debt posed classification problems for contemporaries: 'If to be in debt is so great a crime . . . as to deserve the worst of punishments, perpetual imprisonment', mused Thomas Baston in 1732, 'it is all the reason in the world it should first be determined, if the person has committed this heinous crime before he suffers the punishment.'[14] As David Lieberman points out, 'The practical operation of the law . . . undermined any easy application of the modern categories of "criminal" or "civil" in the classification of legal disputes.'[15] The implications of this categorical indeterminacy for our

[10] Brooks, *Lawyers, Litigation*, 5.

[11] Cited C. Hill, *Liberty Against the Law: Some Seventeenth-Century Controversies* (London, 1996), 278.

[12] Cf. *Litigation Past and Present*, ed. W. Prest and S. Roach Anleu (Kensington, NSW, 2004), ch. 1.

[13] N. Landau, 'Indictment for Fun and Profit: A Prosecutor's Reward at Eighteenth-Century Quarter Sessions', *Law and History Review*, 17 (1999), 536.

[14] T. Baston, *Observations on Trade and A Publick Spirit* (London, 1732), 109.

[15] D. Lieberman, 'Blackstone and the Categories of English Jurisprudence', in *Law, Crime*

purposes remain uncertain, because trends in criminal proceedings during the seventeenth and eighteenth centuries are not clear-cut. Thus while indictment rates for property crime in Essex and neighbouring counties peaked in the later sixteenth century and thereafter fell away until after 1750, equivalent prosecutions in London tended to fluctuate around a higher level from the Restoration onwards, surging in the 1690s, 1720s, and 1750s.[16]

A second difficulty is that the data currently available for what would nowadays be unambiguously classed as civil litigation is far from comprehensive in scope or uniform in type. For the two major central common law courts of Common Pleas and King's Bench, we currently possess a total of only four counts, covering cases at 'advanced stages' in the calendar years 1640, 1670, 1700, and 1750, plus totals for Common Pleas only in 1690 and 1720.[17] The information for Chancery (which in the reign of James I was said to be 'frequented above other the common-law courts at Westminster') is somewhat better, comprising seven tallies of original bills lodged between 1673–4 and 1750, and four estimates of 'active cases' for the entire period 1684–1760.[18] These are regrettably slender foundations for calculating long-term trends in court business, especially since we have no reason to suppose that large annual case load fluctuations were less characteristic of early modern civil jurisdictions than they are of their modern counterparts. Thus, for example, the numbers of bills entered in Chancery in the four years 1745, 1746, 1750, and 1752 are recorded as 1836, 2032, 1827, and 1023 respectively.[19] Clerical mistakes and other anomalies or gaps in the surviving records are an additional source of disquiet; for example, the non-survival of Chancery pleadings, and the failure of mid-eighteenth-century attorneys to bring in entry rolls for docketing, which might and did lead to under-recording.[20]

and English Society 1660–1830, ed. N. Landau (Cambridge, 2002), 141; see also Beattie, *Crime and the Courts*, 457.

[16] P. King, *Crime, Justice, and Discretion in England 1740–1820* (Oxford, 2000), 134–5; J.M. Beattie, *Policing and Punishment in London 1660–1750: Urban Crime and the Limits of Terror* (Oxford, 2001), 40–1.

[17] Brooks, *Lawyers, Litigation*, 31.

[18] National Archives [Public Record Office], SP14/199/177, quoted W.R. Prest, *The Rise of the Barristers* (Oxford, 1991), 16. Brooks, *Lawyers, Litigation*, 30. H. Horwitz and P. Polden, 'Continuity or Change in the Court of Chancery in the Seventeenth and Eighteenth Centuries', *Journal of British Studies*, 35 (1996), 30–1.

[19] Cf. T. Wright and A. Melville, 'Hey, But Who's Counting? The Metrics and Politics of Trends in Civil Litigation', in *Litigation Past and Present*, ed. Prest and Roach Anleu, 102–8. Brooks, *Lawyers, Litigation*, 30.

[20] W.A. Champion, 'Litigation in the Boroughs', *Journal of Legal History* 15 (1994), 221, n. 82; cf. C. Francis, 'Practice, Strategy, and Institution: Debt Collection in the English Common-Law Courts, 1740–1840', *Northwestern University Law Review*, 80 (1986), 810–11, n. 7; Horwitz and Polden, 'Continuity or Change', 29–30 and n. 18 (434 of the 1,544 bills entered in the bill book for 1785 have not survived in the relevant NA class).

Unfortunately our coverage of local courts, both urban and rural, is at present even less satisfactory. The scale of the inadequacy can only be estimated, since we do not even know how many local courts were active during the seventeenth and eighteenth centuries, but there were at least 200 borough courts of record, as well as forty-odd county courts, hundreds of hundred courts, and many thousand manorial courts.[21] While Muldrew has counted the numbers of suits initiated in various town courts at different points between the sixteenth and eighteenth centuries, his fragmentary data extends beyond 1730 only for Bristol, King's Lynn, and Yarmouth. King's Lynn's Guildhall Court and Great Yarmouth's Borough Court are represented by totals for only four sample years between 1700 and 1750, while six year-counts are given for the Bristol Mayor's and Tolzey courts over the same period.[22] Brooks's data for 'Actions in the Newcastle town courts' during the first half of the eighteenth century consists of eight observations for eight separate years, two for the Court of Conscience, three for the Sheriff's Court and three for the Mayor's Court.[23] Even Champion's detailed studies of actions entered in Shrewsbury's *Curia Parva* do not extend beyond 1730, although he also presents four samples taken over three civic years of suits begun in the Ludlow town court during the first half of the eighteenth century.[24] For rural courts – county, hundred, manorial, peculiar – we have very little by way of litigation statistics, let alone runs of data covering the later seventeenth and eighteenth centuries. Much the same applies to the various palatinate, stannary, ecclesiastical, and civil law jurisdictions.[25] Needless to say, the quantitative data on early modern civil litigation currently available has been laboriously won; to point to the desirability of acquiring still more certainly implies no criticism of those whose toil has brought together our current small but precious holding.

In the third place, the unevenness of the information which we now possess might not much matter if all pointed more or less in the same direction. To some extent it does – hence the apparent plausibility of a post-1700 'crisis in

[21] Muldrew, *Economy of Obligation*, 203–4; *idem*, 'Rural Credit, Market Areas and Legal Institutions in the Countryside in England, 1550–1700', in *Communities and Courts*, ed. Brooks and Lobban, 155–7.

[22] Muldrew, *Economy of Obligation*, 219, 222–3.

[23] Brooks, *Lawyers, Litigation*, 40–1.

[24] Champion, 'Litigation in the Boroughs', 201–22; *idem*, 'Recourse to Law and the Meaning of the Great Litigation Decline, 1650–1750: Some Clues from the Shewsbury Local Courts', in *Communities and Courts*, ed. Brooks and Lobban, 179–98.

[25] On ecclesiastical courts, see T. Meldrum, 'A Women's Court in London: Defamation at the Bishop of London's Consistory Court, 1700–1745', *London Journal*, 19 (1994), 1–20; R. Shoemaker, 'The Decline of Public Insult in London 1660–1800', *Past and Present*, 169 (2000), 101; D. Lemmings, 'Women's Property, Popular Cultures and the Consistory Court of London in the Eighteenth Century', in N. Wright, M.W. Ferguson, and A.R. Buck (eds), *Women, Property and the Letters of the Law in Early Modern England* (Toronto, 2004), 66–94: I am grateful to David Lemmings for allowing me to see this paper before it was published.

litigation' or 'steep decline in [court] business'.[26] Yet closer scrutiny reveals considerable variation between individual jurisdictions in the pace and timing of litigatory recession, even supposing we assume that the various proxy measures of court business adopted by different historians were strictly comparable (a point to which I shall return). Thus whereas on Brooks's figures Common Pleas cases in advanced stages fell by some 10 per cent from 1640 to 1670, the King's Bench equivalent measure actually rose by more than a third (from just over eight thousand to just under eleven thousand suits) during the same period. And while Common Pleas cases continued to diminish throughout the eighteenth century (albeit 'trials dropped off almost imperceptibly between 1702 and 1720'), King's Bench business evidently bottomed as early as 1720, although whether this was the true low point or merely an optical illusion resulting from a shortage of observations remains to be seen.[27] Chancery followed a different path: while the numbers of recorded bills lodged in that court actually rose by nearly 20 per cent between 1673/4, 1685/6, and 1700/1, at the next observation a generation later (1734/5) they appear to have contracted by over 40 per cent (from 5,707 to 3,240). This shrinkage seemingly continued until the end of the century (whereas in the Exchequer, Chancery's 'younger sister', the decline in newly lodged bills – yet another measure – was significantly greater between 1685 and 1735, but then partially reversed over the next half-century).[28] An alternative method of measuring Chancery business shows yet another picture, with 'active cases' peaking before the Civil War but still nearly 20 per cent higher in 1684/5 than they had been in 1609/10; twenty-five years later, in 1709/10, they were just below the early seventeenth-century level, which was maintained almost without change over the next quarter-century, dropping decisively to a low point for the century only at George III's accession.[29] Where town courts are concerned, we find business peaking rather earlier, either in the last quarter of the sixteenth century (Exeter, Ludlow, Shrewsbury, Yarmouth) or the early decades of the seventeenth century (King's Lynn, 1610; Taunton, 1625; Bristol, 1635). The process of decline accordingly appears to have been more gradual, if ultimately more severe than at Westminster Hall, despite its interruption by occasional rallies in the 1680s and 1720s.[30]

[26] C. Brooks, 'The Longitudinal Study of Civil Litigation in England 1200–1996', in *Litigation Past and Present*, ed. Prest and Roach Anleu, 33.

[27] Brooks, *Lawyers*, Litigation, 31; a slightly larger figure (8,537) for 1640 King's Bench suits is given at ibid., 11.

[28] Horwitz and Polden, 'Continuity or Change', 30; H. Horwitz, 'Chancery's "Younger Sister": The Court of Exchequer and its Equity Jurisdiction 1649–1841', *Historical Research*, 72 (1999), 168.

[29] Brooks, *Lawyers*, *Litigation*, 30; Horwitz and Polden, 'Continuity or Change', 29–31.

[30] Muldrew, *Economy of Obligation*, 218–24; Champion, 'Litigation in the Boroughs', 205, 216; *idem*, 'Recourse to Law', 183–4. At Newcastle, on the other hand, 'legal business

So the great litigation decline may have begun either as early as the 1580s, or as late as the 1700s, and reached its nadir in the 1720s, or much later, indeed not before the end of the eighteenth century in the case of Chancery, Common Pleas, and many regional jurisdictions. Such wide chronological divergence strongly suggests that we are not confronting a single phenomenon generated by a common cause (or complex of causes), and everywhere exhibiting broadly similar effects – unless perhaps something in the order of a swing of the pendulum, a return to the *status quo ante* after the previous extraordinary litigation boom. Such a notion appears to underlie Muldrew's caveat that

> it is probably best not to look at the general pattern of litigation over the course of the seventeenth century in terms of absolute decline, but rather as a period of adjustment from the enormously and unusually high levels occurring from the 1570s to the early seventeenth century.[31]

But then, fourthly, what exactly is being counted, or measured, when we speak of civil litigation booms and busts? In 1956 J.P. Cooper concluded his contribution to the gentry controversy with the following words:

> Statistics on such subjects in this period are bound to be imperfect, but the counting of manors seems to have effects dangerously akin to the counting of sheep, it introduces us to a dream world, in which, as in our own dreams, reality may not be entirely absent, but appearances are often deceptive.[32]

Cooper's main point was the incommensurability of manors, their enormous variation in value, which made them incapable of providing an index of their owners' wealth. Like manors, law suits were anything but equivalent units, all of a piece. Indeed they were arguably more heterogeneous than manors, which at least had a moderately consistent formal definition and status. As already noted, the nature of the surviving evidence constrains modern historical quantifiers to use at least three different approximations for a law suit. The unit counted may be the first bill, plaint, or writ which signalled the possible commencement of legal action, even though the vast majority of such filings had no institutional sequel. (At King's Lynn in the 1680s, for example, only 16 per cent of initial complaints appear to have left any further trace at all in the records of the Guildhall Court, with as few as 4 per cent going on to trial and judgment.)[33] Alternatively it may be that the surviving evidence only

probably reached a peak a decade or so after the introduction in 1690 of a court of requests': Brooks, *Lawyers, Litigation*, 40.

[31] Muldrew, *Economy of Obligation*, 239.

[32] J.P. Cooper, 'The Counting of Manors', *Economic History Review*, 2nd ser., 8 (1956), 388.

[33] Muldrew, *Economy of Obligation*, 202, 255, 386 n. 19. In 'Tudor Shrewsbury the figure [of cases settled before trial] ran at 80–90 per cent, and between a third and a half of all

permits enumeration of those proceedings where the parties had 'joined issue', or at least reached that point 'at which the defendant had come into court in order to answer the plea of the plaintiff and either put himself on the country or confess the action'.[34] Finally, Horwitz and Polden have devised for Chancery a statistical artefact, the 'active case', which is intended to 'estimate the number of individual, active cases in given years'.[35] Unfortunately these are not three interchangeable measures of court business, nor indeed of lay participation in litigation. Muldrew elaborates the same point when he observes that comparing levels of litigation between different jurisdictions 'is a task fraught with difficulty' because of wide variations in record-keeping practices from court to court, and also the fact that 'ratios between actions and plaints differed from jurisdiction to jurisdiction, and in all probability changed over time'.[36]

Moreover, and fifthly, even if each of these units (initial filing or plaint, advanced case, active case) could be regarded as fully negotiable equivalents of a single 'law suit', merely adding them up can take no account of relevant characteristics which could and did differ widely from one legal action to the next. These include for present purposes the number,[37] socio-economic status, and sex of litigants, the technical form and factual basis of the action, and its duration and eventual outcome. No doubt all such matters are in principle subject to categorization and quantification, provided that the relevant evidence survives, something which can hardly be taken for granted across the board. But it is possible very rarely (and then only after the expenditure of much time and trouble) to recapture some part of the emotional and cultural significance which attached to particular individual suits, not just for the parties directly involved, but also for their families, friends, and communities. The experience of litigation, that is, the subjective dimension and meanings attached to going to law, could vary enormously, as for example between men and women, rich and poor, villagers and townsfolk, plaintiffs and defendants, successful and unsuccessful litigants. Little or no hint of these qualitative aspects and attributes is revealed by the curt and formal common law records, which typically elide or distort the cultural context of individual suits in order to accommodate them to particular institutional categories and procedural

actions may have been resolved without pleading taking place at all': Champion, 'Recourse to the Law', 180.

[34] Brooks, *Lawyers, Litigation*, 29. It should be noted that in the central courts parties 'appeared' via the written mediation or representation of their attorneys, rather than in person.

[35] Horwitz and Polden, 'Continuity or Change', 30.

[36] Muldrew, *Economy of Obligation*, Appendix I: Counting Suits in Borough Courts, 335, 337. These complexities would be considerably multiplied if it were seriously sought to integrate data drawn from other jurisdictions, such as the ecclesiastical courts.

[37] Suits in which one or more individuals appeared as parties were 'a significant minority' in the 1627 Chancery sample of Horwitz and Polden and in over half of their early nineteenth-century sample group: 'Continuity or Change?', 44.

formulae.[38] The depositions in which 'the verbal evidence of inhabitants was transcribed by clerks of equity courts adjudicating in customary disputes' may seem potentially more rewarding, but this evidence was also constrained by the demands of legal formalism.[39] To penetrate beyond the silences and stereotypical formulations it is necessary to adopt a much more intensive approach, supplementing official court records with a variety of other – usually local – sources, as Christine Churches has demonstrated to remarkable effect in her investigations of civil litigation involving the inhabitants of the rising Cumberland port of Whitehaven during the later seventeenth and early eighteenth centuries.[40]

Among other things, Churches has confirmed that going to law sometimes offered a means by which the relatively humble could challenge authority and resist the power of great men, in this case the Lowthers, landed proprietors of most of Whitehaven. Besides manorial tenants challenging their landlords, other sorts of more or less lowly plaintiffs who could and did find litigation a shield and buckler in time of trouble included Dissenters and Quakers confronting various forms of sectarian discrimination and persecution, plebeian women combatting slurs on their sexual reputation, sailors and sailors' wives suing for back wages, and free miners resisting entrepreneurial and state authority.[41] But we simply do not know how widespread such 'litigation from below' was, then, earlier or later. This makes it very difficult to determine to

[38] Compare P.R. Schofield's observation that 'historians are unlikely to be aware of the cultural background to a dispute recorded in a court record because it has typically been forced out by the legal formula of the record': 'Peasants and the Manor Court: Gossip and Litigation in a Suffolk Village at the Close of the Thirteenth Century', *Past and Present*, 159 (1998), 9. See also the thoughtful reflections of J. Bailey, 'Voices in Court: Lawyers or Litigants?', *Historical Research*, 74 (2001), 408.

[39] A. Wood, 'Custom and the Social Organization of Writing', *Transactions of the Royal Historical Society*, 6th ser., 9 (1999), 260. C. Churches, '"The Most Unconvincing Testimony": The Genesis and Historical Usefulness of the Country Depositions in Chancery', *The Seventeenth Century*, 11 (1996), 209–227.

[40] C. Churches, 'False Friends, Spiteful Enemies: A Community at Law in Early Modern England', *Historical Research*, 71 (1998), 52–74; *idem*, 'Business at Law: Retrieving Commercial Disputes from Eighteenth-Century Chancery', *Historical Journal*, 43 (2000), 937–54; *idem*, 'Some Figures Behind the Numbers: Going to Law in Early Modern England', in *Litigation Past and Present*, ed. Prest and Roach Anleu, 44–58.

[41] C.W. Horle, *The Quakers and the English Legal System 1660–1688* (Philadelphia, 1988); Meldrum, 'A Women's Court in London'; P. Morris, 'Defamation and Sexual Reputation in Somerset, 1733–1850', Warwick University Ph.D. thesis, 1985; G.F. Steckley, 'Litigious Mariners: Wage Cases in the Seventeenth-Century Admiralty Court', *Historical Journal*, 42 (1999), 315–45; M.R. Hunt, 'Women, Credit and the Seafaring Community in Early Eighteenth-Century London', unpublished paper prepared for International Economic History Conference, Madrid, Spain, August 1998; A. Wood, 'Custom, Identity and Resistance: English Free Miners and their Law c. 1550–1800', in *The Experience of Authority in Early Modern England*, ed. P. Griffith, A. Fox, and S. Hindle (Basingstoke, 1996), 249–85.

what extent and in what ways civil litigation actually empowered the relatively poor and weak in early modern England, as distinct from serving the interests of the relatively grand, strong, and well-to-do.

What seems incontrovertible is the centrality of debt to most forms of civil litigation, both at the centre[42] and in the provinces. Indeed it has recently been suggested that the contraction of central court business in the later seventeenth and eighteenth centuries can be explained largely in terms of changing credit enforcement practices, especially the increased use of arrest on mesne process, with a consequent reduction in the numbers of Common Pleas and King's Bench cases reaching 'advanced stages'. Certainly, if most of the so-called law suits responsible for the litigation boom in late Tudor and early Stuart England amounted to nothing more than routine anticipatory or preliminary stages of debt collection, 'in which the prospect of contention in court about either the law or the facts was extremely remote', one might well wonder whether the shrinkage of such proceedings amounted to the disempowerment of 'ordinary people' in a litigation crisis.[43] True, the post-1700 shrinkage of Chancery business cannot be accounted for in this fashion. But then Chancery was almost certainly the least socially accessible of all central jurisdictions, even if the representation of 'commercial and artisanal' occupations among its litigants increased somewhat from the later seventeenth century onwards.[44]

Despite the epigraph to this chapter, evidence that contemporaries either noticed or bemoaned a general, protracted reduction of civil litigation in the later seventeenth and eighteenth centuries is not exactly thick on the ground.[45] (Blackstone remarked on the shortage of business at Westminster Hall in Michaelmas term 1751 as a novelty, not a familiar and chronic condition.)[46] Perhaps, as Muldrew suggests, this apparent silence reflects the persistence of broadly disapproving community attitudes towards going to law.[47] Of course the absence of evidence is not usually conclusive. If people at the time were

42 'The vast majority of the civil case-load of the common-law courts . . . involved debt collection': Francis, 'Practice, Strategy, and Institution', 810.

43 C.M. Gray, review of Brooks, *Lawyers, Litigation* in *Journal of Modern History*, 72 (2000), 779–80. For Brooks's prior rebuttal of this line of argument, see *Lawyers, Litigation*, 33–5. Churches notes that more than half the Common Pleas suits involving debt which she has studied were undefended actions, possibly reflecting 'the practice of debtors signing warrants of attorney to confess judgment': personal communication, 26 October 2003.

44 Horwitz and Polden, 'Continuity or Change', 42–53.

45 Cf. Brooks, *Lawyers, Litigation*, 31–2.

46 Professional complaints on this score were heard even during the Elizabethan boomtime: thus 'Serjeant Harris . . . "They talk of a call of sergeants" said he, "but for ought I can see we had more need of a call of clients"': *The Diary of John Manningham of the Middle Temple, 1602–1603*, ed. R.P. Sorlien (Hanover, New Hampshire, 1976), 141. See also J. Harington, *Epigrams* (London, 1615), sig. E4v.

47 Cf. Muldrew, *Economy of Obligation*, 241; E. Law, *Litigiousness Repugnant to the Laws of Christianity* (Cambridge, 1743).

not much inclined either to identify or attach importance to a long-term drop in court business, that does not necessarily invalidate the different perceptions of modern historians, who might be better placed than contemporaries to make such observations. Their silence nevertheless provides further reason to treat the notion of a post-1700 'crisis of litigation' with caution.

Changing attitudes towards the law and lawyers?

Yet if only for purposes of argument, we might choose to disregard all the caveats expressed above. Let us do so now, in order to pursue the logically subsequent questions, those of causes and consequences.

It has been claimed that spreading public dissatisfaction with both law and lawyers was one major reason why many potential litigants turned away from the courts during the first half of the eighteenth century. Whereas sixteenth- and early seventeenth-century critics and would-be reformers had been preoccupied with what they saw as the evils of excessive litigation (a position often embodying crude class prejudice against any resort to litigation from below), from the later seventeenth century onwards the law's excessive costs, unreasonable delays, and inaccessible or inappropriate remedies became the main themes dominating respectable middling-sort and gentry comment. Brooks indeed notes 'a constant stream of complaint about the inefficiency of the administration of justice' from 1690 to 1850.[48] According to Lemmings, there were three main reasons why such complaints had to be taken seriously by those whose vested interests they targeted: the growing influence of commerce and its spokesmen, like William Hutton of Birmingham court of requests fame, who showed no patience with legal delay and obfuscation; an enlarged public sphere in which new forms of print media, particularly newspapers and periodical publications, gave such critiques increasingly broad currency; and a novel willingness on the part of parliament to implement proposals for legislative law reform.[49]

Lemmings's views would seem to gain support from Paul Langford's suggestion that the 'propertied mind' of the eighteenth century scarcely shared the legal practitioners' complacency about their joint inheritance:

> The law itself, the machinery which applied it, and the profession which operated it, were bitterly criticized. The tangled mass of rules and precedents that constituted the common-law doctrine of real estate were denounced for their irrational and gratuitous complexity. There was endless complaining about the bizarre language and often extended proceedings which seemed essential to the most commonplace

[48] *Lawyers, Litigation*, 92.

[49] D. Lemmings, *Professors of the Law: Barristers and English Culture in the Eighteenth Century* (Oxford, 2000), 11–14.

transactions. The matching eccentricities of Chancery, responsible for a vast body of property litigation, were scarcely less despised and execrated.

These complaints were conveyed in some of the most widely read literature of the day.[50]

Denunciation of the law and its practitioners, and proposals for their reform, did not suddenly cease or go underground in 1660, despite the strong conservative reaction to republican and sectarian initiatives of the 1640s and 1650s, with their associated campaigns for codification, simplification, decentralization, and deprofessionalization of English law.[51] Yet it would be quite mistaken to suppose that attacks on the law and lawyers before the later seventeenth century were largely the work of plebeian religious or social radicals, or alternatively that before 1660 would-be law reformers were mainly concerned with the disruptive social consequences of allowing the poor unregulated access to legal remedies. On the contrary, as an anonymous author put it towards the end of the eighteenth century,

> In England particularly, the multiplicity of our forms and 'the law's delays' have been complained of ever since the invention of printing. It has been the favourite theme of ridicule, declamation or of satire, as the writer has been disposed to be witty, moral or severe. Yet our lawyers and our laws have gone on in their old course, the lawyers have generally swallowed the oyster, and left their client only the shell.[52]

Examples abound of pre-Civil War complaints about lawyers and litigation from gentlemen apparently untroubled at the social implications of ready legal recourse by the poorer sort. Thus in his *An Apologie of the Power and Providence of God* (1635) Dr George Hakewill, rector of Exeter College, Oxford and a former royal chaplain, expressed the hope that the lawyer might 'forbear to spin out the suits of his client, to whip him about from court to court'. Another contemporary Oxford don also sympathized with 'the forlorn client . . . tired out with delays, while his advocate demurs about his cause, as long as Simonides did about the nature of God'.[53] Although frequently expressed in assize sermons, such concerns were not confined to dons and clergymen: the author of an Elizabethan broadside warned 'Lawyers that wrest law and matters prolong . . . Woe be to such sayeth Christ.'[54] Indeed the delays and frustration of going to law were literally proverbial. Thus Thomas Gainsford's 1616

[50] P. Langford, *Public Life and the Propertied Englishman 1689–1798* (Oxford, 1991), 48.

[51] B. Shapiro, 'Law Reform in Seventeenth-Century England', *American Journal of Legal History*, 19 (1975), 280–311.

[52] [Anon.], *A Review of the Principles and Conduct of the Judges . . . in Bengal* (London, 1782), 31.

[53] G. Hakewill, *An Apologie of the Power and Providence of God* (Oxford, 1635), 605; W. Hayes, *The Paragon of Persia* (Oxford, 1624), 17–18.

[54] *A new ballad Intituled, Daniels siftyng in these our Dayes* (London, 1572).

collection of aphorisms includes the following maxims: 'Laws are like a pair of terriers; and he that enters into them, is like the treading in a maze, who goeth in with ease, and out with labour. Or if you will, the fellow in the horn; who leapeth lustily into the great end, but is squeezed at the going out of the small.' More pithy advice to the same end was relayed by William Camden: 'Agree, for the law is costly'; 'As a man is friended, so the law is ended'; 'Laws or if you will, going to law, require both charge and travail'.[55]

As these and many other possible examples from this era of buoyant litigation indicate, criticism of lawyers and the law was by no means confined to, or preoccupied with, the consequences of excessive resort to legal remedies by the common sort. Nor were proposals for amelioration of legal abuses the sole province of moralists, clerics, and radical sectaries. Bills for the limitation of lawyers' fees were read in the House of Commons in 1571, 1614, and 1621, when a committee for reformation of courts of justice sat over several months, while in James's last parliament of 1624 the Commons considered measures designed to prevent irregular proceedings in courts, and 'for avoiding vexatious delays caused by removing actions and suits out of inferior courts'; this bill gained a first reading in the Lords and must be set against several early seventeenth-century measures 'for limitation of actions and avoiding suits in law'.[56] In 1607 Sir Edwin Sandys endorsed James I's proposal to 'review our laws and reduce them, in regard of the people, to more order and certainty', 'for whatsoever is the cause, the laws are not in so high reputation as heretofore; let us therefore review them.'[57] Attempts to reform the court of Chancery and to regulate fees levied there and in other jurisdictions were another familiar staple of early Stuart parliamentary debate. Conrad Russell has noted that 'For all the trust Stuart gentlemen had felt in the law, distrust for its practitioners was never very far from their minds.' Russell also cites diary notes from a 1628 Commons' speech against a bill which would have exempted England's marcher counties from the Council in Wales's jurisdiction: 'In Westminster a man be gone thrice to the West Indies before their suits be determined: nay, a man may grow old yet his suits but young. The 10th part of expenses in any courts here shall end a suit there [i.e. at London].'[58] Mercantilist criticism of legal formalism and the common law's lack of accommodation to everyday

55 T. Gainsford, *The Rich Cabinet* (London, 1616), 80; W. Camden, *Remaines, concerning Britaine* (London, 1614), 82, 303; ibid. (London, 1623), 265. Cf. M. Tilley, *A Dictionary of the Proverbs in England in the Sixteenth and Seventeenth Centuries* (Ann Arbor, 1950), 370–1; Prest, *Rise of the Barristers*, 283–91.

56 *Journals of the House of Commons 1547–1691* (London, 1742), i. 93; *Proceedings in Parliament 1614*, ed. M. Janssen (Philadelphia, 1988), 289; *Commons Debates, 1621*, ed. W. Notestein, F.H. Relf, and H. Simpson (New Haven, 1935), iii. 101, n. 30, iv. 345, vi. 434; *Journals of the House of Lords, 1578–1714* (London, 1767), iii. 317.

57 *The Parliamentary Diary of Robert Bowyer, 1606–1607*, ed. D.H. Willson (Minneapolis, 1931), 256n., 259.

58 C. Russell, *Parliaments and English Politics 1621–1629* (Oxford, 1979), 349.

commercial practice was also prevalent well before the end of the seventeenth century.[59] No doubt the proliferation of periodical publications and printed books during the eighteenth century made for more efficient dissemination of attacks and satire upon the law and lawyers. But it would be difficult to show that legal targets were being disproportionately singled out for heavier (let alone more effective) bombardment in the public prints than clerical/religious or medical ones, or indeed that such attacks amounted to something other than the recycling of well-worn stereotypes. Even enlightened sneers at the common law's feudal barbarity and tedious formalism had their pre-1640s antecedents in gibes at legal insularity and bad Latin.[60]

There are always problems with the use of literary evidence as a window on popular cultural and social attitudes, not least the almost irresistible tendency to distinguish a single or dominant outlook (a 'spirit' or 'climate' of the age) from what must usually have been a complex, far from coherent assemblage of different viewpoints and perceptions. But in any case the really crucial question for present purposes is whether the evident hostility of eighteenth-century critics, satirists, and would-be legal reformers significantly impaired the common law's credibility and effectiveness as an ideological construct, prop, and rationale for the existing order of things. Oliver Goldsmith's *Citizen of the World* (1762) purports to reproduce a conversation overheard by his Chinese philosopher persona between a debtor speaking through the grate of his prison, a porter, and a soldier, on the subject of a threatened French invasion:

> 'For my part' cries the prisoner, the greatest of my apprehensions is our freedom; if the French should conquer us what would become of English liberty? My dear friends, liberty is the Englishman's prerogative, we must preserve that at the expense of our lives, of that the French shall never deprive us. . . . 'Ay, slaves', cries the porter, 'they are all slaves, fit only to carry burdens every one of them'.[61]

Of course this is literary artefact masquerading as direct reportage, in order to make an ironic point about the human capacity for self-deception. But the extent of the apparent false consciousness here held up to (admittedly gentle) ridicule is open to question. Given the opportunity to explain themselves, Goldsmith's fictional porter and prisoner might both have maintained that the

59 'Reasons for the Decay of Trade to France, 1641' (British Library Stowe MS 132, ff. 298–9), cited *Seventeenth Century Economic Documents*, ed. J.P. Cooper and J. Thirsk (Oxford, 1972), 496; see also ibid., 71 (Thomas Papillon's testimony to Lords' Committee on Decay of Rents and Trade, House of Lords Record Office, Main Papers, HL, 28 October 1669), and 96 (John Locke's Notes on Trade, c. 1674, Bodleian Library Locke MS c 30, f. 18); J. Child, *A New Discourse of Trade* (London, 1694, first published 1668), 6, 131–4.
60 Prest, *Rise of the Barristers*, 107, 187–9.
61 O. Goldsmith, *The Citizen of the World; Or Letters from A Chinese Philosopher Residing in London* (London, 1762), 11.

afflictions they suffered as individuals paled into insignificance against the broad lack of personal freedoms and weight of worldly burdens carried by their counterparts across the Channel. Indeed it seems very likely that many who embraced the general notion of freedom guaranteed by the rule of law as the Englishman's birthright, simultaneously adopted a critical, dismissive, hostile, or patronizing stance towards particular aspects of the law and its administration.

Thomas Baston's *Observations on Trade and A Publick Spirit* (first published 1713, with two subsequent editions) is therefore quite remarkable for the extent to which its author engages directly with the whole constitutionalist rhetoric of 'Liberty and Property', in order to subvert it:

> O rare Liberty and Property! Blest Constitution . . . We boast we have the best laws in the world, Magna Charta and the Lord knows what. We talk much of Liberty and Property . . . and praise our excellent constitution above all others . . . but all this is little more than a jingle of words. . . . As matters are carried on in England by the lawyers, there is no greater tyranny under the sun . . . The vulgar mistake about this Liberty and Property is, because 'tis not in our Prince's power to oppress us; but 'tis in every one of his subject's power to tyrannize over one another, so that we have only taken this power from him, to lodge it in our selves, or rather the lawyers.[62]

The printing history of this emotional critique of law, lawyers, courts, and legal institutions suggests that Baston must have struck a chord with at least some contemporaries. Yet he stands alone (at least in my reading) in the passion, range, and specificity of his analysis. His book often reads like a throwback to the 1650s rather than a product of the calmer Augustan age, distinct from both the more universalized condemnations of Swift, and the knowing digs and jibes of Arbuthnot, Defoe, Mandeville, and other contemporaries.

Law in the community

So there is more evidence for continuity in expressed public attitudes towards the law and lawyers before and after the Glorious Revolution than some recent writings might lead us to expect. But whether or not the law sank into greater disrepute as the eighteenth century progressed, did 'professional lawyers and courts, on the local as well as the national level, become to a degree disconnected from society at large'?[63] And supposing we were to allow, for the purposes of argument, that some such process of disconnection,

62 T. Baston, *Observations on Trade and A Publick Spirit* (London, 1732), 67, 105–6.
63 Brooks, *Lawyers, Litigations*, 3.

marginalization, or recession may indeed have occurred, would declining volumes of civil litigation be necessary or sufficient to explain the phenomenon?

Let us imagine, for example, despite Namier's assertion that 'in the eighteenth century Parliamentary politics were transacted, to a disastrous extent, in terms of jurisprudence', that the common law and its practitioners could be conclusively demonstrated to have enjoyed less national political influence and standing in the eighteenth century than they had maintained over the previous hundred years.[64] To explain such putative downgrading we should surely look first to the implications of James II's ousting and all those contemporaneous events which have been labelled 'The Triumph of the Lawyers', amounting to the removal of previous perceived threats to the institutional autonomy of the common law, whether from rival codes or arbitrary royal government, rather than to volumes of business passing through the courts.[65] Again, even if it could be established that there was a significant increase after 1689 (or 1700, or 1714) in public expressions of dissatisfaction with legal delays, expense, and uncertainty, might not such a (hypothetical) phenomenon be largely explained in similar terms, by invoking the enhanced independence from executive control and pressures which legal institutions were perceived to enjoy under a new constitutional and political dispensation?[66] Circulation of critical comment was undoubtedly enlarged and intensified by the continued expansion and proliferation of print media, and the lapse of pre-publication censorship from 1695. But how far such wider dissemination may have enhanced the impact of the message is yet another tricky question. The extent to which the emergent cultural prestige of natural philosophy and the post-Restoration fashion of the virtuoso damaged the law's standing among the self-conscious proponents of enlightenment is also difficult to measure, although some such development seems at least feasible. At all events, if the law and lawyers did indeed lose some cultural, political, and social ground after the Glorious Revolution, the explanation need not lie exclusively or largely in the contracting sphere of civil litigation.[67]

This point may be extended. Just as the statistics of court usage, however imperfect, are far better for common law jurisdictions than civil or ecclesiastical

[64] L.B. Namier, *The Structure of Politics at the Accession of George III* (2nd edn, London, 1957), 42.

[65] Cf. M. Landon, *The Triumph of the Lawyers: Their Role in English Politics, 1678–1689* (University of Alabama Press, 1970).

[66] This is not to deny the continued and in some respects heightened political pressures brought to bear on Hanoverian judges: cf. D. Lemmings, 'The Independence of the Judiciary in Eighteenth-Century England', in *The Life of the Law*, ed. P. Birks (London, 1993), 125–49.

[67] Interestingly, Lemmings suggests that not until the late eighteenth century did works of fiction depict the law as an external, alien force; 'early and mid-century novelists like Swift, Defoe, Fielding and Smollett . . . were obviously very familiar with all kinds of legal proceedings': *Professors of the Law*, 320.

or customary courts, so most explanations of case load changes over time relate to the common law courts. This is an unfortunate anomaly; the pre-1640 church courts clearly played a far from insignificant social role, so the reasons for their contracting jurisdiction in and after the later seventeenth century should be of considerable interest. It seems obvious enough that after 1689 this must have owed something to the Act of Toleration's partial legitimization of protestant dissent, and the consequent weakening of excommunication as a sanction, developments which had no comparable impact on the secular courts. In sum, the ecclesiastical courts had plainly become quite marginal institutions by the end of the eighteenth century, but their decline is difficult to integrate with any general explanation of legal recession.[68]

Nor can lack of popular involvement, direct or indirect, in common law civil litigation be necessarily inferred from a drop in the numbers of case filings, unless we are also able to count the numbers of litigants involved in each suit and somehow or other measure the varying extent and nature of their participation. At the same time, it must be recognized that much contact with the law took place out of court and via experiences other than direct participation in litigation as plaintiff or defendant. Thus a mid-eighteenth-century magistrate like the Reverend Edmund Tew JP, rector of Boldon, County Durham, 'provided a vital source of state authority' in his quasi-judicial but domestic role of hearing complaints and promoting settlements among his parishioners and neighbours.[69] Again, Whitehaven's epic legal contests of the late seventeenth and early eighteenth centuries often drew in a far wider range of persons than those formally named as parties to the suits. Churches notes that

> a law suit in Chancery which went beyond a bill of complaint and its answer to the taking of depositions was played out over many months, frequently years, and involved a chain of people from the great merchants who attempted arbitration, partners in ships and cargoes, the servant girl who minded the shop to the cooper who made the barrels and kegs – witnesses and swearers of affidavits who came from many levels of society, all gaining some knowledge of legal process, its possibilities and disadvantages.[70]

The wide range of out-of-court legal services which 'Honest Industrious Tradesmen' might require is illustrated by an undated handbill advertising the services of a cut-price 'CONVEYANCING BUSINESS' conducted from 'No 7, CHARLES COURT, STRAND, NEAR HUNGERFORD':

[68] See however Lemmings, 'Women's Property and the Consistory Court of London', 84–5, which suggests that rising fees reduced access to the London consistory court, as may also have been the case in many secular jurisdictions.
[69] G. Morgan and P. Rushton, 'The Magistrate, the Community and the Maintenance of an Orderly Society in Eighteenth-century England', *Historical Research*, 76 (2003), 54–77.
[70] Churches, 'Business at Law', 947.

> where Gentlemen, Tradesmen, &c. may have Bonds, Agreements, Articles of Copartnership, Leases . . . Mortgages, Bills of Sale, Letters of Licence and Deeds of Composition, Bonds of Arbitration, Releases, Marriage Articles, Settlements, Wills, Letters of Attorneys, Deeds of Trust and Partition, Memorials, Petitions, Letters . . . Advice in Law Matters from One Shilling each Question, N.B. Rents gathered and Debts got in.[71]

The burgeoning print media played no less crucial a part in spreading knowledge of the law than in publicizing its shortcomings. When the cathedral city of Worcester's leading bookseller advertised his wares in 1760, legal titles – including volumes of the statutes, Blackstone's antiquarian and occasional writings, three trial transcripts, and Giles Jacob's *The Complete Parish Officer* (1750) – comprised the largest category among eighty-six stock items listed. Law books also figured prominently in advertisements placed by booksellers in the provincial press, as they did in metropolitan newspaper and journal advertising.[72] Landholders, clergymen, merchants, and parish officers constituted a sizeable secondary market for at least some categories of professional law books. Lay readers could also choose between a wide selection of self-help manuals, a genre headed by Jacob's *Every Man his own Lawyer* (which saw ten editions between 1736 and 1788). While little systematic legal education was provided at the inns of court during the eighteenth century, a plethora of self-help books offered legal advice and information, of admittedly variable quality and utility, to a potentially vast non-professional readership. Another major source of current information about the law was the London-based newspaper and periodical press, which published extensive coverage of legal proceedings, notably trials and judgments, both in criminal and civil cases, as well as occasional columns of 'Law Intelligence' and public apology notices which deflected or more often resolved a prosecution.[73]

So despite powerful countervailing attractions – the pursuit of commercial profit, nature's secrets, and maritime or imperial glory – it seems premature to conclude that eighteenth-century Englishmen and women were generally less knowledgeable about or interested in the law's workings than their parents and

[71] 'To the Public' (n.p., n.d.): collection of A. Taussig, London.

[72] J. Feather, *The Provincial Book Trade in Eighteenth-Century England* (Cambridge, 1985), 75; M. Cooper, 'The Worcester Book-Trade in the Eighteenth Century', *Worcestershire Historical Society, Occasional Publications* (1997), 8, 28. C. Ferdinand, 'Constructing the Framework of Desire: How Newspapers Sold Books in the Seventeenth and Eighteenth Centuries', in *News, Newspapers and Society in Early Modern Britain*, ed. J. Raymond (London, 1999), 164.

[73] J. Oldham, 'Law Reporting in the English Newspapers 1756–1786', *American Journal of Legal History*, 31 (1987), 177–206; D.T. Andrew, 'The Press and Public Apologies in Eighteenth-century London', in *Law, Crime and English Society 1660–1830*, ed. N. Landau (Cambridge, 2002), 208–29.

grandparents.[74] Perhaps the extraordinary pre-1640 surge in civil litigation (even if much of that may turn out to have been little or nothing more than a form of debt collection, or loan registration) had helped effect a permanent change in communal expectations about the law's accessibility and efficacy. Henceforth state power mediated by the rule of law could be assumed to function as part of the complex background context which informed and supported the everyday interactions of subjects throughout the realm.[75] Thus people would hardly have needed to go to court in order to utilize and depend on understandings of the law in countless routine individual transactions. In addition they might well have been increasingly dissuaded from litigation by a new cultural emphasis on the virtues of civility and politeness, together with a rational appreciation of the likely costs and risks: 'so much trouble & vexation, as well as expenses, always attending it, & so great hazard & uncertainty in the Issue, let your cause be ever so good'.[76] If this speculation has any merit, it could go some way towards explaining why the very high per capita rates of involvement in civil actions reported for the later sixteenth and early seventeenth centuries were never subsequently matched, let alone exceeded.[77]

Conclusion

Overarching explanatory hypotheses which stimulate discussion, controversy, and further investigation are always welcome. Given the current lack of consensus in explaining the putative 'massive fall in civil litigation' after the Civil War,[78] it would be shortsighted as well as ungenerous to make too much of the unconvincing nature of some key causal links postulated to date between booms and busts in court business on the one hand, and broad changes in the

[74] Concerns voiced by Blackstone and Bentham about the gentry's legal ignorance were hardly novel; compare B.L., *The Institucion of a Gentleman* (London, 1555), sig. Diiiivvv; R. Mulcaster, *Positions* (London, 1581), 208; T. Fuller, *The Holy and the Profane State*, ed. M.G. Walten (New York, 1938), ii. 24; Edward Hyde, Earl of Clarendon, 'Dialogue Concerning Education', in *A Collection of Several Tracts of the Rt. Hon. Edward, Earl of Clarendon* (London, 1727), 327–8.

[75] For the underlying concept and some of the wording of this passage I am indebted to M. Kyrgier and R. van Krieken, 'The Character of the Nation', in *Whitewash*, ed. R. Manne (Melbourne, 2003), 103.

[76] British Library, MS Stowe 748, f. 148: Rev. John Clough to Edward Cave, London, 17 February 1737 (a letter written to persuade the recipient 'as a Friend, to put an end to it all as fast as possibly you can, & never more engage in Law, unless by the last necessity you are driven to it').

[77] The apparent resurgence of litigation volumes in the later eighteenth century may then be seen to reflect a combination of socio-economic causes, notably rising population and expanding economic activity.

[78] H. Horwitz, 'Changes in the Law and Reform of the Legal Order: England (and Wales) 1689–1760', *Parliamentary History*, 21 (2002), 307–8.

law's cultural and social role on the other. (The problem of explanation is further complicated by the fact that a contemporaneous falling-off in civil litigation appears to have been identified in eighteenth-century France, Germany, and Spain, although apparently not Ireland, a circumstance perhaps pointing to the vital underlying role of demography.)[79] Some scepticism is nonetheless warranted, lest we conclude that whereas the non-criminal law functioned in sixteenth-century England primarily as a tool of popular participation, by the eighteenth century it had become merely another mode of elite oppression. The reality must have been more complex than that, not least because of the great mass of comment from medieval (and indeed Biblical) times onwards which emphasized how cruelly the odds were stacked against poorer litigants, those like Langland's Plowman, and the early Tudor poet who complained that for want of money his cause did not speed.[80] Nor was it only naive laymen who expressed such sentiments; in 1637 the Middle Temple barrister Charles Cocks, 'Exigenter of the Common Bench', set aside £40 p.a. for barristers to act as independent arbiters of poor men's causes, 'having observed that multiplicity of Suits in law tend not only to the disquiet of the Common weale but the Decay of many Familyes'.[81]

The Tudor litigation boom doubtless owed more to client demand than the self-enriching activities of pettyfogging lawyers, notwithstanding much contemporary assertion to the contrary. Certainly the judiciary and parliament both made efforts to curb attorney malpractice, even if the effectiveness of their good intentions must remain uncertain. Yet that '[t]here were of course public complaints about unqualified or dishonest practitioners'[82] seems scant acknowledgement of the vehemence, volume, and persistence of such criticism. Complaints about attorneys stirring up suits among the common people may indeed have become less prominent in the eighteenth century than under Elizabeth and the early Stuarts. Yet attacks on lawyers for fomenting quarrels and otherwise manufacturing business did continue, as for instance in Christopher Smart's assertion that 'Division crowns the labour of the lawyer, and keeps his practice alive', or the near-contemporaneous tract which claimed that 'there are more persons confined in prison, and executed, in England than there are in any parts in Europe proportionately', thanks not least to the lawyers' 'Ignorance, Artifice and Tricks'.[83]

[79] Brooks, *Lawyers, Litigation*, 91. It may also be worth bearing in mind that the later seventeenth to mid-eighteenth centuries saw a marked contraction in public school, university, and inns of court enrolments.

[80] Cf. C. Hill, *Liberty Against the Law* (London, 1996).

[81] Middle Temple Library, miscellaneous manuscripts, indenture tripartite, 27 September 1637 (copy); Cocks's plan seems to have been frustrated by disputes about the properties he bequeathed to his trustees: see *Minutes of Parliament of the Middle Temple . . . 1650–1703*, ed. C. T. Martin (London, 1905), 1160, 1190, 1194–5, 1203, et seq.

[82] Brooks, *Lawyers, Litigation*, 131.

[83] C. Smart, *Index to Mankind* (London, 1757), 13; [Anon.], *A Compassionate Address to*

Even if fewer people (either absolutely, or as a proportion of the total English population – and that distinction may be of some importance in view of the likely post-1650 demographic contraction) were taking advantage of the full range of legal services available in the eighteenth than the seventeenth century – and that case remains at least contentious – the courts also continued to provide non-elite litigants with a channel for redressing grievances and asserting rights. Here are two specific examples. In 1756 a jury at the Middlesex assizes awarded Elizabeth Folkstone, a maidservant under the age of majority, £150 damages for wrongful arrest and imprisonment on a malicious indictment of felony preferred by a dairy farmer, her former master, and his wife (the latter seems to have been largely responsible for 'causing her to be arrested and kept in prison 43 days till presenting the bill of indictment which the jury would not find'). The presiding judge minuted 'I did not express any dissatisfaction at the quantum, though I rather think £50 would have been enough'; the reaction of Elizabeth, her friends and supporters, is not recorded.[84] But an expressive material artefact survives from the aftermath of a trial at the Maidstone assizes before Lord Chief Justice Mansfield in August 1772, in the form of a handsome silver cup presented by the Sea Salters Company of Fishermen to 'Thomas Benson Esqre in Consideration of his Services in the Prosecution of their Oyster Fishery Cause wherein a Verdict was Obtain'd in their Favour against the Tenants of Lord Bolingbroke on a Special Issue'.[85]

However exceptional and isolated they may have been, these (admittedly uncontextualized) fragments are difficult to integrate with the quantitative evidence produced by the scholars to whose labours tribute was paid at the beginning of this chapter. But any overview of law and litigation in eighteenth-century England must surely seek to come to terms with the whole of what was plainly a very complex reality. Not until the pioneering work of Chris Brooks and others is complemented by a great deal more detailed research, especially along occupational, regional, and local lines, will we be anywhere near doing justice to the many-faceted experiences and implications of going to law in early modern England.

the High and Mighty In Behalf of the Poor Distressed Prisoners (London, 1753), 17. See also [Anon.], *The Gentleman Instructed . . . with Reflections on some Modern Practitioners of Law. Pt. III* (London, 1712), 83–4.

[84] Lincoln's Inn Library, 'Legal Notebook of Sir Dudley Ryder (1754–1756)', Document 16, pp. 38–41.

[85] The cup is now accession item 1985–363A&B, Dewitt Wallace Decorative Arts Museum, Colonial Williamsburg Foundation, Virginia. A 'Thos Benson' was listed as attorney in the Crown Office, London, by T. Mortimer, *The Universal Director; or the Nobleman & Gentleman's True Guide to the Masters and Professors of the Liberal & Polite Arts and Sciences & of the Mechanic Arts, Manufactures & Trades, Established in London and Westminster & their Environs* (London, 1763); this information was obtained from CD 1 of the *Biography Database 1680–1830* (Newcastle upon Tyne, 1995).

7

Litigation, participation, and agency in seventeenth- and eighteenth-century England

CHRISTOPHER BROOKS*

Loud complaints have been made against the courts of law, for their procrastination and expence; perhaps with reason.

William Hutton, *Courts of Requests: Their Nature, Utility, and Powers Described, with a Variety of Cases Determined in that of Birmingham* (Birmingham, 1787), 7

Introduction

This chapter considers the relationship between changing patterns of civil litigation and more general changes in the nature of the relationship between state and society over the period from roughly 1500 to 1800. Its starting point is a counter-intuitive and somewhat paradoxical finding that has now been confirmed by a number of scholars. Between about 1550 and 1600, the number of actions entering the central royal courts in London, as well as those coming before local jurisdictions such as borough courts or ecclesiastical courts, underwent what appears to have been a historic and probably unprecedented increase. Apart from a temporary drop caused by the disruption of the mid-century Civil Wars, the volume of litigation remained at high levels during the later seventeenth century, but it then plummeted during the course of the early eighteenth century to a low point around 1750 that contemporaries recognized and commented upon. Litigious legal business grew again in the late eighteenth and early nineteenth centuries, but an increasingly large proportion of cases were then being heard in local rather than central jurisdictions. It is unlikely that either the number of cases entering the royal courts in London, or the overall volume of litigation per head of population, ever again exceeded the levels reached in the reign of James I.[1]

* I would like to acknowledge the British Academy's contribution towards my travel expenses for the conference in Canberra which gave rise to this chapter.

[1] C.W. Brooks, *Lawyers, Litigation and English Society since 1450* (London, 1998), chs 2–4, and statistical material therein.

What is now pretty commonly referred to as the eighteenth-century decline in litigation was not altogether unique. The later fifteenth century and the first three-quarters of the twentieth century reveal similar patterns.[2] But the fact that a precipitate drop followed the unprecedented increases is particularly intriguing. It is clear, moreover, that the flow and ebb of litigation was linked to historic changes in the size and shape of the legal professions, both at the bar and in the world of the general practitioners of the law, the attorneys and solicitors. Watershed increases in the proportion of lawyers to population in the earlier period were followed by significant contraction and attempts to regulate the admission of newcomers.[3] The heyday of the inns of court under Elizabeth and the early Stuarts was followed by a collapse in organized legal education so complete that its institutional foundations had to be rebuilt during the first half of the nineteenth century.[4]

Litigation, law, and participation c. 1560–1700

Historians of the sixteenth and seventeenth centuries now routinely depict the increase in court business as both a consequence and a constituent of significant economic, social, and political changes. Apparently reflecting the growth in the number of economic transactions in a society highly reliant on credit, and where the use of legal instruments of all kinds was so ubiquitous that nearly every phase of the life cycle of an individual left a footprint in the form of a legal act,[5] it accompanied a surge in the commercialization of English society that followed the first sustained population increases since the Black Death of the mid-fourteenth century.[6] At the same time, it has been incorporated into interpretations of the early modern state that recognize the widespread use of courts on the local and regional as well as national levels, and which stress the importance of broadly based social and political participation by social groups ranging from the greatest landowners down to the smaller farmer or the urban tradesman who had some kind of economic stake in civil society, and who may just have been a player in what Keith Wrightson

[2] Ibid., ch. 4.

[3] Ibid., chs 5–6; D. Lemmings, *Professors of the Law: Barristers and English Legal Culture in the Eighteenth Century* (Oxford, 2000).

[4] C.W. Brooks and M. Lobban, 'Apprenticeship or Academy? The Idea of a Law University 1830–1860', in J.A. Bush and A. Wijffels (eds), *Learning the Law: Teaching and the Transmission of Law in England 1150–1900* (London, 1999), 353–83.

[5] For some examples see C.W. Brooks, R.H. Helmholz, and P. Stein, *Notaries Public in England Since the Reformation* (Norwich, 1991), 76–95.

[6] C. Muldrew, *The Economy of Obligation: The Culture of Credit and Social Relations in Early Modern England* (London, 1998). K. Wrightson, *Earthly Necessities: Economic Lives in Early Modern Britain* (New Haven, CT, 2000), 175.

has called the 'politics of the parish'.[7] It sometimes seems that a kind of petty bourgeois proclivity for legal wrangling has replaced coercion and oppression as the principal ligaments of a polity that was nevertheless notably unable to resolve a legalistic constitutional struggle about the nature and sources of political authority without descending into a half-century of civil war and serious political conflict.

Steve Hindle has argued that ignoring litigation as a dimension of governance ignores the extent to which the subjects of the crown might draw upon its institutions as a resource to serve their own interests. Mike Braddick depicts recourse to the courts as a significant ingredient in the state formation (without any hidden hands) that he sees characterizing the two centuries between 1500 and 1700.[8] These views correspond nicely with Mark Goldie's recent attempt to show that participation by middling people in a wide range of local officeholding (which almost always had a strong legal dimension) was a major feature of the *ancien régime* British state up to the reforms of the 1830s, and that such activity allowed sufficient scope for political influence and the achieving of necessary ends that the vast majority could live contentedly under a form of government that fell considerably short of perfect representative democracy.[9]

Everywhere we turn in the period prior to 1660 there are courts which were full of business, many of them organized to a significant degree on the basis of customary practices, and often managed by local authorities such as urban corporations. A number of recent studies have shown that large numbers of people were getting, or at least hoped to get, some benefit out of going to law. Women, for example, appeared in court surprisingly frequently, or at least sufficiently often for it to be a matter of misogynist comment. Their proclivity for suing out actions of slander in the ecclesiastical courts reveals the way in which they contested, negotiated, and shaped sexual and gender roles; despite the apparent disadvantages of coveture, marriage settlements and trusts made it possible for them to enjoy property rights to the degree that they were often argued over in court.[10] Seamen recovered wages; the political elites of towns engaged in partisan politics through the courts; free miners fought against those

[7] K. Wrightson, 'The Politics of the Parish in Early Modern England', in P. Griffiths, A. Fox, and S. Hindle (eds), *The Experience of Authority in Early Modern England* (Basingstoke, 1996), 10–46.

[8] S. Hindle, *The State and Social Change in Early Modern England 1550–1640* (Basingstoke, 2000), 13–15, ch. 9; M. Braddick, *State Formation in Early Modern England 1550–1700* (Cambridge, 2000), ch. 4.

[9] M. Goldie, 'The Unacknowledged Republic: Officeholding in Early Modern England', in T. Harris (ed.), *The Politics of the Excluded* (Basingstoke, 2001), 153–94.

[10] T. Stretton, *Women Waging Law in Elizabethan England* (Cambridge, 1998); W.R. Prest, 'Law and Women's Rights in Early Modern England', *The Seventeenth Century*, 6(2) (1991), 169–87; Laura Gowing, *Domestic Dangers: Women, Words and Sex in Early Modern England* (Oxford, 1996).

who were attempting to take away their means of earning a living; copyholders (small landholders) raised 'common purses' so that they could go to law to fend off oppressive landlords and maintain the rights to their land; those who quarrelled with their neighbours, or who were involved in affrays, might take out a recognisance (a form of penal bond) with a local magistrate that bound the parties to keep the peace with one another.[11] Even the potential exception, the ecclesiastical courts, appear to prove the rule. According to Martin Ingram, they prospered because they met the needs of a population that valued the maintenance of moral and sexual reputations, and which sometimes needed help in managing the making and breaking of marriages.[12]

Easy access to courts was a source of both individual agency and, possibly, a high degree of political consciousness that was diffused more widely than we might expect from considering other kinds of sources. Local attorneys who could take cases to the royal courts in London were readily available in provincial towns; indeed, the commercialization of legal services might be summed up by the fact that noticeable numbers of them not only resided in rooms in urban inns, but actually owned alehouses.[13] Barristers and judges, meanwhile, were busy making arguments that were rehearsed in the legal inns and/or found their way into the earliest published law reports.[14] Legal discourse (rhetoric), some of which had a noticeable populist thrust, and most of which emphasized legally protected self-interest as a primary reason for an individual adhering to authority, was exchanged regularly with the wider public and formed the common currency of political debate at least up until the outbreak of Civil War in 1642.[15]

[11] G.F. Steckley, 'Litigious Mariners: Wage Cases in the Seventeenth-Century Admiralty Court', *Historical Journal*, 42 (1999), 315–45; Paul Halliday, *Dismembering the Body Politic: Partisan Politics in England's Towns, 1650–1730* (Cambridge, 1998). A. Wood, 'Custom, Identity and Resistance: English Free Miners and their Law, c. 1550–1800', in Griffiths *et al.* (eds), *The Experience of Authority*, 249–85; C.W. Brooks, 'Contemporary Views of "Feudal" Social and Political Relationships in Sixteenth and Seventeenth-century England', in N. Fryde, P. Monnet, and O.G. Oexle (eds), *Die Gegenwart des Feudalismus, Présence du féodalisme et présent de la féodalité, The Presence of Feudalism* (Göttingen, 2002), 109–35; S. Hindle, 'The Keeping of the Public Peace', in Griffiths *et al.* (eds), *The Experience of Authority*, 213–48. See also J.R. Dickinson and J.A. Sharpe, 'Courts, Crime and Litigation in the Isle of Man, 1580–1700', *Historical Research*, 72 (1999), 315–45; A. Shepard, 'Legal Learning and the Cambridge University Courts', *Legal History*, 19(1) (1999), 62–74; C. Crawford, 'Patients' Rights and the Law of Contract in Eighteenth-Century England', *Social History of Medicine*, 13(3) (2000), 381–410.

[12] M. Ingram, *Church Courts, Sex and Marriage in England 1570–1640* (Cambridge, 1987).

[13] C.W. Brooks, *Pettyfoggers and Vipers of the Commonwealth: The 'Lower Branch' of the Legal Profession in Early Modern England* (Cambridge, 1986), 188.

[14] W.R. Prest, *The Rise of the Barristers: A Social History of the English Bar 1590–1640* (Oxford, 1986); J.H. Baker, *Readers and Readings in the Inns of Court and Chancery* (Selden Society Supplementary Series, vol. 13, 2000).

[15] I am thinking primarily of the lengthy set-piece speeches that prefaced the 'charges' that

The early seventeenth-century state was tenaciously monarchical, but it was also manifestly juridical. An often repeated theme was that the rule of law separated men from beasts and made civilized life possible by protecting the property and persons of the subjects. Courts, particularly those associated with the commissions of the peace, were important administrative organs. Local economic and political conflicts, no less than the more celebrated clashes between the Stuart kings and their parliaments, were fought out in the form of law suits, and many of the values that were central to the legal life of the realm also found their way into more general political discourse. Thomas Hobbes, for example, was not an admirer of the common law or its practitioners, but one of the key concerns of his political philosophy – how people can be made to keep their promises – was also implicit in the masses of debt litigation that characterized the period.[16] Even though he never seems to have considered a legal career for himself, John Locke, who attacked patriarchalism and arbitrary rule in the 1680s by claiming that those with some stake in civil society had a right to determine its government, was the son of a Somerset attorney whose surviving notebook is in a number of respects a remarkable template of the interests of his son.[17] In addition to a large number of medical recipes and brief observations on religion and moral philosophy, it also records John Locke senior's work as a local lawyer and includes notes on bastardy orders, business at the assizes, and the names of those who composed the grand jury at one of the meetings of the local quarter sessions.[18] Coincidentally, either this John Locke, or more likely a relation, is also named as the foreman of the homage of the manorial court held at Beaminster Prima (in Dorsetshire) in 1651. The court's proceedings included the hearing of presentments about the numbers of sheep that were to be allowed on the commons and the fouling of the streets of the village by dunghills. The tenants had been involved in a Chancery case in 1632. The custom of the manor was that when a tenant died and surrendered his land, the other tenants went to the lord to discuss

were given by judges, lawyers, and country squires at the opening of meetings of quarter sessions and assizes. In addition, of course, lawyers and law figured constantly in the political and constitutional debates of the early seventeenth century. For examples, see Brooks, *Lawyers, Litigation*, chs 8 and 9 and A. Cromartie, 'The Constitutionalist Revolution: The Transformation of Political Culture in Early Stuart England', *Past and Present*, 193 (1999), 76–121.

16 Brooks, *Lawyers, Litigation*, 89.

17 For what appears to be Locke's only significant technical legal argument see J.R. Milton and P. Milton, 'Selecting the Grand Jury: A Tract by John Locke', *Historical Journal*, 40(1) (1997), 155–94. On the close relationship between Locke and his father see Lord Peter King, *The Life of John Locke with Extracts from His Correspondence, Journals and Common-Place Books* (London, 1829), 1–9.

18 B[ritish] L[ibrary], MS Additional 28273. Details of the life of John Locke senior are given in the article on his son in *Dictionary of National Biography*.

whether a new entry fine could be agreed. If it could not, then the manorial jury was to decide.[19]

A similar picture emerges from the writings of another Somerset attorney of the middle third of the seventeenth century, Robert Powell of Wells. He composed one of the earliest published histories of the reign of King Alfred[20] as a companion-piece for an otherwise unremarkable *Treatise of the Antiquity, Authority, Vses and Iurisdiction of the Ancient Courts of Leet.* Having praised Alfred for reducing his anarchic 'kingdom to the subordinate rule of orderly government' by instituting national laws and dividing the country into its most ancient units of local government, shires, hundreds, and tithings, Powell appended to his *Treatise* (published in 1642) an 'Explanation of The old Oath of Legeance' which was due from the tithingmen of the leet to the king. In this he provided one of the earliest examples I have come across of a fully developed argument that the subject's duty of obedience to the monarch was directly related to the degree to which the sovereign protected civil and religious liberties. Castigating the illegality of Ship Money, Powell provided a number of historical examples of clashes between kings and people over such issues.[21]

The decline in litigation: the question of causes

Compared with the interest the high levels of sixteenth- and seventeenth-century litigation have attracted, the eighteenth-century decline has up to now been largely neglected by non-specialists. The phenomenon does not figure to any significant extent in the most recent characterizations of the eighteenth-century state, despite the fact that one strand of interpretation has stressed the ongoing importance of highly participatory forms of local

[19] Dorset Record Office, Dorchester. Accession numbers 6282, 6269, 6290. Court books and eighteenth-century copy of customs of the manor, Beaminster Prima. The known landholdings of John Locke senior were in Pensford, Somerset, about six miles south of Bristol. His family were originally from Charlton Court in Dorset, but there is no other evidence of a personal connection with Beaminster, which is near the border between Somerset and Dorset.

[20] Robert Powell of Wells and of the Society of New-Inne, *The Life of Alfred or Alured: The first Institutior of surordinate government in this Kingdome, and Refounder of the Vniversity of Oxford. Together with a Parallell of our Soveraigne Lord, K Charles untill this year, 1634* (London, 1634).

[21] Robert Powell, *A Treatise of the Antiquity, Authority, Vses and Iurisdiction of the Ancient Courts of Leet, or view of Franck-Pledge, and of Subordination of Government derived from the Institution of Moses, the first Legislator: And the first imitation of him in this Island of Great Britaine by King Alfred and continued ever Since. Together with Additions and alterations of the Moderne Lawes and Statutes inquirable at those Courts, untill this present Yeare, 1642. With a large Explication of the old Oath of Allegiance and the Kings Royall office of Protection annexed* (London, 1642).

government.[22] The eighteenth century has long been, and continues to be, the focus of much of the best British socio-legal history, but most of it has concentrated on crime. Although it seems likely that similar patterns were experienced in other eighteenth-century states, including France and Spain,[23] the suggestion that there was a significant decline in the use of civil courts is a relatively recent finding, and thus far we lack the volume and range of studies of particular courts and types of action that are now available for the seventeenth century. Hardly any of the writers who have attached broader significance to the increase in litigation in the sixteenth and seventeenth centuries have as yet fully explored the possible consequences of its subsequent fall.

Admittedly, any attempt at broader generalization has first of all to confront tricky problems about causation that involve weighing up juridical factors on the one hand and broader social and demographic configurations on the other. For example, an increase in the amount of hard currency in circulation from the 1690s onwards, and technical legal changes that facilitated the negotiability of informal written instruments such as promissory notes and bills of exchange, may have led to a decline in the numbers of actions of debt, a development of considerable importance since debt cases constituted by far the largest single category of litigation brought in local courts and in central jurisdictions such as King's Bench and Common Pleas.[24] Yet this factor alone does not seem to account for all of the observable changes. While it may for example have been a reason for some of the fall-off in the business of the court of Chancery, which had frequently been resorted to in connection with debt cases in the early seventeenth century, the decline in the work of the court in the eighteenth century seems to have occurred across the whole spectrum of its activities. In the ecclesiastical courts, debt was very rarely the issue at stake, and in the court of Common Pleas there was a fall in the total number of cases that were eventually tried before a jury, regardless of the cause of action.[25]

The phenomenon was so widespread, and included so many different tribunals, that there seems to be relatively little scope for explaining falls in one court by increases in others. It may be that actions of slander brought by married women to defend their sexual reputations were to some degree pushed out of the ecclesiastical courts in the second half of the eighteenth century because the stories that were retailed by the litigants were too graphic,

[22] David Eastwood, *Government and Community in the English Provinces 1700–1870* (Basingstoke, 1997). Nor, of course, does it figure in the writings of those who look towards war and the cost of war as the principal driving force. See J. Brewer, *The Sinews of Power: War, Money and the English State 1688–1783* (London, 1989).

[23] Brooks, *Lawyers, Litigation*, 91.

[24] This point is explored at some length in ibid., ch. 3. See also, '*An Exact and Industrious Tradesman*': *The Letter Book of Joseph Symson of Kendal 1711–1720*, ed. S.D. Smith (British Academy Records of Social and Economic History, New Series, 34, Oxford, 2002), lxv–lxx.

[25] See in particular, Brooks, *Lawyers, Litigation*, 32.

or contained too much rough language, for the polite sensibilities of the court officials, who in any case made very little money out of the business.[26] Otherwise, however, hardly any evidence has been uncovered that points definitively towards the decline being the result of either legislative or judicial initiatives, and it is hard to resist the observation that with the exception of Lord Mansfield, chief justice of King's Bench between 1756 and 1786, very few eighteenth-century judges made much of a mark for originality of any kind. In fact of all the juridical factors so far assembled in connection with the drop in the number of civil plaints, increases in court fees and other associated costs of legal services (lawyers' charges) appear to be the most striking, a point I will return to shortly.[27]

By contrast, although there are serious problems in linking cause and effect, a number of general social and structural features of the later seventeenth and early eighteenth centuries appear at least compatible with the alterations in court usage.[28] After over a century in which population doubled, the period from 1650 to 1750 was one of near perfect demographic stagnation. Although increases in overseas trade added to the nation's commercial wealth, in the long term the level pegging of population, coupled with improvements in productivity, led to falling agricultural prices. Resulting in higher real wages, this conjuncture may have been a good thing for those with little or no land, but it also contributed to a notable erosion in the position of small farmers, an important group that had been economically successful under the Tudors and earlier Stuarts and a mainstay in all kinds of participation that stretched from serving as constables or jurors to voting in parliamentary elections.

In terms of litigation, these changes coincide with a general shift of business away from the provinces towards London, and away from regions such as East Anglia and the South West, which had formerly been agricultural power-houses, towards the newly 'industrializing' North and North-east.[29] Furthermore, economic and demographic reconfiguration was most likely accompanied by the conversion of a large number of customary tenures, particularly copyholds, into leaseholds, and the further decline of the institution that had most characterized the juristic life of rural communities in the period up to 1640, the manorial court. Remarkably, the Webbs' book on the manor and the borough, published in 1903, is the last attempt at a serious survey of the state of these institutions during the period, and while they justifiably cautioned about the need to take full account of fairly numerous local

[26] Polly Morris, 'Defamation and Sexual Reputation in Somerset 1733–1850', (Warwick University Ph.D. thesis, 1985), 6, 13, 17, 136, 144, 146, 156, 189. It appears that litigation fell steadily within this jurisdiction through the eighteenth century, though Morris argues that the defamation jurisdiction continued to be important to plebeian women.

[27] See below, pp. 168–9.

[28] Brooks, *Lawyers, Litigation*, 36–9, 52–4.

[29] Ibid., 36–40.

exceptions, their overall conclusion was that by the early eighteenth century manorial courts were nowhere near as active as they had been previously.[30] To a large degree, the role of the manor in village life, both as an institution, and as an arena for participation, appears to have been superseded by the parish vestry,[31] but while the vestry was of critical importance because of the power it wielded in the administration of poor relief, it was not a court in any sense that a lawyer would recognize.[32] Its membership was often determined by collective oligarchy, its meetings were usually held behind closed doors, and it did not have the same powers as the manorial court to try small debts, inflict penalties for minor affrays, or to resolve disputes over public nuisances such as fouling water courses, over-commoning, keeping a dovecote, or failing to remove dung-heaps from the streets. In the seventeenth century, business of this kind contributed to the litigious mill in the localities, and cases involving such matters frequently came from the provinces to London when there were controversies over, or challenges to, local decisions. In the eighteenth century, the laws of settlement and the administration of poor relief led to many cases being brought in the central courts about the responsibility of parishes for paupers, but most of these were brought by one parish against another rather than by individuals.[33] The constitution of the parish seems to have been questioned less often,[34] and, of course, historians of the poor find it difficult to determine to what extent claimants thought that they had a 'right' to relief.[35]

It is often, and quite plausibly, argued that those aspects of the administrative and judicial role of the manor that did not pass to the parish were to a large extent taken over by those quintessential cogs in the judicial machinery, the English justices of the peace.[36] But, interestingly, the dockets of the courts of quarter sessions in the early eighteenth century were also less full than they had been one hundred years earlier, and in some respects the pattern closely

[30] S. and B. Webb, *English Local Government from the Revolution to the Municipal Corporations Act: The Manor and the Borough* (London, 1924 edn), 31, 116.

[31] J.R. Kent, 'The Centre and the Localities: State Formation and Parish Government in England circa 1640–1740', *Historical Journal*, 30 (1995), 363–404; Hindle, *State and Social Change*, ch. 8.

[32] A legal history of the vestry would undoubtedly produce valuable results. As late as the 1630s lawyers thought that the vestry as a secular institution was both lacking in any clear authority and little controlled by law. This is a point confirmed by the Webbs, *The Parish and the County* (London, 1963 edn), 5, where they declare that it would be impracticable to define the legal position of the vestry at the time of the accession of William and Mary.

[33] James Burrow, *A series of the decisions of the Court of King's Bench upon settlement-cases* (London, 1768); *Continuation of the decisions of the Court of King's Bench upon settlement–cases, by four additional years, ending in July 1772* (London, 1772)

[34] Webbs, *The Parish and the County*, 15, 37–40. The Webbs regarded parish government as petty tyranny.

[35] See the papers in T. Hitchcock, P. King, and P. Sharpe (eds), *Chronicling Poverty: The Voices and Strategies of the English Poor, 1640–1840* (Basingstoke, 1997).

[36] Norma Landau, *The Justices of the Peace, 1679–1760* (Berkeley, CA, 1984), 169–74.

mirrors that of civil litigation. According to Norma Landau, during the early eighteenth century, the rural populace appears to have become increasingly disinclined to request magisterial help in resolving disputes.[37] As Peter King has put it recently, between 1650 and 1750 there was a decline, or stagnation, in indicted crime in every non-metropolitan area so far studied until the advent of a new upsurge in the later eighteenth century that continued on to 1840.[38]

At the same time, the commissions of the peace were changing in ways that might have surprised an early seventeenth-century lawyer. The capacity of clerics to hold temporal offices (in cases of blood) was a highly contested topic in the initial stages of the Long Parliament, but by the early eighteenth century, active JPs were increasingly drawn from amongst the clergy, while the gentry, whom Blackstone thought woefully ignorant of the law, and the lawyers themselves were beginning to withdraw.[39] Tudor and Stuart lawyers insisted that justices of the peace were the creatures of statute who should be bound by the letter of the law; indeed, one of the benefits of the notorious court of Star Chamber was that it frequently heard cases where it was alleged that justices had over-reached their authority. In the eighteenth century, on the other hand, it seems that much of the work was done in the parlour of the justice sitting out of sessions, who frequently employed legal instruments, such as recognisances, in a magisterial regime characterized by mediation and judicial discretion, a good deal of which was increasingly sanctioned by parliamentary statute.[40]

Justices such as the rector of Boldon (Co. Durham), Edmund Tew, clearly did what they could to help people of all sorts within their districts who came before them with issues ranging from minor affrays or thefts to the problems associated with domestic violence.[41] None the less, this was evidently a regime in which formal legal thought at best shared the stage either with local manifestations of party politics or with the precepts of Anglican paternalist social theory. A decision by the justices of the peace in Kent that excluded attorneys and justices clerks from making motions before quarter sessions may well have had the effect of diminishing the impact of professional lawyers on the jurisdiction. Even though it was intended to transfer a monopoly over such business to barristers, barristers were both thinner on the ground and more expensive than country attorneys. If repeated in other parts of the country,

[37] Ibid., 194–5.

[38] Peter King, *Crime, Justice, and Discretion in England 1740–1820* (Oxford, 2000), 134–5.

[39] Landau, *Justices of the Peace*, 140ff. King, *Crime, Justice and Discretion*, 362.

[40] Ibid., 123, who comments that historians have failed fully to analyse why the controls on magisterial discretion imposed on felony cases by mid-sixteenth-century statutes were apparently allowed to lapse. Brooks, *Lawyers, Litigation*, ch. 7.

[41] *The Justicing Notebook (1750–64) of Edmund Tew, Rector of Boldon*, ed. Gwenda Morgan and Peter Rushton (Surtees Society, vol. 205, 2000). Interestingly, however, Tew seems to have departed the neighbourhood for holidays during several months of the year!

such measures may have had a part to play in the creation of what King describes as a golden age of discretionary justice.[42] Whereas the earliest printed manuals for JPs had arisen within the educational system of the inns of court in London, and been developed subsequently by leading sixteenth-century barristers such as William Lambarde, the major eighteenth-century work on the subject was produced by the Westmoreland vicar, Richard Burn, who had a doctorate in civil law from Oxford, and who served as an ecclesiastical court judge as well as a JP.[43] Organized in the form of an alphabetical commonplace book, Burn's work was concerned first of all with parliamentary authority and then with that of the reported case law. But he also accurately observed that the last major publication of this kind had been that of Michael Dalton, which was first published in the reign of James I, and he pointed out that there had been no authoritative collections of recent case law since the beginning of the reign of George II.

Perhaps it is not too far-fetched to see in all this the replacement of a legalistic conception of the role of the justice by one that was (to pick up a distinction made by Landau) at first patriarchal and then patrician. Early in the reign of James I, parliament evidently thought it necessary to pass a statute that would make it more difficult for individuals to bring law suits in the central courts against local officials such as constables and justices of the peace, presumably because the numbers were considered troublesome.[44] By contrast, according to Douglas Hay, in the second half of the eighteenth century, there was 'a well understood but largely unmentioned equivocation central to English justice'. Although the high court judges in theory controlled local magistrates, very few cases were brought against the summary decisions they made, and the judges at Westminster Hall seem to have been reluctant to intervene in their activities, even when these displayed incompetence or malicious and abusive conduct.[45]

Turning from rural to urban areas, while depictions of eighteenth-century agricultural society are generally gloomy, with occasional bright periods of revisionist optimism, the towns of the period are now normally described as beautifying centres of consumerism, commercialism, and an appetite for 'polite' recreation and leisure that was built on the affluence of the gentry and

[42] Landau, *Justices of the Peace*, 254; King, *Crime, Justice and Discretion*, ch. 4, 355–6, who also notes the importance of the growing intervention of local attorneys in summary courts after 1800 (85).

[43] *Dictionary of National Biography*. First published in 1755, *The Justice of the Peace and Parish Officer* quickly went through numerous editions and continued to provide the basis for enlargements into the nineteenth century.

[44] 7 James I c. 5; continued and enlarged in 21 James I c. 12.

[45] D. Hay, 'Dread of the Crown Office: The English Magistracy and King's Bench 1740–1800', in N. Landau (ed.), *Law, Crime, and English Society, 1660–1830* (Cambridge, 2002), 21.

provincial middling sort.[46] Of all the orthodox views of eighteenth-century society, this is the one that seems at first sight to sit least comfortably with the decline of litigation, especially when we consider that commercialization now looks a very plausible contender as a principal cause of the late sixteenth-century increase. Nevertheless, there are several features of Georgian urban life that may well have contributed to the decline in court business, which, it will be recalled, was as dramatic in the small debt courts of provincial towns as it was in the royal courts in London.

A case can be made for a deceleration in the English economy during the first half of the eighteenth century. Although the calculations are somewhat dependent on definitions, and although there are notable exceptions, it is also likely that overall urban population growth was significantly more dynamic in the late sixteenth and early seventeenth centuries than it was in the comparatively stagnant demographic conditions of the period from 1700 to 1750.[47] The late seventeenth and early eighteenth centuries are in fact notable for a decline in the remarkable process of in-migration, especially of boys seeking apprenticeships, that had characterized late Tudor and early Stuart towns. With a few exceptions, early eighteenth-century towns were prone to a kind of dynastic economic oligarchy, where sons stepped into their fathers' shoes rather than venturing forth on their own after a period of apprenticeship that might well take them away from home, as was common in the previous period. While the early eighteenth century saw a much less precipitous decline in urban guild organizations than is sometimes suggested (the major change occurred after 1750), it is clear that guilds were increasingly becoming self-recruiting, intergenerational social clubs rather than the loci of the highly participatory, and highly intrusive, regime of local social and economic life that they had been previously.[48]

In the seventeenth century, institutions such as guilds, and corporate urban government itself, had been venues for the resolution of conflict as well as sources of litigation that arose when individuals challenged regulation, or alternatively, when guildsmen or groups of residents set about criticizing or calling for the reform of local institutions. Furthermore, by the end of the 1730s at the latest, the erosion of the test of religious conformity as grounds for purging local officeholders had gradually removed a source of urban faction-fighting that had resulted in many cases coming from corporate towns into the court of King's Bench in connection with writs of *mandamus* and/or *quo*

46 The seminal text is P. Borsay, *The English Urban Renaissance: Culture and Society in the Provincial Town 1660–1770* (Oxford, 1989).

47 Brooks, *Lawyers, Litigation*, 37–9. J. Langton, 'Urban Growth and Economic Change c. 1688–1841', in Peter Clark (ed.), *The Cambridge Urban History of Britain: Volume 2, 1540–1840* (Cambridge, 2000), 462–90.

48 C.W. Brooks, 'Apprenticeship, Social Mobility and the Middling Sort', in J. Barry and C.W. Brooks (eds), *The Middling Sort of People: Culture, Society and Politics in England* (Basingstoke, 1994), 64–9.

warranto proceedings.[49] Though such actions did not altogether cease thereafter, it would seem that the passage of a private act in parliament became the preferred strategy for local groups who wanted to accomplish some objective that was opposed by entrenched officeholders.[50] Meanwhile the development of local government in unincorporated towns, which accounted for much of the urban growth of the period, retained a great deal of local particularity at least in part because relatively few cases concerning them were heard by the central courts.[51] The point here is not that political participation, including that of the formally disenfranchised, ceased; it clearly did not. Rather, in the eighteenth century, unlike the seventeenth, it appears less likely to have been channelled into the courts and the legal system.[52]

No less important, according to Bill Champion, whose study of local courts in Shrewsbury is the most comprehensive investigation yet undertaken of urban legal life across the period, the decline in litigation was accompanied also by a decline in the use by inhabitants of the local leet jurisdictions, which had formally served as fora for personal as well as public prosecution of minor affrays and the enforcement of community regulation. Occurring alongside a drop in small debt litigation in urban jurisdictions, it is hard to say how far this was a reaction against local town authorities and increased fees as opposed to a growing distaste within provincial society for nit-picking judicial invigilation of any kind. In the 1730s, for instance, there was a quite widely based movement within parliament for a drastic reduction in the powers of the ecclesiastical courts.[53] A recent study of London has suggested that the growing anonymity of metropolitan life, as well as a disinclination to get involved in other people's business, led to a drop in prosecutions for social and sexual offences.[54] In any case, Champion concludes that the fall-off in both kinds of legal business was part of the 'demise by 1720 of much of the old regulatory regime, and the massive decline that this entailed for aspects of institutional

[49] Halliday, *Dismembering the Body Politic*, chs 9–10.

[50] Julian Hoppit (ed.), *Failed Legislation, 1660–1800: Extracted from the Commons and Lords Journals* (London, 1997), Introduction [with Joanna Innes].

[51] See the Webbs, *The Manor and the Borough*.

[52] See for example K. Wilson, *The Sense of the People: Politics, Culture and Imperialism in England 1715–1785* (Cambridge, 1995). J. Hoppit, 'Patterns of Parliamentary Legislation 1660–1800', *Historical Journal*, 39 (1996), 129.

[53] Stephen Taylor, 'Tories and Anticlericalism: Ecclesiastical Courts Legislation in 1733', *Parliamentary History*, 19(3) (2000), 329–55. For an example of criticism of the church courts see [Anon.], *A Brief View of Ecclesiastical Jurisdiction addressed to Nathaniel Curzon and the Rest of the Gentlemen of the Committee appointed by Parliament for inquiry into the Abuses and Corruptions of Ecclesiastical Courts and Jurisdiction* (1733), 15. This accused the ecclesiastical and temporal court lawyers in the palatinate of Durham of colluding so that the 'poor client is often forced to bear the rapines and plunderings of both jurisdictions'.

[54] F. Dabhoiwala, 'Sex, Social Relations and the Law in Seventeenth- and Eighteenth-century London', in M. Braddick and J. Walter (eds), *Negotiating Power in Early Modern Society* (Cambridge, 2001), 85–101.

participation', such as pledging and the simple obligation of sitting on civil juries, which 'constitutes one of the most striking changes in English urban society' during the period.[55]

Some consequences of the decline in civil litigation

If the decline in recourse to courts can be placed within a broader context of social and institutional change in the early eighteenth century, its consequences can be measured in both the short and the longer terms. Since we now know that the nadir in court business was associated with a per capita shrinkage in the size of the barristers' branch of the profession, as well as in that of the general practitioners of the law, the attorneys and solicitors, it seems evident that lawyers would have been thinner on the ground, especially in the provinces, in the mid-eighteenth century than they had been in the mid-seventeenth.[56] At the same time, it seems certain that growing ossification in the late seventeenth-century legal bureaucracy,[57] and the effective resistance by officeholders to reform in the early eighteenth century,[58] helped to make increases in legal costs an important contributory cause of the decline in litigation. But what is no less striking is that legal costs continued to increase despite the fall-off in legal business so that escalating fees were also an important consequence of it for the remainder of the eighteenth century and beyond. Attorneys increasingly charged for 'pains taken' (a forerunner of by the hour) and for expenses rather than sticking to the fixed tariff of fees that had largely been maintained in the early seventeenth century, and the barristers seem to have compensated for the fall in the number of cases by multiplying the numbers of motions they made in court.[59] David Lemmings is surely right that

[55] W.A. Champion, 'Recourse to Law and the Meaning of the Great Litigation Decline, 1650–1750: Some Clues from the Shrewsbury Local Courts', in C.W. Brooks and M. Lobban (eds), *Communities and Courts in Britain* (London, 1997), 197.

[56] Lemmings, *Professors*; Brooks, *Lawyers, Litigation*, chs 5, 7. Though it should be kept in mind that the numbers increased again in the late eighteenth and early nineteenth centuries.

[57] There is a need for more research on the legal bureaucracies of the late seventeenth and eighteenth centuries, but see G.E. Aylmer, *The Crown's Servants: Government and Civil Service under Charles II, 1660–1685* (Oxford, 2002), 269–70, who concludes that post-Restoration civil servants were in general more likely to be less well trained and less committed to the public service than those of the Commonwealth and Protectorate. Aylmer is ambivalent about the success of government attempts to control fees.

[58] H. Horwitz, 'Changes in the Law and Reform of the Legal Order: England (and Wales), 1689–1760', *Parliamentary History*, 21(3) (2002), 301–24, who notes the consistent resistance of vested interests to reform in the early eighteenth century.

[59] Brooks, *Lawyers, Litigation*, 93–5. Though largely beyond the scope of this chapter it is worth noticing that one of the reasons for the increasing popularity in the late eighteenth

by the 1790s the bar's '*fin de siècle* culture of restrictive practices and optimising returns' was in large part the product of 'a paradoxical history of declining litigation, low enrolments, and public criticism, but rising fees, elite associations, and self-referencing "apologies and panegyrics"'.[60]

It is also clear that dilatory legal proceedings, high costs, and vexatious law suits could be manipulated to their advantage by those with sufficient inclination and means. For example, the extremely wealthy Cumbrian coal magnate Sir James Lowther apparently learned that the most effective strategy for getting the better of his business enemies was to encourage other people to take out law suits against them,[61] and in 1742, the cleric Edmund Law published an assize sermon that he had delivered at Carlisle which attacked litigiousness and was especially critical of the use of the law for the purposes of revenge.[62] By contrast, however, the effects of high costs and the relative inaccessibility of lawyers on the moderately well off and the poor are more problematic, largely because they can only be judged through complaint literature and a degree of speculation. Since eighteenth-century people were evidently not all that often at law, the historian is forced into the very difficult position of trying to attach some weight to negative evidence.

The trouble with complaint literature is that it has apparently been around and sticking like mud to lawyers and courts for as long as there has been written evidence, but it may be possible to read something into the way it changed over time. For example, the well-known and vocal demands for law reform that erupted in the wake of the fall of the Stuart monarchy in 1649 have often been portrayed as condemnations of lawyers and the courts that are universally applicable to any segment of the early modern period up until the 1830s, when changes along the lines of those advocated by the earlier reformers were finally

century of associations for prosecuting felons was the difficulty and cost of the process. See D. Philips, 'Good Men to Associate and Bad Men to Conspire: Associations for the Prosecution of Felons in England, 1760–1860', in D. Hay and F. Snyder (eds), *Policing and Prosecution in Britain 1750–1850* (Oxford, 1989), 118, 136.

60 Lemmings, *Professors*, 314.

61 The legal affairs of Lowther and other inhabitants of Whitehaven have been meticulously uncovered by Christine Churches, 'Business at Law: Retrieving Commercial Disputes from Eighteenth-Century Chancery', *Historical Journal*, 43(4) (2000), 937–54. Her 'False Friends, Spiteful Enemies: A Community at Law in Early Modern England', *Historical Research*, 71 (1998), 52–74, shows that in his younger days Lowther had not always been so successful in managing his legal business.

62 *Litigiousness Repugnant to the Laws of Christianity* (Cambridge, 1743), 18–19. Law, who was the father of the judge, Lord Ellenborough, also noted that the cost frequently came to more than the value of the loss. On the other hand, the use of law was 'necessary in such a Country as ours, where so much Property is lodged in private hands and at their free disposal; where the transferring of it is so frequent, where so many Contracts must occasion such a variety of Contests, and so many intricate Cases will arise, requiring to have the Sense of Laws explained by persons learned therein' (28).

implemented.[63] Yet it is not certain that any aspect of this formulation is true. One of the principal themes of the Civil War material, the desire to make legal knowledge accessible to the public so that every man could act as his own lawyer, represents the kind of argument for the appropriation (including of course a translation from esoteric languages into the vernacular) of a realm of valuable knowledge that was in fact most likely to be put forward within a community where there was both a high degree of contact with courts and a considerable understanding already of how they worked. At the same time, it is worth asking why most of the ideas put forward by radical thinkers associated with the Leveller milieu got no further than they did. While the evolution of political circumstances and the obstruction of common lawyers certainly played a significant part, something can be learned by looking more closely at the proposals on their own terms. For example, attractive sounding plans that called for the abolition of seigneurial obligations and institutions such as the manorial court could also involve the abolition of customary tenures such as copyholds and their conversion to what would in effect have been leases at market rents. It is not obvious that such a suggestion would have been all that appealing to the average smallholder who understood much of what he called his own in precisely those terms.[64] In any case, as I will show in more detail shortly, the kinds of courts envisioned by Civil War-period reformers, which involved high levels of participation by local gentry and middling sorts acting as both magistrates and jurors, were not the kinds of local institutions that were either demanded or created in early nineteenth-century reforms.[65]

Victorian institutional reforms were a response to the legal world that evolved in the wake of the decline of litigation, not that of the litigious seventeenth century,[66] and the general theme of complaint literature stretching from the 1720s to the 1830s was that legal process was so expensive and complicated that most people gave up their claims, or rights, rather than taking their chances by going to law.[67] The choice of quotations that might illustrate this point is virtually limitless, but one of the most telling remarks comes from the preface of a pamphlet published in 1750, which contains proposals for reducing the number of attorneys and solicitors on the grounds that the

[63] The most comprehensive account is D. Veall, *The Popular Movement for Law Reform, 1640–1660* (Oxford, 1970).

[64] See for example [Nicholson], *The Lawyers Bane or, The Lawes Reformation, and New Modell: Wherein the errours and corruptions both of the Lawyers and of the Law it selfe are manifested and declared. And Also, Some short and profitable Considerations laid downe for the redresse of them* (London, 1647), which is discussed in Brooks, 'Contemporary Views of "Feudal" Social and Economic Relationships', 134–5.

[65] For reform proposals which had some prospect of government support during the Protectorate see N.L. Matthews, *William Sheppard, Cromwell's Law Reformer* (Cambridge, 1989), esp. ch. 4.

[66] Brooks, *Lawyers, Litigation*, 101ff.

[67] Ibid., 44–7.

numbers of practitioners far exceeded the amount of legal business that there was to do. Evidently written by a non-professional, the preface to the work notes that while there was admiration for the English constitution and the common law in general terms, the practical state of affairs was that going to law was tedious, precarious, and expensive, a fact that 'intimidated many from legally asserting their just rights' as well as diminishing the business of practitioners.[68] In the seventeenth century, by contrast, there were many instances of elite remarks about the way lawyers encouraged ordinary people to go to law, or assert their rights, even when their cases were allegedly weak.

There is a need for more detailed research on the social and legal contexts of all kinds of dispute before eighteenth-century criticisms of the legal system can be confidently confirmed or dismissed. For example, complaints from tradesmen about the difficulty of using the courts in order to recover small debts were a particularly persistent theme from the 1720s through to the 1830s, but analyses of central court business suggest that a significant proportion of debt cases continued to be brought for relatively small sums of less than £10.[69] One interpretation of this might be that the complaints were unfounded, or at least that costs may not have been such a powerful deterrent as the complaint literature suggests. On the other hand, however, it is equally possible that the collection of such small sums continued to be of economic importance, but that only a smaller proportion of those with claims to make were able to do so and hence the volume of litigation fell, especially outside London. Similarly, recent studies by Margaret Hunt and Joanne Bailey have shown that ordinary women in areas as different as the North-east of England and metropolitan London knew how to use the law in domestic disputes, but the statistical evidence about ecclesiastical court usage in particular suggests that litigation was probably less often resorted to than it had been previously, and it is likely that the most common strategy for dealing with an abusive spouse was to go to a justice of the peace and ask that he make the offending party enter into a recognisance for good behaviour.[70]

[68] [Anon.], *Animadversions Upon the Present Laws of England; or, An Essay to Render them more useful and less expensive to all His Majesty's Subjects To which is added, A Proposal for Regulating the Practice, and reducing the number of Attornies, Sollicitors With A Supplement, Humbly submitted to the Serious Consideration of Both Houses of Parliament* (London, 1750), 3, 5–7.

[69] H. Horwitz, 'The *nisi prius* Trial Notes of Lord Chancellor Hardwicke', *Legal History*, 23(2) (2002), 152–66, esp. 160–3.

[70] M. Hunt, 'Wives and Marital Rights in the Court of Exchequer in the Early Eighteenth Century', in P. Griffiths and M.S.R. Jenner (eds), *Londonopolis: Essays in the Cultural and Social History of Early Modern London* (Manchester, 2001), 107–30; J. Bailey, 'Voices in Court: Lawyers' or Litigants'?', *Historical Research*, 74 (2001), 392–408. See also M. Berg, 'Women's Property and the Industrial Revolution', *Journal of Interdisciplinary History*, 34 (1993), 233–50. Elizabeth Foyster, 'At the Limits of Liberty: Married Women and Confinement in Eighteenth-century England', *Continuity and Change*, 17(1) (2002), 39–62,

Taking a different tack, Peter King argued convincingly in his study of gleaning that the expense of going to law probably inhibited the propertied from mobilizing legal sanctions that would have facilitated the reshaping of rural social relations through the imposition on the poor of new definitions of property.[71] But in general it is far from clear that the less well off benefited much from the legal regime of the eighteenth century. One of the reasons for the agitation for parliamentary law reform in the 1730s that led eventually to the passage of several measures, including the act of parliament making English rather than Latin the language of record, appears to have been the perceived need in the West Yorkshire clothing districts for more effective ways of enforcing the payment of wages.[72] To give another example, in the seventeenth century 'free miners' in Derbyshire used their customary barmoot court, and raised common purses, in order to defend their rights to dig for lead in the 'Kings Field', but by the middle of the eighteenth century, the high costs of constant struggles with powerful gentry opponents had weakened their position.[73] In the 1760s, those who supported their cause idealized the antiquity of 'mining law', and also contrasted the simplicity of procedures in the local jurisdiction, where every miner acted as his own lawyer, with the dilatory proceedings of the Georgian central courts, institutions where the 'subtle distinctions of the lawyers' and the incompetence of the judges did injustice and was a discouragement 'to all Miners in general'.[74]

Again, although those opposing enclosure of common land were able to mount campaigns against it in the eighteenth century,[75] the increasing use by

argues that only wealthier women were likely to be able to use the writ of habeas corpus in order to free themselves from confinement by husbands, although they were also more likely than poorer women to find themselves confined to madhouses.

71 Peter King, 'Gleaners, Farmers and the Failure of Legal Sanctions in England 1750–1850', *Past and Present*, 125 (1989), esp. 123, 128–30, 138. In most of the gleaning cases it was the substantial farmer rather than the illiterate landless gleaner who was indicted. Since neither the moribund Colchester Monday or Thursday courts, nor the Essex county courts, could hear cases of trespass, it was necessary to bring expensive prosecutions at assizes, and it was feared in any case that jurors would side with the gleaners.

72 Brooks, *Lawyers, Litigation*, 45. It is notable that one of the most comprehensive proposals for law reform in the 1720s was produced by the Yorkshire squire and justice of the peace, Christopher Tancred, *An Essay for the General Regulation of the Law. In which The Great Corruptions and Expenses of Law Controversies are Exposed, and effectual Methods proposed to redress such Great National Grievances* (London, 1727).

73 A. Wood, *The Politics of Social Conflict: The Peak Country 1520–1770*, (Oxford, 1999), esp. ch. 13.

74 BL MS Additional 6681, ff. 126, 186^{v}, 189–89^{v}. In 1653, Edward Manlove, the steward of the Barmoot Court, had composed a long poem that detailed the liberties and customs of the mines. This manuscript is part of a large collection relating to the legal affairs of the Derbyshire mines that was bequeathed to the British Library in 1825 by Adam Wolley of Matlock.

75 J.M. Neeson, *Commoners: Common Right, Enclosure and Social Change in England*

landowners of private acts of parliament made this more difficult and expensive, and in any case tended to preclude access to the central courts. In his magisterial study of the rights of commoners in the eighteenth century, Edward Thompson argued that although the common law to some extent upheld customary rights, the *English Reports* reveal few cases in which poor commoners challenged their lords or great landowners in the highest courts of the realm.[76] Taking cases to Common Pleas or King's Bench was not the labourers' 'thing'. Unless some party with money and a shared interest was on their side, rights were liable to be lost silently and without consent. For the eighteenth-century smallholder, cottager, or small commoner, the law was always something to avoid.[77] Those dependent on use rights, like those who claimed poor relief, were obliged to exercise agency within a context of paternalistic and discretionary justice.[78]

It is true, of course, that some observers have seen the decline in litigation in a more positive light than this. Some years ago, for example, Lawrence Stone[79] suggested that it should be interpreted as part of the evolution during the eighteenth century of a less contentious and more harmonious society, one that frowned on all kinds of interpersonal conflict, including that involving the use of law as well as that which manifested itself in physical violence, or, indeed, public insult.[80] There is, moreover, contemporary support for this hypothesis in the thought of the political economist Adam Smith. Although he overlooked the fact that seventeenth-century observers credited the commercial success of the Dutch at least in part to the effectiveness of their courts, Smith might have attributed the decline of litigation to the achievement of a higher state of economic maturity in which individuals much more readily kept to their contracts, a world that achieved the Hobbesian objectives of security of person and property without the intervention of the state or the law it administered.[81] Looking back on the sixteenth and early seventeenth

1700–1820 (Cambridge, 1996 edn), 124, 153, ch. 9. Neeson also argues that manorial organization was still important in the open field areas of Northamptonshire.

76 E.P. Thompson, *Customs in Common* (London, 1991), 141–2, although Thompson himself seems to have suspected that the rights of the commoner were just as controversial in the seventeenth century.

77 But see also Leigh Shaw-Taylor, 'Labourers, Cows, Common Rights and Parliamentary Enclosure: The Evidence of Contemporary Comment, c. 1760–1810', *Past and Present*, 171 (2001), 126, who reminds us that Thomas Andrew's *Enquiry into the Causes of the Encrease and Miseries of the Poor of England* (1738) indicates that there is an entire unwritten history of the exclusion of the poor from common pasture before enclosure by the simple expedient of manorial by-law. I expect that this is correct.

78 Hitchcock *et al.* (eds), *Chronicling Poverty*, *passim*.

79 L. Stone, 'Interpersonal Violence in English Society 1300–1980', *Past and Present*, 101 (1983), 22–33.

80 R. Shoemaker, 'The Decline in Public Insult in London 1660–1800', *Past and Present*, 169 (2000), 97–132.

81 Adam Smith, *Lectures on Justice, Police, Revenue and Arms Delivered in the University*

centuries, for example, Victorian commentators appear to have been astonished by the webs of regulation and petty contention reflected in all sorts of local courts, and local bylaws, including the regulations laid down for behaviour in the inns of court and Chancery, and they were heartily glad that it had passed away.[82] More recently, Craig Muldrew has argued that it was the high levels of litigation in the sixteenth and seventeenth centuries that were the aberration, and that by the eighteenth century new forms of association, and a growing sense of internalized self-discipline, account for much of the subsequent decline.[83]

As we have seen, it is arguable that some of the institutional and juridical changes of the period support these views, but, overall, there are three reasons for doubting whether the decline in litigation can be explained by some kind of 'civilizing process'.[84] First, in London and Middlesex at least, the appetite for contention seems to have remained robust;[85] in fact recent work has shown that the inhabitants regularly used solicitors to bring actions for misdemeanours such as assault in the criminal courts largely because they could obtain financial settlements more speedily and at a lower cost than was possible in the civil jurisdictions.[86] Second, the great demographic and economic changes of the second half of the eighteenth century (rapid rises in population and the dependence of a larger proportion of the population on wage labour) evidently made little impression on the courts, presumably because traditional local jurisdictions had atrophied and the central common law and equity courts had proven themselves remote and expensive. For example, Douglas Hay's studies of the application of the law of 'master and servant', which governed the relationship between employer and employee, indicate that industrialization during the later eighteenth and nineteenth centuries was accompanied by increasingly harsh use by justices of the peace of summary powers of imprisonment to discipline servants, while servants and employees found it increasingly difficult to use the law in order to collect unpaid wages. Although the common

of Glasgow . . . Reported by a Student in 1763, ed. E. Cannan [1896] (New York, 1964), 253–9.

82 Charles Pugh, 'The Origins and Progress of Barnard's Inn', *Notes and Queries*, 7th Series, II (1886), 101–2, 141–3, 181–3, 221–4, 301, 341–3, 403–4, 482–4.

83 C. Muldrew, 'From a "Light Cloak" to an "Iron Cage": Historical Changes in the Relation between Community and Individualism', in A. Shepard and P. Withington (eds), *Communities in Early Modern England* (Manchester, 2000), 156–79.

84 It is worth noting that fear of fraud in business dealings was a persistent eighteenth-century theme. See, for example, R. McGowen, '"From Pillory to Gallows": The Punishment of Forgery in the Age of the Financial Revolution', *Past and Present*, 165 (1999), 107–40.

85 Brooks, *Lawyers, Litigation*, 55–7. See also Dr Robert Shoemaker's forthcoming book on the London 'Mob', which addresses some of these issues. I am grateful to him for letting me see a chapter in advance of publication.

86 N. Landau, 'Indictment for Fun and Profit: A Prosecutor's Reward at Eighteenth-Century Quarter Sessions', *Law and History Review*, 17(3) (1999), 507–36.

law judges were not universally unsympathetic to the claims of servants, Hay argues that the reported case law of the central courts was not in practice all that significant because it was difficult for wage labourers to bring their cases into them.[87] Similarly, although early industrial occupations ran a high risk of injury, such cases hardly figure in the law reports,[88] and it was also difficult for groups of workers with no tradition of guild organization to justify collective action. After the abrogation of the Statute of Artificers in 1815, disputes over wage rates and conditions of work in occupations such as mining were resolved largely through arbitration, albeit in a form that frequently included a role for local justices of the peace.[89] For whatever reason, cases involving these issues did not enter the central courts in large numbers. Does this help to explain why what one historian has described as largely unregulated industrial capitalism brought in its train a largely unregulated urban environment?[90]

Third, it is of course necessary to take account of the fact that certain kinds of litigation began to increase again in the later eighteenth century.[91] Then, no less than in the seventeenth century, the all important areas of getting and spending, mine and thine, remained critical to poorer and middling as well as richer families,[92] and it is here that studies of the changing characteristics of civil litigation are, maybe, at their most telling. Though the overall volume of litigation began to increase again by the 1780s, over the next hundred years, an ever larger proportion of this went into local courts of request rather than the central courts, and much of it consisted of actions for debt, including debts for tallies and consumer goods bought on credit.[93] Though they had a history that went back to the time of Henry VIII, courts of request

[87] D. Hay, 'Master and Servant in England: Using the Law in the Eighteenth and Nineteenth Centuries', in W. Steinmetz (ed.), *Private Law and Social Inequality in the Industrial Age: Comparing Legal Cultures in Britain, France, Germany and the United States* (Oxford, 2000), 227–64.

[88] Joan Lane, *Apprenticeship in England 1600–1914* (London, 1996), ch. 2. Brooks, Lawyers, *Litigation*, 111–12.

[89] James Jaffe, 'Industrial Arbitration, Equity and Authority in England, 1800–1850', *Law and History Review*, 18 (2000), 525–58. Unlike Jaffe, I am struck by how much the processes he describes appear to mirror the kinds of approach to the resolution of wage disputes that were enshrined in the late fourteenth-century Statute of Labourers.

[90] Eastwood, *Government and Community*, 160.

[91] See Brooks, *Lawyers, Litigation*, 73–4 for a long list of matters sued for in the London court of requests in 1799.

[92] As one contemporary put it, 'Excepting the laws for the support of Government and the maintenance of the Poor, there does not appear to be any of more universal concern than the laws between Creditors and Debtors. No man can buy or sell, borrow or lend, but he may have occasion to appeal to them. They are the laws that belong to every day's business, and equally concern every rank of the State': [Anon.], *Considerations on the Laws Between Debtors and Creditors: and an Abstract of the Insolvent Acts* (London, 1779), sig. B2.

[93] Margot Finn, 'Debt and Credit in Bath's Court of Requests, 1829–39', *Urban History*, 21(2) (1994), 211–36.

were quintessentially eighteenth-century institutions. Most of them were formed when local pressure groups created enough steam to successfully petition parliament for an act creating a new court with a small claims jurisdiction. The judges were self-selected in the localities from amongst local notables, and it was a particular feature of these courts that they usually prohibited any participation by professional lawyers.[94] The majority of the courts of request were established after 1750, and their chronology and placement very closely track the economic and demographic change of the period.[95] Those who argued in favour of their foundation claimed that they were essential if credit was to be extended to poorer members of the community and that this credit was a necessary life-line in the domestic economies of the less well off. Critics argued that the new courts operated without the aid of that most basic ingredient in due process according to common law, trial by jury. Supporters and opponents both agreed that the courts offered the potential for helping to maintain the economic discipline of poorer households,[96] while a few pointed out that, backed up by the power to imprison for debt, they could also be the sources of oppression and hardship.[97]

Conclusions

Viewed in the broader context of the relationship between institutions and society (which I personally prefer to state formation), the history of the courts of request links the history of civil litigation into the same pattern that has been detected in connection with the criminal law at quarter sessions and the parochial administration of the poor law. Ordinary law suits between individuals were carried out predominantly in local jurisdictions that had relatively little to do with either traditional customary law or the common law dealt in by professional lawyers, and where local notables acted with considerable discretion, which they could apply with varying degrees of charity, paternalism, or enlightened realism, to cases that mostly dealt with the family economies of the less well off. In all three spheres local powers might occasionally be challenged, or indeed reinforced, by reference to cases that were brought in

[94] Although there are indications that what might be described as irregular (or unlicensed) female solicitors were sometimes active in some of them. Brooks, *Lawyers, Litigation*, 99–100n.

[95] Ibid., 39–42.

[96] William Hutton, *Courts of Requests: Their Nature, Utility, and Power Described, with a variety of cases determined in that of Birmingham* (Birmingham, 1787), 21–5.

[97] William Hutton, for example, did not criticize imprisonment for debt, but he did believe that punishment should be proportionate to crimes and that the overall state of prisons was deplorable. Ibid., 57, 64–7. Margot Finn, *The Character of Credit: Personal Debt in English Culture, 1740–1914* (Cambridge, 2003), which was published after this chapter was completed, contains a great deal of additional information about courts of request.

the higher courts in London, but more often, in so far as they were monitored at all from above, they were altered by parliamentary legislation. Furthermore, these developments were most likely accompanied by another significant change in the character of legal life. Whatever the forum (manorial court, borough court, guild court, or royal court), and whatever the role (complainant, defendant, witness, deponent, or juror), the decline in litigation meant that in the eighteenth century ordinary English people probably participated in open court less often than their predecessors had done.

Finally, the decline in litigation raises one last question. If eighteenth-century people evidently avoided litigation, or did not feel the need to employ lawyers and go to court all that often, there would seem to be something paradoxical in the fact that modern historians of the eighteenth century have traditionally placed so much emphasis on the role of law as a central ideological component in the social and political life of the period.[98] Contemporary opinion, which was capable of paying lip-service to the symbolic importance of English law, while decrying its cost, complexity, and inaccessibility, may provide part of the answer. Even so, much more work needs to be done on the dissemination, reception, and appropriation of legal thought in the eighteenth century before firm conclusions can be drawn, and, here again, comparisons with earlier periods raise questions worth considering. For example, the break from Rome in the 1530s and the gradual emergence of Protestantism in the sixteenth century were accompanied by a good deal of enthusiasm for making legal knowledge more widely available to the public, even if this seems to have been followed under the early Stuarts by more circumspection and debate about the advisability of such empowerment.[99] In the eighteenth century, by contrast, figures such as Blackstone and Bentham were concerned about varieties of legal ignorance amongst the gentry as well as amongst ordinary people. It is also very hard to imagine making a case for the political importance of lawyers or legal discourse in the eighteenth century that could match the one that can easily be stitched together by mentioning the names of Coke, Selden, Clarendon, Hale, and even Jeffries or Holt, in the seventeenth.[100]

Given the present state of knowledge, it is difficult to say how far, and in what ways, the general character of common law thought changed over the period from 1560 to 1800. An impressionistic comparison of the case law suggests that late Tudor and early Stuart judges were more likely to encounter, and accept, arguments that were based on customary rights or sources of

[98] See, for example, the seminal essays in D. Hay, P. Linebaugh *et al.* (eds), *Albion's Fatal Tree: Crime and Society in Eighteenth-Century England* (London, 1975) and the final chapter of Edward Thompson, *Whigs and Hunters: The Origins of the Black Act* (London, 1975).

[99] Brooks, Lawyers, *Litigation*, ch. 9; R. Ross, 'The Commoning of the Common Law: The Renaissance Debate over Printing English Law, 1520–1640', *University of Pennsylvania Law Review*, 146 (1998), 323–460.

[100] See also Lemmings, *Professors*, 320–1.

authority. At the same time, the place of law in moderating the relationship between the person, the community, and the state appears to have been much more often a central concern of litigation, and, perhaps, of the political process more generally, in the earlier period.[101] On the other hand although the word 'property' no doubt figures more frequently in the writing of influential eighteenth-century authors such as Smith and David Hume,[102] the security of lands and goods was manifestly a central concern in the political and legal disputes of the early seventeenth century. Indeed, even the ideas about law and property that Thompson so brilliantly observed in their transmission to India and Australasia at the end of the eighteenth century had a trial run in the writings of James I's attorney general in Ireland, Sir John Davies.[103]

Continuity as well as change also emerges from an examination of the modes of discourse that characterized those occasions at which legal and political ideas met most regularly, the thousands of charges to grand juries that were given at the start of meetings of assizes and quarter sessions. While there are notable changes in detail, the general content and subject matter remained much the same. Early seventeenth-century charges reveal the complex interplay between an Aristotelian emphasis on participation and the individual, as well as the collective good, versus a neo-Stoic call for obedience to established authority.[104] Those from 1689 through to the 1720s and 1730s offer a great deal of evidence of discussion at the local level of the principles that lay behind the 'Glorious Revolution'. Though as often informed by factional quarrels associated with party politics as by abstract legal theory, a fair number of them referred explicitly to contractual notions of government drawn either from Locke or Richard Hooker; one author even went so far as to provide a history lesson about how princes all over Europe had been deposed for ruling tyrannically. Like their seventeenth-century predecessors, many early eighteenth-century charges also stressed that civil government had been instituted for the governed, not the rulers, and that the laws of England were the laws of 'the people', there to sustain and protect the neighbourhood as well as the state.[105]

[101] Compare, for example, the early seventeenth-century law reports of Sir Edward Coke with Joseph Burchell, *Arrangement and Digest of the Law, in Cases Adjudged in King's Bench and Common Pleas from the Year 1756 to 1794 inclusive* (London, 1796).

[102] H.D. Aiken (ed.), *Hume's Moral and Political Philosophy* (New York, 1959 edn), 49ff. 'Treatise of Human Nature: pt II. Of Justice and Injustice'.

[103] Thompson, *Customs in Common*, 278–83. [Sir John Davies], *A Discoverie of the True Causes why Ireland was neur entirely Subdued, nor brought under Obedience of the Crowne of England, vntill the Beginning of his Maiesties happie Raigne* (London, 1612).

[104] For examples see Brooks, *Lawyers, Litigation*, chs 8–9.

[105] A sample of material is collected in *Charges to the Grand Jury 1689–1803*, ed. Georges Lamoine (Camden Soc., 4th ser., vol. 43, 1992). A much fuller list is given in H.L. Snyder, 'Charges to Grand Juries: The Evidence of the Eighteenth-Century Short-Title Catalogue', *Historical Research*, 67 (1994), 286–300.

Against this background, it is easy to appreciate the stress historians have placed on the role of lawyers and the importance of popular legalism in connection with John Wilkes's battle over the Middlesex elections in the 1760s and early 1770s but, of course, the direct action took place in London, and it is worth pointing out that few similar episodes have come to light (or at least been written up) from the localities.[106] During the 1770s and 1780s and on into the 1790s, moreover, the language of charges became distinctly more conservative. Then, speeches hostile to abstract theories of government stressed the necessity of obedience and were concerned about the threat of combinations of workers against employers. In 1797, Justice Grose told jurors at Hertford that the prime objective of the law was to prevent the subversion of the constitution. Their duty was to teach the 'lower orders' to be upright. All members of society were links in a great chain. The minds and morals of the inhabitants of any country were formed by its laws.[107]

Language such as this obviously owed a great deal to the unstable political situation that accompanied the French Revolution and the wars that came in its aftermath,[108] and some of it would not have been entirely out of place in the equally troubled 1590s. What would have changed however is the composition of the people who were listening to it. As is well known, the social status of grand jurors became increasingly elevated, much more confined to the greater gentry, from 1660 onwards than had been the case previously.[109] It could, nevertheless, be argued that the wider dissemination of print, and particularly of newspapers, made the law and legal ideas at least as readily available in the eighteenth century as they had been previously, and although advocates of a print revolution too easily disregard the efficacy of face-to-face participation and oral transmission, they undoubtedly have a point. Michael Lobban has recently shown that the publication of all kinds of technical legal works tracked surprisingly closely the ebb and flow of litigation,[110] but civil as well as criminal trials were publicized in newspaper reports.[111] Here, though, it may just be worth pondering an analogy with modern day football supporters

[106] The classic treatment is J. Brewer, 'The Wilkites and the Law, 1763–74: A Study of Radical Notions of Governance', in J. Brewer and J. Styles (eds), *An Ungovernable People: The English and their Law in the Seventeenth and Eighteenth Centuries* (London, 1980), 177–205.

[107] Lemoine, *Charges*, 544, 547,

[108] D. Eastwood, *Governing Rural England: Tradition and Transformation in Local Government 1780–1840* (Oxford, 1994), 16, 21.

[109] Landau, *Justices of the Peace*, 39. By the early eighteenth century, many of the members of the grand jury at assizes were justices of the peace.

[110] M. Lobban, 'The English Legal Treatise and English Law in the Eighteenth Century', in S. Dauchy *et al.* (eds), *Auctoritates Xenia R. C. van Caenegem Oblata, Juris Scripta Historica*, xiii (1997), 69–88.

[111] See, for example, James Oldham, 'Law Reporting in the London Newspapers, 1756–1786', *American Journal of Legal History*, 31 (1987), 177–205.

and media representation of the game. The supporters, like those of Wilkes, frequently buy paraphernalia celebrating the team, and, if you overhear their conversations, they will display a lot of knowledge. But they neither go on the pitch or are involved in managing the business. Should their participation be dismissed as at best virtual, and at worst exploitative? Does this explain why working-class radicalism of the nineteenth century was expressed more often in terms of the general rights of Englishmen that had been inherited from the Anglo-Saxon past (and then tarnished by Norman corruption) than in terms of specific cases that could be argued in court?

In conclusion, the decline in litigation can help us to see more clearly that the eighteenth century, measured from the 1720s or 1730s onwards, constituted a distinctive phase in the history of the relationship between the person, the community, and the law. It evidently marked a decline in the willingness of wide cross-sections of the population to use courts in order to defend their reputation, their place in local politics, or their economic interest. At the same time the decline of a wide range of institutions that we lump together as local jurisdictions is just as significant as the drop in central court business. English local courts were the places where the words 'community' and 'neighbourhood' had been articulated regularly (in Latin as well as English) since the middle ages.[112] Yet, while they enjoyed a good deal of local autonomy, in the earlier period their powers and their decisions were frequently characterized by fractious local politics, and they were often the sources of litigation brought before the central courts.

It would appear that between about 1720 and 1770, the involvement of law and lawyers in a wide range of social and economic relationships diminished noticeably, and during the course of the second half of the eighteenth and early nineteenth centuries, the decline of the smaller farmer and proletarianization further undermined the social as well as the institutional basis of the common law world as it existed prior to 1700. When economic change and population growth subsequently put pressure on the makeshift structures, such as the courts of request, that had replaced it, they were ultimately subjected to the same stringent bureaucratic rationalization that characterized most of the early Victorian parliamentary reforms. Some apologists for the new county court system that was finally introduced in 1847 liked to associate it with a return to 'medieval' or 'feudal' jurisdictions which they thought represented an older connection between law and the community, but in fact it had more in common with the reforms of King Alfred, imposed from above rather than generated from below. In the 1850s there were even serious calls for making it a requirement that county court judges should live outside the county over whose court they presided.[113] By the end of the nineteenth century legal

[112] J.H. Baker, *The Legal Profession and the Common Law* (London, 1986), 153–70.

[113] Brooks, *Lawyers, Litigation*, 105–7. Though frequently threatened, the civil jury survived more robustly than is sometimes thought. See M. Lobban, 'The Strange Life of the English

historians such as F.W. Maitland and the Webbs, no doubt suffering from a surfeit of idealism, were left to lament the way in which an older sense of community had been undermined by the 'occidental despotism' of the bureaucratic nation state.[114] Twenty-first century historians have had in turn to rediscover that communities can be litigious as well as harmonious and that law can be participatory as well as hegemonic.

The English legal profession thrived in the early nineteenth century, but the most important alteration in its character appears to have been an unintended consequence of both the imperial state at war and the decline of civil litigation. The slow evolution during the eighteenth century of the right of defendants in felony to have a lawyer present their case in court seems to have arisen at least in part because judges thought it only fair that defendants prosecuted by the Mint, the Treasury, or the Customs should be allowed to have their own lawyers to contest the cases put forward by official prosecutors. By the end of the century, although they only appeared in a minority of cases, and although the activity was concentrated in London, some of the large numbers of barristers who were at best moderately successful in generating significant civil case loads at Westminster were beginning to make up for the deficit in their incomes by work in the criminal courts.[115] The decline in civil litigation and the rise of the 'adversary criminal trial' were not unrelated, and both were central to the watershed that separates the medieval and early modern English legal system from that which evolved from the mid-eighteenth century onwards.

Civil Jury, 1837–1914', in John Cairns and Grant McLeod (eds), *The Dearest Birthright of the People of England: The Jury in the History of the Common Law* (London, 2002), 173–215.

[114] Thompson, *Customs in Common*, 174; Otto Gierke, *Political Theories of the Middle Age*, translated with an introduction by F.W. Maitland (Cambridge, first edn 1900, 1987 edn), xxxiv: Maitland speculated that a German might ask: 'do you not think that some part at least of the appalling mess . . . that you made of your local government was due to a bad and foreign theory which, coupling corporateness with princely "privilege", refused to recognize and foster into vigour the bodiliness that was immanent in every English township, in every rural *Gemeinde*.'

[115] John H. Langbein, 'The Prosecutorial Origins of Defence Counsel in the Eighteenth Century: The Appearance of Solicitors', *Cambridge Law Journal*, 58(2) (1999), 314–65. See now his *The Origins of Adversary Criminal Trial* (Oxford, 2003) and Allyson N. May, *The Bar and the Old Bailey, 1750–1850* (Chapel Hill, NC, 2003).

8

'Making examples' and the crisis of punishment in mid-eighteenth-century England

RANDALL MCGOWEN*

> Indeed these seem to be the only reasons for public executions, which if they do not inspire both pity and terror, and make not a visible impression on the minds of the spectators, are not only useless, but dangerous.
>
> *The Right Method of Maintaining Security in Person and Property* (London, 1751), 44

Tyburn offered one of the major spectacles of eighteenth-century London life. On an execution day, a large throng of rich and poor flocked to the gallows to see how the condemned would meet their fate. Despite the high-flown phrases offered by judges and clerics, and the repeated calls for greater order and decorum in the proceedings, the tumult around the scaffold made a shambles of any pretence of a stage-managed occurrence intended to celebrate the power and legitimacy of the state. Historians have tended to accentuate the scale of the disorder associated with the event. 'By the eighteenth century', Peter Linebaugh writes, 'this crowd had become so unruly that the "hanging match" became well known to foreign visitors and English alike as both a principal attraction of the town and a periodic occasion of disturbance.'[1] Hogarth's brilliant illustration of Tyburn in his series 'Industry and Idleness' (1747) offers a vivid portrait of the chaos and spontaneity that reigned on execution day. The counter-theatre of the mob, Thomas Laqueur has written, decisively trumped the pretensions of the government. The lower orders displayed their contempt for authority; they made heroes of at least some of those who suffered, and they commiserated with the sad circumstances of the rest. The crowd's exuberance and irreverence mocked death; it created a festival of crude humour

* I would like to thank John Beattie, Peter King, Nicholas Rogers, Donna Andrew, Iain McCalman, Michael Meranze, and Simon Devereaux for their comments on earlier drafts of this chapter. It was written, in part, with support from the Humanities Research Centre at the Australian National University.

[1] Peter Linebaugh, 'The Tyburn Riot Against the Surgeons', in *Albion's Fatal Tree*, ed. D. Hay *et al.* (New York, 1975), 67.

and collective emotion that resisted incorporation into the schemes of society's rulers.[2]

This portrait of the execution has gained wide acceptance, despite the fact that it relies heavily upon the words and sentiments of precisely those people who were most critical of the excesses of the 'Tyburn Fair'. We rarely hear from the authorities who were in charge of managing the event. They evidently accepted the value of the execution, even with all the attendant disorder. Only slightly more often do we hear echoes of popular opinion, the report of the crowd contesting a particular execution or the words of a broadsheet describing the career of a celebrated offender. The newspapers, however, tell a different tale; for every episode of riot or of the condemned attacking the justice of their sentences, the journals report many other instances of the crowd attentively watching the proceedings and of victims dying penitent. 'The scaffold crowd reveals much greater complexity than meets the eye,' V.A.C. Gatrell reminds us; 'it wore many faces.'[3] No doubt the responses to the scene varied widely. Just as the execution brought together people of different classes, so the crowd was composed of people with different attitudes towards what happened there, responses often shaped by the identity and character of those who suffered.

The controversy over the crowd's reaction to the spectacle of punishment, inconclusive as it has been, has also tended to obscure other interesting questions about the status and meaning of public executions. In particular, it has diverted attention from the question of the significance of mounting criticism of Tyburn in the history of the changing attitudes towards punishment in eighteenth-century England. The scholarly debate creates the impression that responses to the gallows were sharply polarized but essentially unchanging over the course of the century. It will be the argument of this chapter that, on the contrary, attitudes were fluid and unsettled, and that the period was marked by several dramatic shifts in the way capital punishment was regarded.[4] Indeed, the episode I want to examine, the mid-century crisis over the management of the execution at Tyburn, scarcely fits the familiar narrative of the progress of penal reform. The humanity or inhumanity of the death penalty itself was not an issue. No novel proposals for alternative punishments were offered. Despite a considerable flurry of comment, few concrete changes resulted from

[2] Thomas Laqueur, 'Crowds, Carnival, and the State in English Executions, 1604–1868', in *The First Modern Society*, ed. A.L. Beier *et al.* (Cambridge, 1989), 305–55.

[3] V.A.C. Gatrell, *The Hanging Tree* (Oxford, 1994), 89. For a similar conclusion about an earlier period, see Peter Lake and Michael Questier, 'Agency, Appropriation and Rhetoric Under the Gallows: Puritans, Romanists and the State in Early Modern England', *Past and Present*, 153 (1996), 64–107.

[4] Peter King has emphasized how 'each of the available sanctions' in eighteenth-century England 'underwent subtle and sometimes complex changes' over the course of the period. *Crime, Justice, and Discretion in England 1740–1820* (Cambridge, 2000), 263. This chapter is indebted to Donna Andrew's discussion of changing notions of philanthropy in her book, *Philanthropy and Police: London Charity in the Eighteenth Century* (Princeton, 1989).

the discussions. Rather the importance of this episode lay less in what it achieved than in the profound change in attitude that it marked. It was an occasion when deeper cultural currents bubbled to the surface exposing a transformation in the way punishment was imagined. The crisis did not spring from changes in the conduct of the lower orders. Rather it emerged from the altered perceptions of the execution on the part of the upper classes. Although the discussion occurred in the midst of one of the recurrent panics over a surge in criminal activity following the end of a war, it represented far more than a temporary hysteria. The crisis concerned a growing uncertainty about the ability of the public execution to achieve its ends. The crowd seemed no longer to be 'taking the appropriate message'. These doubts, in turn, indicated an erosion of the notions that grounded and made sense of particular practices of death.[5]

Central to the operation of early modern justice was a belief in the value of using punishments, and especially the gallows, to 'make examples'.[6] This conviction sustained the operation of Tyburn in the face of concerns about the wisdom or moral justification of the extensive reliance upon the death penalty. Yet by the 1750s doubts were being expressed in pamphlets and the press about the capacity of the execution to produce the appropriate lesson. Criticism of what transpired around the gallows mounted to new heights. There was little that was novel in these comments, but the very extent of the discontent represented a significant intensification of the earlier complaints. Though it was London and what happened at Tyburn that produced the anxiety, the provincial press disseminated the discussion across the nation. The sense that something was wrong was far sharper than the idea of what should be done. Much of the commentary focused on the conduct and character of the crowd. More subtly, however, it pointed to changes in the understanding of those who had traditionally accepted the Tyburn ritual without hesitation. In response, some authors sought to reform the way in which executions were conducted, in order to reinvigorate them. Others searched for alternatives, a few proposing greater severity. None of these measures succeeded in resolving the problem. For what had altered was less the conduct of the crowd or the condemned, than the way in which polite society regarded the event. The upshot was that the gallows regime was less securely anchored after the 1750s.

[5] Clive Emsley, *Crime and Society in England* (London, 1996), 260–1. This chapter will cover some of the same ground discussed by Steven Wilf, 'Imagining Justice: Aesthetics and Public Executions in Late Eighteenth-Century England', *Yale Journal of Law and the Humanities*, 5 (1993), 51–78. While I agree with his call to read penal practices more carefully, I have a different approach to the question of why the aesthetics of punishment changed in mid-eighteenth-century England.

[6] I have discussed this issue in 'The Body and Punishment in Eighteenth-Century England', *Journal of Modern History*, 59 (1987), 651–79. Here I want to consider more carefully what was at stake in the idea of making examples and to pinpoint a period when the issue assumed more striking importance.

The idea of the example, the notion that was at the centre of the early modern conception of punishment, had undergone a significant transformation. Punishment was still meant to be exemplary; the principle continued to be invoked. But it was emptied of much of its meaning. The result was that what had been a moment of punishment that appealed to higher sanction for its justification, even if practice seldom realized these aspirations, came increasingly to look squalid and compromised. The tumult that had long surrounded the gallows came to seem more ominous.[7]

'Exemplary correction'

That punishment should be exemplary had long been a familiar way of explaining not only the purpose of penal inflictions but the mechanism by which they worked as well. 'And this, I am persuaded', wrote the author of *Hanging Not Punishment Enough* in 1701, 'will best answer the End of Sanguinary Laws, which are not *chiefly* intended to punish the present Criminal, but to hinder others from being so; and on that account Punishments in the Learned Language are called *Example*, as being design'd to be such to all mankind.'[8] 'Criminals', another writer announced in 1751, 'are considered as public examples.' 'This', he explained, 'is the true language of the law.'[9] Secular and religious authorities agreed on this point. Punishment was less a matter for individuals, either the offender or the victim of crime, than for society as a whole. Once the offenders had been condemned, the crucial relationship was no longer to the crime they had committed but to a spectacle in which they were to participate. 'The use and intent of punishment', a third author concluded in 1754, 'is not to gratify the person injured, but to procure, by exemplary correction, a benefit to the public.'[10] Several important deductions flowed from this belief. Perhaps most important was the conviction that punishment was not simply unfortunate or harmful, a regrettable necessity. The argument asserted that chastisement promoted a social good. Its task was to provide the occasion for conveying a salutary message. Crowds were supposed to attend the event. Everyone should see and learn from it. Precisely because the institution of punishment was seen in a positive light and as

[7] For an interesting treatment of a transformation in the terms of social analysis that paralleled the one I am describing here, see Jonathan White, 'The "Slow but Sure Poyson": The Representation of Gin and Its Drinkers, 1736–1751', *Journal of British Studies*, 42 (2003), 35–64.

[8] *Hanging Not Punishment Enough* (London, 1701), 5. Emphasis in original unless stated otherwise.

[9] *The Right Method of Maintaining Security in Person and Property* (London, 1751), 57–8.

[10] *Proposals to the Legislature for Preventing the Frequent Executions and Exportations of Convicts in a Letter to Henry Pelham* (London, 1754), 15; Gwenda Morgan and Peter Rushton, *Rogues, Thieves and the Rule of Law* (London, 1998), 141–8.

offering a lesson for all eyes, the elite as well as the lower orders were expected to be present. 'In other countries', Sollom Emlyn observed, 'the criminals are sometimes executed in private', but in England it was carried out 'always openly and in public, it being necessary to answer the end of justice, that a public example be made of offenders in order to deter others from the like crimes.'[11] There might be disagreements over the frequency with which death was inflicted; Emlyn was no friend of the capital code as it existed. There was, however, unanimity when it came to the employment of this word to describe the goal of punishment. An example was meant to deter; it was supposed to frighten potential offenders. But the occasion was intended to do more; it was also an illustration, and as such it produced a complex narrative, 'saturated in symbols of sin, redemption, and damnation'. Religion provided far more than a simple rationale for punishment; it helped to structure all aspects of the experience and to lend it dignity. It explained the place of punishment within the life of the community.[12]

It was left to clerics to elaborate on what it meant to describe punishment as exemplary. In doing so they mingled the secular and religious sources of power, so that the latter inflected the meanings associated with the operation of justice. 'There must be some public example', Francis Weber announced in an assize sermon,

> some leading influence of authority to encourage and impress the belief and practice of it amongst the people; there must be some visible form and exterior mode of worship not only to engage the attention by addressing the senses, but even to facilitate the progress of that real goodness and internal virtue of mind, which it is the design of all religious institutions to promote.[13]

No other punishment so perfectly suited this scheme as death. It offered an enormous example, sustained by a potent religious script. Secular authors shared such sentiments. Human justice, wrote the author of *Hanging*, should 'imitate Divine Justice' in inflicting 'an animadversion suitable to such enormous Offenders'.[14] The gallows drama evoked the most familiar and powerful aspects of the Christian narrative, the themes of death, judgement, and eternity. At the gallows pain and suffering supplied the colours for sketching a message that pointed beyond what the body experienced. The execution

[11] Sollom Emlyn, *A Complete Collection of State Trials and Proceedings for High Treason* (London, 1730), iv.

[12] Gatrell, *Hanging Tree*, 81.

[13] Francis Weber, *The Case of Authority Considered as It Respects Religion* (Oxford, 1742), 37.

[14] *Hanging*, 5. One author, in 1716, explained 'that Justice, unless it is mix'd with Mercy, which is another Attribute of God, whom we ought to imitate, rather seems Vindictive than Exemplary'. *Georgicum: or, A Supplement to the Mirror of Justices* (London, 1716), 31. See also Cynthia Herrup, *The Common Peace* (Cambridge, 1987), 193–206.

offered a tableau, an illustration of a series of fundamental relationships, between divine and human authority, subjects and rulers, life and death. No doubt the state sought to appropriate the language and imagery of Christianity to the support of the established order, but these terms also structured how the authorities themselves thought about justice and the way in which they shaped the ultimate sentence of the law. Ministers had a dense and evocative language to employ in describing the task of justice. George Halley reminded his listeners, in a sermon preached to the condemned at York in 1691, that human punishment could be compared to the warnings of divine afflictions that filled the pages of the Bible. They were a providential sign to turn aside from a sinful course before it was too late. He called upon his audience to remember 'that by the Latter End is to be understood not only Death, but, what follows Death, the Judgment, and Appearance before the Dreadful Tribunal of Almighty God'. He pleaded with his listeners that they be 'persuaded by the *Exemplary punishment of these persons*' to amend their lives.[15]

The language of exemplary punishment was everywhere. The very pervasiveness of the notion testifies to how rich and subtle were the meanings associated with the term. The severe earthquake that jolted London in 1750 produced a flurry of sermons interpreting the event as a warning from God to the nation. 'If we consider', the Bishop of London, Thomas Sherlock, announced in a letter to the inhabitants of the metropolis, 'the general government of the world by God, and upon what reasons and motives he acts, when he brings calamities upon any people', it was to have made them 'examples of justice'. Both religious and secular history were full of such lessons. If the English were upright, he advised his flock, they had nothing to fear. If, however, 'our consciences tell us, that we have sinned after their example, what consolation is there to be had against the just expectations of suffering after their example also?'[16] The prevalence of such notions had profound consequences for the understanding of crime and punishment. Without in any way diminishing the awfulness of the suffering inflicted, it nonetheless appeared in a more positive light when understood as part of a divine scheme for the salvation of humanity. The punishments imposed on criminals were seen as on a continuum with the operation of a divine justice that employed penalties as a mode of instruction to all of society. One point of the execution was to remind people of all classes that their predicament was no different from that of the condemned. In 1739, Fifield Allen, the archdeacon of St Albans,

[15] George Halley, *A Sermon Preach'd at the Castle of York to the Condemned Prisoners* (York, 1691), 1–2, 7, 27 (original emphasis). William Dodwell acknowledged that the advantage of human penalties was that they were 'more visible' than divine, even if their intention was to put people in mind of the more awful day of judgement to come. *The Nature, Extent and Support of Human Laws Considered* (Oxford, 1750), 19.

[16] *Gentleman's Magazine*, 20 (1750), 123; Paul Langford, *A Polite and Commercial People: England 1727–1783* (Oxford, 1989), 284–5.

defended this interpretation of God's justice against the charges raised by those whom he called modern antinomians, that harsh penalties were inconsistent with the dignity of humanity. Severe laws, he argued, were needed to restrain the strong and protect the weak. It might be asked, he admitted, why gibbets and whips were necessary when the threat of eternal damnation hung over all. Too few, he answered, responded to this distant threat.

> But where wholesome Severities are exercis'd upon Delinquents legally convicted, and that not only to secure Multitudes from falling a Prey to them, but *in terrorem*, that others may *lay it to Heart*, amend their Lives, and *not come into the same Place of Torment*: Where is the inhumanity in all this?

He noted the frequent charge that the execution was incompatible with the Christian's obligation to show 'Pity and Compassion', and the accusation that 'there is such a Cruelty in all capital Punishments, as is altogether' at odds with the 'gentle Spirit of the Gospel'. But did God, he responded, not appoint death for the Jews? 'For what are earthly Judicatures', he concluded, 'but an Image of God's Tribunal in Heaven?' Charity might be found in defeating the designs of the wicked, and the punishment of them might then appear a tool to save souls.[17] An example thus had a double nature, at once exhibiting terror but also speaking of majesty, offering mercy as well as suffering, suggesting the possibility of salvation as well as damnation. Spectators were supposed to imagine themselves in the situation of the condemned. The offender thus became a pattern to be imitated or a fate to be avoided.

Terrifying as the gallows was, the message presented there was more complicated than simple suffering. The precedent most often appealed to was the choice offered to the two thieves who died next to Christ. The parallel was reinforced by gesture and setting, by the performance of roles and the movement of bodies, at least as much as by what was said.[18] The drama followed a loose script, one that allowed for different parts and even some variation in the way the central role was played. The condemned were allotted a significant place in the production; they were invited to lend themselves to the performance. One minister, addressing the condemned in London in 1695, told them that 'no other benefit to mankind can be expected from you, but only by the examples of your death; and to stand like marks on fatal rocks and sands, to warn others from the same ruin in the future.' He hoped that the misery and shame they suffered would 'make a better impression on others'. 'Therefore,

[17] Fifield Allen, *The Reasonableness and Necessity of Human Laws and Penalties* (London, 1739), 8–12, 13, 15–16 (original emphasis). Another minister called punishment 'a glorious and divine employment'. Robert Fordsham, *The Dreadful Consequences of Sin* (Chester, 1751), 8–9.

[18] Mitchell Merback, *The Thief, the Cross and the Wheel: Pain and the Spectacle of Punishment in Medieval and Renaissance Europe* (London, 1999), 19–22, 27.

surely it should turn our very bowels within us', he concluded, 'to see them perish in such an ignominious death.'[19] The importance of this moment was such that they were left with the freedom to resist their assigned part, because so much was gained if they collaborated. It was also true that something could be made of whatever they chose to do. If they confessed their guilt, told their tales of how one sin led to another, and asked forgiveness, they were then offered reconciliation with the community and given the hope of salvation. Still, even if they died unrepentant, their deaths could be made to serve a useful purpose, for they stood as examples of the destruction that awaited rebellious humanity. Either way the offender was held up to the spectators as a lesson. Here was the moment of high suspense that was intended to elicit the attention of the crowd: Would the condemned relent, confess, and offer themselves for edification, or would they remain obdurate? The journalistic accounts of executions reflected this concern; they seldom mentioned the behaviour of the assembled people, but they usually characterized the conduct of those who died. The words employed were few, but that was because they belonged to a familiar story. The gallows stood as a signpost; it offered the sternest of warnings. At least to the minds of those who lectured society, it called attention to the human condition in a particularly forceful way, in a message which also happened to promote the cause of social order. The individuality of the condemned, though never entirely lost, became subsumed within a universal narrative. The enormity and excess of the penalty, even the disproportion between particular offence and infliction, were vital to the way in which it conveyed this meaning.[20]

Penitent criminals and unruly crowds

Exactly how the crowd took the execution remains unclear. There can be little doubt that the pious wishes of the clergy at best only imperfectly overlapped with the understanding of the spectators. Nonetheless, the condemned on many occasions lent themselves to the purposes of the authorities. Just as significantly, justice had a very particular use to make of them. One newspaper reported with approval the 'commendable' conduct of a man executed in 1736. 'At the place of execution he kneel'd down in perfect Composure, and with

[19] B. Crooke, *Two Sermons Preached before the Condemned Convicts at Newgate* (London, 1695), 1–2.

[20] Peter Lake, 'Deeds Against Nature: Cheap Print, Protestantism and Murder in Early Seventeenth-Century England', in *Culture and Politics in Early Stuart England*, ed. Kevin Sharpe and Peter Lake (Stanford, 1993), 274–7. J.A. Sharpe has written of the need to remember how Christianity shaped early modern responses to executions. 'Civility, Civilizing Processes, and the End of Public Punishment in England', in *Civil Histories: Essays Presented to Sir Keith Thomas*, ed. Peter Burke *et al.* (Oxford, 2000), 220–1.

all visible Marks of Christian Fortitude and Chearfulness.' 'The Solemnity of the Execution', the paper concluded, 'the decent Deportment of the Criminal, the tender Manner in which he took his Leave of all about him, his parting with the World, and meeting Death with so much Serenity and Calmness, drew Tears from many, and greatly affected the Multitude of Spectators.'[21] Here was the approved pattern; submission to punishment and acceptance of the justice of the sentence earned the applause of the public. Such conduct transformed the condemned from the reviled villain into the pattern for human conduct. In 1750 the press was full of the exploits of the highwayman, James Maclain. There was general satisfaction with the way in which he met his death. The papers reported his words and conduct in detail. And, for the most part, they approved of his 'manly firmness' because it revealed a 'true devotion'. He 'took no Notice of the Populace, but was truly attentive to his Devotion'. He met his end expressing the hope that his death would 'be useful'. 'If those in power thought it necessary', he explained

> to make an example of him, in order to deter others, he acquiesced; and begged of God, that such wicked men as he had been might take warning by his example. And he intreated that divine, when he was gone to press his sad example as a warning to young men to shun the courses that had ruined him.[22]

Precisely because so much was expected from the execution, by the late seventeenth century there were critics who complained that the ceremony was being mismanaged in ways that subverted the essential purpose of the death penalty. With mounting frequency those who discussed capital punishment often lamented that Tyburn seemed poorly regulated to achieve its desired effect. In 1695, one author, who identified himself as *Solon Secundus*, characterized the execution day in terms that became familiar to succeeding generations. The gallows, he charged, made no impression on the crowd. ''Tis made a kind of Jest, a Game, a Rendezvous of Mob.' It was a 'holy-Day, or Play-Day'. The 'Hanging', he concluded, 'is nothing at all! only a wry Face, and pist pair of Breeches.' ''Tis in every Body's Mouth, that Laws were made *in terrorem*; Pray', he demanded, 'how was he terrified?' The author, by way of illustration, described attending an execution with several 'Ladies'. Their response, after the event, was to ask if that was all there was to it. Future

[21] *Derby Mercury*, 22 January 1735–36.

[22] *The Universal Magazine*, 7 (1750), 179; *Whitehall Evening Post*, 2–4 October 1750. In 1732, the *Derby Mercury* printed a particularly full account of the execution in Derby of John Hewitt. The report dealt largely with his confession and repentance. 'It is hardly to be conceived', the story concluded, 'with what Earnestness he continued praying for Mercy till the Moment the Cart was drawn away, in the midst of vast Numbers of People, who pitied and prayed for him' (30 March 1732). For a subtle analysis of executions, see Andrea McKenzie, 'Martyrs in Low Life? Dying "Game" in Augustan England', *Journal of British Studies*, 42 (2003), 167–205.

offenders, he warned, left the scene emboldened, impressed by the celebrity status that descended on the condemned. 'Publick Executions', he added, 'will never heal these Breaches of Laws, or prevent the ill Consequences of them.'[23]

Many of these same phrases were used in 1725 by Bernard Mandeville in his vivid description of a spectacle gone dangerously awry. On 'the Day of Execution', he wrote, one would expect 'a deep Sense of Sorrow, with all the Signs of a thorough Contrition'. Yet nothing could be further from the case. Newgate was a scene of noise, quarrelling, obscenity, and laughter. Horrible oaths were uttered; vast quantities of beer and spirits were consumed. It was a holiday, a busy day for industrious pickpockets. 'All the Way, from Newgate to Tyburn, is one continued Fair.' The disorder and scandal increased as the mob approached the gallows. 'These processions', he lamented, 'are very void of that decent Solemnity that would be required to make them awful.' There was far too little ceremony, Mandeville concluded, and too much savage humour, to make the event an effective lesson. The courage displayed by the condemned, arising as it did from drunken bravado, was a large part of the problem. 'The further a Man is removed from Repentance, nay, the more void he seems to be of all Religion, and less Concern he discovers for Futurity, the more he is admired by our sprightly People.' 'Our publick Executions are become Decoys,' he complained. 'Instead of giving warning, they are exemplary the wrong Way, and encourage where they should deter.'[24]

The following decades were peppered with such complaints. A contributor to a magazine in 1731 expressed the fear that 'the present punishment for capital offences has so little solemnity in the manner of it, that it often appears more like a mob-triumph than an execution.'[25] Another critic charged that the English execution was little short of a comedy; 'here people laugh at the dishonour.'[26] A third writer complained that 'the truth is, the frequency of these bloody and mournful spectacles seems to have got the better of our humanity, and so hardened our nature, that we throng with as much keenness, and behold an execution with as much indifference as we do a Merry Andrew on the stage.'[27] In the eyes of one commentator, there was nothing so flawed as an English execution. He was at a loss to say which was worse, 'he who bestows Commendations on the Follies of a harden'd Scoundrel; or the Rascal himself who believes he can blot out his Villanies by expressing neither Remorse nor Regret for having perpetrated them'. 'Instead of applauding the

[23] *Solon Secundus, or Some Defects in the English Law with their Proper Remedies* (London, 1695), 6–7.

[24] Bernard Mandeville, *An Enquiry into the Causes of the Frequent Executions at Tyburn* (1964 reprint of 1725 original, Los Angeles), 18–25, 36–7.

[25] *Gentleman's Magazine* (1731), 60.

[26] *Gentleman's Magazine* (1737), 169.

[27] *Gentleman's Magazine* (1738), 14–15.

silly Speeches, and other Impertinenties, of Villains so hardened as to mock at their Shameful Chastisements', he urged the public to show 'a due Contempt' for the offenders.[28] Admittedly these scattered comments appeared in journals that represented polite opinion, but the unanimity of the authors suggests the gradual spread of discontent with the proceedings at Tyburn. Their indictment contained many of the counts that would be cited against public executions for the next century. They castigated the authorities for permitting what should have been a solemn ceremony to become a celebration of immorality and villainy. Worse still, they saw the shambles of the execution spawning dangerous moral consequences that rippled through society.

There were various suggestions offered for how to remedy what was seen as a growing evil. The author of *Hanging Not Punishment Enough* proposed that the worst offenders should be kept in a 'box or cell' by themselves, so that 'they might not improve each other in wickedness'. He would make 'their confinement more uneasie' before their deaths, so they had fewer opportunities to gain encouragement from each other.[29] Mandeville thought that if the condemned were denied drink, they would soon reveal their true natures. The bravado they exhibited under the influence of alcohol would disappear. He advocated locking them up separately, so they 'never be suffer'd to converse together'. Like other authors, he believed that setting a limit upon the period when pardons could be granted would be a benefit. Beyond that time the offenders should be given three days during which to meditate on their fates. If these measures were instituted, he argued, the ritual might be saved. By curtailing the liberties taken, by imposing tighter control, the example might be made more impressive.[30]

Several attempts were made during the first half of the century to address these complaints. The most significant effort arose when the Lord Mayor and Aldermen of London, in 1735, proposed new rules for the regulation of Newgate prison. Many of them dealt with the treatment of the condemned. No prisoners, they advised, were to be put into the condemned cells before being sentenced, but once judgment had been passed, they were to be 'only one in a cell'. The condemned were 'to have no other Sustenance but Bread and Water'. Clergymen were to have free access to their cells, but no one was permitted to carry food to them. Only one friend at a time was allowed to visit, and never for more than an hour. No one was to be admitted to the Press Yard or the Chapel while the condemned were going to and from service. 'The Sheriffs Officer', the order continued, was 'not to permit the Prisoners, in their Passage from Newgate to the Place of Execution, to drink any Wine, or other

28 *London Magazine* (1737), 152–3.

29 *Hanging*, 20.

30 Mandeville, *Enquiry*, 18–25, 32, 36–7. For a similar proposal, see *Street-Robberies Consider'd* (London, 1728), 53.

strong Liquors, on any Pretence whatsoever'.[31] Although these regulations were, at best, only rarely enforced, they represent an acknowledgement, on the part of those in authority, that the critics of the proceedings at Tyburn had made their point.

It will not do, however, to overstate the case. Certainly some authors felt that the London crowds were growing more threatening. Yet much evidence supports the contention that little had changed in the character of the proceedings. Most reports of executions in the newspapers of the years around 1750 express satisfaction with the conduct of the condemned and seldom note any unusual level of disorder among the crowd. They reinforce the notion that what most interested the authorities was the conduct of the condemned rather than the behaviour of the assembled populace. In February 1749, one paper reported that six were executed, and 'they all behaved with great Decency'. In April of the same year, nine died at Tyburn, and 'they all behaved very penitent'. Similar phrases were used to describe execution days throughout 1749–51.[32] Such reports should not suggest that Tyburn was a place of perfect order, with an utterly cowed populace respectfully accepting every word uttered by a cleric or magistrate. On the other hand, they certainly do not support a portrait of panicked officials desperate because they had lost control of the event.

Mid-century alarms

Nonetheless, by mid-century the chorus of complaint increased dramatically. The background to this explosion of frustration was one of those periodic panics occasioned by a dramatic increase in crime, especially in the metropolis. From 1748 the papers and journals were full of reports of particularly audacious offences. 'Not only pickpockets', one journal remarked, 'but street robbers and highwaymen were grown to a pitch of insolence at this time, robbing in gangs, defying authority, and often rescuing their companions and carrying them off in triumph'. The challenge seemed to grow with each passing month. 'In most counties', one correspondent claimed in early 1750, 'the assizes were greater

[31] *London Magazine* (1748), 389. These proposals to reform the conduct of executions were rather different from other occasions when a dramatic increase in the number of executions was meant to terrorize the criminal classes. For instance, in 1744, amidst a mounting panic about rising crime rates, the government of London sent an address to the king calling for immediate action. There were, the message charged, 'great Numbers of evil-disposed Persons' at large who committed 'the most daring outrages'. It called for 'a speedy, rigorous and exemplary Execution of the Laws' that would strike 'Terror into the Wicked'. In the wake of this appeal, eighteen offenders died at Tyburn. *London Magazine* (1744), 515–16, 618.

[32] *Whitehall Evening Post*, 18–21 February 1749, 25–27 April 1749, 6–8 November 1750, 12–15 February 1751.

than has been generally known, and many were condemned for murder, robberies, and other crimes.'[33] Most marked was the sense of personal threat. Day after day the papers were full of reports of robberies and assaults.

> The Frequency of audacious Street Robberies repeated every Night in this great Metropolis, call aloud on our Magistrates to think of some Redress; for, as the Case is now, there is no Possibility of stirring from our Habitation after dark, without the Hazard of a fractured Skull, or the Danger of losing that Property People are sometimes obliged to carry about them.[34]

The dismay over rising crime was only one aspect of a more general concern about the moral condition and stability of the nation. As Nicholas Rogers has written,

> Fears about plebeian insubordination and disorder undoubtedly resonated throughout the propertied public during the crime wave of 1749–53, when reports about street robberies were accompanied by accounts of turnpike riots in the West Country, keelmen's strikes on the Tyne, and unruly revels at the London fairs, where, it was said, 'the common people are so audacious, insolent, and ungovernable'.[35]

Riots had been a feature of London life for much of the century, but a succession of challenges, including the Forty-Five, the sailors' assault on the brothels in 1749, and the unrest that accompanied the execution of Penlez (the affair that touched Henry Fielding so closely), all sharpened the sense of unease. Against this backdrop, the sudden surge in the volume of crime, especially of a sort calculated to render personal safety more precarious, presented an alarming portrait of public spaces no longer under control. The ever larger crowds attending executions took on a more sinister appearance. A number of authors were ready to read these various features as symptoms of a crisis in the life of the country. Fears about the spread of corruption and of national decline produced a resurgence of calls for moral reformation. Many commentators saw in gin-drinking and gambling the signs of a social disease that demanded the most vigorous action from the authorities. The reassertion of paternalistic regulation of the poor appeared necessary if the country was to be saved.[36]

[33] *London Magazine* (1748), 570; (1749), 94; (1750), 140. On this panic, see Nicholas Rogers, 'Confronting the Crime Wave: The Debate over Social Reform and Regulation, 1749–1753', in *Stilling the Grumbling Hive*, ed. L. Davison *et al.* (New York, 1992), 77–98; J.M. Beattie, *Crime and the Courts* (Princeton, 1986), 219–21, 530–5.

[34] *Whitehall Evening Post*, 14–17 January 1749.

[35] Rogers, 'Confronting', 87; Elaine Reynolds, *Before the Bobbies: The Night Watch and Police Reform in Metropolitan London, 1720–1830* (Stanford, 1998), 28–33.

[36] Bob Harris, *Politics and the Nation: Britain in the Mid-Eighteenth Century* (Oxford, 2002), 85–7, 123, and, more generally, chapter seven.

In the midst of the panic produced by the rising tide of crime, clerical and secular authors alike returned with special fervour to the idea of the singular value of exemplary punishment. They reasserted their faith in the power of a well-regulated example to teach humanity, especially in its ability to arouse emotions that would have a salutary impact upon personal conduct. Yet the very frequency of these appeals hints at some disquiet concerning the efficacy of these demonstrations. It was as if these ministers found it necessary to recall for their readers and auditors the familiar moral. Robert Fordsham, in a sermon delivered at the Chester assizes in 1751, told his congregation that

> example is an unspeakable benefit to mankind; it shows him how to walk and behave himself without the trouble of instruction, and discovers to him his failings and faults, without reproof and upbraiding – This is the noblest charity, and the greatest good that can be done to man: This is, in the truest sense, giving eyes to the blind. Examples certainly prevail beyond the power of all other means and methods; their authority is forcible, and our reason cannot help conforming to them, though our passions are of an other party.[37]

Henry Fielding shared with these clerical authors a belief that the goal of punishment was to create an 'example'. 'Is not the inflicting of Punishment', he argued, quoting Matthew Hale, 'more for Example, and to prevent Evil, than to punish?' 'The Terror of the Example', he continued, 'is the only Thing proposed, and one Man is sacrificed to the Preservation of Thousands.' The authorities, he cautioned, needed to keep this objective in mind as they encountered pleas for mercy. 'Examples of Justice', they should remember, 'are more merciful than the unbounded Exercise of Pity.'[38] Perhaps even more revealing was his response to what he felt was an epidemic of murders, published in 1752, his *Examples of the Interposition of Providence in the Detection and Punishment of Murder*. This work was intended to awaken and instruct his audience with stories of God's direct intervention to expose murderers and bring them to justice. Such examples, he believed, exercised a salutary

[37] Fordsham, *Dreadful Consequences*, 8–9. Other ministers spoke in a similar vein. According to Peter Pinnell, 'there is a commanding force in great examples': *Where the Righteous Are in Authority the People Rejoice* (London, 1750), 9. 'When men', William Dodwell announced, 'are taught by visible Examples, that Iniquity is the Path to Ruin,' then they learned to avoid 'those Paths which they see bring others to Shame and Misery': *Practical Discourses on Moral Subjects* (London, 1749), i. 244–5. 'When the justice of the magistrates', Curwen Huddleston told his listeners in 1754, 'sets before their eyes and sense the tragical effects of vice and wickedness in the example of suffering criminals; this cannot choose but have a most powerful effect upon the most resolute offenders, even upon those who are proof against the threats of religion itself': *The Advantage of an Impartial Administration of Justice* (London, 1754), 7.

[38] Henry Fielding, *An Enquiry into the Late Increase of Robbers* (1998 reprint of 1751 original, Middletown, Connecticut), 167.

influence at a time when irreligion and immorality seemed in danger of overrunning the land.[39] For Fielding, manners alone were no secure foundation for the stability of society. Only sound religion could answer this need. The pressing task of the example was to remind humanity of this basic truth.[40]

Attempted reforms

As the alarm increased during these years, a flurry of pamphlets and articles appeared that took up the issue of what might be done to improve English penal arrangements. They offered a number of proposals, everything from tossing notorious offenders to wild animals, to calls for a harsh regime of forced labour. Especially prominent, however, were expressions of discontent with what Horace Walpole called 'the monthly shambles at Tyburn'.[41] One author complained of the long trip to the gallows, of the excessive drinking on the journey, and of the general disorder that prevented spectators from attending to the crime for which the condemned suffered. If public executions, he wrote, 'do not inspire both pity and terror, and make not a visible impression on the minds of the spectators', they were 'not only useless, but dangerous, as they accustom the populace to look on violent death with indifference, and instead of rendering the punishment terrible, insensibly render it familiar.' The result was that the day became 'a sort of diversion', an outcome 'incredible elsewhere, and would have been so even here but thirty years ago'.[42]

Joshua Fitzsimmonds denied that the problem was the frequency of executions; rather it arose in 'the Manner of performing them, or perhaps rather by the Inattention of the Ignorant, Careless, or Extravagant, who have no Thoughts about any Punishment at all'.[43] Fielding lamented the fact that what should have been the thief's day of shame had become instead his 'Day of Glory'. 'His Procession to Tyburn, and his last Moments there, are all triumphant, attended with the Compassion of the meek and Tender-hearted, and the Applause, Admiration, and Envy of all the bold and hardened.' He,

[39] Henry Fielding, *Examples of the Interposition of Providence in the Detection and Punishment of Murder* (1988 reprint of 1752 original, Middletown, Connecticut), 179–80.

[40] Melvin Zirker, *Fielding's Social Pamphlets* (Berkeley, 1966), 42; C.J. Rawson, *Henry Fielding and the Augustan Ideal under Stress* (London, 1972).

[41] Quoted in Richard Connors, '"The Grand Inquest of the Nation": Parliamentary Committees and Social Policy in Mid-Eighteenth-Century England', *Parliamentary History*, 14 (1995), 310.

[42] *Right Method*, 44. 'Those condemned', wrote another author, 'are made a publick spectacle in our jails, and suffered to carouze, not only there, but in their passage to the gallows': *London Magazine* (1751), 82.

[43] Joshua Fitzsimmonds, *Free and Candid Disquisitions on the Nature and Execution of the Laws of England* (London, 1751), 40. He praised Fielding's proposals.

too, feared that all consideration of the crime vanished in the contemplation of the condemned.[44]

Even before Fielding composed these passages, a new sheriff for London, Stephen Theodore Janssen, took up in 1749, the challenge of reforming the management of the execution. A prominent merchant, Janssen was a supporter of several organizations that promoted the economic and moral well-being of the nation. His guiding principle was the belief that many of the ills afflicting English society could be remedied if the proper authorities paid due attention to their responsibilities. He himself attended each execution in order to oversee the proceedings, and he insisted his subordinates do likewise. He ensured that the procession left Newgate promptly and forbade any of the usual halts for alcohol. Most observers agreed that Janssen's efforts produced immediate and positive results. Fifteen people were executed in October 1749. 'Mr. Sheriff Janssen', one paper reported, 'holding his White Wand, and surrounded by his Officers, attended the Execution on horseback.' 'Though some Tumult was expected on account of the unhappy Rioters (both of whom were expected to suffer), yet none happened; the requisite Quiet, Seriousness and Decency, being seen in every Part of that necessary but dismal Spectacle.' 'A vast Body of Sailors' who had gathered to save the bodies from the surgeons, 'behaved towards the Sheriff with all imaginable Respect'. Janssen was so confident of his ability to control the proceedings that he dismissed a party of footguards who had been summoned to help preserve order.[45] The following February, the sheriff once again asserted his authority. Nine 'malefactors' died. The procession 'set out from Newgate about Nine in the Morning, in four Carts, which (agreeable to antient Custom, though by a new Order) were doubly guarded, all the proper Officers being commanded to attend'. 'Endeavours were used to get the Carts to stop, in order for the Prisoners to drink, but this Favour was very justly refused.'[46] In March there were fears that a violent gang would attempt a rescue. On this occasion the sheriff attended with several hundred constables, the sight of which led many in the crowd to surrender their bludgeons. It was, the *Whitehall Evening Post* reported, 'a remarkable Example of the Influence (superior to any other) of the Civil Power when duly exerted'.[47]

Subsequent execution days saw similar successes, at least in the eyes of the press. In May the procession, with thirteen condemned, travelled to Tyburn with the 'utmost decency', though the decorum may have been purchased in

[44] Fielding, *Enquiry*, 166–7.

[45] *Whitehall Evening Post*, 17–19 October 1749. Harris, *Politics*, 259–60. The author of *Right Method* (48) complained that sheriffs and high constables too often neglected their offices, and instead left matters 'to a few inferior officers and Petty Constables'. The seriousness with which Janssen regarded this obligation was demonstrated when two constables of the Tower Hamlets were tried for neglect of duty in not attending an execution (27–30 October 1750).

[46] *Whitehall Evening Post*, 6–8 February 1750.

[47] *Whitehall Evening Post*, 24–27 March 1750.

part by the discreet concession by the sheriff in ordering that the bodies be given to the crowd of soldiers and sailors, so as to avoid the 'barbarous Custom of fighting for the Bodies after Execution'.[48] Three women were executed in July. Janssen attended with five high constables and 'a very large number' of petty constables. 'The procession was made with great solemnity all the way.'[49] In August, the six victims were carried in two carts. 'Mr. Sheriff Janssen attended (as usual) with the High Constables; as likewise did the City Marshall (for the first time) with his Officers, as far as Holborn Bars. The Procession went on with the greatest Order.'[50] In October, the execution of Maclain and the forger Smith attracted 'the greatest Concourse of People at Tyburn ever known at any Execution'. Yet, 'no Soldiers attended at the above Execution', a paper noted with satisfaction. 'The excellent Regulations made (in this and other Respects) during the late Sheriffalty, have rendered the Aid of the Military Power quite unnecessary.'[51] It says a good deal about the state of polite opinion that these measures were greeted with extravagant enthusiasm, and were widely disseminated in the provincial press. They marked, one author remarked, the revival of 'the former decency and solemnity of executions'. A Bath newspaper reported with approval the arrangements made for the April 1750 executions, and in August congratulated London on its management of the day, while calling upon 'future Magistrates' to follow 'the Example here set them!'[52] Perhaps inspired by the conduct of the metropolis, the university authorities at Oxford made special arrangements to control the students on execution day. The result was that the town avoided 'great Mischief'. The two men who suffered, a paper noted with pleasure, 'behaved decently, and acknowledged the Crimes for which they suffered'.[53] Other proposals for further improvements soon followed. One author in the *London Magazine* complained that some of the condemned travelled to Tyburn in hackney coaches. It was a mistake, he concluded, to allow malefactors to be distinguished one from another. 'For, as all executions are, or ought to be, an example to the living, to deter them from the like end, so, most surely, the ignominy and shame attending thereon, cannot be too much or too openly exposed.' It was, after all, for the purpose of humiliating them that they were carried so far.[54]

The rapid success of Janssen's efforts to secure greater order might have been expected to restore confidence in the execution to an uneasy public. Instead the chorus of complaint swelled in volume. The fact that his achievement did

48 *Whitehall Evening Post*, 14–17 May 1750.

49 *London Magazine* (1750), 331.

50 *Whitehall Evening Post*, 7–9 August 1750.

51 *Whitehall Evening Post*, 2–4 October 1750. These sentiments were repeated in the *Newcastle Courant*, 13 October 1750, and the *Bath Journal*, 8 October 1750.

52 *London Magazine* (1750), 90, 140, 378, 454; *Bath Journal*, 2 April 1750, 13 August 1750.

53 *Bath Journal*, 9 April 1750.

54 *London Magazine* (1750), 378, 454; *Whitehall Evening Post*, 25–27 September 1750.

not quell doubts about the morality and utility of Tyburn indicates that the problem lay elsewhere than in the actual conduct of the event. While there was unanimous agreement that the existing management of the execution was defective, critics advanced a number of different proposals intended to cure the evil. One author demanded that if the nation spared even the worst offenders 'those terrifying circumstances' that attended executions in other countries, 'surely some care should be taken to heighten the solemnity of this spectacle'. As things stood, 'in this last and most interesting scene to the public', there was 'no proper method invented to make these examples a warning to others'.[55] These years saw a variety of proposals for altering the theatrical elements of the execution, either by increasing the horror or by cloaking the highest penalty in more mystery. One author suggested that executions should take place, like those of Sparta, at night, so that the condemned could not be seen to set the law at defiance.[56] Another wrote that 'there can be no reason assigned' why a horrid crime 'should not suffer most acutely in the Flesh'.[57] Near the end of his own pamphlet, given over to a sweeping analysis of the ills he believed afflicted English society, Henry Fielding turned to the execution. He announced his conviction that the trip to Tyburn had become a triumph instead of a tragedy, and so defeated the ends of justice. 'The great cause of this evil', he charged, 'is the frequency of executions.' One could become too familiar with these episodes; they lost their force when they ceased to be rare. Fielding offered an analysis of this situation that was striking for its psychological specificity. The problem, he alleged, arose from the difficulty in uniting 'the ideas of death and shame', since 'all ideas of the latter' were 'absorbed by the former'. As proof of this phenomenon, he asked his readers to imagine a scene: 'tell me, when he hath beheld a poor wretch, bound in a cart, just on the verge of eternity, all pale and trembling with his approaching fate, whether the idea of shame hath ever intruded on his mind?' Even less did the bold villain inspire moral reflection.[58] 'Instead of making the Gallows an object of Terror', he argued in 1752, 'our Executions contribute to make it an Object of Contempt in the Eye of the Malefactor; and we sacrifice the Lives of men, not for the Reformation, but for the Diversion of the Populace.'[59]

Several of Fielding's recommendations echoed those advanced by earlier authors. He was in favour of reducing the time between sentencing and execution. He also opposed 'Examples of ill grounded Clemency'. He joined in the general demand that executions be made more solemn. Yet in one

[55] *Right Method*, 44.

[56] *Proposal to the Legislature*, 19.

[57] Charles Jones, *Some Methods Proposed Towards Putting a Stop to the Flagrant Crimes of Murder, Robbery and Perjury* (London, 1752), 14.

[58] Fielding, *Enquiry*, 163–72.

[59] Quoted in Rogers, 'Confronting', 87.

respect Fielding went well beyond Janssen's efforts to bring greater order to the gallows day, for he had come to doubt whether such measures would ever succeed in making Tyburn useful. His solution was that the execution 'should be in some degree private'. It might be performed in front of the Old Bailey, in the presence of the judges. Fielding's ambition was to regulate more closely who was seeing and what was seen. The eye, he implied, could no longer be trusted. Better was an appeal to the imagination. 'The mind of man', he went on to explain, 'is so much more capable of magnifying than his eye, that I question whether every object is not lessened by being looked upon.'[60] Fielding's partial retreat from the principle of public execution marks an important moment in the history of capital punishment. Even as he committed himself to the goal of reinvigorating the practice of making examples, he conceded that punishment might have to be withdrawn from view in order to make it effective. The visibility of punishment, so long central to its character, could no longer, it seemed, guarantee the symbolic meaning and force of the example.[61]

What had led him to make such a drastic proposal? Tyburn's critics, and Fielding chief among them, were in no doubt about the reason for this crisis; they blamed the crowd for the failure. Writers drew an increasingly grim portrait of a mob so vicious and turbulent that it could no longer be reached by the rituals of the law. The mob was impervious to the significance of the event it witnessed. 'Death is become too familiar to our profligate', one writer complained, 'and no wonder, as it is a jubilee for our butchers apprentices, and loose young fellows of that class, to attend a dozen or score of the most unhappy wretches to Tyburn.'[62] Samuel Johnson could scarcely restrain his contempt for 'that croud of thousands' who attended 'the legal massacre, and look with carelessness, perhaps with triumph, on the utmost exacerbations of human misery'.[63] What is most striking is the absolute insistence upon the idea that the assembled would not and could not interpret the event in the right way. These commentators believed that crowds had grown less manageable and more irreverent. Worse still, the writers assumed a bond had grown up between the condemned and the mob that the authorities were impotent to sever. Tyburn Fair had become for them the epitome of all the evils that characterized the malignant life of London.

Yet even as they affixed on the crowd blame for the situation, these same authors revealed that other emotions and beliefs were involved in the growing

60 Fielding, *Enquiry*, 163–72. One author, in praising Fielding's pamphlet, wondered if the tendency to show criminals dying penitent and being forgiven did not act to encourage crime: *A Letter to Henry Fielding* (London, 1751).

61 Wilf, 'Imagining', 56–7.

62 *London Magazine* (1751), 82.

63 Samuel Johnson, *Works* (New Haven, CT, 1969), iv. 242 (from *The Rambler*, no. 114, 1751).

distance of the respectable classes from the scene of punishment. For more was at stake than the conduct of the unruly mob. 'All executions of criminals', one contributor to the *London Magazine* explained, 'are shocking to every humane and considerate mind.'[64] Physical inflictions were painful to behold. They loomed large in the descriptions offered by these critics of existing arrangements, elbowing out even the drama of repentance that figured so prominently in traditional accounts of the execution. 'The Scenes of Barbarity and Torture that are so often exhibited before the Eyes of the People', one writer warned, 'can administer to no other End, than to extirpate and extinguish the soft and tender Passions of the human heart.'[65] The problem, these authors suggested, was that public punishments interfered with the operation of the civilizing influences that were making the English more sociable and humane. Such penalties were all the more dangerous for the lower orders that had yet to feel the full effect of these beneficial developments. 'We grossly deceive ourselves', one pamphleteer wrote in 1754, 'if we imagine the rack, the gibbet, or any other barbarity a peevish legislator can ordain, will be capable of long deterring mankind from crimes of the blackest die.' Terror might restrain a population for a period, but it soon lost its force and became 'the ridicule and mockery of an audacious vulgar'.[66] What these phrases proclaimed is that it was no longer acceptable to attend an execution. Too much occurred there that could not be tolerated. Attendance indicated a morbid curiosity or a savage lust to see others suffer. There was little room here for the idea that one could learn from such an event, that duty required attendance, and that religion ennobled what happened there. Even in the midst of the enthusiasm for Janssen's efforts, these critics suggested that perhaps the spectacle could not be redeemed.

Politeness, punishment, and the eclipse of the example

In one sense what these commentators testified to was the growing 'polarization of polite and popular culture'. The revulsion against Tyburn was a part of a broader and more diverse movement. They came to believe that the execution shared too much with other sports and festivities, as well as popular rituals, which had come to seem distasteful or immoral. 'It was a measure of the urban elite's profound disengagement from traditional culture', Peter Borsay has written, 'that activities once shared and supported were now perceived as

64 *London Magazine* (1750), 453.

65 *London Magazine* (1746), 638. Public whippings, at least in London, declined dramatically in number over the first half of the century. J.M. Beattie, *Policing and Punishment in London 1660–1750* (Oxford, 2001), 446–7.

66 *Proposal to the Legislature*, 116.

threatening.'[67] The English upper and middle classes were in the process of creating a different kind of world for themselves, above all in London. It was a geography composed of squares and pleasure gardens, of commercial districts filled with shops and offices. Georgian architecture presented a reassuring image of a rational and orderly society. Public and private spaces were devoted to the cultivation of polite sociability. Violence was to be excluded; passions were to be controlled. The expression of rude or exaggerated emotions had become unseemly. Propriety and refined manners not only provided the rules to govern society, they also marked the boundary separating the respectable from the lower orders. No respectable person would want to be associated with events dominated by the boisterous and unruly crowd. 'The pastimes of the polite therefore, emerged as cerebral and enlightened, while those of the common people appeared to be physical, sensual, superstitious, and ignorant.'[68] Of course these values found sanction in religious attitudes, but they spoke as well of a more optimistic view of human nature and of greater confidence in the ability of manners and habits to regulate and refine human behaviour. The polite no longer accepted suffering as an inevitable aspect of the human condition.

Tempting as it is to view this change as one more instance of the 'civilizing process', there are good reasons to avoid this urge. The problem with that term, powerful as it is for capturing prominent features of a vast cultural movement, is its difficulty in accounting for the role of ideas in constituting such a transformation as that described here. For it has been the argument of this chapter that it was the eclipse of the notion of the example that was pivotal to the shift in the meanings and feelings associated with the public execution. The discomfort that arose for the polite at the gallows had both a religious and a class dimension that was not reducible to psychological states. The feelings of unease, the disgust aroused by the spectacle, occurred because the elite no longer believed in the example, in the older sense of that word. The respectable classes, by the 1750s, were rapidly losing faith in the ritual and the religious trappings that accompanied the execution. They also viewed their relationship to the lower orders in a different light.

The example had been a bridge of sorts, at least in the minds of the authorities, between rulers and ruled. It was supposed to bring them together in a mutual understanding in which religion justified the divisions on earth while reminding the assembled of a common condition before the seat of God. Punishment, with the central place allotted to confession, enacted this belief. But it relied upon everyone recognizing a role at the scene of punishment, as

67 Peter Borsay, '"All the Town's a Stage": Urban Ritual and Ceremony 1660–1800', in *The Transformation of English Provincial Towns*, ed. Peter Clark (Bradford-on-Avon, 1985), 248–9, and more generally 228–58.

68 Peter Borsay, *The English Urban Renaissance* (Oxford, 1989), 289, and more generally, 257–308. See also John Brewer, *The Pleasures of the Imagination* (London, 1997), 98–112; Miles Ogborn, *Spaces of Modernity* (New York, 1998), 75–115; Langford, *Polite*, 68–79.

authority, audience, or victim. It required the conviction that public punishment offered an edifying spectacle for all of society. By the mid-eighteenth century, increasing numbers of people were finding no place for themselves in this drama. Rather the unease inspired by the crowd and the discomfort provoked by the penalty itself pointed to a gulf that could not be closed. Even a well-behaved assembly around the gallows produced dismay. Not all members of the respectable classes experienced these feelings equally. But the frequency of the complaints about Tyburn testifies to the spread of the sentiment. It was precisely because the example was so central to their conception of punishment that some authors expressed alarm at what they saw increasingly as its failure. Yet they remained divided about how to attempt to restore its effectiveness, or if this effort was even possible or desirable. The polite found it harder to attend to what was said at the gallows; the drama did not speak to them as powerfully as it once had. They were too distracted by other things. Death might be necessary; few argued for its total abolition. But its public display was not. It might operate on the imagination, but it was hard to see how it could be safely or constructively experienced directly and collectively.

Little legislation arose out of this crisis, and even those bills proposed 'were essentially *ad hoc* conclusions of fact, unguided by any theoretical structure'.[69] Yet one measure bears witness to a remarkable shift of understanding of the sort that this chapter has been trying to describe. The Murder Act, passed in 1752, contains traces of the shifting currents that marked these years and points to the confusing conclusions they might produce. The preamble expressed alarm at the increase in the frequency of murder, especially in London. It aimed to add 'some further Terror and peculiar Mark of Infamy . . . to the Punishment of Death' in cases of the crime. One clause enacted the often repeated suggestion that the court announce a time for execution, and proposed that it should follow two days after sentence was pronounced. The condemned were to be subjected to strict confinement, placed in a separate cell, and allowed no visitors without the explicit permission of the authorities. They were also to be kept on a severe diet of bread and water. The provision that excited the most comment ordered that the body of the executed offender be given up to the surgeons for dissection, unless the judge decided that it should be suspended in chains. Proposals of this sort had circulated for several decades, but parliament now gave the suggestion specific sanction.[70]

[69] Hugh Amory, 'Henry Fielding and the Criminal Legislation of 1751–52', *Philological Quarterly*, 50 (1971), 177. For a discussion of the reasons for this failure, see Rogers, 'Confronting', 77–98. Yet Richard Connors defends this effort, 'Grand Inquest', 312–13.

[70] 25 George II c. 37; Leon Radzinowicz, *A History of English Criminal Law* (London, 1948), i. 206–7; *London Magazine* (1744), 637–9; (1750), 453; Linebaugh, 'Tyburn Riot', 70–4; Beattie, *Crime*, 525–30. For an earlier instance of this proposal, see Eboranus (T. Robe), *A Collection of Political Tracts* (London, 1735), 49–51.

Hanging in chains and dissection, as practices, pulled in opposite directions. Each aimed to heighten the shame associated with death; each sought to use the exhibition of the body as a way of increasing the effect of punishment. Yet they could not have been more different. In one case the remains were exposed to all eyes, the grim fact of the human mortality on display. Still, the body in chains acted as a sign, to be read and interpreted, a reminder of the fate of the mortal body in the scales of eternity. In the other instance, the body was opened to the gaze of professionals, and the practice was justified, at least in part, in the name of science. The seeing was limited to a select audience, whose viewing was not supposed to be voyeuristic, but was intended rather to promote the progress of knowledge. The audience in Hogarth's 'Fourth Stage of Cruelty' looks on with a studied indifference to the fate of the individual. Even as the authorities relied upon the knowledge that dissection would anger, and, they hoped, frighten the lower orders, they also treated these beliefs with a scorn reserved for what was seen as the illiterate and superstitious rabble. It was a punishment that justified itself by being divorced from passion, opposed to delight, and justified as useful to humanity. Here we see hints of a new path charted for the legitimization of penal measures.

With the passage of the Murder Act, the controversy over the Tyburn spectacle subsided for a time. The feeling of unease, however, never disappeared. Complaints about the management of the execution became a staple of reform arguments for an alteration in the criminal law. Even those who defended the death penalty acknowledged that hanging day was poor theatre. Change came slowly. It was only in 1783, in the midst of another criminal panic and in the aftermath of the Gordon Riots, that the procession to Tyburn ended, and executions came to take place outside Newgate prison. Crowds continued to rush to the scene. The Ordinary went on publishing his accounts, while last dying speeches remained a popular literary form. Many people still wanted to see how the condemned would die. Despite mounting unhappiness with public executions, the authorities for long resisted their abolition. Prudence dictated caution. If there was less faith in the ability of the occasion to offer moral instruction, the authorities still hoped it might terrify potential offenders. Only in 1868 did the gallows disappear from view.[71] The long hiatus and the halting character of the movement away from public executions in no way diminish the significance of what was happening in mid-eighteenth-century England. For in this period a profound transformation occurred in the way in which polite and respectable society saw the gallows. The uneasiness with the practice of capital punishment took more than one form in eighteenth-century England. The process of change involved not only the rise of new attitudes and views of punishment, but also the dissolution of older understandings and experiences.

[71] See my 'Civilizing Punishment: The End of the Public Execution in England', *Journal of British Studies*, 33 (1994), 257–82.

The central features of the crisis of the 1750s were the gradual withdrawal of the respectable classes from the place of execution, the mounting fear that public punishment presented a threat to social order, and, in particular, the diminished belief in the principle of the example. Hogarth's portrait of Tyburn did not offer much hope that anything useful could be made of the event. The condemned and his last words are lost amidst a jostling crowd scarcely capable of drawing any valuable lesson from the death. The public execution had become an unsettling occurrence. It was a symptom rather than a cure for the moral ills that afflicted society. It offered only ugly facts and disgusting behaviours. The concern most often expressed was that the gallows failed to inspire the lower orders with proper ideas of justice and morality. The real secret, however, was that it no longer succeeded in doing so for the respectable. While they placed the blame for this failure on the crowd, their words spoke of their own loss of faith in the ceremony as an exemplary occasion with a meaning that operated across class boundaries. Despite the pervasive alarm aroused by the mid-century crime wave, authors offered little discussion of the criminal code or of alternatives to the gallows.[72] Such a critique of existing arrangements only blossomed in the 1760s and 1770s. Nonetheless, the 1750s were linked to what followed, even if only indirectly. The frequent recital of the discomfort occasioned by the imperfect spectacle of public execution hastened the search for alternative punishments. The culture of politeness inspired new ideas about how punishment should work and what its goal should be. When it proved so difficult to make an example of an individual offender, some writers began to look for ways of harnessing social pressure and religious instruction to foster the improvement of prisoners. This quest lay in the future. For the moment uncertainty marked the discussion. What made the mid-century crisis distinctive was the retreat it revealed from a belief in the power of the gallows to deliver a useful, indeed essential, lesson about the human predicament, one that endowed the penalty with a kind of nobility.

[72] Rogers, 'Confronting', 92–4.

9

Virginia and the imperial state

Law, enlightenment, and 'the crooked cord of discretion'

DAVID THOMAS KONIG*

A good caveat to Parliaments to leave all causes to be measured by the gold and straight metwand of the law, and not to the incertain and crooked cord of discretion.

Sir Edward Coke, *The Fourth Part of the Institutes of the Laws of England* (London, 1648), 41

It is a great Unhappiness, that no one can tell what is Law, and what is not, in the Plantations. . . . [W]e are left in the dark, in one of the most considerable Points of our Rights; and the Case being so doubtful, we are too often obliged to depend upon the Crooked Cord of a Judge's Discretion, in Matters of the greatest Moment and Value.

An anonymous Virginian, *An Essay Upon the Government of the English Plantations On the Continent of America* (1701), ed. L. Wright (San Marino, CA, 1945), 23

Introduction

From a constitutional perspective, the North American 'long eighteenth century' falls conveniently into the century from 1689 to 1789 – between news of the Glorious Revolution and that announcing the inauguration of a federal republic under the United States constitution. The triumph of king in parliament ended crude Stuart efforts to erect a Continental-style military empire in North America, as parliament shifted the exercise of its sovereignty from force to statutory intrusion. As Lord Townshend, President of the Board of Trade, reported to the king and Privy Council in 1721 '[I]t hath ever been

* I would like to thank David Lemmings for his helpful comments and insightful suggestions.

the wisdom, not only of Great Britain, but likewise of all other States, to secure by all possible means the intire absolute and immediate dependancy of their Colonies.' Townshend was addressing the fact that '[t]he laws and constitutions of your Majesty's Colonies are copy'd from those of Great Britain, but fall short of them in many particulars.' In such a situation, he warned, 'your Majesty's Colonies can never be put on a right footing.'[1]

To achieve that 'right footing' parliament replaced Stuart force with the more subtle and ultimately more intrusive Whig bureaucratic and legal mechanisms, commencing with the Navigation Act of 1696,[2] which created an administrative and judicial apparatus for extending the reach of the imperial state through law across the seas. In succeeding decades the Privy Council – beholden to and controlled by parliament – rejected local legal usages on appeal and disallowed local statutes on review. Unfortunately for London and the colonies alike, the same bureaucratic inefficiencies and inconsistencies that marred all other efforts to reduce the colonies to serve the interests of the imperial state affected these legal and judicial matters as well. Championed on both sides of the Atlantic as the distinctive hallmark of British identity, the 'rule of law' itself became a field of contest, with different meanings for imperial interests and the colonists who experienced it in their own local courts. Neither side wanted to be subject to 'the crooked cord' of legal uncertainty, and both wanted to replace it with some 'gold and straight' standard. But they differed sharply on the rules and principles that would make it so. The debate was abruptly aborted in 1776, but local legal imperative and the modern state clashed again in 1789, when a federal constitution established a legal regime under the supremacy of the 'law of the land' interpreted by a federal judiciary. For Virginians, the result was a legal déjà vu: where local political leaders had struggled to insulate local institutions from parliamentary power, and where local juries had defied English law for a century, once more province and state were at odds over law.[3]

It is the purpose of this chapter to examine the way that the imperial state attempted to use law and legal mechanisms to achieve that 'dependency' in Virginia, the empire's oldest, most populous, and wealthiest North American province. It is commonly accepted historiographical convention that in eighteenth-century Virginia neither crown nor parliament followed a 'coercive' model of imperial governance but rather promoted the 'significant role of peripheral entities in constructing authority in the extended polities

[1] Board of Trade to king, 8 September 1721, *Calendar of State Papers, Colonial Series, America and West Indies, 1574–1711*, ed. W. Sainsbury *et al.* (London, 1860–1924), *1721*, 444–5 (hereinafter, CSP)

[2] 7 & 8 Wm. III c. 22 (1696), 'An act for preventing frauds, and regulating abuses in the plantation trade'.

[3] F. Miller, *Juries and Judges versus the Law: Virginia's Provincial Legal Culture, 1783–1828* (Charlottesville, VA, 1994).

represented by the new transatlantic empires'. The result was a successful 'quest for power' by colonial elites, whose legislative ascendancy created an 'extraordinary political stability' within an acknowledged 'multicentric' constitutional structure that lasted until disrupted by parliament in the 1760s.[4] This conventional portrait as applied to Virginia remains useful, but it requires revision and expansion, especially in view of the abundant scholarship amply demonstrating the success of the imperial state in flexing its 'sinews of power' in the eighteenth century.[5] Although the present chapter concedes – indeed, re-emphasizes – the 'multicentric' nature of the imperial constitution, it argues that no consensus existed to legitimize it, and that the struggle by colonists to retain control over the meaning and practice of 'law' against encroachment from London remained a point of friction throughout the period of supposed 'salutary neglect'. While this model may have use in describing parliament's posture towards legislative politics in North America, it certainly cannot apply to the law and to those institutions in London working relentlessly to rationalize legal affairs there. To explain why – and to gain a proper appreciation of how law was understood and used on the edges of empire – this chapter will examine the role of law as it affected property, exchange rates, control of an enslaved labouring population, and the procedures of private litigation. From those details, it is hoped, will be revealed a hidden pattern of legal contest between imperial interests and local usage. Focus must be shifted, therefore, from the usual study of the struggle between executives and their recalcitrant assemblies to that between executive administration and colonial courts.[6] Such

[4] This model of colonial legal development is best demonstrated in the work of Jack P. Greene, whose major essays on this point are collected in his *Negotiated Authorities: Essays in Colonial Political and Constitutional Development* (Charlottesville, VA, 1994) and *The Quest for Power: The Lower Houses of Assembly in the Southern Royal Colonies 1689–1776* (Chapel Hill, NC, 1993). Greene's model of colonial legal development explicitly complements and acknowledges that of John Phillip Reid, in that both argue 'the dispersion, not the concentration, of authority' as 'a central fact of its [the Atlantic empire's] legal and constitutional character'. Reid describes the eighteenth century as an 'epoch of two constitutions in Great Britain and the American colonies' in *Constitutional History of the American Revolution*, abridged ed. (Madison, WI, 1995), 4.

[5] As exemplified by J. Brewer, *The Sinews of Power: War, Money, and the English State, 1688–1783* (New York, 1989).

[6] The power of courts – and not just legislatures – to effect legal change in a positivist manner has been challenged by R. Epstein, 'Social Consequences of Common Law Rules', *Harvard Law Review*, 95 (1982), 1717–51. But the major factors adduced by Epstein and others – a disorganized court system, lack of standing by interested parties seeking influence, and a low volume of cases affecting the desired outcome – did not apply in eighteenth-century Virginia, as the present chapter will show. David Millon argues, moreover, that the modernist paradigm of legal positivism overlooks the ways in which earlier societies imposed their own consistent normative judgment through juries without explicitly articulated rules. 'Positivism in the Historiography of the Common Law', *Wisconsin Law Review*, 1989 (1989), 669–714. On the impact of jury norms on early American legal development, see W. Nelson,

a focus concedes, as Lord Hardwicke grudgingly admitted after decades of failure to lead colonial legislatures to reform, 'As they are Legislative Bodies, I can see no help for it.'[7] Instead, he recognized that 'the administration of justice and execution of laws is the principal point of government.'[8]

The contest over law in an 'enlightened' empire

In 1698 Francis Nicholson returned to Virginia to begin a second term as lieutenant-governor of that royal province, the crown's 'Old Dominion' as dubbed by a Charles II grateful for its loyalty to him during the Civil War.[9] But Virginia's loyalty – though undiminished at the turn of the eighteenth century – had required the stern imposition of Stuart coercion after Bacon's Rebellion in 1676, when the provincial government fell into chaos and the royal governor was put to flight. Nicholson was a reminder of the way that Stuart autocracy might resort to force: he had been active in suppressing Monmouth's Rebellion, and had followed his military career with executive service in Maryland and New York, as well as a prior term as lieutenant-governor of Virginia from 1690 to 1692. Nevertheless, his first term there had been a success; as a military leader in a desperate time of war, his experience and energy were welcomed by grateful colonists willing to overlook his autocratic rule and personal abuse for the relatively short time he was there. But his military background and style, though typical of royal governors sent to North America in the decades before and after 1700, ill suited the contours of the imperial state emerging more clearly in his second term. No longer would the maintenance of empire rely on the patterns of Hobbesian authoritarianism that had driven not only England's imperial thrust but those of its French, Spanish, and Portuguese rivals.[10] In its place would emerge a paradigm of imperial control more typical of the enlightenment, with rule by administrative agencies seeking consistency and rationality. Hobbes was replaced by Locke

Americanization of the Common Law: The Impact of Legal Change on Massachusetts Society, 1760–1830 (Cambridge, MA, 1975).

7 J. Henretta, *'Salutary Neglect': Colonial Administration Under the Duke of Newcastle* (Princeton, NJ, 1972), 341.

8 *The Parliamentary History of England*, xiv. 20 (House of Lords debate on the bill for abolishing the hereditable jurisdictions in Scotland, 17 February 1747).

9 Nicholson was among the first colonial executives to serve as lieutenant-governor under an absentee titular 'Captain General and Governor in Chief', in this case George Hamilton, Earl of Orkney, who received half the income of the position as a sinecure. Nicholson was being rewarded for his service under the Duke of Marlborough. It has been estimated that 60 per cent of colonial executives from the Restoration through the 1720s were military officers. Stephen Saunders Webb, 'The Strange Career of Francis Nicholson', *William and Mary Quarterly*, 3rd ser., 23 (1966), 513–14.

10 On this model, see Elizabeth Mancke, 'Empire and State', in D. Armitage and M. Braddick (eds), *The British Atlantic World, 1500–1800* (New York, 2002), 175–95.

in colonial administration just as in domestic politics. Not the army, but the Privy Council and the Lords Commissioners of Trade and Plantations (better known as the Board of Trade when created in 1696) would reshape the empire. English law, not continental-style force, would extend and strengthen the reach of the imperial state, and in 1700 the Board asked all colonial governors to 'report as to the method of proceedings in the Several Courts upon trials of all sorts of causes'.[11] It is fitting that among the most vocal advocates of the Board was the statistician Sir William Petty, author of *Political Arithmetick* (1690), and that one of the strongest influences on the Board in its formative years was John Locke, secretary to one of England's most active colonial entrepreneurs, Anthony Ashley Cooper, third Earl of Shaftesbury. Expertise, based on patiently and carefully gathered knowledge, would provide the enlightenment project of administration. Not arbitrary and erratic force, but 'a set of rationally conceived policies' would govern the colonies.[12]

Nicholson had not adapted to the changes now inexorably altering imperial relations after the Glorious Revolution. During his time in New York he had made it known that he shared the military 'principle that parliaments are roots of rebellion and Magna Charta sprung out of them'. 'Magna Charta, Magna Farta', he is said to have remarked before fleeing the colony when news of the Glorious Revolution reached it in 1689.[13] When Nicholson returned to Virginia in 1698 as governor, Virginian Robert Beverley reported that he arrived 'not then with that Smoothness on his Brow, he had carry'd with him' before.[14] Beverley recorded this fact in his *History and Present State of Virginia*, which he wrote while in London in 1703 and 1704 defending an appeal to the Privy Council by an adversary supported by Governor Nicholson, who had presided at the Virginia appellate court and expressed his own dissenting opinion against Beverley. But Beverley was no ordinary litigant, and the appeal epitomized the legal contestation emblematic of a new chapter in the history of the empire. Beverley had served in some of the most important (and lucrative) legal offices of the colony: clerk of the General Assembly (the lower house), clerk of the Council (the upper house) and clerk of the General Court (the colony's highest judicial body, where the governor presided over the Council meeting in a judicial capacity). As clerk of those bodies, Beverley possessed the apparently mundane but highly strategic power to record and store the records that Virginia rivals might demand in their attempts to punish their enemies, or that English officials might wish to consult in searching for

[11] *CSP (1700)*, 447.

[12] Peter Laslett, 'John Locke, the Great Recoinage, and the Origins of the Board of Trade: 1695–1698', *William and Mary Quarterly*, 3rd ser., 14 (1957), 370–402, at 381. C. Andrews, *The Colonial Period of American History* (New Haven, CT, 1934–8), iv. 281, 291–94.

[13] Webb, 'Francis Nicholson', 522.

[14] R. Beverley, *The History and Present State of Virginia* [1705], ed. L. Wright (Chapel Hill, NC, 1947), 105–6.

evidence of actions antithetical to royal authority. In effect, the clerk was a very well compensated curator of the colony's political and legal legacy. Few men in the colony, moreover, were as skilled in the ways of the courtroom as Beverley, who had come by them naturally: a contemporary had described his father, Major Robert Beverley, as 'best acquainted with the practice part' among all lawyers in the colony. As clerk of the House during the Restoration, the major had been jailed for refusing to surrender its records and then ordered to be removed by James II. The younger Robert and eight other Beverleys sat in the House in the eighteenth century, and the family was allied by marriage to several other Virginia dynasties.[15]

Robert *fils* proved to be a worthy successor to Robert *père* both as politician and lawyer, though it was his attempt to act as both in his ill-fated law suit that undid him and sent him into retirement cultivating wine. In 1699, using his political connections, Beverley arranged to be awarded land which he claimed had escheated to the colony for lack of an heir, but he was sued by a family claiming to have occupied the land since 1671 by right of a valid testamentary bequest.[16] No record of the trial exists, but depositions gathered for it suggest that Beverley was able to prove his factual case before a jury at the Elizabeth City County court. The legal issues were simple, and the tactics straightforward: two conflicting factual claims, which were resolved by a jury in Beverley's favour. It took four years for his defeated opponents to regroup and resume their legal assault on Beverley, but this time the litigation would be far more complicated. Before it ended, it would proceed from the Elizabeth County courthouse by certiorari to the General Court at Williamsburg and by writ of error to the Privy Council in London, and would reveal painstaking attention to legal and factual nuances. It would reveal, too, how confused and contradictory was the body of law governing Virginia, and how contested its control was.

By 1703, both parties had prepared legal and factual arguments to claim title through the tangled thicket that was English inheritance law. At the General Court Beverley's adversaries based their civil action of ejectment on the existence of a bequest, which that court gave 'to the Jury to weigh what it will'. He countered with a deposition sworn in London by 'Rachel Viscountess Dowager Faulkland' alleging descent to the intestate. To his dismay, the Virginia high court refused to admit the deposition for not having been sworn in the colony and gave judgment against Beverley. Shocked but undeterred, he obtained a stay of execution for additional pleading. The jury that had

15 Richard L. Morton, *Colonial Virginia* (Chapel Hill, NC, 1960), i. 304–5, 323.

16 Basic documents from this case, along with genealogical matter, are published in a collection of materials relating to the settlement of this location, known by its Indian name of 'Kecoughtan' before its inhabitants rejected its 'savage' name in 1619 and Anglicized it to 'Elizabeth City County'. See 'Old Kecoughtan', *William and Mary Quarterly*, 1st ser., 19 (1910), 83–131.

decided against him, he argued, had not been legally empanelled. But his opponents pleaded that the error was harmless because 'all those mistakes were aided by the Statute of 21st King James Cap. 13 Entitled an Act for the further reformation of Jeofayles (which statute was read).' This statute was commonly pleaded in colonial courtrooms, as it 'aided' (or cured) minor defects of precise pleading or notation. Despite its widespread customary use in the colonies, it was not at all clear that the statute legally applied: though enacted after settlement, it did not mention the colonies and thus arguably did not apply across the seas. Such omissions would become a constant source of dispute over whether or not a law might be applied in the American provinces, a question too often settled by 'the Crooked Cord of a Judge's Discretion'.

Beverley therefore responded with a Virginia statute on jury trials directing that they be conducted 'as near as may be to the laws of England (by which wee are to be governed) as our present capacities will admit',[17] and he produced in court a copy of 'Dalton's Office of Sheriff (shewing what a Pannel was)'.[18] Insisting on the procedure set out by this well-known and much relied on manual, Beverley moved that 'for want of such Form it cant be taken for a Legal Pannel and therefore does not come within the said [Virginia] statute.' After Beverley cited a prior Virginia decision as precedent, the bench agreed, accepted the motion, and reversed its prior decision. Presiding at the General Court, however, Governor Nicholson entered his own opinion that the statute of jeofails had cured the defect, '& that a Case that at Tryall was mentioned . . . was no more like this case than a Horse is like a man'. The losing appellants, emboldened by this dissent, appealed to the Privy Council through a writ of error. Beverley's presence at St James's Palace was unavailing; the Council, deciding law not fact, reversed the Virginia decision in 1704.[19]

The only thing left clear by the Privy Council was that the status of English law in the colony of Virginia was entirely open to question and subject to various determinations by different judges. Beverley was outraged, and it was this decision, which had confirmed Nicholson's remark (that Beverley's cited precedent was no more like the case at hand 'than a Horse is like a man'), that prompted him to write three letters home calling Nicholson a 'viper', and accusing him of harbouring 'designs of ruin & Slavery to our poor Country'. Lamenting his loss as he prepared to leave London in 1704, he wrote, 'My cause is over & gone against me, having had as unfair a Trial here as ever I had there.'[20]

[17] Laws of 1662, ch. 37, *The Statutes at Large; Being a Collection of all the Laws of Virginia, from the First Session of the Legislature, in the Year 1619*, comp. W. Hening (Richmond, VA, 1819–23), ii. 73–4.

[18] Michael Dalton, *Officium vicecomitum: the office and authority of sheriffs: gathered out of the statutes and books of the common laws of this realm* (London, 1682).

[19] 'Old Kecoughtan' documents, 98–9.

[20] *Executive Journals of the Council of Colonial Virginia* (Richmond, VA, 1925–8), ii. 391, 392, 395.

The antagonism of the litigation touched off a running feud. The governor called Beverley's accusations 'part scandalous, & part malitious', and advised him 'to get himself close shaved, and make friends with the Governors of her Maj[es]tys hospital of Bethlam and get a place there: and there he may meet with real chains instead of imaginary ones'.[21] Behind the heated rhetoric lay substantive disputes about law. The land title case had revealed several basic areas of sharp disagreement. The question of statutory application had surfaced in a pamphlet circulating since 1701, written anonymously but so parallel in its contents to Beverley's own struggles and opinions that it was long attributed to him by twentieth-century scholars.[22] The author, whom we only know to be a Virginian, observes,

> It is a great Unhappiness, that no one can tell what a Law is, and what is not, in the Plantations; some hold that the Law of *England* is chiefly to be respected, and where that is deficient, the Laws of the several Colonies are to take place; others are of Opinion, that the Laws of the Colonies are to take first place, and that the Law of *England* is of force only where they are silent; others there are, who contend for the Laws of the Colonies, in Conjunction with those that were in force in *England* at the first Settlement of the Colony, and lay down that as measure of our Obedience, alleging, that we are not bound to observe any late Acts of Parliament made in *England*, except such only where the Reason of the Law is the same here, that it is in *England*; but this leaving too great a Latitude to the Judge; and some others hold that no late Acts of Parliament of *England* do bind the Plantations, but those only, wherein the Plantations are particularly named. Thus we are left in the dark, in one of the most considerable Points of our Rights; and the Case being so doubtful, we are too often obliged to depend on the Crooked Cord of a Judge's Discretion, in Matters of the greatest Moment and Value.[23]

Stating what would be repeated many times in the next decades, he urged '[t]hat some Rule be established, to know what Laws the Plantations are to be subject to, and particularly how far the late Acts of Parliament [i.e., those since 1607] do affect them, where they are not expressly mentioned'.[24]

Neither Beverley nor his anonymous compatriot mentioned another factor that lurked within the entire affair. The only avenue of appeal – if the untechnical use of the term might be excused – to England lay by writ of error. 'Appeal' in its modern American usage raises questions of fact as well as law, but the

[21] Ibid., 394.
[22] *An Essay Upon the Government of the English Plantations on the Continent of America* (1701), ed. L. Wright (San Marino, CA, 1945) with Beverley's authorship asserted by the editor with support from another scholar. More recent scholarship has refuted this, but no consensus exists on authorship. R. Davis, *Intellectual Life in the Colonial South 1585–1763* (Knoxville, TN, 1978), ii. 1453, discusses the possibilities.
[23] *Essay Upon Government*, 23.
[24] Ibid., 39.

writ of error allows only questions of law apparent on the record to be reviewed, permitting no inquiry as to whether the lower court had erred in dealing with questions of fact.[25] The record sent to London included no evidence presented at trial, nor any reasons (if any) given by the jury, or the court's holding on the applicability of rules or statutes. Beverley's initial strategy before the Virginia General Court had been to join issue on the facts, obtain a jury verdict on the factual question, and thus shield the judgment from appellate review in London. But he was undone by the shift of the question to one of law – the applicability of an English statute in Virginia, which was decided in London by 'the Crooked Cord of a Judge's Discretion' – in this case by the law lords of the Privy Council. Defeated at law, Beverley returned to Virginia in 1704 to spend the rest of his life as master of his plantation 'Beverley Park' and as presiding justice of the peace of King and Queen County. Retiring from colony-wide politics, he spent his final years cultivating wine, of which he produced four hundred gallons in 1715.[26]

But Beverley had brought with him from London the unfinished manuscript of *The History and Present State of Virginia*, which he completed and published the next year.[27] Framing the contours of a debate over the way the imperial state administered its colonies that would remain unsettled until the collapse of the first British empire at the end of the century, the *History* raised issues of law that have been overshadowed by attention to legislative contest. And its author named names that the anonymous writer of the *Essay* had omitted. Of Nicholson's predecessor as lieutenant-governor, Francis Howard, Lord Howard of Effingham, Beverley wrote,

> though he pretended no great Skill in legal proceedings, yet he made great Innovations in their Courts, pretending to follow the *English* Forms. Thus he created a new Court of *Chancery*, distinct from the General Court, who had ever before claim'd that Jurisdiction. He erected himself into a Lord Chancellor, taking the Gentlemen of the Council, to sit with him as meer Associates and Advisers, not having any Vote in the Causes before them.

He had, moreover, closed these deliberations, moving them from the capitol to 'the Dining-Room of a private House'.[28]

It was Effingham that Nicholson succeeded in his first term as lieutenant-governor in 1690. Nicholson's strategy of control revealed the difference between legislative and judicial manipulation, as he 'was a strict Observer of

[25] Millon, 'Positivism', 685–6.

[26] A. Bagby, Jr, 'Beverley Park and the Knights of the Golden Horseshoe', *William and Mary Quarterly*, 3rd ser., 9 (1900), 508–10.

[27] Beverley revised and republished his volume in 1722. Four editions were published in French between 1707 and 1718.

[28] Beverley, *History*, 97 (this and the following quotations from the same source preserve the original emphasis).

the Acts of assembly, making them the sole Rule of his Judgment, where-ever they happen'd not to be silent. But his Behaviour in Council at the same time', Beverley charged, 'did not square with that Regularity; For, there he was so Arbitrary and Imperious, that they could not bear it, and several of the Councellors writ Letters to the Court of *England* against him.'[29] At the end of Nicholson's second term Beverley could tap a vein of disaffection with the way that Virginians were losing control of their own courts of justice. He spoke from experience as clerk of the General Court:

> In the General Court, of which he is chief Judge, he has often behaved himself in that boisterous manner, that neither the rest of the Judges on the Bench, nor the Lawyers at the Bar, cou'd use their just Freedom. There 'tis usual with him to fall into excessive Passions, and utter the most abusive Language against those that presume to oppose his Arbitrary Proceedings.

To the king's attorney, whom Nicholson had choked for refusing 'some hard piece of Service, as being against Law', the governor said, '*That he knew of no Laws they had, and that his Commands should be obey'd without Hesitation or Reserve*'. As a veteran army officer he had no qualms about saying '*That they were Dogs, and their Wives were Bitches; that he knew how to govern the Moors, and would beat them into better manners*'. The Virginians, he averred, '*had no Right at all to the Liberties of* English *subjects, and that he wou'd hang up those that should presume to oppose him, with* Magna Charta *about their Necks*'.[30] The county courts attracted his ire, too: in a land dispute with the colony auditor, Nicholson had browbeaten witnesses during trial there and derisively refused to accept the verdict of a 'Chickahominy [i.e., Indian] Jury', threatening to appeal to the Privy Council. Rather than do so, he fired the auditor.[31]

Nicholson ran afoul of other political forces in the colony, however, and was replaced by Lieutenant-Colonel Alexander Spotswood, who arrived in Williamsburg to assume his duties as lieutenant-governor of His Majesty's royal colony of Virginia in 1710. That he met resistance ranging from social ostracism to political warfare should have come as no surprise to him, for North American colonists were reluctant to provide the fruits of patronage that strengthened the emerging imperial state, and they responded to imperial intrusions with political cunning, malice, and even violence.[32] In New York in 1708, Governor Edward Hyde, Viscount Cornbury, was driven from the colony in disgrace, the victim of gossip sent to London alleging that he

[29] Ibid., 100.

[30] Ibid., 106–7.

[31] L. Dodson, *Alexander Spotswood, Governor of Virginia 1710–1722* (Philadelphia, 1932), 166–7.

[32] On the struggle over gubernatorial patronage, see B. Bailyn, *The Origins of American Politics* (New York, 1965).

appeared in public dressed in women's clothing; Horace Walpole repeated the rumour that Cornbury even had 'opened the Assembly dressed in that fashion'. Two years later – the year of Spotswood's appointment – Governor Daniel Parke, a native Virginian serving as governor of the Leeward Islands, had been stripped naked, torn from limb to limb, and his body left in the sun by a mob of colonists who also killed eleven soldiers in venting their rage at his autocratic rule and predatory sexual activity.[33] Within six years, an embattled Spotswood would complain to the Board of Trade,

> I am charged in plain words as Guilty of breach of Trust, breach of Oath, breach of the King's Instructions, breach of faith in my publick Contracts, of tricking an Assembly out of £1,350, of Extortion, of Murder, of stirring up Sedition and Rebellion, &c.[34]

Like the other governors representing the imperial state, Spotswood had also antagonized powerful local interests and had evoked fears of continuing the high-handed rule of those who had preceded him.

Spotswood was personally less bellicose and politically more skilful than Nicholson, but he inherited a legacy of colonial resistance to the efforts of the imperial state, which they saw as attempting to curb their control over and participation in legal affairs. Given a mandate to collect all revenues owed to the crown, Spotswood had undertaken to end the corrupt system of land distribution from the royal demesne and to assure full and complete payment of the quit-rents due on such grants.[35] Nicholson had failed miserably in his contest with the 'mighty dons' and 'parvenues' who controlled the system, the members of the Council who served not only as the colony's upper house of assembly but also as an executive body and the colony's highest court. For all practical purposes these men held life tenure; only the king could remove them, an action rarely taken. They remained in office, evading back taxes due on their land grants, when Nicholson was sent packing, and they remained to resist him successfully in his second term, too. Spotswood thus had the unenviable task of reforming a system of entrenched local practice protected by an entrenched local judiciary.

The result defied even the most skilful efforts of executive manipulation of the legislature. In 1713 Spotswood had managed what few thought possible: passage of a law declaring forfeit all land grants on which quit-rents had not

[33] On Cornbury, see Patricia U. Bonomi, 'Lord Cornbury Redressed: The Governor and the Problem Portrait', *William and Mary Quarterly*, 3rd ser., 51 (1994), 108. On Parke, see Cyril Hamshere, *The British in the Caribbean* (Cambridge, MA, 1972), 120.

[34] Spotswood to Board of Trade, 16 January 1717, in *The Official Letters of Alexander Spotswood, Lieutenant-Governor of the Colony of Virginia, 1710–1722*, ed. R. Brock (Richmond, VA, 1882), ii. 189.

[35] M. Voorhis, 'Crown Versus Council in the Virginia Land Policy', *William and Mary Quarterly*, 3rd ser., 4 (1946), 499–514.

been paid for three years. He had done so by allowing loopholes making it easier for claimants to establish that they had 'seated and stocked' the land sufficiently to legitimize claims.[36] But he had not reckoned on the fusion of legislative and judicial powers of the Council: namely, 'That, as an Upper House of Assembly, they may concur in making Laws, which afterwards, when their Opinion is ask'd as Councillors, they may, nevertheless, think unfit to be pass'd.' Writing to the Board of Trade in 1715, he could not 'forbear taking notice' of 'this strange distinction'. Spotswood believed this anomaly to be a matter that he

> must submitt to Y'r Lo'ps' better Judgmrnt, only taking Notice that if, as an upper house of Assembly, they can separate themselves from the duty of Councillors they are under no Oath at all, And if such a distinction be allowed it may be hereafter extended to other occasions of the Government.

By 1718 the Council fulfilled his prediction when, acting in its judicial capacity, it held that the three-year forfeiture clause applied only to lands granted after the 1713 law – in effect, judicially nullifying the statute. Appeal to the Privy Council was for all practical intents out of the question, he wrote to the Board, owing to the power of 'the Governing party of the Council, who are also the Judges of the General Court, and the last Resort here in all Cases under £300 Value'. As large as the unpaid quit-rents were, they fell below that sum in individual cases, '[b]y which means that Act is rendered useless'.[37] In a long report he had made to the Board the year before, Spotswood had sought to deflect criticisms sent to London complaining about his administration, including his land policy. His reform of the land system was, he confessed, 'a restraint on the ancient Liberty which some people here made use of'. Nevertheless, he continued, such a local 'Liberty' to amass more land than anyone 'could reasonably be supposed of ability to cultivate' injured not only other Virginians but the crown. 'I must own I have been in an Error in restraining that Liberty,' he conceded in anticipation of defeat.[38]

Spotswood was caught between competing notions of 'liberty', and he might offend that of British merchants as easily as he might antagonize Virginians. In 1714 he attempted to bring order out of the chaotic and disruptive trade between Virginians and their Indian neighbours. He did so by proposing the creation of a monopoly trading company, the 'Virginia Indian Company', whose subscribers would have the exclusive right to conduct business from a single location, where local tribes would settle and undergo Christianization.

[36] *The Statutes at Large; Being a Collection of all the Laws of Virginia, from the First Session of the Legislature, in the Year 1619*, comp. W. Hening [1819–23] (Charlottesville, VA, 1969), iii. 39, 41.

[37] Spotswood to Board of Trade, 7 March 1718, *Letters*, ii. 266.

[38] Spotswood to Board of Trade, 16 January 1717, ibid., ii. 216.

The plan received only lukewarm support in Virginia, but it generated strong disapproval among London merchants who saw their own 'liberty' under attack. They fought the proposal in the Board of Trade on legal grounds, arguing that the act violated the governor's instruction to approve no law affecting the trade of the empire, as well as provisions of the Navigation Act of 1696 assuring the rights of English merchants within the empire.[39] Spotswood replied that 'it seem'd necessary to restrain such a generall liberty' of unregulated trade, and that the Board should construe the act favourably to its purpose. He explained to the Board's secretary that 'that Restraint extends only to trading through Virginia, and that for only a limited time', and that subscription was open to all who wished to buy stock. Moreover, he argued that the Navigation Act 'seems only to point to that sort of Commerce which is to be so carryed on by the Brittish navigation, and not to a Trade severall hundreds of miles within Land'. He pleaded that 'such an Exposition . . . of the Act of Parliament' was injurious to the long-term interests of the crown, but the Board's lawyer accepted the arguments of the English merchants, and the Privy Council repealed the law on his recommendation.[40]

Spotswood faced the insuperable obstacle of reconciling imperial interests with the specifics of local problems and customary practices. As governor, he had to submit the names of any new councillors for royal approval, and gradually the Council, a self-perpetuating oligarchy, came to include many who owed their approval to him. Nonetheless, such gratitude did not extend to willingly giving up the perquisites of power and jurisdictional reach that the Council had established in more than a century of development. The Navigation Act of 1696 had created a system of vice-admiralty courts for the colonies, and the councillors had to yield their grudging acquiescence when Governor Andros appointed only one of them to its four-man bench. Local control slipped still farther away with the absence of juries and the way vice-admiralty judges construed the law favourably to the crown. In a 1699 case its judges rejected a plea to its jurisdiction based on construction of the 1696 statute, and the next year interpreted coastal shipping as coming within its authority and the restrictions of the act. Factual sufficiency was for the court to decide; if necessary, Nicholson wrote to the Board of Trade in 1700, trial in England might overcome any 'Quibles and niceties of the Law' concerning 'good proof'.[41]

The councillors jealously guarded their judicial authority from this kind of encroachment, and reacted vehemently when early in his administration Spotswood began planning to create and staff another new court. He proposed establishing a court of oyer and terminer to try convicted felons more promptly

[39] Dodson, *Spotswood*, 83, 89. CSP (1716–1717), 72.

[40] Spotswood to William Popple, 16 April 1717, *Letters*, ii. 234–5.

[41] *Proceedings in the Vice-Admiralty Court of Virginia 1698–1775*, ed. G. Reese (Richmond, VA, 1983), 6–7, 15, 41–2, 48–9.

than was possible by the semi-annual sessions of the General Court, which had exclusive jurisdiction over matters of life and limb. What seemed to him to be an act of streamlining judicial administration only aroused two of the colonists' most deeply held local fears: punitive political prosecutions and slave resistance. Virginians still recalled the brutal reaction to Bacon's Rebellion in 1676–7, when two companies of English soldiers had given force to the judicial retribution meted out by Governor Sir William Berkeley, who saw to it that his most vexing opponents were hanged after court martial.[42] Nor had they forgotten the more recent vengeance of New York's aptly named Governor Henry Sloughter, who had had eight of his enemies convicted as traitors and sentenced to be hanged, disembowelled, decapitated, and quartered for their unwise seizure of power after the Glorious Revolution in New York.[43]

The councillors did not accuse Spotswood of harbouring such designs, but they had not yet perceived London's new strategy of control and feared that loss of control of judicial institutions might mean a return to Stuart autocracy. 'Tho' we have the most entire confidence in your hon'r's Justice, and do firmly believe That in all things you will act according to the nicest Rules of Integrity and honor, yet in times to come it may be our misfortune, in your Stead, to have a Governour who may make a very dangerous use of this Precedent,' wrote the Council in explaining its opposition to his plan.[44] Virginians were entering a new era of anxiety, not yet convinced that the old patterns had ended and fearful of new terrors. The worst of those fears concerned control of a rapidly increasing population of enslaved African labourers.[45] Crucial to control were force and fear – the arbitrary exercise of violence to subdue the enslaved through plantation 'correction' or state execution. After a slave rebellion in 1710, the Council had ordered that two leaders – an Indian slave and an African slave – be hanged, quartered, and decapitated as 'exemplary punishment [that] may have a due effect for deterring other Slaves from entering into such dangerous Conspiracys'.[46] Despite his military background, Spotswood was uneasy with such a policy, and in 1710 had commented that 'freedom wears a cap which can without a tongue, call together all those who long to shake off the fetters of slavery.'[47]

[42] On Berkeley's vengeance and the humiliations he inflicted on his victims, see Morton, *Colonial Virginia*, 274–7.

[43] D. Lovejoy, *The Glorious Revolution in America* (New York, 1972), 354–8. The eight were ultimately hanged and decapitated.

[44] Council to Spotswood, received 1 May 1713, *Letters*, ii. 221–3.

[45] Slave imports began to increase sharply after 1700, and Spotswood had supported efforts to raise the import duty on slaves as a way of reducing the trade and slowing the increase of tobacco production in order to boost its price. London and Bristol merchants succeeded in killing this effort and subsequent ones for the rest of the colonial period.

[46] *Executive Journals of the Council*, iii. 242–3.

[47] Morton, *Colonial Virginia*, 417.

The governor also had misgivings about the brutal way slave owners disciplined their slaves, and he questioned the way a local 'Jury's Inquest and County Court' had refused to convict a woman for 'Whipping her Slave to death'. He thereupon ordered the attorney-general to prosecute her, a prosecution labelled by one outraged slave owner as 'contrary to Law, for the Death of her slave under a very Moderate Correction'. Spotswood accepted the challenge and informed the Board of Trade that upon exhumation of the 'suddenly and secretly Buried' body, the coroner's jury had reported the charge of murder. He insisted,

> [T]ho' the Querist can, with a barbarous unconcern, call it a very moderate Correction under which an hail Negro gave up the Ghost . . . I think it indispensably my Duty to take care that such Proceedings be not stifled, but that a legal Tryal do ensue thereupon, for how unpopular soever the Doctrine may be in this Country, Yet until your Lord'ps condemn it, I will dare stand to my Charge to a Grand Jury here, vizt: that in this Dominion no Master has such a Sovereign Power over his Slave as not be liable to be called to an Account whenever he kills him; that at the same time, the Slave is the Master's Property, he is likewise the King's Subject, and that the King may lawfully bring to Tryal all Persons here, without exception, who shall be suspected to have destroyed the Life of his Subject.[48]

Spotswood would not be the last Virginia politician to run afoul of racial fears, and his efforts to protect the rights of Africans as the king's subjects would echo long into American history in the form of federal attempts to enforce civil rights in the modern American South. But his efforts also bespoke an enlightenment disgust at popular brutality and a disapproval of the private recourse to violence as an accepted part of local justice.

'Virginia merchants', Virginia planters, and the force of imperial law

The 'Crooked Cord' that had ensnared Spotswood grew no straighter in the following decades, for expanding trade multiplied the occasions for Virginians to clash with London merchants. As Beverley had written in his attack on Nicholson from London in 1704, English merchants were not satisfied 'in making a Trade of us in the sale of our Tobaccos, and return of our goods', but 'they had busied themselves in matters of State to keep us underlings and poor, prying into our Laws and improvements.'[49] Well acquainted with the tobacco trade, Beverley was also well acquainted with the so-called 'Virginia merchants', a group that has been described as 'perhaps the most powerful lobby of Anglo-American merchants' of their day. Meeting in London coffee

[48] Spotswood to Board of Trade, 7 February 1716, *Letters*, ii. 202–3.

[49] Ibid., 74. *Executive Journals of the Council*, ii. 392.

houses to co-ordinate their efforts, they repeatedly used their influence to lobby the Board of Trade to recommend that the Privy Council disallow any Virginia statute harmful to their profits.[50] But the London merchants knew how to make their case to the Privy Council in legal matters, too.

In the chapter of his *History* treating 'Of the Courts of Law in Virginia', Beverley asserted that Nicholson 'has endeavour'd to introduce all the quirks of the *English* Proceedings, by the help of some wretched Pettifoggers, who have had the direction both of his Conscience and his Understanding'.[51] Were such 'quirks' merely the technicality of English writs, the specific minutiae of pleading that rustic Virginia lawyers might not have mastered? In looking at litigation in eighteenth-century Virginia, especially at the General Court, one is struck by the Virginians' attention to proper common law pleading and their awareness of English cases available in the published reports of English decisions.[52] The anonymous author of the *Essay* provides a clue to understanding the problem by emphasizing the way the law actually operated, in particular in the law of obligations where the common law had developed fewer substantive rules than in the law of property.[53] At the root of the problem was the fluctuating rate of exchange between sterling and Virginia currency, which was based on the price of tobacco. These changes, he explained,

> give Opportunity to some sharp *English* Merchants to put such tricks upon us, as we cannot foresee; they have great Advantages of us, if their Inclinations tend that way; they are skilful in Trade and Exchange, which we cannot pretend to; they have much the larger Purses, and can outdo us at any thing, whenever they please.

English merchants also had better access to news of events – such as the outbreak of war – that might affect the price of the colonial staple: 'and besides all this, they have daily Opportunities of looking abroad in the World, and may have many Prospects of Advantage, which we that are shut up in *America* know nothing of.'[54] In that short comment, Beverley summed up the nature of the problem and pointed to the intersection – or, more aptly, the *collision* – of imperial and provincial law.

The Privy Council's reversal of Robert Beverley's skilfully prepared case in 1704 had foreshadowed the ever more significant impact of the imperial state in the eighteenth century. Despite the decline of the Council in English politics

[50] A. Olson, 'The Virginia Merchants of London: A Study in Eighteenth-Century Interest-Group Politics', *William and Mary Quarterly*, 3rd ser., 40 (1983), 363–88.

[51] Beverley, *History*, 256.

[52] This skill is apparent in reports circulating in manuscript in the colony. *Virginia Colonial Decisions: The Reports of Sir John Randolph and by Edward Barradall of Decisions of the General Court of Virginia 1728–1741*, ed. R. Barton (Boston, MA, 1909).

[53] On this contrast, see Millon, 'Positivism', 671.

[54] Anon., *Essay*, 42–3. On currency as a topic of imperial concern, see Laslett, 'Great Recoinage', 378–80.

after the fall of the Stuarts[55] and a focus by American historians on its 'only partly effective' review of colonial legislation,[56] the advent of the long eighteenth century marked a major redirection of its remaining concerns. Ironically, the changes that diminished its traditional role served to increase its new one. Shorn of its control over internal matters, it concentrated more on those parts of the realm deemed to be of lesser constitutional stature, such as Ireland or Britain's more distant possessions in North America. The Privy Council, now much more subject to parliamentary influence, would reflect the interests of the powerful commercial groups that were gaining ever tighter control of parliament during the Whig ascendancy.

Its more focused concerns meant, too, that the Council was reorganized, with activities concentrated into a committee of the whole. As perceptively noted in the most important study of its appellate role, 'The segregation of colonial administration to a particular committee was thus abandoned, and plantation affairs were merged with domestic and with matters arising from other dominions of the crown outside the realm.'[57] This internal change not coincidentally occurred almost contemporaneously with the creation of the Board of Trade, which funnelled a steady flow of information and recommendations to the Council. But the Board of Trade held only advisory power: it depended on the Privy Council (or parliament) to implement its advice. While parliament's troublesome control of the colonies after 1763 remains central to the historiography of early America, that of the Privy Council in the six decades before that must be recognized, too.

A law suit in 1724 between the largest merchant house dealing in Virginia and one of the most prominent planter families of the colony places this conflict in sharp relief. As the early generation of the Atlantic trading community died off, it was replaced by a newer generation less inclined to indulge personal relations and more pressed by economic stress, especially after the collapse of the South Sea Bubble in 1720. The London trading house of Micajah Perry and Company had been trading with the wealthy Randolphs of Virginia since William Randolph had begun the trade with Micajah in 1686. Before his death in 1711, William's debts to the Perrys had mounted steadily; much to his annoyance, he had written, 'the interest was twice as much as the principle'. His estate executors tried mightily to bring them down and succeeded in reducing them from almost £3,260 to £2,465 within six years. 'Old Perry', as Spotswood called him, had influenced appointments in the colony and blocked unfavourable colony laws, but had treated his Virginia

[55] Edward Raymond Turner, *The Privy Council of England in the Seventeenth and Eighteenth Century*, 2 volumes (Baltimore, 1927) remains a standard account.

[56] Greene, *Quest for Power*, 18. The Council disallowed only 469 of the 8,563 colonial acts submitted to it.

[57] J. Smith, *Appeals to the Privy Council from the American Plantations* (New York, 1950), 135.

debtors leniently and allowed their debts to accumulate. His death in 1721, however, signalled a new chapter in transatlantic relations – full-bore debt collection through litigation. The next year a new generation of Perrys sued the Randolph estate for the balance due.[58] The General Court appointed its own commissioners to report on the amount of the debt, and they reported that the Randolph estate owed only £80 as original principal without any interest, or £2,465 with compound interest and the addition of insurance charges. Presented with these facts, the jury rejected the charges for 'Insurance and for Interest and interest upon interest' and, moreover, accepted the estate's claim of a set-off, or moneys owed by the Perrys to Randolph. Altogether, they awarded the plaintiffs nothing.[59] On appeal to the Privy Council, however, the Perrys gained all that they had failed to win at the General Court of Virginia. In March 1725 the Council sent the accounts to four London merchant referees of its choice, selected, as it said, for their ability to report what was 'fair and just and agreeable to what is always Charged, and allowed in Accounts of this nature by the constant usage of merchants trading to the Plantations'. Two of the four decided for the Perrys' version of the obligation, and a third concurred without comment; the fourth sided with the Virginians. The Council found the Virginia decision 'erroneous', overturned the jury's verdict, and awarded the Perrys their claim in full.[60]

The reversal provoked panic and desperation in Virginia, for the insulation of factual determinations by local juries from review in England had been a time-honoured safe haven for Virginians. Despite the Assembly's formulaic language softening its 'humble Address to the Kings Majesty', its protest touched on points so sensitive that Lieutenant-Governor Hugh Drysdale tried to prevent its transmission to London. Distancing himself from the joint Council–Burgesses 'Representation', he sent it to the Duke of Newcastle, the Secretary of State, 'very unwillingly' and with 'nothing to recommend itt'. Had he not been compelled by his royal instructions to forward it, he would have 'left this to bee presented to H.M. by another way'. The address assailed the Council's action as contrary to settled legal practice and the due process of law guaranteed them as Englishmen. The General Court had acted only 'by the Consent of the Plaintiffs and Defendants and conformable to the practice of the Court in like Cases' in sending the dispute to referees, whose report made 'the matters in dispute more clear and Perspicuous to the Jury'.

[58] Morton, *Colonial Virginia*, 414. J. Price, *Perry of London: A Family and Firm on the Seaborne Frontier, 1615–1753* (Cambridge, MA, 1992), 69–70.

[59] *Journals of the House of Burgesses of Virginia*, ed. H. McIlwaine (Richmond, VA, 1905–15), *1717–26*, 421–2.

[60] On the increasing resort to arbitrators to make factual reports on the bewildering variety of commercial practices in this age, see *The Mansfield Manuscripts and the Growth of English Law in the Eighteenth Century*, ed. James Oldham (Chapel Hill, NC, 1992), i. 94, 151–2, 155. *Journals of the House*, 423. *Acts of the Privy Council of England, Colonial Series* (Hereford, 1908–12), *(1720–45)*, 70.

Issue was joined, and 'A trial was had accordingly by twelve good and Lawful men.' The verdict was lawful, and the plaintiffs had accepted it, neither asking for a stay of judgment nor moving for a new trial.[61] The implication was clear: by rejecting any factual re-examination, the plaintiffs revealed that they were not seeking justice, but rather to trump the colonial judges through recourse to a distant higher court. If they could not win on the facts – which Virginians determined – they would try to win on the law – which Englishmen would decide.

The reversal affected more than the fortunes of one of the colony's most eminent families. To the Virginia Assembly, this case was fraught with 'Consequences which A Precedent of this nature may have on the trade and properties of your Majesties good Subjects of this Colony'. The Assembly denied the demand for interest, insisting that 'no such Custom or Usage hath Ever hitherto prevailed or been allowed among the Merchants trading to this Colony whereby Interest or Interest upon Interest hath been or can be recovered upon Open runing Accounts.' That is, not even simple interest was calculated on the sorts of accounts – open and 'runing' book debts – at issue here unless expressly assessed by a jury.[62] Such was not only Virginia practice, but the common law, for a jury 'by the Laws and Customs of *England* (to which Our procedings here do as near as can be conform) are the only proper Judges' of an assumpsit. The Assembly pointed out that 'your Majesties Subjects in this Colony have alwaies without interruption had and Enjoied the benefits of a legal Trial by Juries' in common law actions. The decision of the 'Lords of the Committee for hearing Appeals from the Plantations' thus struck at the root of English liberties and subverted due process of law. It also had ignored a Virginia practice, that of the set-off, which was not recognized at common law courts in England.[63]

[61] *CSP(1726)*, 115. *Journals of the House*, 423, 425.

[62] Following the common law rule, Virginia practice was to award simple interest only on specialties or mortgages unless a jury said otherwise. Randolph, however, had written 'at the foot of this Account . . . Interest till repaid'. It was the opinion of William Thomson, a Virginia attorney consulted on this case, that 'Upon a running Account no Interest will be allowed', but that Randolph's written admission had changed that: *Virginia Colonial Decisions*, B22. Whether this obliged Randolph to pay *compound interest* was another matter. By statute, interest was limited on colonial debts to 8 per cent, but commercial communities had devised numerous ways to evade that limit, and courts recognized that 'hazard' justified rates in excess of the usury limit. Oldham, *Mansfield Manuscripts*, i. 638. Nevertheless, when merchants trading to Virginia made claims for compensation after the Revolution they did not seek compound interest. J. Price, *Capital and Credit in British Overseas Trade: The View from the Chesapeake, 1700–1776* (Cambridge, MA, 1980), 8. Interest allowed on colonial debts exceeded that on inland obligations. By 12 Anne c. 16, rates were fixed at 5 per cent in England, and 6 to 8 per cent in the colonies.

[63] The set-off would not be so recognized in English courts until late in the nineteenth century. James Steven Rogers, *The Early History of the Law of Bills and Notes: A Study of the*

Altogether, the process of review seemed arbitrary: appeal had been granted despite the fact that no 'rules of the Common law hath ever been allowed or Established' for 'Examining the Judgments of your General Court'. Plaintiffs should have sought 'A new Trial and Verdict', but instead had obtained a legal order through a proceeding that did not even qualify as a trial, heeding evidence provided by unsworn merchant referees, who 'are Ever inclined to favor one another'. With that bias and the force of the Privy Council behind it, appeals to London would be the ruin of the colony. If such men 'be admitted to Overrule the Verdicts of Legal Juries', the Assembly predicted, Virginia debtors 'will be liable to whatever Charges and impositions their factors and Correspondents in *Great Britain* think fit to load them with'. Pleading for due process in appeals, it concluded with the request that the crown '[e]stablish for the future such a Regular Course for Examining and reforming the Judgments given in your Supreme Courts here that your Subjects of this Dominion may still Enjoy the benefit of Trial according to the Laws and Customs of *England*'.[64]

Opportunity to strike back came soon, when Lieutenant-Governor Drysdale returned to England, making the president of the Council, Robert 'King' Carter (perhaps the wealthiest planter in Virginia, and a signer of the protest) acting executive. Where Drysdale had dragged his feet in the affair, Carter used his office to write to the colony agent in London and reiterate his personal fears. Gloomily reflecting that the Assembly's remonstrance never had had a chance of convincing a body that represented the interests of mercantile Britain, he confessed, 'In confidence it may be observ'd, if the merchants can worry us out of our estates by loading us with interest upon interest we shall be in a bad condition.' The best remedy, he noted, citing a long held but never realized goal, would be to stay out of debt.[65]

How and why Virginians were trapped by debt was a lively topic among those ensnared in the system. Obviously, extravagance was an easy target, but even thoughtful observers knew that the problem was more complex, and they laid the blame at the system of credit and currency exchange over which they had no control. John Wayles, whose daughter married Thomas Jefferson, from his perspective as agent for an English merchant wrote in 1766 that 'many are ignorant of the true cause'. But Wayles was also a Virginia planter, whose debt-ridden property Jefferson's wife inherited. For his part, Jefferson the planter-lawyer knew that 'The advantages made by the British merchants on the tobaccoes consigned to them were so enormous that they spared no means on increasing those increments.' Enticing the planter with 'good prices and credit', they controlled the 'powerful engine' of credit and debt.[66]

Origins of Anglo-American Commercial Law (Cambridge, 1995), 192. *Journals of the House*, 424.

64 Ibid.

65 *CSP (1726–7)*, 227.

66 Wayles and Jefferson are quoted by B. Ragsdale, *A Planters' Republic: The Search for Economic Independence in Revolutionary Virginia* (Madison, WI, 1996), 24–5.

Jefferson was right that the credit system, as shaped and enforced by law emanating from London, was a way of 'increasing those increments'. Even Lieutenant-Governor William Gooch, Drysdale's successor, came to the defence of Virginia planters when he wrote a long report to the Board of Trade in 1731. Gooch provided a simple example of a situation repeated often in the transatlantic tobacco trade: 'A planter consigns 10 hhds of tobacco to his merchant in London, desiring him to sell them and out of the produce to send him such and such goods.' They repeat this arrangement over several years, with the planter running up a debt to the merchant. However, as Gooch explained, it often happened that 'the merchant sends the planter a letter telling him that the tobacconist to whom he sold the four or five hogsheads of his first consigned tobacco is broke, that the money is lost, and the planter must repay it.' The merchant sues the planter in Virginia where, of course, 'no Court or Jury can possibly charge the planter with this loss.' But such legal protection, afforded by a jury local to the planter, would likely be lost on appeal to England.[67]

Such appeals were not common in 1731, with appeals limited to those exceeding £300, but Gooch was reflecting a growing fear that the rules of the game were changing, as British merchants trading to Virginia were pressing the Privy Council to repeal laws they regarded as discriminatory. In the wake of the catastrophic South Sea Bubble, the tobacco market had plunged into a decade-long depression, and by the 1730s British merchants were seeking to shift some of the burden away from themselves. On the same day that his report was read, so, too, was a draft bill that would tilt legal process sharply against the colonists. British merchants had petitioned that the appellate limit be lowered to £100, which would open the gates to a flood of appeals. Worse still, explained Gooch,

> the poor planter knowing no man in England to whom he can entrust the defences there, and considering the charge he must be at of at least £70, or £80 on the tryal in England, will find it more to his interest to pay what is unjustly charged him than defend himself at such an expence. Many more instances may be given as I am told of the like hardships in the matter if acco[un]ts which the planters here must submit to, if appeals be allowed for so small a sum.[68]

It was this manipulation of the legal and administrative apparatus that worried Virginians as the imperial state strengthened its support of British merchants at colonial expense. Already, Virginia creditors had learned that they could make little use of England's bankruptcy act, since the time-consuming transatlantic journey made it virtually impossible for them to get to England before

[67] *CSP (1732)*, 172. Gooch's report, dated 10 July 1731, is at 168–73. It was not read until 18 January 1732.
[68] *CSP (1732)*, 172–3.

bankruptcy commissioners had made their accounting and distribution of assets.[69] Direct control by British officials in America, therefore, was not always needed: the law and its administration would suffice.

In a series of petitions in 1731, therefore, the London merchants had made other proposals for more efficient remedies to collect debts due from Virginians and other colonial trading partners. 'They have great sums due to them from the inhabitants', complained the merchants of their colonial debtors, 'and as the laws now stand in some of the Colonys and Plantations, H. M. subjects residing in Great Britain are left without any remedy for the recovery of their just debts, or have such remedy only as is very partiall and precarious.'[70] In the wake of *Perry* v. *Randolph*, for example, the Virginia Assembly had responded with its own usury law, limiting recovery to 6 per cent.[71] It also countered the Privy Council's 1730 repeal of its 1705 statute of limitations[72] with artful new laws barring the admissibility of notarized English accounts and by refusing to enact a colonial bankruptcy law that would protect British creditors.[73]

Perhaps the most worrisome of proposed parliamentary intrusion was a legal change that would place Virginian real property rights on a basis inferior to the common law status enjoyed by landowners in England – namely, a law making land and slaves liable to recovery on simple debts. Merchants trading to Virginia were not the only creditors who chafed at being unable to touch debtors' assets tied up in land or slaves. Massachusetts law provided for recovery against land, but by a clause cleverly inserted into its charter of 1691 had barred appeals to the Privy Council in real actions. British merchants therefore could sue and recover land in Massachusetts courts, but they had to contend with hostile local juries. For those trading to Jamaica, slaves subject to judgment debts 'are frequently driven away into the woods or mountains out of the Marschall's way'.[74] To protect their valuable assets in land and slaves, the Virginia Assembly had deemed slaves real property and thus, at common law, not liable to seizure unless secured by mortgage. Gooch spoke for the colony's planters when he pointed out that 'making of lands lyable to the payment of debts is not treating the people in the Plantations as if they were English subjects: lands here are held by the same tenure as in England, and are now lyable to the payment of debts in the same manner as lands in England are.' If parliament changed the rules, however, British merchants would have much

[69] J. Hemphill II, *Virginia and the English Commercial System, 1689–1733: Studies in the Development and Fluctuations of a Colonial Economy Under Imperial Control* (New York, 1985), 175.

[70] *CSP (1731)*, 225.

[71] Laws of 1730, c. 12. Hening, *Statutes*, iv. 294–6.

[72] Laws of 1705, c. 35. Hening, *Statutes*, iii. 377–81.

[73] These manoeuvres are explained by Hemphill, *Virginia and the English Commercial System*, 178–9.

[74] *CSP (1731)*, 294–5.

less trouble seeking justice in Virginia through their agents, but Virginians would have great difficulty suing or defending causes in England. 'Common justice', he averred, 'requires that legal remedies should be reciprocal.'[75]

For themselves, the Virginia Council's petition in 1732 reiterated the discriminatory nature of making real property liable to seizure on simple contracts; 'it would make too severe a distinction between H.M. loial subjects here and those in Great Britain.' Virginians would take strong exception 'when they find out they have not equal Justice with the rest of their fellow-subjects'.[76] At least two members of the Virginia Council sending this memorial knew all too well of the outrage sparked in the province, and in private correspondence they predicted dire consequences if land and slaves were made liable for simple debts. Robert 'King' Carter wrote to Micajah Perry III that such a law 'rais'd so general a fury in the Assembly' that Perry would read of further protests and actions from other Virginians. John Custis warned a Bristol merchant that 'however you may Flatter yourselves to be gainers by that Act you will find that you have so incens'd the Country; that you will force them as soon as convenient to have nothing to do with you.'[77]

Parliament's response, 'An Act for the more easy Recovery of Debts in His majesty's Plantations and Colonies in North America', did not lower the threshold of appeal from £300, but it gave London's 'Virginia merchants' two of their main requests.[78] They could now prove their debts by oath in Britain, and if successful at law could take execution on land and slaves. Virginia planters' bitterness at these grievances abated somewhat with the return of good times for the tobacco trade. But the pattern set in this clash of law would remain, and would rise to the level of constitutional protest. The Privy Council's reversal of *Perry* v. *Randolph* in 1726 had provoked the request by the Virginia Assembly for 'a Regular Course for Examining and reforming the Judgments given in your Supreme Courts here', and the next year the Privy Council established a Committee for Appeals.[79] But as Joseph H. Smith's masterful and exhaustive study has shown, no regular policy ever emerged defining what laws applied in the colonies.[80] The Virginia Council, in the heat of the debates of 1731, had focused the problem even more sharply. Challenging a demand by British merchants 'that an act may pass to hinder any law from being made in the Plantations that may affect the Trade or navigation of Great Britain', it predicted that such an authority would empower the Privy Council with a dangerously broad interpretive authority. '[I]t will be almost impossible', explained its remonstrance, 'to frame any law that may not

75 Ibid., 172.
76 *CSP (1732)*, 15.
77 Hemphill, *Virginia and the English Commercial System*, 189.
78 5 Geo. II c. 7 (1732).
79 *Acts of the Privy Council, Colonial (1720–45)*, 153.
80 Smith, *Appeals*, 465–522.

be construed some way or other to affect the Trade or navigation of Great Britain.' Discretionary judicial interpretation would affect laws ranging from the gauge of barrel staves to 'the just payment of debts'.[81]

Epilogue: the contest redux

The constitutional dimension of this struggle has become part of the *longue durée* of Anglo-American legal history. The creation of a federal judiciary in the United States constitution provoked some of the sharpest debate in the Virginia ratifying convention of 1788, where Virginians feared the imposition of a federal common law at variance with local understanding, construed and declared by federal judges following the interests of mercantile forces hundreds of miles away. Citing legal terms in the text of Article Three of the constitution, Patrick Henry pointed out that the specific wording of the judiciary article served as no protection. 'What is meant by such words in common parlance?' he asked. The constitution made reference to appeals on 'law and fact', which might enable a federal court to overturn a local jury.[82] William Grayson, who would soon be chosen as one of the state's two senators, reminded listeners that debts to British merchants would, by the Treaty of Paris, be tried in federal courts under the federal law of the land. He argued that these debts had been incurred before 1776 and under expectations of repayment and remedy now no longer to be counted on. Virginia courts had been notoriously slow in providing justice, and Grayson alluded to this when he stated, 'I presume, when the contracts were made, the creditors had an idea of the state judiciaries only. The procrastination and delays of our courts were probably in contemplation by both parties. They could have no idea of the establishment of new tribunals to affect them.'[83] Indeed, neither they nor judges and constitutional law scholars who followed them would know for certain how 'the Crooked Cord of a Judge's Discretion' might affect them. Because the problem of divided sovereignty had provoked the Revolution but had not been settled by it, the question remains. Present-day debates on federal pre-emption and the reach of the Commerce Clause rage over this division of authority. It is a question inherent in the modern state, and central to the problems addressed in this volume.

[81] *CSP (1731)*, 322.
[82] *The Debates in the Several State Conventions, on the Adoption of the Federal Constitution*, ed. J. Elliott (Philadelphia, 1836–59), iii. 540, 579.
[83] Ibid., iii. 274, 566.

10

Judges and the application of imperial law in eastern Australia, 1788–1836

Resistance and reception

BRUCE KERCHER

I never thought anything of Jeremy Bentham. He was the most pretentious person that ever lived.

Lord Denning, *What Next in the Law* (London, 1982), 17

Introduction

For some time now, legal historians have been fascinated by broad questions about the reception of English law in the colonies. These concern the formal and informal ties between colonial and English law. Many recent studies of British colonial law have concluded that, particularly in the early years, the law used in the colonies was markedly different from that of England. Early colonial judges in North America and Australia, for instance, bent harsh English debt recovery laws by allowing instalment orders, payment in chickens, wheat or other produce, making work orders instead of ordering payment in money, and so on.[1] With the commencement of more formal courts after some decades of a new colony's existence, there often came closer attention to legality, particularly through stricter application of the rules governing the reception of law. This often meant the colony's law losing its distinctive qualities.

[1] See for example, B.H. Mann, *Neighbors and Strangers: Law and Community in Early Connecticut* (Chapel Hill, NC, 1987); B. Kercher, *Debt, Seduction and Other Disasters: The Birth of Civil Law in Convict New South Wales* (Sydney, 1996); and see C.H. Dayton, *Women Before the Bar: Gender, Law, and Society in Connecticut, 1639–1789* (Chapel Hill, NC, 1995); D. Langum, *Law and Community on the Mexican Californian Frontier: Anglo-American Expatriates and the Clash of Legal Traditions, 1821–1846* (Norman, 1987). More recently, see P. Karsten, *Between Law and Custom: 'High' and 'Low' Legal Cultures in the Lands of the British Diaspora – the United States, Canada, Australia, and New Zealand, 1600–1900* (Cambridge, 2002).

This should be related to another broad question, about the nature of law. Some historians suggest that the nature of 'law' changed in the course of the long eighteenth century. They point to the change from the common law tradition of Coke, Hale, and Blackstone, to the positivism that eventually came to dominate legal thought in the former British empire until well after the middle of the twentieth century. The suggestion is that enlightenment rationalism led to a shift from law as custom and tradition, to a notion of law as command, via legislation.[2]

If this is sound analysis, then what of the colonies and, particularly, what of the penal colonies where law as command might be expected to have been prominent, particularly in the eyes of the British government and colonial governors? Did the colonial judiciary and populace accept this characterization of law, or did they insist on notions of law as custom and tradition, that is, on the idea of law from below? The hypothesis to be tested is that the colonial judiciary gradually shifted from one model to another, from tradition to command, while the governors relied on command alone.

Before testing this hypothesis, it is necessary to say a little about the traditional common law method. In the seventeenth century, Coke emphasized the difference between the artificial rationality of lawyers and judges, and the rationality of legal laypersons.[3] Only those trained in the law could understand the common law, he argued, and only they could be trusted to develop it, even through legislation. While it satisfied the demands of natural law, Coke argued, the common law gained its authority through its acceptance since time immemorial, and through being subject to the process of rational development by the judges. The consent of the general population to their ancient customs, developed by artificial reason, led to the perfection of the common law. Coke's emphasis was on reason, while in subsequently developing the common law method, Hale placed greater emphasis on the general consent underlying the customs that had been in existence for centuries. To both of them, the common law method was based on what came to be known as the declaratory theory.

According to Coke and Hale, instead of law being made by the judges, it was discovered by them, and refined through their artificial reasoning until it became the wisdom of ages. This did not require a strict theory of precedent, as the cases were not the law so much as evidence of the law. Judges could get it wrong, and be declared wrong subsequently. Bad decisions were simply not law.

[2] See, for example, D. Lemmings, 'Law', in I. McCalman (ed.), *An Oxford Companion to the Romantic Age* (Oxford, 1999), 73–81.

[3] This part is based largely on A. Cromartie, *Sir Matthew Hale 1609–1676: Law, Religion and Natural Philosophy* (Cambridge, 1995), Introduction and chps 1, 2, and 7; as well as G. Postema, *Bentham and the Common Law Tradition* (Oxford, 1986), ch. 1. I thank David Lemmings for the suggestion to read these, and for the hypothesis on which this chapter is based.

The crucial issue concerns the common law method's attitude to legislation. While he accepted the theory of parliamentary omnipotence, Coke's version of the common law method allowed legislation to be undermined via statutory interpretation. In interpreting any statute, he said, it was important to begin with the common law, then to see what mischief or defect there was in it that parliament aimed to remedy, then to examine the statutory remedy, and finally to construe the remedy to meet the mischief according to what the judges took to be the true intention of the legislature. But further than that, he allowed a more radical challenge to legislation when it attacked fundamental common law doctrines. When an act was contrary to common right and reason, repugnant, or impossible, he is believed to have said in *Bonham's Case* in 1610,[4] the judges could even declare it void. Thus it was possible for example, to challenge legislation that declared a person or an institution to be judge in its own cause.

The essential elements of the common law tradition then, were a strong belief in the timeless rationality and majesty of the common law, rooted according to its various proponents in natural law, custom, and rationality. On this view, it was the common law that gave statutory law its validity, not the reverse.

These ideas were all evident in Blackstone, whose four volumes accompanied the colonial judges across the British world.[5] Importantly for colonies that were likely to develop their own legal customs, Blackstone particularly emphasized the customary basis of the common law, whether general customs (which term he used interchangeably with the common law) or the customs of particular places, such as Kent. Local customs were recognized as law when they were:

- in use as long as memory of man runneth (that is since 3 September 1189);
- continued since then without interruption;
- peaceable and acquiesced in;
- reasonable and certain;
- compulsory on those bound by them, rather than voluntary;
- and consistent with one another.

Blackstone wrote that statutes were of two kinds, declaratory of the common law, and remedial of it. The latter were to be interpreted through the historical method outlined by Coke. Blackstone was not as expansive as Coke, however, when dealing with repugnant or unreasonable statutes. He said that acts that were impossible to be performed were of no validity, 'and if there arise out of them collaterally any absurd consequences, manifestly contradictory to

[4] *English Reports*, lxxvii. 638: 8 Co. Rep. 107a (1610).

[5] See in particular, W. Blackstone, *Commentaries on the Laws of England* (1st edn, Oxford, 1765–9, repr., Chicago, 1979), i. Introduction, section 3.

common reason, they are, with regard to those collateral consequences, void'.[6] Unreasonable consequences, collateral to the purpose, may be assumed to be oversights by parliament, he said, and may be dealt with through statutory interpretation to avoid those consequences. In this way, any grant of jurisdiction would be read against a person or institution given power to be a judge in its own cause. But this only applied at the margins. There was nothing to prevent parliament from enacting unreasonable statutes if it did so in evident and express words so that its intention was clear. It would be 'subversive of all government' to place the judicial power above that of the legislature, Blackstone said.[7]

Blackstone had a profound influence on the colonial judges who sailed around the world in the early nineteenth century to dispense British justice in the new colonies, but by then those whom Brian Simpson calls the iconoclasts were also smashing away at the common law tradition.[8] Bentham was not the only critic who argued that the common law method was so utterly fluid that its outcome was the result of the will of the judges, rather than determined through artificial reasoning as they claimed.

At the same time, reformers such as Peel, Romilly, and Brougham were also battering away at the perfection of the common law, making important changes to the criminal law in particular. The Blue Books of the early nineteenth century British parliament are full of proposals for law reform. What Coke and Blackstone described as the perfection of reason, the members of these parliamentary select committees saw as irrational, fiction-laden complexity, rooted in archaic values. To these people, law should be made by parliament in a series of planned, rational reforms. Colonial judges had to decide which of these statutes were in force in the colonies, and what they meant.

The colonial judges also participated in changes in the common law method during the nineteenth century. According to Tony Blackshield,[9] the reform bill of 1832 and its successors led to a change in the nature of the legitimacy of the judiciary. It had once been based on the paternalism of a natural ruling class and through custom, but under a broader franchise, law was now seen to be legitimate because it had been made by a representative parliament. The legitimacy of the judiciary now came to rely more strongly, Blackshield argues, on the skills of the judges. Parliament made law, not judges. Judges continued to find correct answers to legal questions through the techniques first described extensively by Coke. But by the end of the nineteenth century, a strict and

[6] Blackstone, *Commentaries*, i. 91.

[7] Ibid.

[8] B. Simpson, 'Legal Iconoclasts and Legal Ideals', *University of Cincinnati Law Review*, 58 (1990), 819.

[9] A.R. Blackshield, 'The Legitimacy and Authority of Judges', *University of New South Wales Law Journal*, 10 (1987),155.

complete legalism controlled judicial method. This was another version of positivism, one that treated case law as if it were statutory authority.

This required a much stronger version of precedent in a strict hierarchy, Blackshield tells us. Lower courts obeyed the decisions of those above them, and before the end of the nineteenth century even the highest tribunal in England, the House of Lords, declared itself to be bound by its own decisions, a stance it did not abandon until 1966. Case law was no longer merely evidence of the law, but was now the law itself. Every binding judgment was based on a *ratio decidendi*, a clear decisive rule, while all else that the judges said was merely *obiter*, persuasive at best. What was once a search for principle, or a reasoned decision, now became a search for authority.[10] Bad decisions were now as binding as good ones. Strict authority now ruled both kinds of law, statutory and judge-made. Top down law became almost entirely dominant.

New South Wales, 1788–1836

The question is just how much of this was evident in the superior courts of New South Wales from the time of their commencement in 1788 until the 1830s? Particularly in the permanent Supreme Court, which began operation in 1824, how much influence did these intellectual currents have in the penal colony? (This chapter concentrates on the case law during the period on the bench of Francis Forbes, the first chief justice of New South Wales, 1824–36.) How did the Supreme Court judges deal with the reception of statute and common law, and what did they do with it once they accepted that it was part of the colony's law? Did they assume that all law came from an English above, or was there any evidence of law being made from below, through the customs of the people of the colony?

The hypothesis concerning a shift in judicial reasoning works well in the first period of New South Wales law, from 1788 until 1814. The colony was founded through British legislation and Letters Patent, and the first judges held office under limited circumstances. They had the title of judge advocate, and until 1809 they were bound to obey the governors 'according to the rules and disciplines of war'.[11] The governors in the period covered by this chapter were all military or naval officers. Until the first major reform took effect in 1824, they were at the head of the military and administrative structures in the colony, they sat alone as the Court of Appeal in civil cases, and as there was no legislature they made orders and proclamations of general effect. That is, within the colony the governors were unchallengeable in formal law,

[10] See also W. Twining and D. Mieirs, *How to Do Things with Rules* (2nd edn, London, 1982), 269–75; and see P. Parkinson, *Tradition and Change in Australian Law* (Sydney, 1994), 84–6.

[11] A.C. Castles, *An Australian Legal History* (Sydney, 1982), 48.

whether in their legislative, executive, or judicial powers. When pressed with a legal argument, Governor Bligh (in New South Wales from 1806 to 1810) responded 'the law Sir! Damn the Law; my will is the law, and woe unto the man that dares to disobey it.'[12] That was a perfect response of a man in as perfectly an autocratic position as any British official of the nineteenth century. He was, however, bound by his instructions from the crown, and the judge advocates were bound to follow the applicable laws of England. The governors also found that they needed some degree of co-operation from the ordinary people of New South Wales.

Even Bligh found that his orders were not always obeyed. The convicts and free population of New South Wales refused to comply with many of the governors' orders, no matter how autocratic their formal powers. The people refused to keep their pigs off the streets, they bought and sold land in completely informal ways despite registration orders, and convicts refused to stop issuing promissory notes when ordered to do so. The people of New South Wales quickly developed customary ways of dealing with one another, and there was little that the governors could do to control it. Worse, the governors soon found that even the judge advocates sometimes disobeyed their orders. When faced with a choice between supporting a customary practice and giving effect to a formal order by a governor, even the barrister Judge Advocate Ellis Bent occasionally ignored the governors' orders.[13] This fits the hypothesis perfectly, at least as far as colonial law was concerned: customary resistance to positive law had the backing of a judge who was trained in the common law method.

From 1824 onwards, the penal colonies' structures more closely matched those of the other British colonies. They were becoming places of ordinary liberties. Under the New South Wales Act (4 Geo. IV c. 96 (1823)), New South Wales and Van Diemen's Land each acquired a Supreme Court headed by a chief justice, with the same jurisdiction as the superior courts at Westminster. The statute also provided for a nominated Legislative Council with explicit power to make law. The judges of the Supreme Court were English and Irish barristers, supported by qualified officials. There was a clear expectation that both the courts and the legislature in the colony would follow English law. As explained later, the colonies' constitutions allowed judicial review of local legislation, to check that it followed British legal propriety.

The first chief justice of New South Wales, Francis Forbes, was also a member of both the Legislative Council and the Executive Council. Although

[12] *A Charge of Mutiny: The Court Martial of Lieutenant George Johnston for Deposing Governor Bligh in the Rebellion of 26 January 1808*, ed. J.D. Ritchie (Canberra, 1988), 161: evidence of Richard Atkins. On this early constitutional structure, see Kercher, *Debt, Seduction*, ch. 1.

[13] See B. Kercher, 'Resistance to Law under Autocracy', *Modern Law Review*, 60 (1997), 779–97.

colonial judges lacked judicial tenure, Forbes thus held a powerful position. In the absence of competent legal advice from the colonial Attorney General or Solicitor General, the governors often relied on Forbes to draft their legislation, after which he had an opportunity to judge its validity. We can already see that the application of the hypothesis is becoming complicated: the judge who might have applied customary law was also up to his ears in the making of positive law.

Reception of English law

Blackstone wrote that English law was the birthright of British subjects in settled colonies, but he qualified this as follows: the colonies received 'only so much of the English law, as is applicable to their own situation and the condition of an infant colony'.[14]

The first substantial debate in New South Wales about the reception of law took place even before the first barrister was appointed to judicial office in the colony in 1809. The only lawyers there at that time were disgraced former attorneys who had been transported as convicts. Blackstone's formula was first cited by the most prominent of these outcast lawyers, George Crossley, when arguing a succession case. Crossley was the first to develop the argument that New South Wales had been founded in a *terra nullius*, under the settled colony category. His opponent in the succession case was a wealthy former convict, Simeon Lord, who was acting as a lay attorney. Lord did not reject the basic test, but he thought it had quite a different meaning from that put by Crossley. Crossley assumed that the formula stood for the strict reception of English laws, while Lord took a broader view. Lord said that he relied on justice and 'the Law of England, in its pure Construction and the law of equity and Reason in every sense'.[15] He saw the law in terms of its spirit, rather than as a body of strict rules.

In fact the reception of English law should have been at issue in the very first civil action heard in Australia, *Cable* v. *Sinclair*. This was decided by the

[14] W. Blackstone, *Commentaries on the Laws of England* (9th edn, London, 1783, reprinted, Garland Publishing, New York, 1978), i. 108. These qualifying words did not appear in the first edition: Blackstone, *Commentaries*, 1st edn, i. 104–5.

[15] *In re Stogdell* (see Mitchell Library, Sydney, MS A2019: P.G. King, 'Letter Book: Legal: Correspondence with Judge Advocates, Reports of Appeals, etc.', 1800–1806, Vol. 4, pp. 179–80). Lord eventually won the case, on appeal to the Privy Council: see *Printed Cases in Indian and Colonial Appeals Heard 1807–1826* (unpublished, in the office of the Judicial Committee of the Privy Council, London), and National Archives [Public Record Office]: PRO PC2/171: Council Register 1 August 1806 to 30 December 1806, 423, 441. On this debate, see B. Kercher, 'A Convict Conservative: George Crossley and the English Legal Tradition', *Law in Context*, 19 (1998), 17. The Privy Council case is now online at http://www.law.mq.edu.au/pc/LordvPalmer,1809.htm.

Court of Civil Jurisdiction in July 1788, just a few months after the first fleet entered Sydney harbour. Two convicts successfully sued the master of the ship that had carried their baggage across the world. When the defendant's ship arrived, some of the plaintiffs' baggage was missing. Judge Advocate Collins ignored the fact that each of the plaintiffs had been convicted of capital crimes in England and sentenced to death, after which their sentences were commuted to transportation. By English law, they were subject to felony attaint, under which they should not have been able to sue or own property until the expiry of their sentences of transportation. It was later argued in New South Wales that at least some aspects of the law of attaint were not received in the colony's law because of the sheer impracticality of applying it in a penal settlement, but in *Cable* v. *Sinclair*, the judge advocate dealt with technical law in a way that became characteristic of the earliest civil courts: he simply ignored it.[16]

After the permanent Supreme Court began operation in 1824, issues of reception of law were treated more seriously. A debate over the date of reception of statutory law led to the enactment of a statutory version of the reception of law test in 1828. In that year, the British parliament passed the Australian Courts Act (9 Geo. IV c. 83). Section 24 stated that all the laws and statutes of England in force at the time of the passing of the act shall be applied in the administration of justice, so far as they can be applied. This test, apparently taken from the law applying to Newfoundland,[17] applied in both New South Wales and Van Diemen's Land.

The statutory test was applied in many New South Wales cases, most notably in *Macdonald* v. *Levy*, 1833.[18] The point in issue in this case was whether the usury laws of England applied in the colony. Interest rates in New South Wales had often been much higher than English law would have allowed, and the question for the three judges of the Supreme Court was whether to recognize this colonial customary practice of high interest loans, or to follow English statutory law.

The Supreme Court split two to one on the issue. The majority judges were Forbes CJ and Dowling J, the two who most often recognized local customary practices against the strict importation of English law. Forbes said that the statutory test was the same as the old common law test of reception of English law. Under this, it was necessary to see whether the English law in question suited the needs of the colony.

For our hypothesis, the important point was that this was a clash between the positive law of the English statute and a local customary practice of lending

[16] *Cable* v. *Sinclair* has been the subject of extensive commentary. See, for example, D. Neal, *The Rule of Law in a Penal Colony* (Cambridge, 1991), 1–7.

[17] 32 Geo. III c. 46, s. 1 (1792); 49 Geo. III c. 27, s. 1 (1809).

[18] Opinions and cases cited here just by name and date are online at www.law.mq.edu.au/scnsw.

at high interest rates. Forbes said that this practice was not a formally recognized local 'custom', but was evidence that the colony's population and its judges had never accepted that the usury laws of England had been received in the colony. Forbes was liberal towards local legal practices and towards the rights of British people, even in a penal colony. He said

> The only legitimate object of all laws, is to provide for the protection and necessary wants of mankind – beyond this, every law is unnecessary; and, in proportion as it is inapplicable, it becomes a useless burthen. Of all evils upon society, I know of none more to be deprecated, than to be governed by unsuitable laws – they interfere with the daily habits and pursuits of mankind; they are opposed to their feelings and opinions, and carry in them all the consequences of oppression.

To Forbes, the fact that the local population had never considered a particular English law to be in force was a good reason for thinking that it was not applicable in the colony's circumstances. 'The first, and leading principle should be, whether such laws are applicable in their nature and object, to the state and condition of the colonists.' Relying on English case law, he drew a distinction between laws that were of a 'general and fundamental kind, upon which the constitutional government, and social rights of the community depend, and such as are of a political and local nature, calculated to suit the exigencies of particular times and places'. The latter might or might not be part of colonial law. He went on:

> Let me not, however, be mistaken; the laws of England are our birth right, where they apply to our condition, and can be administered to us with advantage; but where they are inapplicable, they are not in force; and where they are silent, then there is no law, unless established by the general consent and usage of the colony at large, or the local legislature; both being alike subordinate to the great and sovereign principle, that our local laws and usages must be reasonable in themselves, and not repugnant to the general laws of the parent country.

General usage could become law, he went on to say, when it was incorporated as an implied term of all of the colonists' contracts.

The minority judge, Burton J, took the opposite view to that of Forbes in this and many other cases. There was no 'custom' in New South Wales, he said, since local customs had to have been in existence since 1189 before they could be recognized by the common law, and the colony was obviously founded since then. Local practices of high interest rates were not evidence of lawful customs or practices, but of looseness and irregularity.

Burton took a positivist line, relying on the exact words of the imperial statute. He emphasized the word 'can' in s. 24. The only question was whether the particular law 'can' be applied in the colony. In this case there was no reason why not, he held, so that the English usury laws were in force in the colony. The judge's duty was to decide according to the law. Only parliament could change the law. Burton's positivist method, his emphasis on statute rather than custom, matched his views of the colony. To him, the only good law was the law of England as well as any law passed by the local legislature with the authority of the parliament at Westminster. Legal authority came from an English above.

Burton hated what he thought of as the looseness and irregularity of law in New South Wales, and claimed he suffered personally as a result of the colony's outrageously high interest rates. In letters to his family and friends, he wrote that this dissenting judgment was his 'one grand stand against . . . usurious practices', in which he was in a 'glorious minority of one'. He complained of the 'capricious adoption of some English statutes & the libertine abandonment of others'. While he thought Forbes was clever, he also said that he presided over a court with loose practices and application of laws, and that he could only describe the lawyers who appeared there as 'Botany Bay lawyers'.[19]

In *Macdonald* v. *Levy*, Forbes drew a clear distinction between local customary practices and statutory law, finding for custom, while Burton did the reverse. Forbes placed no emphasis on the words of the reception provision, 'so far as the same can be applied'. To Forbes, Burton's emphasis on the word 'can', a concern with the 'physical possibility of applying a law or not within the colony', was inappropriate. In their judgments it seems clear that Forbes and Dowling, the other majority judge, operated on premises underlying the old common law method. In these judgments at least, law was a matter of custom, not positive rule, gaining its legitimacy by its use or non-use by the people of New South Wales. This was an argument over method as much as content, and the two could not be separated. In this judgment, Forbes clearly showed his common law heritage: it was rooted in custom, even the customs of the British people in a penal colony. By contrast, Burton preferred English statute law to colonial practices, and did so through a positivist method.

The same split between these judges occurred in *R* v. *Maloney*, 1836, the last case decided by Forbes before returning to England in the vain hope of recovering his health. He and Dowling held that the English Marriage Act did not apply in New South Wales, and thus that Roman Catholic marriages conducted in the colony were valid, while Burton was in dissent again. Burton would have declared Catholic marriages invalid, and Catholic children to be bastards. Forbes again used his familiar common law method. He relied on natural law, Coke's method of interpreting statutes, and the consent of the community to its laws, to hold that the long-standing practice of Catholic marriages in the colony was valid. He said that

> To maintain a contrary doctrine, to hold that Parliament intended to force the whole mass of English laws – the laws of an old and settled society, which have

[19] For Burton's correspondence, see *Macdonald* v. *Levy*, 1833, footnote 1. Some of his correspondence is online at ww.law.mq.edu.au/scnsw/html/burton_letters.htm.

> grown out of occasions, during a long course of years, and which are become more refined and complicated than the laws of any other country in the world – to apply all these laws at once to an infant community, without limitation or restraint, 'is a proposition much too inconvenient in its consequences, to be perfectly just in its principle'.[20]

While Forbes usually allowed colonial customs to take effect, sometimes he changed his mind after doing so in the first place. The most alien custom was that of the Aboriginal peoples. In *R* v. *Ballard*, 1829, he and Dowling held quite clearly that the Supreme Court had no jurisdiction when one Aborigine killed another. Forbes's argument rested on the practice in both North America and New South Wales of not interfering with such cases unless the victim had come to a British town to seek sanctuary. In most cases, Aborigines were allowed to rule their own lives according to their own customs. At first Forbes stuck to this position in *R* v. *Murrell*, 1836. But when the case reached the Supreme Court in Banco, he changed his mind. Like Dowling, he acquiesced in Burton's judgment affirming that the Supreme Court had jurisdiction over all crimes within New South Wales, no matter who was involved.[21] The recognition of Aboriginal customs was abandoned and the theory of *terra nullius* affirmed.

Forbes showed inconsistency of a different kind over landholdings. When he was chief justice in Newfoundland, he made some important decisions that recognized the customary practices of the local people over landholding. The British government had been discouraging permanent settlement there, and these judgments were a boost towards the island reaching formal colonial status. In New South Wales, there were similar informalities in landholdings, caused by the loose practices of the governors in granting land and the equally loose practices of the local people in conveyancing. Forbes might have been expected to recognize these practices in New South Wales, but instead he took a very formal line. When the crown's title was in issue, he made no allowance for the fact that the majority of the colony's land titles were held informally. He held that the crown was in possession of land that it had not granted formally, even when everyone else assumed that the land had passed into private hands. There were so many invalid titles for this reason that the Legislative Council passed the Crown Land (Claims) Act 1833. Under it, a Court of Claims was given power to recommend the exercise of the crown's discretion on behalf of those who had bought land or spent money on the basis

[20] Forbes was quoting here from an unknown source.

[21] See B. Kercher, 'The Recognition of Aboriginal Status and Laws in the Supreme Court of New South Wales under Forbes C.J., 1824–1836', in A. Buck, J. McLaren and N. Wright (eds), *Land and Freedom: Law, Property Rights and the British Diaspora* (Aldershot, 2001), 83–102.

of unenforceable promises of crown land grants. That would not have been necessary if Forbes had recognized the customs in the first place.[22]

Forbes was also inconsistent on the question of convict evidence. In *R* v. *Gardener and Yems*, 1829, he was one of a unanimous court of three to decide that attainted convicts could give evidence in the courts of New South Wales. At common law, one of the consequences of felony attaint was that the person was unable to sit on a jury or give evidence. If the rule had been applied strictly, this would have caused many crimes to go unpunished in the colony, where so many people were attainted according to English law. Forbes, Dowling, and Stephen held in *Gardener* that it was permissible to allow a convict at the Port Macquarie penal settlement to give evidence concerning a crime that had taken place there. Forbes said that 'the uniform practice has been to admit the testimony of such persons from the necessity of the thing.' In short, the rule was inapplicable in the state of the colony. Once again, his reasoning followed common law's emphasis on the consent of the community. Convicts had always been allowed to give evidence. (By contrast, Aborigines could not give evidence. Forbes reluctantly applied the English rule against infidels or heathens giving evidence, calling it a 'very barbarous notion', though one that was in force in New South Wales.[23])

Yet in *R* v. *Farrell*, 1831, Forbes reached an uncharacteristically cautious conclusion on a closely related point. In this case, the question was whether a person who had been doubly convicted, in both England and New South Wales, could give evidence concerning a crime committed in the middle of Sydney. Forbes said that the law against attainted evidence could be ignored in the penal settlements like Port Macquarie, where necessity required it, even in cases of double convictions. In other parts of the colony, only the evidence of those simply transported from England or Ireland could be admitted. They had been sent to the colony in the hope of rehabilitation, and had good reason to tell the truth in court. Those convicted a second time in the colony were in an entirely different position, according to Forbes. In dissent, he opposed the admission of the evidence of such people. The majority, Dowling and Stephen JJ, held as they had in *Gardener*, emphasizing the flexibility in the reception of law test.

The difference between the majority and minority in *Farrell* was not one of method, since Forbes used the same basic principles as he had in *Gardener* and *Macdonald* v. *Levy*. Instead, it was a conflict over the character of the

[22] See especially *R* v. *Cooper*, 1825; *R* v. *Steele*, 1834; discussed in B. Kercher and J. Young, 'Formal and informal law in two new lands: land law in Newfoundland and New South Wales under Francis Forbes' (unpublished, 1999). In other areas, Forbes was more consistent between Newfoundland and New South Wales: see B. Kercher, 'Establishment, Freedom of Speech and the Church of England: Pew Disputes in Early Nineteenth Century New South Wales and Newfoundland', *Australian Journal of Legal History*, 6 (2000), 135.

[23] See *R* v. *Fitzpatrick and Colville*, 1824.

English law of evidence, Forbes holding that it was a fundamental law of England, and the others that it was a mere rule of practice of the courts. Forbes said that only extreme necessity would allow doubly convicted people to give evidence. He showed no concern about the local practice in *Farrell*, which since 1788 had been to allow the evidence of all convicts to be admitted, by one means or another. The reason for Forbes taking such a strict line here may have been that the lives of the prisoners were at stake. It was a matter of life and death whether such evidence should be admitted.

After Burton arrived as the new judge of the Supreme Court to replace Stephen, he and Forbes formed a majority against the admission of the evidence of doubly convicted convicts. Yet they did not take advantage of that to change the law. Each of them, and a later judge named Willis, concluded that the Supreme Court was bound by its formally reached decision in *Farrell*.[24] *Farrell* was the law, even if they did not like it. A bad law was still law. This was evidence of a change in judicial style, as Tony Blackshield might have expected. Authority asserted itself over principle as early as the 1830s, and even when it was simply the authority of the judges' own court.

Repugnant colonial legislation

The colonial judges had an opportunity to test statutory law against the standards of the common law that was unavailable even to the most eminent of English judges. By s. 29 of the New South Wales Act 1823, new acts of the colony's Legislative Council were required to be certified by the chief justice that they were not repugnant to the laws of England. This was altered by the replacement act in 1828, the Australian Courts Act (9 Geo. IV c. 83, s. 22). Under that, the duty of reviewing colonial legislation was spread across all of the Supreme Court judges. The chief justice's veto power in the 1823 legislation was replaced, in effect, by a mere opportunity for any of the judges to issue a solemn warning. These powers of review of colonial legislation gave rise to some of the most controversial opinions of the Supreme Court. Since the governor introduced legislation into the Legislative Council, an attack on his legislation was as much a matter of judicial review of administration as it was the review of legislation. These cases give us a good opportunity to test the hypothesis.

The most dramatic use of this power was by Forbes CJ in 1827, when he refused to certify newspaper legislation introduced by Governor Darling. Darling used every legal technique he could find to muzzle a hostile local press. This included imprisonment of newspaper editors for sedition and criminal libel, and licensing and stamp duty legislation. He had reason to be confident

[24] See R v. *Ryan, Steel, McGrath and Daley*, 1832; R v. *McCabe*, 1833; R v. *Humphreys*, in *Sydney Herald*, 3 November 1840. (The latter is not online.)

about his legislation: English press laws of this period were very repressive, the British government had instructed him to introduce bills of this kind, and similar bills had received a certificate of consistency with English law from the chief justice of Van Diemen's Land. Despite that, Forbes refused to issue his certificate of compliance to key provisions of the licensing bill, and ultimately to the stamp duty bill.[25]

Forbes's concern in his *Newspaper Acts Opinion*, 1827 was not with the customs of the colony's people, but with the general freedoms of British people. These general principles were fundamental, not peripheral laws: the colonial legislature was 'not allowed to alter the fundamental laws of the land'. He said that Darling's legislation interfered with constitutional rights to the freedom of the press, and allowed property to be taken without a prior hearing. He believed that if there had been no provision for the chief justice's certificate, it would have been his duty to strike down repugnant legislation in any event. He said that the role of the chief justice was to certify that the proposed colonial law was not contrary to the spirit of English law, by which he meant broad, fundamental, constitutional principles. Forbes's view of this function was consistent with his attitude to the reception of English law. He said:

> The laws of England are an exhaustless fund of legislative wisdom, from which enough may always be drawn to satisfy the exigencies of a small community; the power of selecting and modifying according to circumstances is committed to the subordinate legislatures of the Colonies; but they are not allowed to alter the fundamental laws of the land.

Privately, Forbes said that the governor's object was to eradicate all but the sycophantic *Sydney Gazette*, which would operate as a propaganda arm of government.[26] In return, Darling saw nothing but cunning in the chief justice. He thought that Forbes was in league with the reformist press.[27] The British government accepted Forbes's legal arguments, but warned both the governor and the chief justice that it would no longer tolerate the bitter dispute that had developed between them.

Seven years later, the judges returned to the issue of repugnancy in another important case. By 1834, the new version of the repugnancy provision was in force, under which any of the judges could object to new acts of the Legislative

[25] On these disputes, see B. Edgeworth, 'Defamation Law and the Emergence of a Critical Press in Colonial New South Wales (1824–1831)', *Australian Journal of Law and Society*, 6 (1990), 50; J.J. Spigelman, 'Foundations of Freedom of the Press in Australia', *Quadrant*, 394 (2003), 9.

[26] The correspondence and other details of the legislation are discussed in the footnotes to the *Newspaper Acts Opinion*, 1827.

[27] See, for example, Mitchell Library, MS A 1203, Reel CY 536, Governor's Despatches to the Secretary of State for the Colonies, Vol. 14, September–December 1828, 17–20: Darling to Hay, 1 September 1828.

Council. The act in question was one of the renewals of the Bushranging Act that had first been enacted in 1830. Under this legislation, any person could be retained in custody until the person proved that he or she was not an escaped convict. There was also a reversed onus of proof in a firearms offence, and an acceleration of capital punishment for some offences.

This time it was Burton who declared the act repugnant, while Forbes and Dowling were of the opinion that it was consistent with English law.[28] Forbes had drafted the act, and was a close ally of the liberal governor of the time, Governor Bourke. He and Dowling thought that the extreme state of a penal colony during the bushranging crisis justified extreme measures. Burton took two approaches: first he compared the colonial statute point by point with the laws of England, and then he referred broadly to general constitutional principles, particularly the presumption of innocence. Forbes did not complain about Burton's reference to broad principles, as it was the approach he had taken in the *Newspaper Acts Opinion*. He did object, however, to Burton's point by point approach. That reasoning was too narrow, Forbes said. On that basis, he pointed out, any difference from English law would make colonial law invalid. That would have invalidated the laws of slavery in the American colonies, for example. Given the circumstances of the colony, Forbes said, the Bushranging Act was consistent with the broad principles of English law.

Although Burton had taken some of Forbes's approach in the newspaper opinion, the Bushranging Act controversy also had characteristic elements of the conflict between his approach and that of Forbes. Forbes looked for broad principles, for the basic spirit of English law, and even if that was breached in a colonial law, he looked for any colonial circumstances which might have justified a departure. As in the reception of law cases, Burton was narrower in his general approach, and much less willing to accommodate differences between colonial and English law.

Declaring colonial statutes to be invalid was one thing, but it was something entirely different when the Supreme Court was asked to declare a provision of an imperial statute to be void. That raised the ghost of Coke, with his declaration in *Bonham's Case* that common law judges could declare some acts of the parliament invalid. The Supreme Court of New South Wales was invited to do that in *R* v. *Hayes*, 1829. This was a prosecution of a newspaper editor for seditious libel of Governor Darling. At the time, serious crimes were still tried in the Supreme Court before a panel of seven military or naval officers in place of a civilian jury. Hayes's counsel argued against the composition of the panel that they were soldiers under the governor's command, that they were paid for jury service at his discretion, and that he had nominated their membership. This made the governor judge in his own cause. The trial judge,

[28] See Burton to Bourke, 25 August 1834, *Historical Records of Australia* (Series 1, Sydney, 1914–25), xvii. 524–33; Mitchell Library, MS A 121 (CY 545), 947–56 (Forbes Papers): *R* v. *Elliott*, 1834.

Dowling J, rejected these arguments, and the defendant was tried and found guilty. His counsel, the reformist barrister W.C. Wentworth, then moved to have the verdict set aside. He claimed that s. 5 of 9 Geo. IV c. 83 (1828) (the Australian Courts Act) was void because it had absurd consequences, manifestly contradictory to common reason. The absurdity was in allowing the person allegedly defamed to be judge in his own cause by having such an influence over the panel of officers.

Forbes recognized the constitutional significance of the point, and argued expansively. He said that the laws of England generally conformed with the universal laws of nature. However he was able to avoid the spectacle of a colonial judge declaring some of the legislation of the parliament at Westminster to be void, by finding that the governor had not acted in his own cause. To be judge in his own cause, the governor would have had to preside at the trial, hear the case, and declare his own verdict. None of that was evident here. While Forbes said he had the highest respect for trial by jury, the parliament had made a deliberate decision to depart from it in the Supreme Courts of New South Wales and Van Diemen's Land. Any analogy with jury trial must fail. Forbes said that it was not possible to interpret the statute so that any person could be protected by the criminal law except the colony's governor.

Applying the hypothesis, we see a positivist side to Forbes's reasoning here. He concluded that 'What the Act clearly directs, or authorises, may be done in virtue of the Act, without being restrained in its operation by the common law.' When the crunch came, legislation was superior to the common law. (Forbes felt quite differently about the colonial legislature: one reason he gave for declaring Governor Darling's press licensing bill to be repugnant to English law, was that in some situations it would have allowed the governor to be judge in his own cause.)[29]

The supremacy of the imperial parliament was even clearer in the judgment of Dowling J. He rejected Blackstone's suggestion that some consequences of legislation could be declared void. He cited Christian's edition of Blackstone as follows:

> if an Act of Parliament is clearly and unequivocally expressed, with all deference to the learned Commentator, I conceive it is neither void in its direct nor collateral consequences, however absurd and unreasonable they may appear. If the expression will admit of doubt, it will not then be presumed that the construction can be agreeable to the intention of the Legislature, the consequences of which are unreasonable; but when the signification of a statute is manifest, no authority less than that of Parliament can restrain its operation.

Justice Stephen dissented, but not by holding the statute void. He held that it was possible to avoid these consequences by appointing a panel from officers on half-pay and from naval officers. He would have ordered a new trial.

[29] See *Newspaper Acts Opinion*, 1827.

None of the judges accepted Wentworth's invitation. Much as these three still practised the old common law method, none of them was willing to entertain a declaration that even a small part of an imperial act was void.

Conclusion

Francis Forbes, the first chief justice of New South Wales, was in office during a transitional period, one in which older and newer methods of legal reasoning often conflicted. Forbes and Dowling were expert in the traditional common law method. Forbes in particular used Coke's method of statutory interpretation, referred to natural law, and justified the common law by reference to custom. He took the reception of law to be a reception of broad constitutional principles rather than a set of strict rules that were analogous to statutory law.

In the first important constitutional law case in Australia,[30] *R* v. *Magistrates of New South Wales*, 1824, Forbes showed that he could use statutory interpretation creatively. The New South Wales Act 1823 provided for courts of quarter sessions to handle middle level criminal trials, but was silent as to whether juries should sit on them. The Supreme Court had no civilian juries, but Forbes interpreted the silence in the act concerning the quarter sessions trials to be an intention to include trial by jury. He concluded that 'It would not merely be against the express language of *Magna Charta* to try free British subjects without the common right of a jury, but against the whole law and constitution of England.' Exactly the same question arose in Van Diemen's Land in 1825, when Pedder CJ reached the opposite conclusion in *R* v. *Magistrates of Hobart Town*, 1825.[31] Pedder had much in common with Burton.

Burton often took a stricter approach than Forbes, partly through his literal interpretation of the word 'can' in s. 24 of the Australian Courts Act 1828. That was his device for attempting to import nearly the whole of English statutory and common law and for striking down colonial innovations. Yet he too invoked the broad principles of law at times, particularly in his Bushranging Acts opinion. Like all judges, he sometimes used whatever resources were available to him, and this did not always result in consistency of approach. Burton, too, was schooled in the common law tradition.

Forbes and Burton were not necessarily nor always in different methodological camps then. Burton was certainly more authoritarian in style and more likely to support the decisions of Governor Darling. Forbes was willing to resist the governor's decisions by referring to the grand constitutional freedoms of the British people, but he did this at great cost. He was hated by the conservative supporters of Governor Darling, the colony's exclusive faction.

[30] Castles, *An Australian Legal History*, 185–6.

[31] This is online at www.law.mq.edu.au/scvdl.

No litigants appealed from the New South Wales Supreme Court under Forbes to the Privy Council. Doubts about whether there was power to appeal from this court were resolved only in 1844.[32] This did not mean, however, that the judges were free of imperial supervision. Their repugnancy decisions were subject to review by the Colonial Office, which had oversight on all colonial legislation. This did not mean that there was a policy of tight conformity of colonial law to the law of England. The Office's James Stephen Jr had a similar attitude to Forbes over colonial legal innovations, stating in 1827 that 'it certainly has never been required that the Law of England should be made the inflexible model for all Colonial Legislation.'[33] Lord Glenelg, the colonial secretary, also upheld the view of Forbes and Dowling over that of Burton in the Bushranging Acts opinions. In the judges' advisory capacity, points of law were sometimes referred from New South Wales to the Attorney General and Solicitor General in London. In the *Newspaper Acts Opinion*, 1827, for instance, Forbes was aware that his view would be scrutinized by the law officers. There, as in most others where he was in conflict with the governor or with Burton, the British government accepted Forbes's view of the law.[34]

Forbes's willingness to follow the views of the British crown lawyers does not mean that he lacked independent judgement. Despite lacking judicial tenure, in 1829 Forbes knowingly interpreted the Transportation Acts in the opposite way to that of the Attorney General and Solicitor General in London. In doing so, he denied Governor Darling the chance to control convicts once they were assigned to work for private masters. In his judgment, Forbes described the views of the law officers as 'clearly untenable'. When they reiterated their opinion however, Forbes buckled, saying that he was glad to be corrected by their superior judgement.[35]

Burton's greater attachment to orders from above did not always make him a positivist in approach. It was logically possible for a judge who took Coke's approach to the common law to reject most of the customs of new colonies. Yet there was some connection in practice between the pairs of opposites. Among the first judges of the New South Wales Supreme Court, those who

[32] See *Flint* v. *Walker* (1845, 1847), 5 Moore's Privy Council reports, 179 at 193 (*English Reports*, xxiii. 459 at 464); and see *Lord* v. *Wentworth*, 1829. Absence of appeals: see unpublished *Printed Papers* and MS *Minute Books* in the office of the Judicial Committee of the Privy Council, London, and MS *Council Registers* in the National Archives [Public Record Office], group PC2.

[33] P. Knaplund, *James Stephen and the British Colonial System 1813–1847* (Madison, WI, 1953), 231, and see ch. 9.

[34] See also *Transportation Opinion*, 1826. Bushranging Act: see *Historical Records of Australia*, ser. 1, xviii. 94–5: Glenelg to Bourke, 5 September 1835. On this paragraph, see B. Kercher, 'Why the History of English Law is not English: Second Alex Castles Lecture in Legal History, October 2000', *Flinders Journal of Law Reform*, 7 (2004), 177–204.

[35] See *In re Jane New*, 1829; and see *Convict Assignment Opinion*, 1828. See the footnotes to these decisions for the correspondence.

took a broad approach to the common law method and its basis in custom tended to allow greater latitude to colonial law than those who were more strict in their approach to authority.

Forbes and Burton were most often in conflict over the respect to be paid to colonial customs. In many cases Forbes held that they were legitimate sources of law, usually as evidence of the colonial practice of the non-reception of law. Forbes took a strong version of the old approach to custom, one in which it was not confined to the customs of English people, nor even confined to Blackstone's version of the common law rules on the recognition of colonial customs. At times, Forbes even recognized colonial custom as a true source of law, filling gaps left by English law or its absence. The device he used was an implied term in contracts, the kind of law-making by judges when they denied that they were making law. At times we can see him operating as Robert Cover might have expected, choosing from among the many sources of law generated by the ordinary people of New South Wales.[36] At other times, however, he simply bowed to authority from an English above, statute law, English case law, or the law officers of the crown.

Burton saw nothing good in colonial customs: when they were in conflict with English law, he thought, that was not evidence of something new and legitimate, but only proof of the rottenness of New South Wales legal practices. This had a deeply political meaning in the colony, of course, but it was not simply a matter of politics. There was a sharp difference in the judges' respect for colonial practices, no matter what the subject matter of the case in question.

All of the judges showed some of the positivist approach that would later become dominant. Forbes was certainly not opposed to legislation. He drafted much of the New South Wales Act 1823, as well as some of the bills introduced by the governor into the New South Wales Legislative Council, on which he sat. He supported the Bushranging Act even when Burton attacked it on broad constitutional grounds. He was also keen to find that the imperial parliament's criminal law reforms were in force in the colony.[37] He took the unconventional view that the date of reception of statutory law was not the date the colony was founded, 1788, but the date of commencement of the colony's Legislative Council, 1824. This allowed much of the criminal law reforms to take effect.[38]

[36] See F.G. Snyder, 'Nomos, Narrative and Adjudication: Toward a Jurisgenetic Theory of Law', *William and Mary Law Review*, 40 (1999), 1623. Cover's fiendishly difficult article 'Foreword: Nomos and Narrative', *Harvard Law Review*, 97 (1983), 4, is among the most quoted of all law review articles. In it, he argued that there are multiple versions of law in multiple communities, from which judges must pick one for recognition.

[37] *Applicability of Criminal Laws Opinion*, 1828.

[38] See *Brown* v. *Mannix*, 1828; State Records of New South Wales, 4/6651, Chief Justice's MS Letter Book, 127–8: Forbes to Darling, 26 December 1827; *Historical Records of Australia*, ser. 4, i. 678: Forbes to Horton, 15 December 1826. See also Castles, *Australian Legal History*, 394–6, showing that Forbes had developed this theory in Newfoundland, which went

He also took a liberal view of the reception of these reform statutes even after the reception date.[39] If anyone was a Benthamite reformist in New South Wales, it was Forbes, not Burton. There was no simple match between their approaches to judicial technique and their politics.

Furthermore, Forbes and Burton both felt bound by the decision in *R* v. *Farrell*, 1831, even though each of them felt strongly that it was wrong, and even though they were in a majority on the Supreme Court once John Stephen left the court and Burton arrived. Burton differed from the more liberal judges over the test to be used for the reception of law, but even Forbes and Dowling refused to consider the possibility of declaring an imperial statute to be void. Even before the reform bill of 1832, all of the judges recognized that imperial statute law was above all other versions of law.

Colonial judges were in a very different position from their counterparts in England, on whom they were supposed to model themselves. In some cases, they were forced to consider the legitimacy of deeply held colonial customs which had not been in existence long enough to meet the old common law test for local customs. In others, they were forced to do something that was abandoned in England following the English Revolution. Imperial statute law required colonial judges to engage in the judicial review of colonial legislation. Judicial review was not an invention of the United States Supreme Court in *Marbury* v. *Madison* (1803) 5 US 137. It was an unavoidable consequence of the creation of colonial legislatures which had less than complete powers. The British legal empire of the early nineteenth century operated like a federation of states under a metropolitan government. The two principal devices used to define the relationship of these federal parties were the reception of law, and the repugnancy doctrine. When inferior and superior laws were in unavoidable conflict, the superior, imperial laws prevailed.

Judicial review did not mean judging imperial statute law by common law standards, but it did sometimes mean that for colonial statutes. Judges like Francis Forbes did not take these repugnancy provisions to mean just a conflict of one particular rule with another, but took a much broader, constitutional approach. The deep values of the common law, the spirit of the laws as he sometimes called it, provided a standard by which to judge colonial legislation. In this sense, Forbes retained an older approach to the common law method. He had much in common with Coke and Hale, in his reliance on a peculiar version of custom, and in his willingness to judge legislation by grand constitutional standards. But his judgments also showed something of the positivism to come.

without a legislature for centuries. The date of establishment of the colonial legislature was commonly used in North America: see Philip Girard, 'Themes and Variations in Early Canadian Legal Culture: Beamish Murdoch and his *Epitome of the Laws of Nova-Scotia*', *Law and History Review*, 11 (1993), 101 at 112.

[39] See *Applicability of Criminal Laws Opinion*, 1828; and see *In re Jane New*, 1829.

Index

9 781843 831587

Printed by Libri Plureos GmbH in Hamburg, Germany